1 MONTH OF
FREE
READING

at
www.ForgottenBooks.com

By purchasing this book you are eligible for one month membership to ForgottenBooks.com, giving you unlimited access to our entire collection of over 1,000,000 titles via our web site and mobile apps.

To claim your free month visit:
www.forgottenbooks.com/free73935

* Offer is valid for 45 days from date of purchase. Terms and conditions apply.

HORACE AND HIS AGE

A STUDY IN HISTORICAL BACKGROUND

BY

J. F. D'ALTON, M.A., D.D.

PROFESSOR OF ANCIENT CLASSICS, ST. PATRICK'S COLLEGE, MAYNOOTH

LONGMANS, GREEN AND CO.

39 PATERNOSTER ROW, LONDON

FOURTH AVENUE & 30TH STREET, NEW YORK

BOMBAY, CALCUTTA, AND MADRAS

1917

PREFACE.

IT too often happens that Classical texts are read with little consideration of the character of the age in which they were written. We are usually so engrossed with the linguistic study of an author, so intent on grappling with the subtleties of his grammatical structure, so satisfied with the plain and obvious meaning of his words, that we neglect to probe deeper, and search for the influences, which helped to colour his thoughts, and determine his outlook upon life. We are inclined to leave Higher Criticism as a practical monopoly to Biblical scholars, forgetting that writers are in most things children of their age, that they are immersed in its spirit, which often affects their intellectual being as profoundly and as intimately as their bodies are affected by their physical environment. Authors may themselves be at times unconscious of such influence, and its working may be revealed only by a phrase struck in harmony with some reigning sentiment, by a metaphor cast under the spell of some prevailing current of thought. How difficult it would be at the present day for a writer, even if he made a conscious effort to do so, to escape completely from the web of influence woven round him by the

titanic struggle now in progress, with all the issues it
involves. We should then in our study of a Classical
text search for the " Time-spirit," which helped to mould
it into its present shape. Its discovery or even partial
discovery will serve to illumine many a passage, for the
full meaning of which we were previously but dimly
groping. Virgil assuredly was writing under the influence
of Actium, with all its wealth of significance for a patriotic
Roman, when he penned those lines vibrating with concentrated scorn and passion in the Ninth Æneid (598 *et
seq.*), in which East and West are set in such violent contrast, in which the poet, as it were, forbids the banns on
a suggested union of their civilizations. The Troades of
Euripides was produced in the spring of 415 B.C., one of
the most fateful years in Athenian history. In the Prologue (cf. 78 *et seq.*) Athena and Poseidon, in clear and
ringing words, prophesy destruction for the Greek fleet
ready, flushed and triumphant, for its homeward journey
after its cruel sack of Troy, in which no horror was
spared to the ill-fated city. A few months before the
Troades was staged, the Athenian fleet had returned
from its ruthless repression of the little island of Melos.
In the summer that followed, literally with a flourish of
trumpets, it set out for Sicily on an expedition, that was
soon to come to a tragic and disastrous close. There is
no need to imagine Euripides endowed with the gift of
prophecy, or to believe that in the Troades he was in-
dulging in political allusion, but still he wrote "under the
influence of a year,[1] which to him had been filled full
of indignant pity and dire foreboding". In that year at
Athens, in spite of the brutal sophistries of the " Melian

---

[1] *Vide* Murray, Introductory Note to the Troades.

Dialogue," the air must have for many been oppressive with the memory of the sack of that island population, and charged with gloomy anticipations of retribution to follow in its wake. In the light of such knowledge it would not be difficult to invest many lines in the Troades (cf. 365 *et seq.*) with a more poignant pity, and a greater depth of meaning, and that without any undue straining of the text. Instances might be multiplied indefinitely to show how a knowledge of the historical background will aid us in eliciting the full import of many a passage, which otherwise would have concealed half its meaning from our search.

From all that has been said it will be clear what has been my aim in this study of Horace. I have tried to view him in the light of the various movements of his time, to recapture, as it were, the atmosphere in which he moved, to estimate portion at least of the influences, under which many of his thoughts were bodied forth. The late Dr. Verrall pointed out the way in Horatian study by applying, within a limited sphere, the method of Higher Criticism to Horace, but his work suffered somewhat from his almost complete entanglement in the Murena Episode, which he finds running like some thread of dark hue through the texture of so many of the Odes. I have endeavoured to approach the study of the poet without being weighted down by any preconceived theories, determined to let theories shape themselves in the light of the evidence that came my way. Horace has been treated amply on the domestic side, and we are acquainted with the story of his loves and frolics, and with almost every detail of his friendship for Mæcenas and his attachment to his Sabine farm. This aspect of his character has become traditional, and stands for the portrait of the whole man in the minds of many, who see in him only the gay light-hearted poet, the bon-vivant, linked inseparably to his Sabine retreat, where he dwells in unalloyed happiness, careless of what the morrow may bring. That, however, Horace had his serious side even a superficial reading of his poems will reveal. It might argue a due want of perspective to insist too forcibly on this serious side, but it would no less argue a due want of perspective to ignore it. One who was the friend of statesmen and Emperor could not in the nature of things have escaped the influence of movements, of which they were the centre and propelling force. So, Horace's songs are not always of love and wine. He shows that he was keenly alive to many of the phases of Roman life in his day, so that his interests could range from Roman politics to the moral ills of his age and their remedies, and pass readily from the tale of Canidia's witchcraft to the relative merits in literature of the Ancients and the Moderns. The poet, indeed, is often a surer guide on such questions than many of his contemporaries. He is gifted with a vision denied to meaner mortals, his imagination is more alert, his sympathy more responsive, his capacity to pierce to the heart of things greater than most of his fellow-men. We must not forget, however, that a complete reconstruction of any period in the Past is practically beyond our reach. Even if we had all possible evidence before us, and attempted to wrest their secrets from literature, inscriptions, and material monuments in turn, we would still at many points probably have to confess ourselves baffled in our search. For one thing, it is not easy always to divest ourselves of our modern standpoint, and

place ourselves at the point of view, say, of a Roman in
the time of Augustus.   Besides, a period like the Augustan Age is too complex and many-sided, too full of sub-
terranean influences to admit of its complete penetration.
All the more must we be content with partial results,
and at times with mere conjecture, when we are conscious
that some of the evidence, that would have been of value
to us, is lost beyond recall.   For instance, if we were in
possession of the whole of Varro's works on the Roman
drama instead of the few fragments that we have, we
would be in a securer position to appreciate the value of
many of Horace's judgments on the literary tastes of his
contemporaries.   A study such as this can thus at least
but represent an approximation towards an ideal.   Though
the ideal may never be fully realized, it is well to work
steadily towards it.   Even with the materials at hand,
we can do much to seize the broader aspects of the
period, within which Horace's literary activity lay, and
discern the chief influences, which helped to lend colour
to his verse, and determine the current of his thoughts.
    To pass to some points of detail, I may say that the
chapter on the Augustan Revival did not form part of
the book as originally planned, but I felt that it was impossible to approach the consideration of Horace's Religious and Philosophical views, before I had first cleared
the ground by dealing with the chief aspects of the Revival, and setting forth its character and aims.   I doubt
if there is any other event in the Augustan Age, that
exercised a more profound influence on contemporary
poets, especially Virgil and Horace, than the religious
movement inaugurated by Augustus.   The danger of
starting with an idea such as this is that one might be

tempted to wrest everything in Procustean fashion into harmony with it, and see the influence of the Revival in passages where it does not exist. I have endeavoured not to overstep the limits of the evidence supplied by Horace, and I hope I have not been unsuccessful. At times, I have had to enter into rather wearisome detail, as, for instance, in dealing with the Parthians and with the Roman land-question, thus running the risk of resembling the Epic writer, who begins the history of the Trojan war "gemino ab ovo," but I felt that without such detail, it would have been difficult to put things in their proper setting, and see the significance of many of Horace's references. The titles of the various chapters speak, I hope, sufficiently for their contents, and for the general plan of the book. In conformity with my general plan, I have, in the chapter on Literary Criticism, dealt not with Horace's literary criticism as a whole, but only with such portions of it as I believe to have had a bearing on contemporary movements in Literature.

In conclusion, I must acknowledge my obligation to Professor Phillimore, of the University of Glasgow, for his kindness in reading a portion of the proofs. My only regret is that unforeseen circumstances prevented him from reading them all, as I found his criticism very helpful in many points. I have to express my thanks, too, to Professor Semple, of University College, Dublin, who read the work in proof, and suggested several improvements.

J. F. D.

May, 1917.

CONTENTS.

PREFACE v

CHAPTER I.

HORACE AND ROMAN POLITICS.

The Civil Wars, 1; The Struggle at Actium, 5; Roman Ideals, 10; Parthian Affairs, 13; Victory of Diplomacy, 20; The Conquest of Britain, 22; Revolt in Spain, 24; The Northern Peoples, 27; The German Danger, 29; Augustan Peace, 31; The Elbe Frontier, 32.

CHAPTER II.

THE AUGUSTAN REVIVAL.

The Spell of Greece, 36; Individualism, 37; Greek Philosophy, 39; Foreign Cults, 40; Motives for Revival, 43; Limits of the Revival, 46; Restoration of Temples, 47; Antiquarianism, 48; Augustus, 50; Honours for Augustus, 51; Deification, 53; The Cult of the Emperor, 57; Genius Augusti, 59; Favoured Deities, 61; Apollo Worship, 63; Moral Reform, 68; Ludi Saeculares, 71.

CHAPTER III.

HORACE IN RELIGION AND PHILOSOPHY.

Early Training, 76; At Athens, 77; The Golden Mean, 80; Epicurean Tendencies, 84; The Rigour of Stoicism, 85; The Stoic Paradoxes, 86; Roman Stoicism, 90; Changed Views, 92; Horace's Conversion, 95; The Message of Lucretius, 96; Hedonism, 96; Religious Revival, 99; Stoic Elements, 101; The Cults of Egypt, 103; Cybele, 107; Faded Deities, 108; Prominence of Apollo, 109; Fortuna, 111; Rustic Deities, 112; Imperial Apotheosis, 115; Augustan Peace, 116; Decay of Temples, 119; Reverence for Antiquity, 120; Efforts at Reform, 121.

xi

CONTENTS

CHAPTER IV.

THE PERIOD OF THE EPISTLES.

The Philosophic Mind, 126; Change of Outlook, 127; Eclecticism, 130; The Highest Good, 131; Stoicism Predominant, 133; A Breath of Epicurus, 136; Love of the Country, 137; The Poet's Health, 140; Worldly Wisdom, 142.

CHAPTER V.

HORACE AND SOCIAL PROBLEMS.

The Ager Publicus, 145; Gracchan Legislation, 147; Confiscation, 149; Decline of Agriculture, 150; The City Proletariate, 154; Extent of Latifundia, 155; Latifundia in Horace, 157; Feeling of Insecurity, 159; The Poet's Ideal, 160; Bread and Games, 161; Slavery, 163; Number of Slaves, 164; Sympathy for Slaves, 166; Roman Luxury, 167; Commercial Activity, 169; Influence of Wealth, 173; The Burden of Wealth, 174; Roman Villas, 175; Marble and Mosaic, 177; Artistic Taste, 179; Metal Work, 181; Painting, 184; Furniture, 185; Personal Luxury, 186; Precious Stones, 188; Luxury of the Table, 191.

CHAPTER VI.

HORACE AND POPULAR BELIEFS.

Survivals, 198; Power of Magician, 199; Hecate, 202; Workers of Magic, 203; Magic in Italy, 205; The Dead in Magic, 207; The Moon in Magic, 208; Prophylactics, 209; Carmina, 211; Venena, 212; Sympathetic Magic, 214; The Magic Wheel, 217; Necromancy, 218; Sources, 220; Stoicism and Astrology, 222; Spread of Astrology, 223; Influence of the Stars, 225; Determinism, 225; The Nature of the Soul, 228; The Abode of the Blest, 229; Apotheosis, 230; Life beyond the Grave, 232; Necessity of Burial, 242; Omens, 244; Nature Worship, 246; Efficacy of Numbers, 246.

CHAPTER VII.

LITERARY CRITICISM.

Literary Activity, 251; The Rôle of Critic, 252; The Ars Poetica, 253; The Origin of Drama, 255; Development of Satire, 264; The Faults of Lucilius, 268; The Augustan Age, 269; Inspiration, 270; The Poet's Limitations, 272; Ancients and Moderns, 273; Archaism, 278; Purists, 280; Alexandrianism, 281; Conventional Criticism, 284; Dramatic Activity, 286; Dramatic Taste, 289.

INDEX 293

CHAPTER I.

HORACE AND ROMAN POLITICS.

A READER of Horace will be struck by the frequent reference
in his works to both Home and Foreign politics. He was
evidently keenly alive to the political movements that went
on around him, and possibly, too, such questions might have
formed the subject of discussion in the circle of Mæcenas, to
which he had been admitted. Though he denies[1] any knowledge of these affairs from such a source, it is evident[2] that the
public gave him credit for it. With all his levity of character
and changeful moods, it is clear that Horace had a deep love
for his country, a high[3] sense of patriotism, and an unshakeable[4] belief in the destiny of Rome, and in the endurance of
her greatness. To a thoughtful man surveying the history of
the last century of the Republic, it must have seemed the irony
of fate that the Rome, which had grown from a small city-state
by the Tiber into a great world-Empire, should have been the
incessant prey of internal discord, that the sword, which the
Roman should have unsheathed[5] only against the enemies of
his country, should have been turned against his brother. It
was a spectacle calculated to depress the spirits of every sincere
patriot, and it is little wonder that such depression has left its
mark on contemporary literature. The outlook of Lucretius
upon life is at times dismal in the extreme. Apart from the
pessimism springing from his general theory, that man is en-

[1] Sat. II. vi. 42 *et seq.* [2] *Ibid.* 51.
[3] Odes, III. ii. 13 ; IV. ix. 52. [4] *Ibid.* xxx. 8.
[5] *Ibid.* I. ii. 21 ; xxxv. 38.

gaged in a hopeless struggle with the overmastering forces of Nature, apart from the story of the love-philtre, that is supposed to have clouded the poet's intellect towards the close of his career, there is an element of profound melancholy running its sombre threads through his poem, and above all a disgust with the strivings[1] of inordinate human ambition.[2] The dark and dreary period of internecine strife, through which he lived, which had made "a steaming slaughter-house of Rome," left its impress on his genius, and deepened his poetic colours. Virgil,[3] too, who had suffered a personal loss by the confiscation of the paternal farm, shows that the lessons of the Civil Wars had not been lost upon him, and the spectacle of Roman fighting against Roman helped to intensify the natural sadness of his character.

Horace himself had passed through the crucible of those terrible days following upon Cæsar's death, and he seems to have emerged chastened from the ordeal, with his old Republican ardour considerably lessened. Whether he was ever an extreme Republican we cannot tell. There is no need to bring forward proof of his change of temper. His association with Mæcenas, and the favours he received from that statesman, and subsequently from Augustus himself, combined to win him over to all that Mæcenas and his Imperial master stood for. In an ode,[4] in which he proclaims his sense of security, "as long as Cæsar rules the earth," it is possible to see, as Verrall has done, in the closing lines a veiled reference to Philippi. One might detect an apologetic note in the words "calidus juventa". The doings, he would suggest, of these days were due to the heat of youthful enthusiasm. Again,[5] in a later explicit reference to Philippi, it seems to me that there

---

[1] Lucr. iii. 70; v. 1131 et seq.   [2] Ibid. i. 29; v. 380 et seq.

[3] Virg. Ecl. i. 71; Georgic, i. 489 et seq.; ii. 510; Æn. vi. 280, 612, 825 et seq.; cf. Prop. I. xxii.

[4] Odes, III. xiv.; cf. Verrall, "Studies in Horace," p. 161.

[5] Ep. II. ii. 47.

is a note of apology in the phrase "civilis æstus," a suggestion that it was the fevered excitement of the times that led him to range himself against the arms of Cæsar Augustus. Like [1] many of the young Romans then pursuing their studies at Athens, Horace,[2] who was never a doughty warrior, seems to have been carried away by the magnetism of Brutus' personality, but the disaster at Philippi,[3] which stripped him of everything, was not calculated to enhance his Republican sympathies. It is to his credit, however, that, though he abandoned his Republicanism, and became an enthusiastic supporter of the new regime, he was manly enough never to revile the party to which he had given his allegiance in former days. He could still sing of the valour [4] of his comrades at Philippi, of Cato's [5] "noble death" and "unconquered soul".[6] Though, however, a halo may have hung round these early struggles and their heroes, he was fully conscious of the moral of these dark days. He was conscious of the evils [7] "the dread friendships of the great" had brought upon his native country. He felt that in this fratricidal strife Latin [8] blood had been spilt to no purpose in many lands, that the prestige [9] of Rome had been shaken, that her name had become a mockery instead of a terror to her enemies, and she herself almost [10] an easy prey to their attacks. He has a clear conception, too, of the moral [11] evils, that followed in the wake of the Civil Wars, religion in decay, altars ruined, and no depth of crime left unfathomed. There is frequent in him a sense of melancholy and depression, a conviction of the blood-guiltiness [12] of his generation, which has brought upon it the vengeance [13] of Heaven in the shape of various disasters. Dr. Verrall,[14] true to his general theory,

---

[1] Plutarch, "Life of Brutus," xxiv.   [2] Epode i. 16.

[3] Ep. II. ii. 49.   [4] Odes, II. vii. 11.   [5] *Ibid.* I. xii. 35.

[6] *Ibid.* II. i. 24.   [7] *Ibid.* 3.   [8] Epode vii. 3; Odes, II. i. 27 *et seq.*

[9] Epode xvi. 2.   [10] Odes, III. vi. 13.

[11] *Ibid.* I. xxxv. 33 *et seq.*; cf. Catullus, lxiv. 397 *et seq.*

[12] Odes, III. v. 17; Epode vii. 1, 17; xvi. 9.

[13] Odes, I. ii. 1 *et seq.*   [14] Op. cit. p. 5 *et seq.*

connected the element of depression and pathos, that is evident, especially in many of the Odes, with the Murena episode. Though that may have contributed to it, it is due, I believe, in greater measure to the impression left on the poet's mind by the tragedies of the Civil Wars. If he is inclined to dwell in sadness on the vicissitudes of Fortune, it is not Murena alone he had in mind, but the very noblest of his countrymen, who on many a battlefield had perished at the hands of brother Romans, and the countless others who, in the proscriptions that followed, were reduced from opulence to the direst poverty. It is little wonder that Horace, as an expression of disgust and despair, suggests[1] as a remedy the abandonment of the city, and urges his fellow Romans to wander with him over the ocean, and search in the fabled Isles of the Blest for the happiness they cannot find at Rome. We are not surprised that he welcomes[2] the rule of Octavian, as offering a way out of this senseless bloodshed, and the hope of settled government. He shows his anxiety, too, lest, when settled government is within their grasp, it may be snatched from them by some fresh revolution. This is assuredly the meaning of the well-known Ode I. xiv., with its allegory of the ship of State. A good deal of ingenuity has been expended upon the Ode, but it seems to me to best suit the time immediately after Actium, when the supremacy of Octavian was practically assured, when the chaos of civil strife seemed likely to be ended by his victory, but yet the recalcitrants among Antony's party seemed bent on destroying these golden hopes. For we may be certain that, though[3] the victory of Augustus was received with almost universal acclamation, still there were extremists, who did not readily acquiesce in the new order of things. We know[4] that a number of conspiracies took place in the first twelve years of the reign of the new Emperor, which

---

[1] Epode xvi. 17 *et seq.*; cf. Livy, xxii. 53.
[2] Odes, III. xxiv. 25; cf. *ibid.* IV. xv. 17.
[3] Tac. Annals, I. c. i.   [4] Suet. Oct. xix.

proves that opposition to his rule was a factor always to be reckoned with. Over and above that, his efforts at reform, embodied in the "Leges Juliae," which probably had been foreshadowed for several years before they became law, were bound to provoke serious resistance. Hence in the allegory[1] of the struggle of Jupiter against the Giants, the victory of Jupiter is a symbol of the victory of Augustus over the forces of disorder (*vis consilii expers*). Horace suggests[2] that the conduct of Augustus throughout was characterized by gentleness and moderation. We shall see something later of the extravagant praises lavished by the poet upon the Emperor, but it is interesting to watch the evolution of his feelings towards Augustus from the first almost timid references to him in the Satires,[3] till he becomes an enthusiastic admirer of him and his policy, and gives us many[4] glowing eulogies of the "Pax Augusta," marked by no fear of enemies abroad, and by complete prosperity and happiness at home.

Now, in spite of a certain measure of opposition, the power of Augustus was practically consolidated by the victory at Actium. It is interesting to see what significances the battle had in the eyes of contemporaries. We are fortunate in having a number of references in Horace and his fellow-poets to the campaign of Octavian against Antony, and it is clear that the struggle between the two was viewed, not so much as a struggle between individuals, as a battle of East against West, and a conflict of opposing civilizations. It is strange indeed to find[5] that twice again the same struggle of East against West was

---

[1] Odes, III. iv. 42 *et seq.*; cf. *ibid.* I. xii. 52.

[2] *Ibid.* 41; cf. Velleius, ii. 86, on his victory at Actium, "victoria vero fuit clementissima"; Ferrero, "Greatness and Decline of Rome," vol. iv. p. 34, for his change of temper after his victory over Sextus Pompey.

[3] Sat. I. iii. 4; *ibid.* II. i. 11.

[4] Odes, III. xiv. 14; IV. v. 16 *et seq.*; xiv. 41; xv. 4 *et seq.*; Car. Saec. *passim.*

[5] Vide Mahan, "The Influence of Sea Power on History," p. 13.

to be fought in the neighbourhood of Actium, at the battles
of Lepanto and Navarino.   The orientalizing[1] tendencies of
Antony,[2] his relations with Cleopatra, and the ambitions of
that designing woman, had excited the fear[3] and disgust[4]
of patriotic Romans.   After his victory in Armenia (34 B.C.),
Antony had proclaimed Cleopatra,[5] "Queen of Kings," and
had offered an insult to Roman pride by celebrating his
triumph not at Rome, but at Alexandria.   The "Donations[6] of
Alexandria" revealed, perhaps more strikingly than any other
fact, the designs of Cleopatra, and the extent of her power over
the proconsul.   The fears[7] of his countrymen at home were
probably carefully fostered by Octavian and his followers for
party interests, but the spectacle of Antony in bondage to the
Egyptian Queen, and the fact of the Donations must have
given thinking Romans pause.   It hardly needed the bitter
invectives of Octavian in the Senate House, when the deed of
the Donations was read there, to awaken profound distrust and
anxiety as to the drift of Antony's Eastern policy.   Above all,
when the fact of Antony's marriage, and his divorce of Octavia
became known, when his will,[8] naming his children by Cleopatra as his heirs, was opened at the instigation of Octavian,
this fear and anxiety became doubly intensified.   It is hard
indeed to believe that the Romans ever seriously entertained
the idea that their power was imperilled from the East.   If
they did, one might argue from it the degeneracy of the Roman
spirit, and draw the moral that the Civil Wars had undermined
the valour and prestige of Rome.   Neither can it be argued, as

---

[1] Dio, l. 4; Velleius, ii. 82; Suet. Oct. xvii., "degenerasse eum a
civili more"; Mommsen, "Roman Provinces," vol. ii. p. 25; Ferrero,
op. cit. vol. iv. pp. 52-3.

[2] Virg. Æn. viii. 688; Prop. II. xvi. 37 *et seq.*

[3] Hor. Odes, III. vi. 14; Prop. III. xi. 58; Dio, l. 4.

[4] Prop. IV. vi. 45 *et seq.*   [5] Hill, "Roman Coins," p. 132.

[6] Ferrero, op. cit. iv. p. 268 *et seq.*

[7] Vide Dio, l., opening chapters, for the mutual recrimination of the
leaders; cf. Ferrero, iv. pp. 83, 116.

[8] Suet. Oct. xvii.

Ferrero[1] endeavours to do, that all these rumours about the East were so many bogies to frighten the Roman people, invented by Octavian and his adherents. Antony's military capacity, and the uncertainty of his plans gave grounds for genuine fear. The reports of his conduct in the East, even though exaggerated, supplied Octavian with a splendid catch-cry to gather men to his standard. One would think that he had but to raise the battle-cry of West against East, and set himself up as the national champion, to rally Romans in countless numbers to his support.

It speaks eloquently for the popularity of Antony, and the distrust of Octavian in the minds of many, that the former, the story of whose wild orgies in the East, richly embellished by his enemies, was still fresh in the public mind, could count on the co-operation of a number of leading Romans. The mistrust of Antony in the minds of many Romans, however, was accompanied by an equal or greater mistrust of Cleopatra. That ambitious woman, intending to use Antony as her tool, entertained dreams of the creation of an Egyptian Empire that would be a serious rival to Rome. One has to make allowance for the licence of poetry, but in the excitement of the crisis, Roman imagination had conjured[2] up to itself the spectacle of the Capitol in ruins, and the Egyptian Queen holding high revel there with her band of eunuch slaves. Roman prejudice had always been strongly marked against the East and its ways. This prejudice was apparently not based upon colour, even in the case of Egypt and Numidia, for the colour[3] question seems never to have presented a serious difficulty to Roman Imperialism. It was a prejudice based rather upon race and traditions, on Rome's pride in her free

---

[1] Vol. iv. p. 106.

[2] Hor. Odes, I. xxxvii. 6; Prop. III. xi. 31-32; Dio, l. 5, where Cleopatra's ambition is said to be τὸ ἐν τῷ Καπιτωλίῳ δικάσαι.

[3] Lucas, " Greater Rome and Greater Britain," p. 97; Lord Cromer, " Ancient and Modern Imperialism," p. 129 et seq.

institutions in contrast with the servility of the Eastern nations under the sway of despotic monarchies. Roman " gravitas " was offended at the spectacle [1] of Roman soldiers enslaved to the service of a woman, above all such a woman as Cleopatra, of whom contemporary poets can hardly find epithets [2] sufficiently strong to express their condemnation. The old Roman virtue, decayed but not dead, recoiled in disgust from all the trappings [3] of luxury that distinguished Cleopatra and her hosts, from her eunuch slaves, from her sistrum and mosquito curtains. Of course, in reading the poets, one has to take into account the fact that they were strong partisans of Octavian, and so inclined to take the " official view," but still they are probably voicing a large body of public opinion in Rome, when they set down the war as essentially a war of civilizations, in which the fine Roman traditions of manliness, dignity, simplicity, steadfastness are arrayed against the licentiousness and decadence of the East, in which the gods [4] of the Tiber are ranged against the gods of the Nile. All their better instincts rose in revolt against the danger from Antony's barbaric hosts, and even Virgil's gentle soul could be roused to a bitter [5] scorn alien to his nature. The victory of Actium is thus set down as a victory of Roman traditions, and of Western ideas and institutions, against a threatened invasion of Orientalism. It can hardly be doubted that the poets, though desiring to compliment Augustus, are in some measure reflecting popular enthusiasm in the rapturous outbursts with which they commemorate the victory. This seems to me especially true of Horace. Epode ix. was written apparently in the first access of popular rejoicing, when the news of the battle

---

[1] Hor. Epode ix. 11.

[2] Hor. Odes, I. xxxvii. 21, " fatale monstrum "; Prop. III. xi. 39, " meretrix regina ".

[3] Hor. Epode ix. 15-16; Prop. III. xi. 42 *et seq.*; cf. Varro, R.R. II. x. 8, on Roman ideas of the effeminacy of mosquito curtains.

[4] Prop. III. xi. 41; II. xxiii. 20; Virg. Æn. viii. 698.

[5] *Ibid.* 685 *et seq.*

reached Rome, before, however, the full details were known, and before it was yet clear [1] what were the movements of Antony and Cleopatra after their defeat. The Cleopatra Ode (I. xxxvii.), as we might call it, was composed in the following year, when, after the Alexandrian campaign, the account [2] of the Queen's death had been brought to Rome. Horace probably reflects popular opinion more faithfully than either Virgil or Propertius. They wrote when the "legend" of the battle had been inaugurated, and when popular feeling had been in some measure moulded by the crafty policy of Augustus, in order to put in more favourable light his own rôle in the conflict. Horace gives him honourable mention, but speaks of him merely as a human agent, who has defeated his rival without supernatural intervention. New elements come into play in the versions of his brother poets. The victory is especially associated with the intervention of the gods, above all Augustus's protecting deity Apollo.[3] They wrote, when the Augustan Revival had been set on foot, and probably under its influence. Augustus wished to enhance [4] his victory in the popular mind, and had begun to exploit Apollo soon after the battle. He wished to appear as the saviour of Rome and her national ideals, but as an agent divinely appointed, acting under the special guidance and protection of the gods. He celebrated a triple [5] triumph in 29 B.C. for the war in Dalmatia, the victory at Actium, and the taking of Alexandria. Though official [6] acts and honours are not always a safe guide, still it is clear that many greeted the

[1] Epode ix. 29 *et seq.*

[2] Odes, I. xxxvii. 21 *et seq.*

[3] Virg. Æn. viii. 705 ; iii. 280 *et seq.* ; vi. 69 ; Prop. III. xi. 69 ; IV. vi. 57.

[4] Suet. Oct. 18.

[5] Mon. Ancyr. c. 4 ; Dio, li. 21 ; Suet. Oct. 22 ; Prop. II. i. 31 *et seq.* ; Hill, " Roman Coins," p. 134.

[6] Rushforth, " Historical Inscriptions," p. 1 ; Hill, op. cit. p. 136 ; cf. Cohen, " Médailles Impériales," vol. i. p. 62.

victory with enthusiasm, especially as likely to put an end definitely to civil war. Popular opinion was thus a favourable soil in which to sow what legend he pleased. It is evident that he wished to keep prominently before the public gaze the national [1] aspect of the struggle, and this was to serve a useful purpose in his subsequent policy. For one who was effecting a revolution in government, and endeavouring to consolidate his power, it was a decided advantage to stand forth as the saviour of cherished national traditions, and Augustus was sagacious enough to sound the national note in many of his reforms.

There was an inevitable reaction [2] against the spell of the East, and an appeal to the national sense to restore those qualities,[3] by which the Latin name had grown great, and the Empire of Rome had spread over East and West. Horace condemns the soft Ionian dances [4] which the Roman maiden is taught, while the Roman boy, he tells us, is more skilled [5] in Greek games than in the manly Roman sports, that would mould his character on true Roman lines, and make him fitted [6] to meet the foes of Rome in the field. The Romans, of course, had certainly in early days a strong prejudice [7] against the Greek theory of physical culture, and the exercises of the palaestra. Hunting,[8] riding, the game of ball in the Campus Martius, followed by a swim in the Tiber, were considered pastimes better suited to the Roman youth and the national character. But the emphasis Horace lays, in the many pas-

---

[1] I find that Ferrero has anticipated this view, vol. iv. pp. 60, 82, 108.

[2] Hor. Odes, I. xxxviii. 1.

[3] *Ibid.* III. vi. 33 *et seq.*; IV. xv. 12 *et seq.*; Car. Saec. 58.

[4] Odes, III. vi. 21; cf. Macrob. "Saturnalia," iii. 14, for Roman ideas on dancing.

[5] Hor. Odes, III. xxiv. 52 *et seq.*; Sat. II. ii. 9 *et seq.*

[6] Hor. Odes, III. ii. 4.

[7] Wilkins, "Roman Education," p. 31.

[8] Hor. Odes, III. vii. 25 *et seq.*; xii. 7; Epode ii. 31; Ep. I. xviii. 49, where hunting is called "Romanis sollemne viris opus," A.P. 162.

sages I have quoted, on sports distinctively Roman, points to a strong reaction in favour of purely Roman pastimes. The well-known Ode (III. 3), where Juno forbids the rebuilding of Troy, has caused great searching of hearts, but it seems to me to admit of a comparatively simple explanation, if viewed in the light of Actium, and the trend of Augustus's policy after the battle. It sets up an impassable barrier between East and West, and guarantees the continuance of Roman power on one condition only, that Romans shall not, through attachment to their origin, show honour to the country of their founder by rebuilding Troy, and all that it stood for. It is a summons to Romans never to forget their national heritage, a proclamation that, if a union were ever attempted between the two civilizations, Roman national sentiment would rise up to forbid the banns. The Ode has been connected with the rumour,[1] that Julius Cæsar had at one time intended to transfer the seat of government from Rome to Alexandria or to Troy. That scheme, however, if it was ever seriously entertained, had died with its originator. It is much more likely that the Ode took shape (officially inspired perhaps) out of the disgust which people had felt for the conduct of Antony, who had cast aside all his Roman pride, and had practically become an Oriental, and out of the feelings associated with the struggle at Actium. It is the same feeling of Roman pride and hostility to Eastern ways, that excites Horace's indignation at the thought of Roman soldiers, forgetful [2] of Rome and her institutions, joined in wedlock with a barbarian wife. Again, the same feeling has probably inspired Virgil's [3] fine passage, where the contrast between East and West is so vividly depicted, where Virgil proclaims the superiority of the West, and sends the Phrygians and their effeminate civilization back in

---

[1] Suet. J. Cæsar, 79.

[2] Hor. Odes, III. v. 5 *et seq.*, " Anciliorum et nominis et togae oblitus, Aeternaeque Vestae ".

[3] Æn. ix. 600 *et seq.*

summary fashion to their native land.   We have always to remember this national aspect of the policy of Augustus, and
we shall see some further effects of it, when we come to deal
with his Revival of Religion, not the least of them being his
exclusive [1] attitude to foreign cults.   It was the effort to con-
serve distinctively Roman sentiment that impelled the Emperor
to insist on the more general [2] use of the toga (which many
apparently had begun to discard), for this was considered the
outward symbol [3] of Roman gravity and pride.   It was this
too, that caused him to be so reluctant about conferring Roman
citizenship on foreigners, except on rare occasions, wishing,
says Suetonius,[4] "to keep the people free from any taint of
foreign or servile blood ".

We see the significance of Actium again, in Augustus's
general policy towards Egypt during his reign.   It was reserved
as an Imperial province, and its government [5] was entrusted
to an Equestrian Prefect.   The reason was, of course, partly
economic, for in the days when agriculture in Italy [6] had declined, and Rome was dependent [7] for her corn upon Egypt
and other countries, whoever held [8] the " claustra annonae "
had the city at his mercy.   The Emperor therefore forbade
Senators or illustrious Knights to enter the province without
his permission,[9] lest it should become the playground for the
designs of some ambitious man.   The fate of Gallus showed
how dangerous it was to even appear to harbour such ambitions.   But over and above the economic importance of Egypt,
the temper [10] of its people, their customs and traditions, their

---

[1] Suet. Oct. 93.   [2] *Ibid.* 40.

[3] Virg. Æn. i. 282 ; cf. Tac. Hist. ii. 20 ; Seneca, Rhet. Controv. viiii.
3 (26), 13.   [4] Oct. 40.

[5] Greenidge, " Roman Public Life," p. 436; Tac. Annals, ii. 59 (there
quoted) ; Frank, " Roman Imperialism," p. 350.

[6] *Vide infra*, p. 150 *et seq.*   [7] Suet. Oct. 18.

[8] Tac. Hist. ii. 82; iii. 8.

[9] For a similar fear on the part of J. Cæsar, *vide* Suet. J. Cæsar, 35.

[10] Tac. Hist. i. 11, " Superstitione ac lascivia discors et mobilis,"
" inscia legum ".

lawless and unstable character in marked contrast to Roman love of discipline, were felt to need a strong restraining hand, and the Emperor's own unceasing vigilance. We have spoken of the exclusive attitude of Augustus towards foreign cults generally,[1] "except those that were ancient and well-established," but towards Egyptian worships he showed actual hostility, not unmingled with contempt. This hostility was part of his wider policy of appearing as the champion of all things national. But, moreover, it is probable that there was a strong party at Rome to whom all things Egyptian were taboo. The elder Pliny [2] mentions an incident, trivial in its way, that seems to point in that direction. The Emperor for a time used a seal with the image of the Sphinx, but "ad evitanda convicia," he had to discontinue its use and substitute in its place an image of Alexander the Great.

In reading the Augustan poets one is struck by the numerous references to the Parthians. If we were to judge by the poets alone, we might conclude that they occupied a larger space in Roman politics at this time than any other foreign people. The references to them always exhibit a note of marked, and sometimes of fierce hostility. At times a feeling of race-hatred [3] emerges, but almost in every case the hostility is the outcome of the disgrace, which the Roman army had suffered by its defeat and the capture of its standards on the fatal field of Carrhae. This was not to be the only defeat, which the Romans were to suffer at the hands of the Parthians, but this alone would account for the tone of bitterness, which marks almost every reference to this people, and was certainly the root of the prejudice against them in the popular mind. But to all who were keenly interested in Roman Imperialism, it was clear that as long as such a formidable military power remained unbroken, and ever threatening to violate Roman

---

[1] Suet. Oct. 93.   [2] N.H. xxxvii. 4.

[3] Hor. Odes, III. v. 5 ; cf. Dio, liv. 8, which throws some light on Horace.

territory, the prestige of Rome in the East would be insecure. One wonders, too, whether here again the enmity does not rest in part on the fundamental difference between two civilizations.[1] Parthia had originally formed part of the old Iranian Empire. Its people were Iranian in race and language. This native population was, however, conquered by a tribe (called Scythian[2] by the Greeks) issuing, under its leader Arsaces, from the Steppes east of the Caspian Sea. The power of the House of Seleucus had been broken by the battle of Ancyra (c. 240 B.C.),[3] and under the Arsacid dynasty Parthia was erected into an independent state, and began a career of conquest for itself, especially under the sixth Arsacid, Mithridates I (c. 175-136 B.C.), who subdued the old Bactrian kingdom, and wrested to himself Persia, Media, and Babylonia.[4] "The Arsacids regarded and professed themselves throughout as the successors of Cyrus and Darius," and as the heirs of the old Achaemenid kingdom. Horace refers[5] indifferently to this Eastern people as Parthi, Medi, or Persae. Now, in spite of such incidents as the acting[6] of the Bacchae at the Parthian Court, this Arsacid power was essentially an Oriental and non-Hellenic power.[7] "The Parthian State was based on a national and religious reaction, and the old Iranian language, the Order of the Magi,

---

[1] For the history and development of the Parthian State, *vide* Bevan, "The House of Seleucus," vol. i. pp. 262, 284-9; Mommsen, "The History of Rome," vol. iii. pp. 58-60 (Everyman Library); Hogarth, "The Ancient East," pp 242-3.

[2] Gardner, "Parthian Coinage," p. 2, for Scythian costume on coins of the Arsacids.

[3] *Ibid.* op. cit. p. 4, gives date as 246 B.C.

[4] Mommsen, "Roman Provinces," vol. i. p. 4; cf. Hor. Odes, II. ii. 17.

[5] In Mon. Ancyr. *c.* 32-3, a distinction is made between Medi and Parthi.

[6] Plutarch, Crassus, xxxiii.

[7] Mommsen, Hist. vol. iii. p. 59; cf. "Roman Provinces," vol. i. p. 5 *et seq.* For the non-Hellenic character of the Parthians, cf. Hogarth, op. cit. pp. 249-50; Mahaffy, "The Greek World under Roman Sway," p. 170; Cumont, "Les Religions Orientales," pp. 163-5; Wendland, "Die Hellenistisch-Römische Kultur," pp. 26-7.

the worship of Mithra, the oriental feudal constitution, the cavalry of the desert, and the bow and arrow first emerged therein in renewed and triumphant opposition to Hellenism." The Romans first came into conflict with this mighty Eastern power in the time of Sulla, and the conference between him and the Parthian envoy on the banks of the Euphrates was justly celebrated. As the result of it, the Euphrates was recognized as the boundary line between Parthian and Roman power. Pompey[1] reversed this policy for one of aggressiveness. Though he had previously[2] agreed to do so, he refused to regard the Euphrates as the limit of Roman conquest. He declined,[3] moreover, to give the Parthian monarch the title of "King of Kings," and actually handed over to Tigranes of Armenia territory nominally subject to Parthia. It was undoubtedly this irreconcilable attitude of Pompey, which sowed the seeds of the disaster reaped by Crassus at Carrhae (53 B.C.), the conclusion of an expedition which Plutarch[4] considers a real tragedy, which ended in the deaths of Crassus and his son, the almost complete destruction of the Roman army, and the deepest disgrace of all, the loss of its standards. The Romans might attribute[5] their defeat to the obstinacy of Crassus in proceeding to battle, when the auspices were unfavourable, but the keener-minded among them must have seen clearly that they had come into conflict with a military power of the first magnitude, with soldiers[6] unrivalled as horsemen and archers, against whom the Roman infantry was powerless. Their peculiar tactics, along with their capacity for retreating into the desert, made their position practically

---

[1] Mommsen, " History of Rome," vol. iv. pp. 130-2.

[2] *Ibid.* p. 110.　　　　　　[3] Plutarch, Pompey, 33.

[4] Crassus, xxxiii.; cf. Appian, B.C. ii. 18.

[5] Hor. Odes, III. vi. 9 ; Velleius, ii. 46 ; cf. Plutarch, Crassus, 19, on his αὐθάδεια.

[6] Hor. Sat. II. i. 15 ; Odes, I. ii. 22 ; xix. 11 ; xxix. 4 ; Virg. Georgic, iii. 31 ; Prop. III. xi. 54 ; IV. iii. 36 ; Ovid, Fasti, v. 527 ; cf. Hill, op. cit. p. 130 ; Mommsen, Hist. vol. iv. p. 312.

impregnable.   They were essentially a warlike people, restless
and turbulent, and ever inclined to make incursions into Roman
territory.   We can get no better insight into their lawless and
aggressive character than from the Correspondence of Cicero,
when about to leave Rome as governor of Cilicia (51 B.C.), and
during his year of office.   Before setting out,[1] his mind is beset
with uneasy forebodings of danger from the Parthians, and
during his absence in the province his Letters contain frequent
allusions,[2] that reveal anxiety as to their designs.   The Civil
wars did not help to re-establish Roman prestige in the eyes of
the Parthians.   Pompey,[3] laying aside his Roman pride, con-
descended to negotiate for the help of Orodes before the battle
of Pharsalus, and some years later, when Cassius revolted in
Syria, he called the Parthian monarch to his aid, and Parthian
mounted archers fought on the Republican side at Philippi.
As long of course as Carrhae remained unavenged, the Parthian
question was always a living one for Roman statesmen.   Over
and above this consideration, it must have been clear to many
that the integrity of the Parthian Empire was a standing men-
ace, and could hardly co-exist with Roman supremacy in the
East.   Under such circumstances a Parthian expedition was
always a popular one, and, for an ambitious Roman,[4] probably
the surest way to win power and influence at home.   It was
an expedition, too, calculated to appeal to a soldier of imagination, to carry the Roman standards into regions rendered half-
legendary by their distance, to surmount incredible obstacles,
to give battle to a vast horde of brave and cunning warriors,
who employed other weapons and other tactics than the Roman
legionary, and to humble that power which made precarious
Roman dominion in the East.   Success would have been, for

---

[1] Ad Att. v. 12 : " velim Parthus quiescat ".

[2] Ibid. 20; Ad Fam. viii. 5; Caelius in a letter to Cicero says : " nunc
si Parthus movet aliquid scio non mediocrem fore contentionem ".

[3] Mommsen, " Roman Provinces," vol. i. pp. 21-2.

[4] Vide Ferrero, op. cit. vol. iv. p. 151.

him who achieved it, one of the greatest triumphs in Roman military annals.

We are not surprised then that Julius Cæsar, who was gifted with imagination, if ever a Roman leader was, contemplated such an expedition shortly before his death. There is one incident, in connection with this proposed expedition, that is worthy of note.[1] An oracle was reported to have been discovered, which declared that only a king could conquer the Parthians. This incident, insignificant in its way, sheds some light on popular opinion as to the seriousness of a Parthian expedition. Unless this opinion had existed, it would have been absurd for Cæsar or his supporters to have invoked such an oracle to further their political designs. The murder of Cæsar, however, brought to nought all these splendid plans of Parthian conquest. A few years later (40 B.C.), the Romans were to suffer a further humiliation at the hands of their old enemies, when Decidius Saxa was defeated[2] by Pacorus aided by the renegade Quintus Labienus. This defeat was in a measure retrieved by the victory of Ventidius Bassus at Gindarus (38 B.C.), but two years later the Roman legions, this time[3] under the leadership of Antony himself, once again succumbed to Parthian valour. The invading force had advanced as far as the Capital of Media (Phraaspa), but was unfortunate in having its siege-train surprised and destroyed by Phraates, the Parthian leader. The Parthians came on in overwhelming numbers, and inflicted a severe defeat upon the Romans. Antony's skill and resource as a general were never more conspicuous than in his retreat, and though he lost many men, he saved his army from complete disaster. This failure

---

[1] Suet. J. Cæsar, 79; cf. Appian, B.C. ii. 110; iii. 8, 24.

[2] Mommsen, " Roman Provinces," vol. ii. p. 22; Hill, op. cit. p. 128; Cohen, " Médailles Impériales," p. 29, for a coin struck by Orodes in honour of Labienus *Parthicus.*

[3] Mommsen, " Roman Provinces," vol. ii. p. 31; Ferrero, op. cit. vol. iv. p. 23 *et seq.*

did not cause him to abandon the design of conquering
Parthia. Twice afterwards he thought of renewing the expedition, but he was foiled, once by the cleverness of Cleopatra,
who had destined Antony for a different rôle in her political
schemes, and again, when he had gathered an army at
Ephesus for the invasion of Parthia, he was forced to abandon
the attempt by the events at home, which culminated in
Actium.

It is little wonder that the bitter memories of these defeats
rankled in Roman breasts. Above all, the capture of their
standards was felt to be a lasting disgrace to the arms of
Rome, and a serious injury to its prestige. Horace is merely
reflecting popular opinion when he speaks of the Parthians as
the bitterest[1] foes of Rome, and prays for their destruction
through internal strife, when he represents them as lying[2]
and treacherous enemies—qualities which the Romans were always able to discover in formidable opponents—and wishes[3]
Apollo to drive amongst them a pestilence that was raging in
Rome. He tells us, too, with a certain note of satisfaction, of
the internal[4] dissensions with which the Parthian kingdom was
torn. Phraates IV had succeeded Orodes (38 B.C.), but after
some years of tyrannical government was expelled, and the
throne passed to Tiridates, another member of the Arsacid
House. Phraates was soon restored, and Tiridates fled with
an infant son of Phraates to seek the aid of Augustus, probably
when he was journeying[5] through Asia after the battle of

---

[1] Hor. Epode vii. 9.   [2] Hor. Odes, IV. xii. 23 ; Ep. II. i. 212.
[3] Odes, I. xxi. 15.

[4] The sequence of these events, and their dates are, to say the least of it,
problematical. I follow Verrall's version of them in the main, who recognizes two distinct rebellions on the part of Tiridates, and a double restoration of Phraates, " Studies in Horace," p. 117 *et seq.* ; cf. Mommsen,
" R.P." ii. pp. 34-7; Wickham, Introduction to Horace, Odes, p. 7;
Dio, li. 18 (there quoted) ; Mon. Ancyr. c. 32-3.

[5] Ferrero, op. cit. iv. p. 227, makes the visit of Tiridates coincide with
Augustus's absence in Spain. For a visit of Tiridates to Rome, *vide* Dio,
liii. 33.

Actium. Augustus gave him little help, and endeavoured to play off one prince against the other, with the object of recovering the lost standards. Some years later (*c.* 27 B.C.), however, Tiridates succeeded in expelling Phraates, who was himself restored [1] once more, probably in the following year, with the aid of the Scythians.

Now, after the battle of Actium, when Augustus was in supreme power at Rome, it is clear that there was a strong [2] popular demand for an expedition against the Parthians, and the recovery of the Roman standards. Probably there was a section of aggressive [3] Imperialists, who would not be content with a mere punitive expedition, but who had larger designs, and wished the sphere of Roman conquest in the East further extended, at the expense of their old enemy, the Parthian. Augustus, we are told, [4] will be hailed as a god if he adds the Parthians and Britons to the Empire. It is equally clear that Augustus did not favour such a policy of expansion. He was not endowed with the high military genius of Julius Cæsar, and an even less far-seeing man than he, above all with the memory of recent defeats still fresh, would have hesitated before embarking on such an expedition. Augustus claims [5] himself never to have been an aggressive Imperialist. Though in the case of Germany, he consented to an attempt to extend the Roman frontier to the Elbe, still his last message [6] to the Senate showed the innate conservativeness of his character, when he advised it to keep the Empire within the limits

---

[1] Hor. Odes, I. xxvi. 3 ; II. ii. 17 ; III. viii. 19 ; xxix. 27.

[2] Hor. Sat. II. v. 62 (written probably soon after Actium) ; Odes, I. ii. 51 ; xii. 53 ; xxix. 4 ; III. ii. 3. Odes, II. ix. 21, is merely an anticipation ; cf. also Virg. Æn. vii. 606 ; Prop. III. v. 47 ; IV. ii. 35 ; vi. 83.

[3] Hor. Odes, III. iii. 44 ; Prop. III. iv. 2 *et seq.* ; cf. Lord Cromer, op. cit. p. 25 *et seq.*

[4] Hor. Odes, III. v. 2.   [5] Mon. Ancyr. c. 26 ; Suet. Oct. 21.

[6] Tac. Annals, i. 11 ; cf. Frank, "Roman Imperialism," p. 354 ; Pelham, "Essays on Roman History," for Augustus's organization of the frontiers of the Empire.

already attained, and aim at no further expansion. With
regard to Parthia, he must have seen (as the Emperor Hadrian
saw in later times, when he relinquished the conquests of
Trajan) that the Euphrates was a natural boundary for Roman
power, and that Roman arms could not venture across it with
any guarantee of safety or success.   In the light of these facts,
it is not easy to account for Horace's attitude.   No one could
be stronger or more insistent than he is in his demand for a
Parthian expedition.   It is certainly going too far, I believe,
to conceive Horace, as Ferrero[1] has done, as the spokesman
of the extreme Imperialists.   If Horace had been acquainted
with the Emperor's views on the Parthian question, it is unlikely that he would have made his poetry the vehicle of
demands so directly opposed to them.   One can, of course,
raise the whole question as to how far the poet was acquainted
with the Emperor's political designs.   It is a question that
does not admit of an easy answer, but on the face of things it
is probable enough that the poet, who co-operated so loyally
with Augustus in his domestic policy, was not wholly ignorant
of his views on a topic of such burning interest as that of a
Parthian expedition.   Yet we find him in the very Odes,[2] in
which he extols the domestic reforms of the Emperor, clamour-
ing for a vigorous offensive against the Parthians.   Augustus
felt bound to take some action, but he was determined to wipe
out the stain upon Roman arms, and win back the standards,
not by a great military expedition, which might prove disastrous, but by the easier path of diplomacy.   I believe also
that Augustus, from the time of his coming into power, fostered
the illusion that an expedition against Parthia would take
place, and that the clamours of the poets, and of Horace in
particular, may have been partly inspired by the Emperor
himself.   It is significant that when the expedition[3] under
Aelius Gallus was setting out for Arabia Felix (24 B.C.),[4]

---

[1] Op. cit. vol. iv. p. 14.   [2] Odes, III. ii. 3 ; iii. 43 ; v. 4.
[3] Dio, liii. 29.   [4] Odes, I. xxix. 4.

Horace leaves one under the impression that it would not confine its activity to Arabia, but would be directed also against Parthia, though, as far as I know, there is no evidence from any other source that it was destined for so serious an undertaking.   Probably this was the impression which Augustus desired to create among the general public.   The standards were at length restored [1] (20 B.C.), as the result of Tiberius's [2] mission to the East.   They were placed in the "temple" [3] of Mars Ultor, probably a small shrine of the god on the Capitol, specially built to receive them, and were destined [4] ultimately for the great temple in the Forum of Augustus, which was not dedicated till some years later (2 B.C.).   Augustus, as Dio tells us, was very proud of his achievement.   Yet, though Roman honour was appeased, it is unlikely that a mere diplomatic triumph was sufficient to satisfy the ambitions of the extreme Imperialists.   If Horace, as Ferrero suggests, was the mouthpiece of this party, it is not probable that he would have shown the enthusiasm [5] he does over the bloodless victory, which restored the standards, but left the Roman frontier where it stood.   As far as official acts go, the victory was greeted at Rome with much enthusiasm.   It was celebrated by the erection of a Triumphal Arch [6] to Augustus in the Forum, of which merely the foundations remain at the present day.

---

[1] Mon. Ancyr. c. 29; Dio, liv. 8; Suet. Oct. 21; *ibid.* Tib. 9.

[2] For this mission, *vide* Mommsen, "Roman Provinces," ii. pp. 37-8; Hor. Ep. i. 3; Tac. Annals, ii. 1.   Tiberius also settled affairs in Armenia, and restored Tigranes to power; cf. Hor. Ep. I. xii. 26; Tac. Annals, ii. 56; Cohen, op. cit. p. 64, for coin with device "Armenia Capta"; Hill, op. cit. p. 145.

[3] Ovid, Fasti, v. 525 *et seq.*

[4] Dio, liv. 8; cf. Hor. Odes, IV. xv. 6, where he says that the standards were dedicated to Jupiter; Hill, op. cit. p. 141, for a discussion of the Temple.

[5] Ep. I. xii. 27; xviii. 56; II. i. 256; Odes, IV. v. 25; xv. 6; Car. Saec. 53; cf. Ovid, Fasti, vi. 399; Prop. II. x. 13; IV. vi. 79.

[6] Huelsen, "Roman Forum," p. 157.

The event was celebrated on numerous coins,[1] and at least in one work[2] of Roman Art, the statue of Augustus, now in the Vatican. But it is a question whether all this enthusiasm was a spontaneous outburst, or, as the enthusiasm of Horace may well have been, artificially created to drown the disappointment of those, who had hoped for greater achievements.

It was probably the same section of advanced Imperialists, who dreamt of universal Empire,[3] and who were eager for a Parthian expedition that also demanded an expedition against Britain. Julius Cæsar's second expedition to the island had been more fruitful than his first,[4] which had rather been of the nature of a reconnaissance, but, even in the second, he had conquered merely the fringe of the country, and his achievement is justly appraised by Tacitus, when he says[5] that " he rather pointed out the island to his successors than handed it down as a legacy ". Cæsar may have thought[6] that the conquest of Britain was essential to the complete subjugation of Gaul, but now that Gaul was comparatively secure in the grasp of the Romans, Augustus, naturally cautious and conservative in character, would be unlikely ever to seriously consider an expedition to Britain that would have merely spectacular results. Still, the glamour of Cæsar's exploit had not yet faded, and we can well understand how those who looked for ever fresh victories from Roman arms would have demanded that Cæsar's conquest be resumed and extended. Once before Actium (34 B.C.), Augustus, who by the Treaty of Brundusium had secured control of the Western half of the Empire, seems

[1] Hill, op. cit. p. 138; Cohen, op. cit. vol. i. p. 99.

[2] Amelung and Holtzenger, " The Museums and Ruins of Rome," vol. i. p. 34; cf. Furtwángler and Urlichs, " Greek and Roman Sculpture," p. 234.

[3] Frank, "Roman Imperialism," p. 349; cf. Hor. Odes, III. iii. 45.

[4] Cæsar, B.G. iv. 20; cf. Belloc, " Warfare in England," pp. 60-1.

[5] Agricola, c. 13.

[6] Cæsar, B.G. iv. 20; cf. Mommsen, " R.P." vol. i. p. 172.

to have contemplated an invasion [1] of Britain. He did not yet enjoy sole power, and he may have wished to perform some exploit that would rival,[2] if not surpass, Cæsar's achievement, strike the popular imagination, and so win him favour with his countrymen at home. He had actually proceeded to Gaul with the avowed object of invading Britain, but he was recalled by a rebellion in Dalmatia. Though the attempt, if it was ever seriously contemplated, was thus frustrated, the thought of it, as is clear from the literature [3] of the time, lived in the public mind, and the hope was not abandoned of adding Britain to the list of Roman conquests. The Britons could not be regarded as enemies in the same sense as the Parthians, or be marked out for the same hostility, though Horace recalls [4] their cruelty to strangers, and in a passage [5] already quoted, couples them with the Parthians as a people, on whom Apollo is to send a pestilence raging at Rome. Some years after Actium, when Augustus was now in comparatively secure possession of power, he seems to have once more [6] left the public under the impression that he was about to undertake an expedition against Britain. The attempt had a second time to be abandoned owing to a rising among the Salassi. We may again entertain a doubt as to whether Augustus seriously intended the expedition, which had no obvious military value, though it might be an impressive demonstration of Roman power. The attempt was never again repeated by Augustus, and Tacitus [7] well styles this "long forgetfulness" of Britain a settled policy of the Emperor. It is clear, however, that a certain weight of

---

[1] Furneaux, Introduction to the Annals of Tacitus, vol. ii. p. 127; Dio, xlix. 38 (there quoted).

[2] As Dio, loc. cit. suggests, " κατὰ τόν τοῦ πατρὸς ζῆλον ".

[3] Hor. Epode vii. 7; Virg. Georgic, i. 30; iii. 25 (possibly all written about the same time); cf. Panegyr. Messallæ, 149.

[4] Odes, III. iv. 33.   [5] Ibid. I. xxi; cf. Prop. II. xxvii. 5.

[6] Hor. Odes, I. xxxv. 29; Dio, liii. 22; ibid. 25.

[7] Agricola, 13. The chapter contains an interesting review of Roman relations with Britain.

opinion continued in favour[1] of an expedition. Probably, as in the case of the Parthians, Augustus desired to create the impression that he had not wholly relinquished his design of a forward policy, though here again he was content with diplomatic triumphs.[2] Some British princes fled to him for protection, and Strabo[3] recounts the arrival of embassies from Britain, and their rendering of certain acts of homage to Cæsar. These events at any rate were an indication that the majesty of the Roman name, and of the power[4] of Cæsar, was recognized even in distant Britain, and though in a measure they served to soothe Roman pride, they must have seemed hollow victories to all who were eager for expansion.

We shall find that Horace, as long as he continued to write, reflects, with a good deal of fidelity, the various phases of Roman Imperial policy. There had been trouble for Roman arms in Spain almost since the death of Julius Cæsar, and though many generals[5] had won triumphs as the result of Spanish campaigns, that was no indication that a stage of settled government of the country had been reached. The unrest was to continue under Augustus, and was particularly acute among two tribes in the North-West of Spain,[6] the Asturians and Cantabrians. These Northern tribes were, as a whole, distinctly more warlike than the tribes of Southern Spain. When Horace refers to Spain, in almost every case he speaks only of the Cantabrians, partly because they were the most formidable opponents of Rome, partly adhering to his custom of selecting some typical name as representative of a whole people. In one Ode[7] he refers to their warlike qualities, and again[8] describes them as yet untaught to bear

---

[1] Hor. Odes, III. v. 3.   [2] Mon. Ancyr. c. 32.
[3] L. 5, 3, quoted by Furneaux, op. cit. ii. p. 128.
[4] Hor. Odes, IV. xiv. 47.   [5] Mommsen, " R.P." vol. i. p. 63.
[6] Dio, li. 20; *ibid.* liii. 25; Bouchier, " Spain under the Empire," p. 21.
[7] Odes, II. xi. 1; cf. Ep. I. xviii. 55.   [8] Odes, II. vi. 2.

the Roman yoke. We know[1] that, in the year 29 B.C., the
Cantabrians, the Asturians, and the Vaccaei revolted against
Rome, and were subdued by Statilius Taurus. The subjugation, however, was not complete, and three years later they were
once more in arms. This time Augustus led the expedition ✓
against them in person. Ferrero[2] suggests that the Emperor
was especially anxious for their conquest in order to get possession of the gold mines in their district, and relieve financial
pressure at home. The expedition was beset with many difficulties recounted by Dio,[3] and, to crown the misfortunes of the
Romans, Augustus was attacked by a serious illness, and was
compelled to go into retirement at Tarraco. The campaign[4]
was ended by Caius Antistius and T. Carisius, the legates
of Augustus, and the Emperor[5] returned to Rome (24 B.C.).
The temple of Janus[6] was once more closed as a sign of universal peace. The peace, however, was not of long duration,
though Augustus, during his two years' absence in Spain,
accomplished much in reorganizing[7] the government of the
peninsula. A new division of provinces was made, and
Tarraco was constituted the capital of Hither Spain, which
was known thenceforth as Hispania Tarraconensis. New
roads[8] were built, and a number of colonies founded, including Emerita Augusta (Merida), Pax Augusta (Badajoz), and
Cæsar Augusta (Zaragoza). But, in spite of such measures,
the very year of Augustus's departure from the province was
marked by another revolt[9] of the Cantabrians and Asturians,

---

[1] Dio, li. 20.   [2] Op. cit. vol. iv. p. 157.   [3] liii. 25.

[4] Hor. Odes, III. viii. 22, refers probably to this campaign, not to the later
victory of Agrippa. It was probably in this campaign also, that Augustus
recovered the standards mentioned in Mon. Ancyr. c. 29.

[5] *Vide* Hor. Odes, III. xiv. for the poet's joy on his return.

[6] Dio, liii. 26 ; cf. Hor. Odes, IV. xv. 8.

[7] Mon. Ancyr. c. 28 ; cf. Bouchier, op. cit. pp. 21-3 ; Mommsen,
" R.P." p. 64 ; Rushforth, " Historical Inscriptions," p. 99 ; Verrall,
op. cit. p. 58 ; *ibid.* p. 161.

[8] Bouchier, op. cit. p. 31.   [9] Dio, liii. 29.

which was suppressed with exceptional cruelty by Lucius Aemilius. A few years later (19 B.C.) we find Agrippa waging a savage campaign [1] against the Cantabrians. He finally succeeded[2] in crushing the resistance of those hardy mountaineers. Numbers of them seem to have perished before the Roman onslaught, while to prevent the recurrence of a serious uprising, many of them were removed to the plains, where they could be watched with greater vigilance by the Roman garrisons. No further trouble occurred in Spain during the reign of Augustus, nor for many years afterwards. While the northern portion of the peninsula was thus disturbed, the process of Romanization [3] had been making steady progress in the more peaceful districts. Intercourse was easy and constant between Italy and Spain. A number of communities were established with full Roman citizenship, and Tarraco was soon to become one of the most prominent centres [4] in the provinces for the cult [5] of the Emperor. Roman coinage had supplanted the native coinage, and the use of the Roman toga, Roman Law, and the Roman tongue had become widely diffused, even among those Spaniards who did not enjoy Italian burgess rights. Spain indeed was one of the provinces that, in spite of long resistance to its conquerors, accepted with most readiness and most completeness the heritage of Roman civilization. We may be sure that a taste for Roman literature grew up side by side with this leavening of the native population with Roman manners. Horace suggests as much, when in the closing Epistle of his first book he apostrophizes the completed volume, and tells it that, as soon as its popularity at Rome has waned, its destiny may one day be to

---

[1] Dio, liv. 11.

[2] Hor. Ep. I. xii. 26; Odes, IV. v. 28; xv. 40; Mon. Ancyr. c. 26; Suet. Oct. 21.

[3] Mommsen, " R.P." vol. i. p. 68 *et seq.* ; Bouchier, op. cit. p. 32.

[4] Boissier, " La Religion Romaine," vol. i. p. 131; cf. Rushforth, op. cit. p. 49.

[5] *Vide infra,* p. 57 *et seq.*

travel to Ilerda.[1]   All this was a preparation and a forerunner of the great Spanish names, that were to make their mark in Roman literature in the first century of the Empire.

We cannot, of course, expect from Horace, when referring to such events, the clearness and definiteness of a historian. My object in this chapter is not to build up from the study of the poet a complete history of Roman policy during the period in which he wrote, but to show how contemporary political events are reflected—often vaguely it is true—in his poetry.   He wrote as a poet, and enjoyed the licence of a poet.   He was content to seize events in their broad outlines, without solicitude for the mastery of detail, and frequently only such events, or aspect of events, as were of supreme interest for the moment, or such as were calculated to lend picturesqueness and colour to his verse.   We have already [2] seen in his reference to Parthian affairs his want of precision in the use of names.   This characteristic of his is even more marked when he deals with the Northern tribes, such as the Dacians, the Scythians, the Getae, the Geloni, that sometimes infringed on Roman interests.   The Scythians dwelt in the neighbourhood of the Don, which Horace calls a "Scythian [3] river," but he describes [4] their life, as well as that of the Getae, as mostly nomadic in character, and in one of his puritan moods he favourably contrasts it, for its simplicity and inno-cence, with the life of the decadent society in the Rome of his generation.   The Scythians had entered indirectly into Roman politics by their interference [5] in Parthian affairs, though it is possible that the poet sometimes employs the name "Scythian" to denote generally the peoples of the North.   They are once [6] spoken of in terms that seem to better suit the Dacians, while

---

[1] Ep. I. xx. 13 ; cf. Odes, II. xx. 19 ; Pliny, Ep. ii. 3.
[2] *Vide supra*, p. 14.
[3] Odes, III. iv. 36 ; x. 1 ; xxix. 28 ; IV. xv. 24.
[4] *Ibid.* I. xxxv. 9 ; III. xxiv. 9 *et seq.* ; IV. xiv. 42.
[5] *Ibid.* I. xxvi. 5 ; II. xi. 1.
[6] *Ibid.* III. viii. 23 ; cf. Wickham, op. cit. p. 5.

the Geloni also are referred [1] to in a manner, that recalls Roman measures against the same people. The truth is, that Horace is particularly vague when he speaks of all these tribes in the neighbourhood of the Danube, the Don, and the Black Sea. To the imagination of the poet, living in his warm Southern climate, they represented distant tribes, living in the cold [2] frozen regions of the North, at the very boundaries [3] of the known world. He was not concerned with making nice distinctions between them. One can see from even a late writer like Dio,[4] how misty were the notions prevailing at Rome with regard to these far-away peoples. The Dacians, however, figured more prominently in Roman politics than their Northern neighbours. They were a wild,[5] restless, lawless people, who occupied, roughly speaking, the further bank of the Lower Danube [6] (Modern Transylvania, Wallachia, and Moldavia), and were ever inclined to make incursions into Roman territory. Julius Cæsar had planned [7] an expedition against them, which never materialized. Augustus, after the Dalmatian war, was preparing [8] to resume Cæsar's design, but he was compelled to abandon it when the struggle with Antony began. The Dacians were then well organized under their chief Cotiso, and the protagonists in the conflict each courted [9] his alliance. The memory of Octavian's projected campaign influenced the Dacians, who decided to support Antony. Their aid was, however, rendered nugatory by internal dissensions, though a Dacian invasion of Italy was a continual dread [10] during the struggle, which led to the downfall of Antony. Soon after Actium a war [11] was begun against the Bastarnae and the

---

[1] Odes, II. ix. 23.   [2] Ibid. I. xxvi. 4; IV. v. 25; cf. Prop. IV. iii. 9.
[3] Odes, II. xx. 18.   [4] li. 22; liv. 20.
[5] Odes, I. xxxv. 9.   [6] Ibid. IV. xv. 21.
[7] Suet. Julius Cæsar, 44; Oct. 8.   [8] Mommsen, " R.P." vol. i. p. 10.
[9] For Antony's version of the negotiations of Octavian, vide Suet. Oct. 63; Dio, li. 22.
[10] Hor. Sat. II. vi. 53; Odes, III. vi. 13; cf. Virg. Georgic, ii. 497.
[11] Dio, li. 23; Mon. Ancyr. c. 30; Mommsen, " R.P." vol. i. p. 14.

Dacians by Marcus Crassus, who in two successive campaigns (29-28 B.C.), drove those tribes across the Danube, and conquered the whole territory of Moesia. Horace's reference [1] to the fall of the host of Cotiso may well point to the victory of Crassus. The Ode was clearly written at a time when Mæcenas was left in charge at Rome, and the period after Actium, when Augustus was endeavouring to settle affairs in the East, would well suit its context. This, however, was not the end of the trouble with the Dacians. We find them making frequent [2] incursions into Roman territory across the Danube, and as late as A.D. 5 it was deemed necessary [3] to send against them a large Roman force under the command of Lentulus. It was one of the great aims and achievements of Augustan policy to secure the Danube as the Roman frontier in the North, and by creating a succession of new provinces, Vindelicia, Raetia, Noricum, Pannonia, and Moesia, Augustus succeeded in making the Danube [4] a Roman river, practically along its whole course. Augustus mentions,[5] as a matter of pride, in the Monumentum Ancyranum that "the Bastarnae and the Scythians and the kings of the Sarmatae, who are on either side of the Don," sought his friendship, while so great was the prestige of the Roman name that he tells us, in the same context, that ambassadors were sent to him from the kings of India,[6] "a thing never before seen in the case of any Roman ruler".

In our discussion of Roman politics we must not pass over Germany and its relations to Rome during those years, though on this point Horace gives us little insight. During the time

---

[1] Odes, III. viii. 18.   [2] Dio, liv. 20, 36.

[3] *Ibid.* lv. 30 ; Mommsen, op. cit. vol. i. p. 42.

[4] Mon. Ancyr. c. 30 ; cf. Hor. Odes, IV. xv. 21.

[5] Mon. Ancyr. 31 ; cf. Suet. Oct. 21 ; Florus, IV. xii. 62 ; Hor. Odes, IV. xiv. 42 ; Car. Saec. 55.

[6] Mon. Ancyr. c. 31 ; cf. Suet. Oct. 21 ; Dio, liv. 9 ; Hor. Odes, IV. xiv. 42 ; I. xii. 56 ; Car. Saec. 56 ; Virg. Æn. vi. 794.

when Horace was writing, there was trouble [1] with the German tribes, who were ever prone to make sudden raids over the Rhine, and violate Roman territory; but still, no serious conflict took place between them and Rome during the reign of Augustus, till the Romans sustained their defeat under Lollius. The Sygambri, who were aided by the Usipetes and the Tencteri, took the leading part in an incursion over the Rhine, and overran a portion of Gaul. They overwhelmed the Roman force under Lollius, but the defeat was not a serious one [2] from the point of view of numbers, as he had only a single legion under his command. Lollius did not apparently fall into disgrace [3] as the result of his defeat. [4] In an Ode written about that time, we find Horace addressing him in complimentary terms, unmixed with any note of condemnation. This incursion of the Germans was evidently considered likely to be the prelude to a more serious movement, and it was feared [5] lest the turbulent elements in Gaul, which had increased in recent years owing to the exaction of the tribute, might join hands with the Germans to throw off the Roman yoke. For these reasons Augustus was induced to go in person to Gaul. The German tribes, learning that Lollius was repairing his forces, and that the Emperor himself was about to march against them, made peace, [6] and withdrew to the further side of the Rhine. Horace looks [7] forward to the day, when Augustus will lead these

---

[1] Dio, li. 21; Mommsen, "R.P." vol. i. p. 26. Agrippa crossed the Rhine in 38 B.C. to punish the German tribes, and soon after Carrinas conducted an expedition against them; cf. Virg. Georgic, i. 509.

[2] Suet. Oct. 23, says it was "majoris infamiae quam detrimenti".

[3] He afterwards fell into disgrace for taking bribes from the Parthian King, during the expedition to the East under Gaius (A.D. 2). For his character, *vide* Velleius, ii. 102; Ferrero, op. cit. vol. v. p. 285.

[4] Odes, IV. ix. 30 *et seq.*

[5] Agrippa at this time realized the German danger and its threat to Roman power in Gaul, and determined to strengthen the Rhine defences. He gave some territory on the hither side of the Rhine to the loyal Ubii (16 B.C.); *vide* Ferrero, op. cit. vol. v. p. 97 *et seq.*; *ibid.* p. 129 *et seq.*

[6] Dio, liv. 20.   [7] Odes, IV. ii. 34; cf. Odes, IV. v. 26; xiv. 51.

Sygambri captive in his triumph down the Sacred Way. He breaks off unfortunately at the most interesting juncture of German affairs. His Fourth Book of Odes was written[1] for the special purpose of celebrating the victories of Drusus and Tiberius in Raetia and Vindelicia. He had resumed, we are told, lyrical composition solely for that reason, at the request of the Emperor, though in reality a very small portion of his Fourth Book is devoted to these victories. One would imagine that his appointed task had been rather to pronounce a panegyric on "Augustan peace," than to sing the praises of Tiberius and Drusus. At the time when Augustus had succeeded in straightening out affairs in Gaul, and in disposing, temporarily at least, of the German danger, the Empire generally was comparatively peaceful. When the Emperor returned from Gaul (13 B.C.), an altar of Peace was erected in his honour. Horace considered himself in duty bound to join in the chorus of praise for the benefits of the Augustan regime. He dwells repeatedly[2] at this time on the victories of Augustus, on the peace that reigns throughout the Empire, with no trace of civil war, on the respect for the Roman name, that was felt even among the most distant nations. In these passages he gives us a kind of Imperial survey, which is well worth comparing in many details with the survey of his achievements given by the Emperor himself in the Monumentum Ancyranum. Horace sets before us in brief space the trials and triumphs of Rome, the dangers on her frontiers, her battles and her victories within the Empire. Strong in the security of the Imperial sway of Augustus, his subjects at home can enjoy the blessings that a bounteous Nature confers on them. If the Suetonian tradition of the origin of the Fourth Book of Odes is correct, and it can hardly be mistaken, it is strange how

---

[1] *Vide* Odes, IV. iv. xiv.; Suet. Life of Horace; Rushforth, "Historical Inscriptions," p. 37.

[2] Car. Saec. 53 *et seq.*; Odes, IV. v. 25 *et seq.*; xiv. 41 *et seq.*; xv 17 *et seq.*

comparatively little space the poet devotes to the appointed subject of his song. He finds it a more congenial task to sing the glories of "Augustan peace". We must remember too, that Horace began these Odes soon after the Saecular Games. He felt constrained, as it were, to write in the spirit [1] of these games, and of the new content given them by Augustus. The Past had been buried, and a new and more glorious era of universal peace and prosperity had opened with unclouded prospect. Hence at this time, it is the spirit of the "Carmen Saeculare" that dominates his work, rather than the victories of Tiberius and Drusus.

The Fourth Book would leave one under the impression that the peace of the Empire was so securely established that never again was it likely to be disturbed. These later Odes of Horace were barely given to the world, when the political horizon was again overcast, and the danger once more came from Germany. The German danger was always a living one. Tacitus in later days, with that rare insight which so frequently distinguishes his judgments, declares [2] that the threat from Germany was always a more serious one for the Empire than could ever come from Parthia. Soon after Augustus had returned to Rome (13 B.C.), it was decided to undertake the conquest of Germany. It is possible, as Ferrero suggests,[3] that the desire to safeguard Roman interests in Gaul was mainly instrumental in causing Augustus to embark at this time on a policy of expansion, though we may be sure that there was not wanting the encouragement of a body of advanced Imperialists, who were always active in advocating such a policy with regard to Germany. The Germans, mainly again the Sygambri, the Usipetes, and the Tencteri, took the offensive, determined to forestall the Roman attack. Drusus, who was in command of

---

[1] *Vide infra*, p. 71 *et seq.*   [2] Germania, c. 37.

[3] Op. cit. vol. v. p. 143 *et seq.* Gaul was one of the richest of the Roman Provinces, in fact a province of infinite possibilities owing to its resources. Cf. Mommsen, " R.P." vol. i. p. 26 *et seq.*

the Roman forces, won a series [1] of brilliant victories, and with the co-operation of the fleet acquired the North Sea coast to the mouth of the Elbe. He next attacked and subdued the tribes of the interior, and brought the Roman standards to the Elbe, but, on his return, these victories were largely counter-balanced by the general's death through a fall from his horse. His work was, however, continued by Tiberius,[2] who made the Roman occupation secure between the Rhine and the Elbe, thus extending the Roman frontier [3] to the latter river. The brilliancy of these victories must have helped to overcome the natural aversion of Augustus to any such extension of the frontiers, whatever scruples may have beset him in the abandon-ment of his usual cautious policy. He certainly lived to re-pent of his forward policy, on the terrible defeat [4] sustained by Varus at the hands of Arminius (A.D. 9), which robbed Rome of its recent conquests, and put the Roman frontier once again at the Rhine. However, of the German campaigns of Drusus no mention appears in Horace. His lyric poetry had ceased for some years before his death, and moreover, in those later years, he was occupied chiefly with the task of literary criticism, and has only the rarest allusion to political events.

There were many minor campaigns, such as that of Carrinas against the Morini (28 B.C.), of Messalla [5] against the Aquitani (27 B.C.), of Murena [6] against the Salassi (25 B.C.), of Silius [7]

---

[1] Dio, liv. 32, 33, 36. For Drusus' plan of campaign, *vide* Ferrero, op. cit. vol. v. p. 193.

[2] Suet. Tib. 9; Dio, lv. 6; Tac. Annals, ii. 26; Ferrero, op. cit. vol. v. p. 234.

[3] For a discussion of the Elbe frontier, *vide* Mommsen, "R.P." vol. i. p. 56; cf. Frank, "Roman Imperialism," p. 352.

[4] Suet. Oct. 23; cf. Mon. Ancyr. c. 26, where Augustus refers to German conquests, but omits all mention of this defeat. Hence it has been dis-puted whether the Mon. Ancyr. is an epitaph, where only fortunate events are narrated, or "an account of Augustus's administration".

[5] Suet. Oct. 21.

[6] Dio, liii, 25; Suet. Oct. 21.   [7] *Ibid.* liv. 20.

against the Vennones and Cammunni (16 B.C.), of which our poet makes no mention. Such campaigns as these created no great sensation at Rome, and did not profoundly affect Roman policy. It was especially the big frontier movements, or campaigns likely to end in an extension of Roman territory, or those, with the conduct of which the Emperor or members of the Imperial household were personally associated, that claimed the attention of the poet.

CHAPTER II.

THE AUGUSTAN REVIVAL.

THE story of the Augustan Revival forms in many respects the most fascinating episode in the religious history of Rome. It is a subject that has been very adequately dealt with by a number of scholars.[1] In this chapter, though I shall necessarily have to traverse ground that is already familiar, I will endeavour to bring into prominence such aspects of the Revival as will furnish a background for the study of the religious thought of Horace.

A word must first be said on the causes[2] of the decay of Roman religion. This religion in its earliest stages was an animistic[3] worship. The Powers believed to control the Universe were vaguely conceived and ill-defined, and thus could be multiplied indefinitely. A spirit could be found to preside over every act of life from the cradle to the grave. These Powers were not endowed with a clear-cut personality like the Greek Olympian gods, and hence the Roman fashioned no image in his worship of them. The native

[1] *Vide* Warde Fowler, "The Religious Experience of the Roman People," Lecture xix.; Carter, "The Religion of Numa," p. 146 *et seq.*; Wissowa, "Religion und Kultur der Römer," p. 73 *et seq.*; Wendland, "Die Hellenistisch-Römische Kultur," p. 142 *et seq.*

[2] *Vide* Boissier, "La Religion Romaine," vol. i. c. 2; Cumont, "Les Religions Orientales," p. 47 *et seq.*; Carter, op. cit. p. 104 *et seq.*

[3] *Vide* Warde Fowler, op. cit. Lecture vii. *passim;* Jevons, "Introduction to Plutarch's Roman Questions," p. 56 *et seq.*; "Idea of God," p. 16 *et seq.*; Döllinger, "Gentile and Jew," vol. ii. p. 7 *et seq.*; cf. Cornford, "From Religion to Philosophy," pp. 37-9.

Roman religion never evolved a mythology of its own, while it was barren of that artistic inspiration which brought Greek Art to its full perfection. It was a religion of cold formalism, calm and unemotional, appealing especially to the intellectual faculties, and such a religion, void of strong appeal to feeling and sensation, was not likely in time of stress and excitement to afford the comfort which afflicted souls demanded of it. It was a religion without fixed or settled dogmas, a loosely-knit Polytheism, or more correctly Polydaemonism, that found little difficulty in admitting[1] foreign deities and foreign cults into its sacred circle. As Roman power expanded, external influences, at first Greek and Etruscan, began to modify the primitive worship of the Romans. Greek ideas had at an early period begun to leaven Roman religious belief. When the Olympian gods invaded Italy, those supernatural beings, who had hitherto claimed the allegiance of the Romans, became identified with them, or assumed many of their attributes. The Sibylline[2] books, with their introduction of the "Graecus ritus," became in process of time one of the dominant influences in the religious life of the Romans. All these Hellenic elements helped to revivify and transform the old beliefs, to give them a touch of the human, by the introduction of the anthropomorphic gods of Greece, to add dignity and solemnity to native ritual. While this was the contribution of Greece towards the religious life of Rome, it was from Greece, too, that some of the strongest forces of disintegration ultimately came./ It was especially at the time of the "Liberation of Greece" that the full flood of Greek influence poured into Rome. Roman statesmen and generals, now come to a knowledge of the real Greece, were brought directly and intimately under the spell of its Art and Literature, and felt the charm of a people beyond the sway of Rome. The Roman mind expanded under this new influence, which helped

[1] *Vide* Warde Fowler, op. cit. Lecture x.
[2] Carter, op. cit. p. 62 *et seq.*; Warde Fowler, op. cit. pp. 316-19.

to break down the narrow, almost insular prejudice, which hitherto had dominated Roman society, and thus contributed in a measure towards the weakening of the bonds of devotion to national ideals. The Scipionic circle, which aimed at transplanting Hellenism to Roman soil, was the finest fruit of this new intercourse, but its action constituted what seemed to men of conservative mind a dangerous break with the traditions of the Past. We must remember that religion and the State were indissolubly bound together in Ancient Rome. Any deflection from unquestioning loyalty to the State would react upon religious belief, and tend towards a lowering of its prestige. Roman education from the earliest times was directed towards the production of a type of disinterested patriotism, which owed unquestioning obedience to the State. The State was supreme, and the individual was expected to sacrifice his private interests to its advancement, and to the increase of its power. But the day came when the individual refused to sacrifice himself further on the altar of State interest. Indications of such individualism had appeared as early as the days of the Scipios. It appeared in the region of thought, when the members of the Scipionic circle refused to be fettered by the old formulas of Roman education, and maintained their right to introduce new elements of culture, which their fathers had not known. In the region of action, in military matters, the same phenomenon revealed itself, especially during the closing century of the Republic, in the increased importance of the individual commander, and the devotion of his soldiers to his person rather than to the State. Possibly, when the Roman Empire was in its infancy, and Rome was beset by formidable rivals, men may have felt less inclination to question their duty to the Republic. But when Rome held sovereign sway in Italy, and above all when her great rival Carthage had been reduced to impotence, this stimulus to patriotism was largely removed. The reforms[1] of Marius,

---

[1] Mommsen, vol. iii. pp. 187-91; cf. Sallust, Bellum Jug. 84.5.

however, dealt the first serious blow to the fabric of State
supremacy. By democratizing the army, by increasing the
power of the commander to reward his soldiers, he laid the
foundation of that personal devotion to the individual leader,
that was to have such disastrous consequences for the Republic, and end in its dissolution. When Sulla marched his
army to the gates of Rome, in defiance of Senatorial decrees,
he gave the death-blow to the idea of unquestioning loyalty to
the State, which had hitherto swayed Roman feeling. Now
personal ambition begins to dominate Roman history, and
was to issue in that long and dreary series of civil wars, which
cast their gloom over the closing years of the Republic. We
feel that, when Cæsar[1] obtained his command in Gaul, he
wished by his victories, not so much to extend the boundaries
of the Roman Empire, as from his army to fashion a military
instrument, that would help him to achieve his ambitions.
When the Republic fell, and when the Julio-Claudian House,
that for many years had ruled the destinies of the Empire, had
become extinct, this personal ambition of commanders again
reasserted itself, and the army discovered "the secret[2] that an
Emperor could be created elsewhere than at Rome". It
is possible that the extravagant honours paid to Roman
generals and provincial governors, especially in Greece and in
the Eastern provinces, helped, as time went on, to intensify
this growing individualism.[3] History had hitherto concerned
itself with the glories of the State; now biographies were
written, the personal element began to appear more frequently
in historical writing, and the microcosm of the individual, his
trials, his sufferings, his triumphs, were brought into greater
prominence.

After the liberation of Greece, as I have said, came the
greatest influx of Greek ideas into Rome. Greece then took

---

[1] Suet. J. Cæsar, c. 38; *ibid.* 68.   [2] Tac. Hist. i. 4.
[3] For some aspects of Individualism, *vide* Sellar, "Virgil," p. 290;
Cumont, op. cit. p. 46; Wendland, op. cit. p. 45 *et seq.*

captive its savage conqueror of later days. But the Greece of the time was a decadent Greece. It was a Greece, which had lost[1] its reverence for the Olympian gods, whom it had clothed indeed with human attributes, but had endowed too with every human frailty. These had not only fallen from their high estate, but had frequently become the butt for the ridicule of the Comic Stage. When the Romans came to a knowledge of Greek Literature (which they had done even before the liberation of Greece), with its overmastering beauty they drank in, too, its spirit of scepticism and irreverence for the Olympian gods and their Roman counterparts. But the greatest legacy of Greece to Rome at this time was its philosophical speculation. Two rival systems struggled for the mastery, each in its own way acting as a solvent to established beliefs. Stoicism from many points of view tended to undermine the fabric of Roman religion. By insisting on the value[2] of the individual soul, it helped to increase the spirit of individualism, with all the consequences of which I have spoken. It taught, too, a doctrine of "Cosmopolitanism". All men were members of the same commonwealth[3] (which for the Stoics was coextensive with the Universe), having a common bond of citizenship, which Cicero calls "communis humani generis societas".[4] Another follower[5] of the Stoic school, in depicting his ideal of the Stoic as embodied in Cato, tells us that "he believed himself not born for himself but for the world". Seneca proclaims that "Nature has made us all kinsmen". The spread of such ideas would tend to destroy the isolation of the Roman, and as the barriers of the old narrow rigid patriotism were broken down, loyalty to the national gods was involved in the same process of disruption. Stoicism contributed to the same re-

[1] Murray, "Four Stages of Greek Religion," p. 103 *et seq.*
[2] Glover, "The Conflict of Religions in the Early Roman Empire," p. 39; Lecky, "History of European Morals," p. 239.
[3] Cic. De Fin. III. xix. 64.   [4] De Offic. iii. 6.
[5] Lucan, "Pharsalia," ii. 383.

sult in its efforts to compromise[1] with the existing beliefs of Rome. It identified Jupiter, the supreme Roman god, with the Power it itself recognized as controlling the Universe, called by various titles, such as Reason, Soul, or God. The other gods of the Roman Pantheon were conceived as merely attributes of this one supreme deity. This was a purer form of religion than any yet evolved on Roman soil, a milestone on the road to Monotheism, and as such it contributed to the collapse of the structure of the older Polytheism.

The rival system of Epicureanism,[2] especially as expounded in the glowing pages of Lucretius, in language vibrating with the passionate sincerity of one who was conscious of a mission, must have furthered still more the process of the decay of traditional beliefs. Its denial that the gods have anything to do with the government of the Universe, coupled with its denial of the immortality of the soul, struck at the very roots of religion. The popularity of the poem of Lucretius, at least among the educated, gives us perhaps a measure of its destructive effect on the religious life of Rome.

Another cause of the disintegration of what we might call the Græco-Roman religion, was the introduction of the Oriental cults. The old forms of worship had lost their power, and even the splendour of the ceremonial prescribed by the Sibylline Books failed to satisfy the religious needs of the masses. It is significant that such a change becomes apparent for the first time towards the end of the Second Punic war. The long struggle, through which the Romans had passed, when Hannibal's cleverly planned scheme for the dismemberment of the Latin League, and the destruction of Roman power, had wellnigh been successful, had left its impress on the popular mind. As is clear from Livy's narrative,[3] this was a period of intense

---

[1] Boissier, op. cit. vol. ii. p. 125 et seq.; Warde Fowler, op. cit. p. 362; "Roman Ideas of Deity," pp. 52-3.

[2] Vide infra, p. 95 et seq.

[3] Especially Books xxi.-xxii.; cf. Warde Fowler, "The Religious Experience," etc., Lecture xiv.

religious excitement, and in the darkest hours of the conflict it is little wonder that the Romans lost faith in the protecting deities of their city, turned eventually to strange gods, and had recourse to protectors from outside, that were considered more potent. The introduction [1] of the worship of Cybele (204 B.C.) opened the door for a further invasion of Oriental cults. The wild orgiastic rites associated with that goddess formed a strange contrast to the staid and sober forms of worship, to which the Roman had hitherto been accustomed. The dangerous qualities of such a cult, which contained many repulsive elements, and its detrimental effect upon the national character soon became apparent. Restrictions followed, and native Romans were forbidden [2] to enrol themselves as priests of this foreign goddess. The taste for such exciting forms of worship was an evidence that the "gravitas," on which the Roman of the old type had prided himself, was being gradually undermined. A few years later (186 B.C.), Bacchic rites had become so prevalent at Rome, and had led to such flagrant abuses, that they were suppressed by a decree [3] of the Senate that is still extant. The Bacchae of Euripides helps us to appreciate the ecstatic nature of this cult. The whole atmosphere of the play is one of unrestrained delirious excitement. The initiated, possessed by the god, as they believe, while their frenzy lasts, career in mad course over hill and dale to the music of their mystic cries. The wild ridges of Cithæron were a fitting background for this drama of lawless revelry. A beginning had thus been made with the Mystery religions by the introduction of the worship of Cybele, which, as the Roman Empire expanded, and as Roman commerce increased, was to be followed by the cults of Mithra, and of the deities of Syria and of the Nile. These religions had new attractions to offer to men, who were weary of a

---

[1] Livy, xxix. 10; Cumont, op. cit. c. iii.; *vide infra*, p. 107.
[2] Cumont, op. cit. p. 64; cf. Prop. II. xxii. 15.
[3] Bruns, "Fontes Juris Romani," p. 160.

"creed outworn". There was the element of ecstasy about
their ritual, the hope of a happy immortality held out to the
initiated. By initiation, each individual soul was given a new
value, and raised, as it were, to a higher plane, while a bond of
brotherhood was established with all, who had shared in the
ceremony.

It is little wonder, when Roman religion was thus in the
melting-pot, that men lost their bearings amid this welter of
confusion, and many found refuge in Agnosticism. Religious
indifference, or professed scepticism seems to have been particularly rife among the educated classes. If we take Cicero [1]
as a typical example, it is clear that when he reveals his real
self, when he is not defending a position in Philosophy, he has
no fixed or well-established beliefs. Again, if we read the letter [2]
of consolation written by Sulpicius to Cicero on the occasion of
the death of his daughter, Tullia, we can see how little religious
considerations weighed with the educated at such a solemn and
sacred moment, how little their sorrow was relieved by a well-
grounded hope of happiness in another life. The demoralization of society, consequent upon the Civil Wars, must have
brought still further to decay the already crumbling edifice of
the national religion, though it is possible to argue that a reaction was inevitable, that at any rate men, who had passed
through the horrors of those years, whose families had been
depleted, who had been the victims of proscription and confiscation, would not rest content with the cold, cheerless dogma
of annihilation expounded by Lucretius, but would look for
a readjustment of the balance to a life beyond the grave.

I have had in this rapid survey to touch lightly on the chief
causes of the decline of Roman religion, but such as the survey
is, it will enable us to appreciate the condition of things, when
the Republic ceased to exist, and when Augustus became the

[1] On this question, *vide* Warde Fowler, "Social Life in the Age of
Cicero," p. 319 *et seq.*; cf. Cic. Ad Fam. xiv. 4.
[2] *Ibid.* iv. 5.

supreme ruler of the Roman Empire. The decline of religion
had been accompanied by a corresponding and inevitable decline of morality. The old simplicity of Republican manners,
which had helped to build up the greatness of Rome, seemed
dead beyond recall, and wealth, luxury, and licence had followed in the wake of Empire. Augustus, shrewd politician
that he was, must have early seen that such conditions were
unfavourable to one who hoped to legalize a revolution and
aimed at settled government. When his position was rendered
comparatively secure [1] by the victory of Actium, he set himself
to the task of reform, and his Religious Revival was in harmony
with his general policy. It is never easy to weigh motives,
but for one thing, Augustus,[2] like a number of his contemporaries, must have been impressed by the value of religion as
a conservative force, and a device, if nothing more, for keeping
the common people in check. This, the politician's view of
religion, had found favour in Rome as early as the days of
Polybius.[3] There is no need to give credence either to the
direct statements or the innuendoes of Suetonius'[4] "chron-
ique scandaleuse" to impugn to some degree at least the
sincerity of the Emperor's efforts at a Moral and Religious
Revival. It is clear enough that Augustus was not wholly
actuated by zeal for religion in his Revival, and that the
"alliance between the altar and the throne"[5] was dictated
partly by self-interest. Such a Revival harmonized well with
one of the dominant features of his policy,[6] which inspired his
aim at creating the illusion that the Republic had been restored, and that the powers he possessed were strictly consti-
tutional.[7] With the restoration of the Republic were to be

---

[1] For some elements of opposition, *vide* Boissier, "L'Opposition sous
les Césars," p. 53 *et seq.*; cf. Suet. Oct. 19.

[2] For Augustus's superstition, cf. Suet. Oct. 90-92; Pliny, N.H. ii. 5.

[3] Polyb. vi. 56.   [4] Oct. 68-71.

[5] Cumont, op. cit. p. 48.   [6] Mon. Ancyr. c. i. ; *ibid.* c. 34.

[7] *Ibid.* c. 6; Tac. Annals, i. 2; Greenidge, "Roman Public Life,"
p. 338.

revived those forms of worship, that reverence for the gods, which had helped to raise Rome to the position of greatness it enjoyed. In examining the Augustan Revival, one can detect in it two apparently conflicting tendencies, but this apparent conflict is resolved in the light of the Emperor's general policy. Augustus lived a double life. He possessed, and was fully conscious of possessing power, unconstitutional and practically absolute, but he sedulously fostered the belief that his power did not overstep the limits of the constitution. The Revival was at once national in character, antiquarian we might call it, in the sense of being a reversion to those old forms of worship so characteristic of the earlier Republic. This aspect of the Revival fitted well with the illusion that the Republic, and all it stood for, had been restored. But there were other aspects of it that harmonized with the absolute character of his rule. Augustus was clever enough to exploit the Revival for dynastic ends.

We have already seen[1] the significance of the struggle at Actium, how Augustus put himself forward as the champion of Roman ideals against the dangerous and seductive charm of Orientalism. He wished to appear, too, as the guardian of national ideals in religion, especially against the invasion of those Egyptian worships, which he held in contempt. Virgil[2] seems to give special prominence to the fact that Augustus offered his vows to the Italian deities, when the gods of the Nile had been conquered at Actium. Again, the very reverence for the Past, which he wished to encourage,[3] could be used in his interest, and the spirit of liberty be replaced by a spirit of pride in the greatness of Rome. The ceremonies, which had fallen into abeyance could, when revived, be given a new

[1] *Vide supra*, p. 5 *et seq.*

[2] Æn. viii. 715 ; cf. Prop. II. xxxiii. 20 ; IV. i. 17.

[3] For his care for the memory of the great figures of Roman history, *vide* Suet. Oct. 31. In his Forum he erected a kind of " Siegesallee," with statues of them in triumphal garb; cf. Æn. vi. 756 *et seq.*; viii. 626 *et seq.*; Hor. Odes, I. xii. 32 *et seq.*

content, that would reflect the glories of the Emperor, and help to invest him with a religious awe, that would silence the murmurs of the discontented. Men were not allowed to dwell wholly in the Past, but were taught, too, to look to the Future. Great as the Past had been, its greatness would be overshadowed by that of the Future, as long as the destinies of Rome were committed to the care of Augustus. The Golden Age would be restored,[1] through the agency of this Heaven-sent ruler, long promised as the Saviour of a distracted country. Though Augustus wished to inculcate reverence for the glories of Ancient Rome, he wished also gradually to break with Republican traditions. It was a similar policy that inspired[2] Julius Cæsar to build a new Forum, and change the orientation of the Roman Forum, a place so intimately associated with the great struggles for freedom under the Republic. Augustus, too, wished to shift the centre of gravity of the State. So he built a Forum of his own, surrounded with especial pomp and fostered devotion to the divinities,[3] that were bound up with the fortunes of the House of Cæsar. In no work of the period are the dominant ideas of the Revival more faithfully reflected than in the Æneid. That was a fascinating theory,[4] that saw in Æneas the counterpart of Augustus, and the temptation was strong to follow out the parallel in detail. But, even though one may not accept the theory as a whole, still a formula might be extracted from Virgil's great Epic, that would include the fundamental conceptions of Augustan policy in the Revival. The formula might run as follows :—Rome, rising under Providence from small beginnings to a greatness, that finds its culmination in the House of Cæsar. Those divergent tendencies in the Revival, one looking to the Past, the other

---

[1] Virg. Æn. vi. 792 ; cf. Conway in " Virgil's Messianic Eclogue," p. 37 et seq.

[2] Wissowa, op. cit. p. 77 ; cf. Stuart Jones, " Classical Rome," pp. 56, 151 et seq.

[3] Cf. Horace's phrase " tuos præbente deos," Odes, IV. xiv. 33.

[4] Saint Beuve, " Étude sur Virgile," p. 63 et seq.

to the Future, one antiquarian in character, conserving the almost vanished relics of a former age, the other pregnant with the hopes of a coming era, subserving the interests of the new Imperial regime, were turned into a single channel, when the worship of Rome and Augustus coalesced. Augustus to all intents and purposes became Rome.

It is not easy to define the limits imposed on himself by Augustus, when he undertook the task of reviving religion. It was probably the supreme object of his labours to drive home the lesson, that Rome owed its greatness to the protection [1] of the gods, and that it was only by securing the " Pax Deorum," that it could maintain its position of supremacy. Disaster would inevitably follow, if the worship of the gods was neglected, and their temples allowed to crumble in ruin. We are given certain details of what Augustus accomplished, in the Monumentum Ancyranum, in Suetonius, and in Dio, but we are left in the dark as to whether he had set himself any clear or well-defined limits in his task of revival. Manifestly he could not have thought of wholly reverting to the earliest period, when Roman religion was in the animistic stage, though from that remote time he could revive many of its old ceremonies, its brotherhoods and priesthoods, and much of the picturesque pageantry of ancient ritual. His thoughts must have been turned especially to the principal deities of that Græco-Roman polytheism, which flourished in a later period of the Republic till the chaos of the Civil Wars and the corroding influence of scepticism had done their work. One would have thought that any attempt to revive the worship of a number of these deities was doomed to failure from the outset, weighted down as they were with the

---

[1] Readers of the Æneid will remember how strongly Virgil insists on the idea of Providence guiding the destinies of Rome. The following passages may be noted: Æn. i. 205, 257, 382; ii. 294, 777; iii. 395; iv. 224 et seq., 345; vi. 66, 461; vii. 239; x. 31 et seq.; cf. Prop. III. xi. 65.

mythology of the Greek Olympians, which was sufficient to undermine and discredit even a more attractive religion. Augustus, however, even though his motives were not wholly disinterested, was in a position to give fresh life to the cult of these deities, by reviving the externals of worship and investing them with a new splendour.

What might be called the material aspect of the Revival was easy of accomplishment, and met with comparative success. Many causes, as we have seen (not the least of them the demoralization [1] consequent upon the Civil Wars), conspired to bring about the neglect of the worship of the gods, and the decay of their temples. Propertius could with justice [2] complain of the cobwebs that clung to deserted shrines. Augustus displayed special activity in building and restoring temples. Many details are given [3] us in the official account of his deeds and in Suetonius, and furnish a formidable list. His activity in this direction began soon after the battle of Actium. Suetonius refers [4] to his solicitude for adorning the temples with splendid gifts, and makes special mention of a lavish offering to the shrine of Jupiter Capitolinus. The Emperor was careful, too, [5] to replace in the temples throughout the cities of Asia the ornaments of which they had been despoiled by Antony. He was not content with mere personal achievement, but he induced [6] many leading citizens to erect new buildings, both sacred and profane, or to restore and embellish those that had fallen into decay. It was through his encouragement that a temple of Diana was built by L.

---

[1] *Vide supra*, p. 3.   [2] Prop. II. vi. 35 ; III. xiii. 47.

[3] Mon. Ancyr. c. 19, 21 ; cf. Supplement, c. 2 ; Suet. Oct. 29-30 ; Ovid, Fasti, ii. 63. In Mon. Ancyr. c. 20, he says he restored eighty-two temples in his sixth consulship.

[4] Oct. 30, 57 ; cf. Mon. Ancyr. c. 21.   [5] *Ibid.* c. 24.

[6] Suet. Oct. 29. For the building of the Pantheon by Agrippa, cf. Dio, liii. 27.

Cornificius, and the temple [1] of Saturn by Munatius Plancus. If we survey the list of temples, on which Augustus concentrated his activities, we shall see that they are those especially of the great divinities, whose worship had long been established in Rome, or throughout Italy.

Augustus devoted himself with no less zeal to what I have styled (if the term be permitted), the antiquarian side of the Revival, which consisted of the restoration of ancient ceremonies, brotherhoods and priesthoods. Ritual was always of prime importance [2] among the Romans. It was their first duty to placate, by sacred rites, the Powers they believed to control the Universe, even when, as often happened, they had no very definite beliefs about them beyond the fact of their existence. This was certainly true of the early period, but even when contact with Greece, and the process of syncretism that followed, made the outline of these supernatural beings more clearly defined, ritual continued to hold its position of pre-eminence. The exact performance of sacred rites was essential as a means of securing the "Pax Deorum". If, through the neglect or inadvertence of the officiating minister, the sacred rite was vitiated, it might bring upon the whole community the anger of the deity, in whose honour it was performed. The decay of such rites was an index of the loss of confidence in the protecting deities of Rome. With their revival it was hoped that confidence would be restored. But, over and above this, many of those rites were believed to go back to a remote, almost legendary age, and for some, the flavour of antiquity about them constituted their chief attraction. Antiquarianism was in fashion owing to the researches

---

[1] Suetonius must refer to the restoration of the original temple at the end of the Forum, dedicated 498 B.C.; cf. Huelsen, "Le Forum Romain," p. 77.

[2] Warde Fowler, "The Religious Experience," pp. 170-1; Pelham, "Essays in Roman History," p. 99.

of Varro.[1] For many minds antiquity will ever possess an unfailing charm, and of supreme interest is that portion of it, that appertains to the religious life of a people. Now, under the guidance of Augustus, men's thoughts were turned more and more to the origins of Rome. They sought to gather up the scattered threads of history and legend, to reconstruct the Past of their ancestors, to piece together the secret of the habits and character of the infancy of that Imperial race, that had achieved a world-wide greatness. Many of the rites restored by Augustus were national in the best sense of the word. They were interwoven with the very fibre of the Roman people in its first struggles, they re-echoed its aspirations, and reflected the earliest achievements of its civilization. Viewed in this light, every vestige of antiquity became sacred, and a halo of romance hung round those memorials of a vanished age. Readers of the Æneid will remember how lovingly Virgil[2] dwells upon details of ancient custom and ritual, how tenderly, with Evander as guide, Æneas lingers[3] on the spots, that were destined to be hallowed by the great associations of historical Rome. The later books of the Æneid especially are steeped in the atmosphere of primitive Italy, and of the cradle of the Roman race. Virgil[4] was not alone among the Augustan poets in coming under the spell of this antiquarian side of the Revival, and the prevailing passion for antiquity. Augustus began his restoration of the old rites by a master-stroke of policy. He opened his campaign against Antony by a declara-

[1] Varro attributed the decline of Roman religion chiefly to the ignorance and neglect of its ceremonies.

[2] Æn. ii. 238; iii. 404 *et seq.*; v. 76 *et seq.*; 600 *et seq.*; vii. 600 *et seq.*; viii. 269 *et seq.*, 284, 343. For a discussion of Virgil's knowledge of ritual and Pontifical law, *vide* Macrobius, "Saturnalia," III. i. *et seq.*

[3] Æn. viii. 314 *et seq.*

[4] Cf. Prop. III. iii. 2 *et seq.*; ix. 49 *et seq.*; IV. i. *passim*; IV. iv., ix., x.; Tib. II. v. 23 *et seq.* Ovid's Fasti is a monument to the renewed interest in the sacred Festivals of Rome; cf. Carter, *op. cit.* p. 152.

4

tion [1] of war through the Fetiales, according to their ancient ceremonies. He thus at once received the sanction of an ancient priesthood in the struggle, and stood forward as the guardian of Roman traditions. In general, he showed a scrupulous regard for the details of religious practice, and insisted [2] upon the same in the case of others. He restored such ancient ceremonies as the Augurium Salutis, [3] in which the Augurs prayed, year by year, for the prosperity of the State, and revived such distinctly primitive festivals as the Lupercalia [4] and the Compitalia. The office of Flamen Dialis was filled [5] once more, and communities like the Fratres Arvales, [6] one of the oldest of the Roman brotherhoods, the Sodales Titii, the Salii, were brought back to their former pride of place. In general, says Suetonius, [7] he increased the number, the dignity, and the privileges of the priesthoods, and showed especial generosity towards the Vestal Virgins. Thus were the externals of religion revived, not only for the glory of the gods, but, as we shall see, also for the glory of the House of Cæsar.

It was one of the great objects of Augustus, as I have said, to invest his person and his office with a religious reverence. This trend of his policy might have been apparent to keen observers, when he assumed the name of Augustus [8] (27 B.C.), a name that, through many associations, was charged with religious significance. Again, Augustus was himself a member [9] of the various priestly colleges, and this fact alone enabled him

---

[1] Dio, l. 4; cf. Livy, I. xxiv.   [2] Suet. Oct. 35.

[3] Dio, li. 20; Suet. Oct. 31; Wissowa, op. cit. p. 525.

[4] Suet. Oct. 31. It was revived, with possibly some new details; Warde Fowler, "The Religious Experience," pp. 478-80; cf. Diels, "Sibyllinische Blätter," p. 69.

[5] Dio, liv. 36; Wissowa, op. cit. p. 76.

[6] On the Arval Brethren, *vide* Warde Fowler, op. cit. p. 434 *et seq.*; Carter, op. cit. p. 156; Pelham, op. cit. p. 113.

[7] Oct. 31.

[8] On the significance of the name, *vide* Dio, liii. 16; Suet. Oct. 7; Ovid, Fasti, i. 559; cf. Hill, "Roman Coins," p. 136; Mon. Ancyr. c. 34.

[9] For the list of the sacred offices held by him, *vide* Mon. Ancyr. c. 7.

to shape them to his ends. By his power of "commendatio," and above all by the patronage, which he exercised, when as Pontifex Maximus[1] he became the religious head of the State, he was in a position to secure that none would be admitted to the membership of these bodies except those subservient to his views. These priestly associations certainly played an important part in impressing the popular imagination with the sacred character of the Emperor and his family. He himself tells us[2] that by a decree of the Senate, his name was included in the Salian hymn, and it was not the least important function[3] of the Fratres Arvales, when revived, to offer prayers and vows on important occasions for himself and the members of his household. A grateful or fawning Senate found numberless opportunities of offering him honours, which tended to create the impression that Augustus was no longer an ordinary[4] mortal. Special prayers for the safety of the Emperor and his House were decreed[5] to be added to the solemn prayers, annually offered for the safety of the Republic. He relates[6] himself that " the Senate decreed, that every fifth year vows for my good health should be performed by the consuls and the priests. In accordance with these vows, games have often been celebrated during my lifetime, sometimes by the four chief colleges, sometimes by the consuls. In private also, and as municipalities (*privatim etiam et municipatim*), the whole body of citizens have continually sacrificed at every shrine for my good health." Such vows were considered especially necessary, as Augustus was generally in a precarious[7] condi-

---

[1] Greenidge, " Roman Public Life," p. 350.
[2] Mon. Ancyr. c. 10.   [3] Warde Fowler, op. cit. p. 437.
[4] Suetonius, with a touch of humour, in recounting the honours paid to Augustus (Oct. 57), says he will pass over those decreed by the Senate " quia possunt videri vel necessitate expressa vel verecundia ".
[5] For the honours paid to him after Actium, *vide* Dio, li. 19.
[6] Mon. Ancyr. c. 9.
[7] Suet. Oct. 59, 81 ; Dio, l. 18 (quoting a speech of Antony's) ; Hor. Ep. I. xiii. 3.

tion of health. In Dio's[1] narrative we are told that "when
letters were brought to Rome about affairs in Parthia, it was
decreed that his name should be inserted in the hymns, on an
equal footing witn the gods". When his influence was missed
for a time, through absence in the provinces, the Senate was
particularly careful to shower[2] on him the most lavish honours
upon his return. Thus, when he returned from the East (19
B.C.) "having arranged matters in Sicily, Greece, Asia, and
Syria," an altar[3] was erected near the Capene Gate to Fortuna
Redux, and upon it the Pontiffs and Vestal Virgins were to
offer yearly sacrifice. The anniversary of the day of his return was to be accounted a feast day, and was to be called
the Augustalia. Again, when he returned from Spain and
Gaul (13 B.C.), "having successfully arranged the affairs of these
provinces," an altar[4] of the "Augustan Peace" was consecrated
in his honour in the Campus Martius, and it was ordered that
the magistrates, the priests, and the Vestals should there offer
sacrifice on each anniversary of his return. In his thirteenth
consulship,[5] "the Senate and the equestrian order, and the
entire Roman people" bestowed on him the title of "Pater
Patriae". The Roman knights,[6] "sponte atque consensu,"
celebrated his birthday for two successive days, and there was
scarcely an important act of his life, that was not commemor-
ated in some striking way. Now, all these honours, many of
which were undoubtedly inspired by Augustus himself, this
solicitude for his welfare, the numerous prayers and vows

---

[1] li. 20.

[2] Suet. Oct. 57; cf. Hor. Odes, III. xiv; IV. ii. 20; v. 2 et seq.

[3] Mon. Ancyr. c. 11; Dio says (liv. 10), πολλὰ καὶ παντοῖα ἐψηφίσθη, but
he refused everything except the altar to Fortuna Redux; cf. Cohen,
"Médailles Impériales," Aug. 102-8.

[4] Mon. Ancyr. c. 12; Dio, liv. 25; vide infra, p. 117.

[5] Mon. Ancyr. c. 35. He insists on the universality of the act; cf.
Suet. Oct. 58; Ovid, Fasti, ii. 127; Boissier, "La Religion Romaine,"
vol. i. p. 100.

[6] Suet. Oct. 57.

offered for his health, tended directly towards giving the Emperor, even in his lifetime, a species of divine worship. You had here Imperial Apotheosis in the making, a phenomenon deserving of some attention, as being one of the strangest products of religion under the Empire.

It had its foundation, in reality, in the honours [1] "too great for mere mortal" conferred on Julius Cæsar, which reached their climax in the closing years of his life. Statues and altars were erected to him, and it was decreed to build a temple to him, under the title of Jupiter Julius.[2] A special priest was appointed, and an additional college of the Luperci [3] brought into being, to minister to the worship of this new god. His death was marked by strange portents,[4] and his reception among the gods was heralded by the appearance of a comet in the sky. His divinity was acknowledged, says Suetonius,[5] not only by a decree of the Senate, but by the conviction of the vulgar. The Senate promised [6] (42 B.C.) a temple to Divus Julius, now formally enrolled among the gods of the State. It was built on the spot where the dictator's body had been burnt, but for various reasons it was only in 29 B.C. that it was dedicated [7] by Augustus. Now, the idea of man being raised to divinity was one altogether foreign [8] to native Roman religious beliefs, and arose only when these were infused with the spirit of Etruria, Greece, and the Orient. In Roman thought there is at times a trace of the belief that man was

---

[1] Suet. J. Cæsar, 76, 88; Appian, B.C. ii. 106. For a discussion of the honours paid to Cæsar, *vide* Warde Fowler, " Roman Ideas of Deity," p. 112 *et seq.*; cf. Boissier, op. cit. vol. i. p. 121 *et seq.*

[2] This, however, is a statement of Dio, xliv. 6, which is now generally discredited; cf. Warde Fowler, op. cit. p. 119.

[3] Suet. J. Cæsar, 76.

[4] Virg. Georgic, i. 466 *et seq.*; Tib. II. v. 70 *et seq.*

[5] J. Cæsar, 88.   [6] Dio, xlvii. 19.

[7] Mon. Ancyr. c. 19; cf. Huelsen, op. cit. p. 153 *et seq.*

[8] Warde Fowler, " Roman Ideas of Deity," p. 86 *et seq.*, gives a very clear analysis of the rise of Apotheosis in Italy.

capable by his nature of something more than human, but the
possibility of attaining divinity was never attributed to him.
In primitive times it was customary enough to associate[1]
magical or divine powers with king or chief, but there is no
clear proof[2] that divine kings were ever believed to exist in
Italy, while the idea of descent from a divine being was one
that arose in Rome only when native beliefs had been recast
under influences from outside. The conception of a deified
man only very gradually took shape out of that strange medley
of beliefs, that continued to pour into Rome, through various
channels, after she had become the head of a great Empire.
Whether the conception was good or bad, Rome had to pay
for her conquests by the abandonment or transformation of her
primitive beliefs, through contact with other lands and other
peoples, and the expansion of the Roman mind. Greece had
indulged in hero-worship[3] from very early times, and a long
list of men could be quoted, to whom divine honours were
paid. It is little wonder, in a way, that Alexander, whose
brilliant exploits must have seemed to many more than human,
was honoured as a god by his contemporaries. It was, moreover, a settled policy with him to encourage such worship, but
it was an altogether strange experience for the Roman Flaminius,[4] the " Liberator of Greece," to be honoured at Chalcis on
an equal footing with Hercules and Apollo. This practice
of deification was in reality not Hellenic in origin, but was
borrowed from the East, from Syria, and especially from Egypt,
that land where the cult[5] of divine kings had at an early

---

[1] Frazer, "The Golden Bough," vol. i. p. 332 *et seq.*

[2] Warde Fowler, op. cit. p. 96.

[3] *Ibid.* p. 98; cf. Strong, "Apotheosis and After Life," p. 63 *et seq.*;
Ridgeway, "The Origin of Tragedy," p. 27 *et seq.*

[4] Strong, op. cit. p. 63; Plutarch's "Life of Flaminius," c. xvi. (quoted
there); Toutain, "Les Cultes Païens," vol. i. p. 22.

[5] Frazer, "The Golden Bough," vol. i. p. 418 *et seq.*; Murray, "Four
Stages of Greek Religion," p. 133 *et seq.*; Cumont, "Astrology and Religion among the Greeks and Romans," p. 179 *et seq.*

period reached a high state of development. The cult of the ruler was particularly prominent in the case of the Ptolemies, and the Græco-Syrian Seleucids. Recent studies [1] have shown that the two main symbols of Apotheosis in Roman Imperial Art, the eagle and the wreath, have been derived from the East, and are found frequently on Syrian monuments. The eagle is believed to be the messenger of the sun, and is entrusted by its master with the task of bringing back to the heavens the soul that is liberated from the body. The wreath, so often worn by the Cæsars, was "symbolic of the ultimate triumph of the soul". However, all this exaltation of man tended to lead to the degradation of the gods. A rationalistic explanation of their origin had been propounded by the Greek Euhemerus,[2] who held that all the gods had originally been human beings, who were deified for their services to humanity. Cicero puts the question [3] whether by his theories he strengthened religion or destroyed it. His theories brought down the gods from the lofty heights they occupied, but they had the effect, too, of placing divinity within the grasp of every great benefactor of the human race. His work was translated into Latin by Ennius, and must have had its share in the development of the idea of Apotheosis among the Romans. But another set of beliefs [4] contributed strongly to the same result. Stoicism had proclaimed, as one of its great doctrines, that the soul of man was a spark of that divine fire, which they conceived to be the Soul of the Universe. At death, it was reabsorbed into the universal fire, though the Stoics allowed to some souls a personal existence for a time after their separation

---

[1] Strong, op. cit. pp. 62, 182. This discovery is due especially to the labours of Cumont. For the eagle on the altar in the Vatican, in which J. Cæsar figures as Divus, *vide* Strong, p. 67. It occurs, too, on the Vienna Cameo, *ibid.* p. 72.

[2] Warde Fowler, "Roman Ideas of Deity," p. 100 *et seq.*; Wissowa, op. cit. p. 68.

[3] De Nat. Deorum, i. 42, 119; cf. *ibid.* iii. 16-40; Tusc. Disp. I. xii. 28.

[4] *Vide infra,* p. 228 *et seq.*

from the body. Now Stoicism, as expounded by Posidonius, one of the great leaders of the Roman school, had come under the influence of the mystical speculations of the Orphics and Pythagoreans, and the beliefs of the Astrologers, upon the nature of the soul. They generally held the soul to be of the same substance as the stars, which they believed to be divine. They set up a dualism of soul and body. The soul was declared to be infected by its contact with the body, but when freed from its prison-house, it would return to its home among the stars, to dwell there in blissful immortality, and share the companionship of the star-gods.

But the Astrologers, for instance, did not always clearly define on whom was to be conferred the privilege of sidereal apotheosis. It was granted [1] at first to the great monarchs, who, even when living, had been raised by the reverence of their fellowmen to the position of divine beings. In all this speculation, however, the tendency was to associate the privilege with all who by the invention of the arts, or by some other signal service had contributed to the material improvement, the culture, or civilization of the world. The "Soter" [2] or the "Euergetes," who had helped to save or uplift humanity, was marked out for Apotheosis before all others. This is a point of cardinal importance for the history of Apotheosis at Rome, for it is clear, both from Augustan poetry, from contemporary Art, and the Art of the succeeding age, that Augustus was honoured pre-eminently as a type of Euergetes. For men, who had been nurtured upon ideas such as I have outlined, who had seen out of the chaos of the Civil Wars order gradually evolved by the new ruler of Rome, the Pax Augusta securely established, and the prestige of Roman power reach its highest point of greatness, the temptation was strong to accord the Emperor extravagant and even divine honours. The cult of the Em-

---

[1] Cumont, "Religion and Astrology," p. 179 *et seq.*

[2] Warde Fowler, "Roman Ideas of Deity," pp. 110-12, 118; Strong, op. cit. p. 75; Norden, Introduction to Æneid, vi. p. 36.

peror was destined to become in many respects the dominant cult of the Empire, and tended to dwarf all others. It was to have its effect upon Imperial Art, and old principles[1] of composition, such as isolation and frontality, were revived to give it expression. In a group, the Emperor, the central figure, was isolated from the surrounding figures to mark his pre-eminence, and represented in a frontal attitude, as if offered to the adoration of those present. As we have seen, Apotheosis had its original home in the East, and it was probably at first repugnant to true Italian feeling. It is not unlikely, as Mr. Warde Fowler suggests,[2] that the attempt to deify Cæsar, even in his lifetime, was due to Antony, who was well acquainted with the ways of the East. Now that Cæsar was dead, and his cult officially recognized, Augustus was particularly anxious to regulate it,[3] by eliminating all objectionable elements, and place it as far as possible on a true Roman footing. Julius, whose official title was Divus, was formally enrolled among the gods of the State. A special priest was set apart to minister in his newly erected temple, and a public holiday appointed each year (12 July) in his honour.

Augustus was not less solicitous about keeping his own worship within due bounds. In the Eastern Provinces, where the tradition of deification was strong, the Emperor was worshipped as a full-blown divinity, though in order to soothe Roman feelings,[4] he insisted that his worship be united with that of Roma. This latter cult was an old one,[5] and had been

---

[1] Strong, op. cit. pp. 77 *et seq.*, 90, 103, for some interesting examples.

[2] "Roman Ideas of Deity," p. 117.

[3] *Ibid.* p. 122; Wissowa, op. cit. p. 342 *et seq.*; Carter, op. cit. p. 171 *et seq.*; Toutain, "Les Cultes Païens dans l'Empire Romain," vol. i. p. 26.

[4] Suet. Oct. 52.

[5] Toutain, op. cit. vol. i. pp. 19 *et seq.*, 37 *et seq.*; Tac. Annals, iv. 56; Warde Fowler, "Roman Ideas of Deity," p. 130.

established at Smyrna as far back as 195 B.C. It was a worship offered to the spirit of that great protecting power, that was supreme over the Mediterranean basin. The worship of the "Numen Augusti" was offered to one, who was the living symbol of the strength and organization of the Roman Empire. This united cult became quickly diffused[1] in the East, and was soon found also, though with less frequency, in the Western provinces. We hear of an altar being erected to Augustus at Tarraco in 25 B.C., and the inhabitants of Narbonne bound themselves by special vow (10 A.D.), "to honour perpetually the divinity of Cæsar Augustus, the Father of his Country". This would go to show that, in spite of Augustus's endeavours, his cult showed variety[2] of form in individual communities. It is not easy to speak with confidence of Italy.[3] That the cult of the Emperor existed, both by itself, and in conjunction with that of Roma, is beyond doubt. But it is clear, from the difference of form it exhibits, that it was local, and was without official sanction or organization. It appeared especially in communities, that were bound to Augustus by special ties of obligation, and in a number[4] of port towns, where native traditions had been weakened by frequent contact with strangers from other lands. In Rome itself, Suetonius tells us,[5] Augustus obstinately refused to receive such honours in his lifetime. Still, the honours, that were granted to him, came at times perilously near deification, if they did not quite overstep the limits. It is probable that there were many at Rome, who wished to give

---

[1] Boissier, "La Religion Romaine," vol. i. p. 130 et seq.; Rushforth, "Historical Inscriptions," p. 44 et seq. (for the organization of the cult in the provinces); Toutain, op. cit. vol. i. p. 29 et seq. (valuable as giving the evidence of inscriptions).

[2] Ibid. p. 43 et seq.; cf. Ferrero, op. cit. vol. v. pp. 151, 261.

[3] Dio, li. 20; Boissier, op. cit. vol. i. p. 132 et seq.; Rushforth, op. cit. p. 51 et seq.; Wissowa, op. cit. p. 80; L. Ross-Taylor, "The Cults of Ostia," p. 46 et seq.

[4] Also, as might be expected, in the Greek cities of Southern Italy.

[5] Oct. 52.

the Emperor the full Apotheosis, that might be granted to an Oriental monarch. This Augustus wished particularly to avoid, from fear of offending Roman susceptibilities, and he sought to obviate the danger by encouraging the worship not of himself, but of his Genius,[1] that higher spiritual self, which each male Roman was believed to possess.

This new departure of Augustus is particularly interesting as a striking illustration of how the Emperor was ever on the alert to turn his religious reforms to account, in support of the Imperial idea. The festival of the Compitalia,[2] which had lapsed for many years, was revived. This was originally a festival of the country, held at points where roads crossed (*compita*), and where consequently the boundaries of several farms converged. Here chapels were erected in honour of the Lares, who were regarded as the protectors of the land. The Compitalia was essentially a festival of the " familia "[3] of the farmstead, associated especially with the slaves[4] of the household. In process of time the cult extended to the city, and the Lares were honoured at the crossings of the streets. Even when transplanted there, the cult preserved its plebeian[5] character, and the Compitalia became one of the most popular festivals with artisans, slaves, and the common people generally. Collegia (with the " magistri vicorum " at their head) were founded to organize and maintain this newly arrived cult. These associations, however, became in time centres of political

---

[1] For the analysis of Genius, *vide* Wissowa, op. cit. p. 175 *et seq.*; cf. Warde Fowler, " Roman Ideas," p. 90. The " Juno " corresponded in the case of the woman.

[2] Suet. Oct. 31 ; Wissowa, op. cit. p. 166 *et seq.* ; Carter, op. cit. p. 177 *et seq.* ; Warde Fowler, op. cit. p. 123 ; Strong, op. cit. p. 70.

[3] Wissowa, p. 168; Warde Fowler, " Roman Festivals," pp. 279-80 ; " The Religious Experience," pp. 77-9. The " Lar Familiaris " was brought by the slaves from the farm into the house and worshipped there. For the Lares as protectors of the farm cf. the " Enos, *Lases*, juvate," of the hymn of the Fratres Arvales. Cf. Tib. I. i. 20.

[4] Hor. Sat. I. v. 65 ; Epode ii. 65.

[5] Döllinger, " Gentile and Jew," vol. ii. p. 21.

intrigue, and were suppressed[1] by the Senate (64 B.C.), revived
by Clodius (58 B.C.), and again suppressed by Cæsar.[2]　It was
one of the reforms of Augustus to reorganize[3] the city, which
he partitioned into fourteen regions, which were subdivided
into a number of quarters (*vici*).　Each of these quarters was
administered by four functionaries (plebeians), who were called
"magistri vicorum,"[4] one of whose chief duties was to keep
the chapels of the Lares in repair, and to maintain year by
year the Compitalia and the Ludi Compitalicii.　There was
however, a new element in the cult, as restored by Augustus.
The Emperor[5] ordered that the statues of the Lares (of which
there were two) be crowned twice a year with spring and
summer flowers, but henceforth between the statues of the
Lares was placed an image of the "Genius Augusti".[6]　It was a
time-honoured custom at Rome for the members of a household to honour the Genius of the master of the house, and it
was not an unnatural extension of the custom for the great
family of the State to honour the Genius of its head, Augustus,
the Father of his country.　Thus the Emperor elevated and
spiritualised his own worship in a form, which was no violation
of Roman feeling.　Here, moreover, was an attempt[7] to enlist
the lower classes, artisans, freedmen, and slaves, for the sup-

---

[1] De Marchi, "Il Culto Privato," vol. ii. p. 81 ; Warde Fowler,
"Roman Festivals," p. 280.

[2] Suet. J. Cæsar, 42.

[3] *Ibid.* Oct. 30 ; Dio, lv. 8 ; Ferrero, op. cit. vol. v. p. 237.

[4] Boissier, op. cit. vol. i. p. 139; C.I.L. VI. i. 445-54 ; Rushforth,
op. cit. p. 58 *et seq.*　For a scene of sacrifice by the *Vicomagistri* on an
altar in the Palazzo dei Conservatori, *vide* Strong, "Roman Sculpture,"
pp. 73-4.

[5] Suet. Oct. 31.

[6] Ovid, Fasti, v. 145.　The whole was sometimes referred to as
"Lares Augusti et Genius Cæsaris".　For the significance of the
phrase, *vide* Rushforth, p. 60; cf. Wissowa, op. cit. p. 172.　For private
worship of Augustus, *vide* Hor. Odes, IV. v. 32.

[7] Boissier, op. cit. vol. i. p. 142; Wissowa, op. cit. p. 171; Pelham,
"Essays," p. 111 (with references).

port of the Emperor. They were thus given new privileges and increased importance, which bound them to the power, from which these emanated. It was one of the great aims of Augustus's policy to win to his person the various orders of the State. As the nobles had been complimented by the revival and enhanced splendour of the priestly colleges, and the knights[1] by the gift of the lesser priesthoods, so this new institution bound the plebeians[2] to him by ties of loyalty and gratitude.

I have said that Augustus fostered, with especial care, the worship of those deities, that were associated by policy or tradition with the House of Cæsar. The cult of Venus had come originally[3] to Rome from Mt. Eryx in Sicily, and in its train had followed the Æneas legend, and the story of the Trojan origin of Rome. Venus figured as the mother of the Trojan line. Julius Cæsar claimed, like so many[4] other Romans, descent from the Trojans, and he traced his lineage[5] back to Julus, and thus to Venus herself. That great master of policy had seen the possibilities of the goddess, and to further his ambitions had exploited his divine descent. At the battle of Pharsalus he had vowed a temple to Venus Victrix, but when the temple came to be dedicated (46 B.C.), that title was changed[6] for the significant one of Venus *Genetrix*, the mother of the Julian line. Her worship was

---

[1] For his policy towards the knights, *vide* Pelham, pp. 129-34.

[2] Augustus sought also to win over the Plebs by numerous largesses, by the splendour of the games, and by his care for the corn supply; Mon. Ancyr. c. 15; *ibid.* c. 22-3; Suet. Oct. 41; Dio, li. 21; liii. 28; liv. 29; cf. Pelham, p. 137 *et seq.*

[3] Wissowa, op. cit. p. 290; Boissier, " Promenades Archéologiques," p. 139; cf. Hor. Odes, I. ii. 33.

[4] Virg. Æn. v. 117 *et seq.*

[5] Suet. J. Cæsar, 6; *ibid.* 42; Virg. Æn. i. 286; vi. 790; Hor. Sat. II. v. 63; Car. Saec. 50; Odes, IV. xv. 31.

[6] Warde Fowler, " Roman Ideas of Deity," p. 113; Wissowa, op. cit. p. 292. The temple was in the new Forum Julium; cf. Stuart Jones, " Classical Rome," p. 151; Suet. J. Cæsar, 78; *ibid.* 84.

naturally perpetuated by Augustus, who united[1] it with that of
Mars Ultor, of which we shall speak presently.   The union of
Venus and Mars was well known in Greek religion, and when
the legend of the origin of Rome began to take shape, the
tendency was again inevitable to effect a union[2] of Venus,
the mother of Æneas, and Mars, the father of Romulus, the
founder of the city of Rome.   Cæsar was another Romulus, a
second founder of Rome.   What more natural than to com-
bine the cult of Mars with that of Venus, the foundress of his
line?   But Mars was brought now into very special relation
with the House of Cæsar, and under the new dispensation was
given a place of great prominence among Roman deities.   It
was the aim of Augustus from the first to safeguard and uphold
by every device the majesty of his House.   The foundations
of such a structure were laid broad and deep, when Cæsar had
been enrolled among the gods, a temple built to him, and his
cult duly established.

But something more was needed.   Augustus, during the
campaign of Philippi, "undertaken to avenge his father," had
vowed a temple to Mars Ultor.[3]   The title suggested that the
god himself was sharing in the task of revenge.   The temple
would be a monument of the deity's vengeance, that would
deter evil-doers in the future from a similar outrage upon a
Cæsar.   It was built in the new Forum of Augustus,[4] "in
privato solo," and must have been one of the dominating

---

[1] Ovid, Tristia, ii. 296.   For the combination in the " Feriale Cuma-
num," vide Rushforth, op. cit. p. 52.

[2] Wissowa, op. cit. p. 290.   For the statue of Venus in the Pantheon,
cf. Dio, liii. 27.

[3] Suet. Oct. 29.   Cæsar had himself projected a temple to Mars (Suet.
J. Cæsar, 44).   For the fate of Cæsar's murderers, cf. Suet. J. Cæsar, 89.
For Augustus as " Cæsaris ultor," cf. Hor. Odes, I. ii. 44.

[4] Mon. Ancyr. c. 21 ; Suet. Oct. 29.   The temple was not finished and
dedicated till 2 B.C. ; cf. Ovid, Fasti, v. 491 et seq.   Meanwhile Augustus
consecrated a small temple to Mars on the Capitol (20 B.C.), in which the
Parthian standards were placed, when restored, vide supra, p. 21.   For
games in honour of Mars, cf. Mon. Ancyr. c. 22 ; Dio, lx. 5.

features of it, as even to-day its ruins are impressive. The Emperor, however, had designed that Mars Ultor should play a still more important [1] rôle in his Imperial policy. It was decided that henceforth the Senate was to consider, in his temple, questions of war and claims of triumphs, that those, who were starting for the provinces with a military command, were to be escorted from there, and to it victorious generals on their return should bear the insignia of their triumph. In it certain barbarian chiefs were compelled to take an oath that they would loyally keep the peace, for which they sought. It was there that the members of the Imperial family assumed the "toga virilis," and there also the nail was driven by the Censors at the end of each lustrum. Thus, not only was this deity of the Julian House brought into intimate relation with the wars and victories, and the military [2] greatness of the Rome of Augustus, but many of the privileges, that had hitherto belonged to Jupiter on the Capitol, were transferred to Mars Ultor. Jupiter Capitolinus, the great national deity [3] of the Romans, whose history was bound up with the traditions of Republican freedom, was a god that could not be easily manipulated for Imperial ends. All this interesting development of Mars-worship was a far cry from the time, when the god had no temple within the city walls, when he still retained some relics of the character [4] of a "spirit of the outland," the protector of crops and herds against the sudden raids of enemies.

Augustus's exaltation of Apollo is another proof of his policy of enhancing the glory of deities, reputed to be

[1] Suet. Oct. 21; *ibid.* 29; Wissowa, op. cit. p. 78; Carter, op. cit. p. 174.

[2] For a scene on one of the Boscoreale cups, in which Mars leads conquered provinces to the feet of Augustus, *vide* Strong, " Apotheosis and After Life," p. 74.

[3] Carter, op. cit. p. 160; *ibid.* p. 164.

[4] Warde Fowler, "The Religious Experience," pp. 131-34; " Roman Festivals," pp. 40-1; Carter, p. 111.

specially connected with the Julian family. There is no need
to credit the unsavoury details (emanating from Antony and
an anonymous writer), which Suetonius[1] gives of Augustus's
own share in Apollo-worship. The same writer quotes[2] the
Theologoumena of Asclepias of Mendes for the story, that
Octavian was believed to be the son of Apollo. This may
possibly show his early devotion to that deity, but it is
especially after Actium that Apollo stands out prominently
as the protector of Augustus, as the god who had helped[3]
him to win his victory over the enemies of Rome, and of
Western civilization. In gratitude, the Emperor enlarged[4] the
old temple of Apollo near the scene of his victory, and also
built an open-air shrine in honour of the god. But the great
monument of Augustus's devotion to Apollo was the temple he
erected[5] to the god upon the Palatine, which must have been
one of the noblest structures of its time. Propertius witnessed
its dedication, and his description[6] helps us to realize the
splendour of the building and its adornment.[7] He gives us
one detail, that is particularly interesting. On the roof of the
temple were placed two chariots[8] of the sun, which would go
to indicate that Augustus wished to emphasize that aspect of

---

[1] Suet. Oct. 70. Augustus appears with the attributes of Apollo.

[2] *Ibid.* 94.

[3] Virg. Æn. viii. 704; *ibid.* iii. 275; Prop. III. xi. 69; IV. vi. 27 *et
seq.*

[4] Suet. Oct. 18; Dio, li. i. He also instituted the Actian games at
the new city of Nicopolis; cf. Æn. iii. 280.

[5] It was begun in 36 B.C., dedicated 28 B.C. Suet. Oct. 29; Dio, xlix.
15; liii. i.; Mon. Ancyr. c. 19; Hor. Odes, I. xxxi. 1. For a discussion
of a representation of the temple on a coin of Caligula (Cohen 9), and
the symbolism of its figures, *vide* Richmond in "Essays Presented to
Wm. Ridgeway," p. 203 *et seq.*

[6] Prop. II. xxxi.

[7] For Augustus's gifts to the temple, cf. Mon. Ancyr. c. 24; Suet. Oct.
52; Dio, liii. 22.

[8] For the significance of the quadriga as a symbol of the sun on coin-
types, cf. Warde Fowler, "Roman Ideas of Deity," p. 57.

Apollo, in which he was identified with the Sun-god. Faint traces of sun-worship[1] had begun to make their appearance in Rome in the time of Cicero, through the influence of Posidonius, who was well acquainted with the religion of Astrology, and was steeped in Oriental speculation. This tendency became more marked under Augustus,[2] though Sun-worship was then far from enjoying the position it enjoyed in later times,[3] when the cult of Sol Invictus became the dominant one throughout the Empire. Now, it is important to note that the new temple was on private ground,[4] "in that part of his (Augustus) house on the Palatine, for which the soothsayers proclaimed the god showed a preference by striking it with lightning". It was thus "in its origin theoretically the private chapel of a Roman family".[5]

Augustus, however, was not slow to invest this deity of the Julian house with increased dignity and importance.[6] When he became Pontifex Maximus (12 B.C.), on the death of Lepidus, one of his first acts was to order[7] a new recension of the Sibylline books. The revised volumes were deposited, not, as was the custom in former times, in the temple of Capitoline Jove, but "under the pedestal (basi) of Palatine

---

[1] Warde Fowler, "Roman Ideas of Deity," p. 56 *et seq.*, for a discussion of Sun-worship at Rome.

[2] Especially among the educated. This is probably the key to Hor. Odes, IV. ii. 46; C. S. 9; cf. Sibylline oracle quoted by Zosimus, verse 17. With others he was worshipped rather as the Healer, cf. Wissowa, op. cit. p. 297.

[3] Cumont, "Les Religions Orientales," p. 176 *et seq.*; "Astrology and Religion," pp. 95-9.

[4] Suet. Oct. 29.

[5] Carter, op. cit. p. 166.

[6] *Ibid.* p. 164 *et seq.*; cf. Wissowa, op. cit. pp. 74-5, for Apollinism under Augustus.

[7] Suet. Oct. 31. Augustus probably had contemplated this change many years before; cf. Mayor in "Virgil's Messianic Eclogue," p. 102; Virg. Æn, vi. 69 *et seq.* (there quoted).

Apollo ". There was, it is true, an inseparable connection[1] between Apollo and the Sibylline oracles. Apollo-worship had come to Rome together with the Sibylline books, and the god was thus the leader of the band of Greek deities, that followed their introduction. The honour of guarding the precious volumes had long rested with Jupiter Capitolinus, and their transference to the Palatine at this stage was significant. It was designed to curtail the privileges of the great deity of the Capitol, and to raise what in its inception had been a private cult of the family of Cæsar into a State-worship. It was part of a movement to change the religious centre of gravity in Rome, to wean men's thoughts from the associations of Republican glory, and to dazzle them with the splendour of the new order of things. It was natural to expect that the favour shown by Augustus towards Apollo should have had its influence upon his contemporaries. Virgil, in his prophecy of the regeneration of Rome, had already familiarized Roman minds with the idea that the world in its last era[2] (" ultima Cumaei carminis aetas ") would be ruled over by this deity, who would bring back to men the innocence and blessings of the Golden Age. We shall see, when we come to deal with the Saecular Games, what prominence is given to the god among the deities, whose assistance is invoked at the festival. He gets a high place of honour in Augustan literature, and the Apollo-cult of the Emperor set a fashion, which did not fail to react[3] upon the Art of the period. Attached to the

---

[1] Wissowa, op. cit. p. 293. The oracles were called " Fatorum praedictiones Apollinis"; Diels, " Sibyllinische Blätter," p. 5 ; cf. Tib. II. v. 1 et seq.; III. iv. 47 et seq.; Hor. Sat. II. v. 60; Virg. Æn. iv. 345 for Apollo as god of prophecy.

[2] Eclog. iv. 4; ibid. 10; cf. Æn. vi. 793; cf. Mayor, op. cit. p. 121 et seq.

[3] Friedländer, " Roman Life and Manners," vol. ii. p. 298 ; cf. Strong, " Roman Sculpture," p. 38, for the Munich relief of Actian Apollo; ibid. p. 61 for swan sacred to Apollo on the Ara Pacis. For statue of Augustus in the Vatican with figure of Apollo, cf. Furtwängler and Urlichs, " Greek and Roman Sculpture," p. 235.

temple on the Palatine were porticoes,[1] and a Greek and Latin library.   Here a kind of Literary Academy was set up, which set the seal of its approval[2] upon contemporary works.   It is certainly significant to find Augustus wishing to bring Roman literature into intimate relation with his protecting deity.   It was an effort to consecrate literature also to Imperial needs. Horace, referring to the temple of Apollo and the adjoining library, speaks[3] of the "temple that has niches for Roman bards".   It would be interesting to know how in such a case Augustus would define "Roman".   We may be sure that among contemporary writers none would be admitted,[4] whose spirit ran counter to his reforms, none that were too Republican in tone, or that sounded a note of hostility to the established regime.

When the Emperor became Pontifex Maximus on the death of Lepidus, he assumed the religious as well as the civil head-ship of the State.   He signalized his accession to the office by transplanting[5] the cult of Vesta from its old temple in the Forum to the Palatine.   Hitherto it had been customary for the chief Pontiff to reside in the Regia,[6] his official residence beside the temple of Vesta, but Augustus made a gift of this to the Vestals, and determined to continue to live in his house on the Palatine, a portion of which he had consecrated to the wor-ship of the goddess.   This was in many respects the most radical of his innovations.   It was, as it were, an uprooting of old institutions, for the temple of Vesta in the Forum, in which the sacred fire had been kindled for centuries, had been under the Republic the very heart of the religious life of Rome.

---

[1] Mon. Ancyr. c. 19; Suet. Oct. 29; Dio, liii. i.; cf. Boyd, "Public Libraries in Ancient Rome," pp. 5, 32.

[2] Hor. Ep. I. iii. 17; II. i. 216; ii. 94.   [3] Ibid. ii. 94.

[4] Ovid represents himself (Tristia, III. i. 59 et seq.) as seeking in vain for an entrance.

[5] Wissowa, op. cit. p. 76; Carter, op. cit. pp. 176-7; Wendland, op. cit. p. 146; Döllinger, op. cit. vol. ii. p. 45.

[6] Huelsen, "Le Forum Romain," p. 191.

But the change meant something more.   In this case also, it
transformed what was in reality a private worship of Cæsar's
household into a State-worship.   Vesta and the Penates of the
house of Augustus and of the State became identical.   The
change set the crown upon the edifice the Emperor had been
rearing, and his Palace became thenceforth the religious centre [1]
of Rome.

Augustus essayed an even more formidable task, as a com-
plement to his religious revival, in attempting a reform of
morality.   It is clear from many sources [2] that luxury and
licence had more than kept pace with the increase of wealth
at Rome, as the Empire expanded.   The erotic poetry of
Tibullus and Propertius, as well as the lascivious verses of Ovid,
may with justice be regarded as a mirror of the decadence of
their age.   Adultery and divorce were occurring with a frequency, which resulted in the almost complete subversion of
the sanctities of married life.   The purity of the home was
poisoned at its source, and, as a consequence, licentiousness
had grown amongst the young to an extent, that caused serious
anxiety to all who were genuinely interested in Roman welfare.
Women had become "emancipated" to a greater degree than
in former days, and it was the prevailing tendency with them
to convert their new-found liberty into licence.   Slavery, too,
had its detrimental effect upon society, offering, as it did, increased temptations to vice, and affording increased opportunities for its indulgence.   Amongst men, who had degener-
ated to effeminacy, the military virtues were often decried, [3]
and it is little wonder that we find many passages of contemporary literature pointing the contrast between the manliness and simplicity of old Rome, and the extravagance and

---

[1] Boissier, op. cit. vol. i. p. 106; cf. Ovid, Fasti, iv. 869.

[2] Livy in the Preface to his History draws a dark picture of the moral
evils of his time; cf. Ferrero, op. cit. vol. iv. p. 195 et seq.; vol. v. p. 157
et seq.; Döllinger, op. cit. vol. ii. p. 257 et seq.; Pelham, "Essays," p.
119; Friedländer, op. cit. vol. i. p. 228 et seq.

[3] Prop. II. vii. 14; IV. iii. 19; Tib. I. i. 75 et seq.; x.; II. iv. 16.

licentiousness, that characterized the Rome of the present period. Now, Augustus (whose own record in such matters, if we can trust Suetonius,[1] had not been perfect) took many measures to remedy these deep-seated evils. He made stricter the regulations [2] for taking part in the Lupercalia, and for viewing the public games and shows, excluding women altogether from athletic contests, and forbidding them to witness gladiatorial fights, except from the upper seats of the theatre. He prohibited young people of either sex from attending any entertainment by night during the Ludi Saeculares, unless accompanied by some relative of mature years. He punished [3] and degraded certain knights, whose conduct had been unworthy. He introduced laws [4] to check bribery at elections, and restrain extravagance in living, setting limits especially to the expenditure at banquets and denouncing prevailing fashions in dress and adornment. In the matter of extravagance he himself set a salutary example by the simplicity [5] of his house and furniture, and of his general way of living. But his great measures for the reform of morals are those known as the " Leges Juliæ ".[6] The " Lex Julia de Adulteriis," for the first [7] time in clear and unmistakable terms, subjected to the rules of legal procedure the offence, with which it dealt, restricting the right of private vengeance, and the right

---

[1] Oct. 68 *et seq.*

[2] *Ibid.* 31, 44. To judge by Ovid, Ars. Am. i. 85 *et seq.*, such restrictions were very necessary.

[3] Suet. Oct. 39.

[4] *Ibid* 34; Gellius, N.A. II. xxiv. 14; Dio, liv. 2 ; *ibid.* 16; cf. Ferrero, op. cit. vol. v. p. 67.

[5] Suet. Oct. 72 *et seq.*

[6] These were passed, 18-17 B.C.; Suet. Oct. 34; *ibid.* 89, where Augustus read for the Senate a speech of Q. Metellus (139 B.C.), " De prole augenda "; cf. Pelham, " Essays," p. 114 *et seq.*; Ferrero, op. cit. vol. v. p. 58 *et seq.*; Bruns, " Fontes," p. 114; *ibid.* p. 118. For humorous references to these laws, cf. Apuleius, Met. vi. 22; Juv. Sat. ii. 37.

[7] Other laws dealing with this crime had been passed, but practically nothing is known about them.

of punishment of the paterfamilias. The penalties were heavy, not only for the offending parties, but for all who were accomplices in the crime. The powers of the law were extensive, and dealt also with various other forms of immorality. An even more important and comprehensive measure was the " Lex Julia de maritandis ordinibus," the aim of which was to encourage marriage and the founding of families. The law put an end to certain restrictions against marriage, which had hitherto existed, removing the barriers against a second marriage, and setting aside whatever obstacles might be placed on heirs by the provisions of a will. It legitimized unions with freedwomen, except for senators and their sons for two generations in the male line. The law offered certain privileges[1] to those who married, especially if their union was blessed with issue. Such persons, too, secured relief from many public burdens. But the penalties of the law were severe. Bachelors were excluded from the festivals and public shows, and numerous limitations were put to their right of inheritance. . Suetonius, in speaking of this latter law, says[2] that Augustus, having emended it so as to make more stringent changes in it than in the case of the other laws, was unable to carry it, owing to the violence of the opposition it encountered, until he had increased its rewards, and abolished or mitigated a portion of its penalties. Now, it is probable that Suetonius here refers not to a mere emendation of the law in its original form, but to a supplementary measure passed in A.D. 4, called by Ferrero[3] (conjecturally) the " Lex Julia caducaria ". This law, which, as regards penalties, placed bachelors and the childless (*orbi*) on the same footing, was an attempt to deal with the evil of childless marriages, which had become a serious one in the years succeeding the passing of

---

[1] Suet. Oct. 44. [2] *Ibid.* 34; cf. Dio, liv. 16; *ibid.* lvi. 1.
[3] Op. cit. vol. v. p. 295. The whole subject of these laws is difficult, but Ferrero's explanation is one of the most plausible that has been offered.

the former measure. Men had married to evade the former law, but had refused to shoulder further the burdens of their state. According to the provisions of the present measure, bachelors and " orbi " alike were declared incompetent to inherit, and legacies left to them passed to the Treasury, not as formerly to their next of kin. The opposition to the law was so strong, especially from the knights, who had been among the chief offenders, that its operation was suspended, first for three years, and then for two. In A.D. 9 a law was passed known as the " Lex Papia Poppaea,"[1] which, yielding to opposition, reduced the penalties on " orbi," while leaving bachelors still incapable of inheriting.

In concluding this chapter, I will discuss briefly the revival of the Ludi Saeculares by Augustus, an event which illustrates, perhaps more strikingly than any other, the Emperor's policy of giving old forms a new content for the glory of the reigning house. When the Leges Juliae had been passed, Augustus wished to create the impression that the success of his reforms was assured, and that a new era in the history of Rome was being inaugurated. He must have realized full well the difficulties of effecting moral reforms by legislation, and many years later (A.D. 9), Dio attributes[2] to him a speech, which contains frequent confessions of failure. In B.C. 17 the ten years had elapsed, for which Augustus had consented to assume the burden of State control. He could look back upon great achievements. There was peace within the wide borders of the Empire. He had done much to effect a revival in religion, and it was hoped that his recent enactments would secure the necessary reform of morality. In these circumstances, even abstracting from his ordinary political sagacity, Augustus might well have claimed that the dawn of a new era was about to break on Rome. In that year, he determined to celebrate

---

[1] Ferrero, op. cit. vol. v. p. 322; cf. Tac. Annals, iii. 25; Furneaux, Excursus at the end of Annals, Bk. III.

[2] lvi. 2 *et seq.*; cf. Prop. II. vi. 25 *et seq.*; vii.; xxii. 47.

once more the Ludi Saeculares,[1] but to stamp them with an entirely new character. These games, "quos nec spectasset quisquam, nec spectaturus esset," had been celebrated in the past to mark the burial of an era just expired (*saeculum condere*), which was variously estimated at 100 or 110 years' duration.[2] Now on previous occasions, the character of purification [3] had been predominant in the games. The outgoing era was laid to rest with all its burden of guilt. When the games were celebrated in 249 B.C., they were carried out according to the "Graecus ritus" ordained by the Sibylline books. At a spot in the Campus Martius, called "Tarentum," was a pool fed by sulphur springs, which, on account of the fiery vapours it emitted, was in popular belief connected with the infernal regions.[4] Here an altar was set up, and for three successive nights black victims were offered to the Greek deities of the underworld, Dis and Proserpine. When Augustus wished to revive the games,[5] men were found who, by computations, the secret of which was known to themselves, brought the new festival into line with previous celebrations. The Quindecemviri, always ready to subserve the Emperor's designs, had discovered a Sibylline oracle [6] ordering the games, and giving instructions on the ceremonies to be observed during the festival. We are fortunate in having further material for the

---

[1] Mon. Ancyr. c. 22; Suet. Oct. 31; Dio, liv. 18; Hill, " Roman Coins," p. 148. For an account of the games, *vide* Wissowa, op. cit. pp. 430-32; Warde Fowler, "The Religious Experience," p. 438 *et seq.*; Carter, op. cit. p. 167 *et seq.*; Boissier, op. cit. vol. ii. p. 86 *et seq.*; Ferrero, op. cit. vol. v. p. 82 *et seq.*

[2] Hor. C.S. 21.

[3] Kukula, " Römische Säkularpoesie," pp. 2-4.

[4] For the connection of sulphur springs and volcanic places in Italy with the underworld, cf. Geikie, "Love of Nature among the Romans," c. xvi.; Frazer, "Adonis Attis Osiris," vol. i. p. 204 *et seq.*

[5] Technically, a " saeculum " might begin at any time.

[6] For the text of the oracle, as preserved by Zosimus, with the historian's own account of the games, *vide* Wickham, Introduction to C.S.; cf. Diels, op. cit. p. 127 *et seq.*

study of this revival, both in an invaluable inscription,[1] or rather series of inscriptions discovered in Rome in 1890, near the site of Pons Triumphalis, and in Horace's "Carmen Saeculare," composed by order of Augustus to be sung on the concluding day of the festival. The inscription contains the preliminary instructions of Augustus, two decrees of the Senate, and a number of records of the Quindecemviri, whose duty it was to superintend the ritual of the games. The festival was held, not only for three nights as was customary in former celebrations, but also for three days, while a number of new deities were honoured, and their assistance invoked. By night offerings were made to the Moirae,[2] who were asked to grant a still greater destiny to Rome, to Ilithyia,[3] the Greek goddess of childbirth, who was invoked to increase the progeny of the Roman race, and to Tellus,[4] who was petitioned for further productiveness of crops and herds.

By day sacrifices were offered to the Capitoline deities, Jupiter and Juno, and to the deities of the Palatine, Apollo and Diana. White victims were offered to these as gods of the upper world. The Saecular Games are thus no longer merely a festival of night and of the underworld, but are held, too, by day, and share their honours with the gods above. For their change in spirit, and their place in Augustan policy, we must have recourse in particular to Horace's "Carmen Saeculare," which was sung on the third day of the festival by

[1] Now in the Museo delle Terme in Rome; cf. Boissier in "Revue de Deux Mondes," Feb. 1892, p. 75 et seq.

[2] For the origin of the Moirae, cf. Cornford, "From Religion to Philosophy," ii.

[3] She is thus brought into relation with the recent reforms of Augustus in the Julian Laws.

[4] For the conception of Tellus, as the "fruitful and kindly mother," on the reliefs of the Ara Pacis, cf. Strong, "Roman Sculpture," p. 43 et seq.; on the Vienna cameo, ibid. p. 88; on the statue of Augustus in the Vatican, cf. Furtwängler and Urlichs, op. cit. p. 235.

a choir of twenty-seven youths and twenty-seven maidens,[1] specially selected, as having both parents alive. We feel that the games are being celebrated, not so much to commemorate the burial of an outworn age, as the founding of a new and more glorious era. Throughout Horace's hymn, there is a note of triumph and rejoicing in the success of the Emperor's policy, foreign and domestic. The poet, after he has alluded to the Emperor's reforms, prays for the fertility of man, beast, and crop, and as if his prayer had been already granted, he tells of the peace and plenty,[2] that reign in the land, and the splendid prestige, that the Roman name enjoys throughout the world. But the prominence given to Apollo and Diana in the hymn is especially significant. Horace apparently received orders from the Emperor to commemorate in his hymn[3] all the deities, that had been honoured during the festival, but, even as compared with the Capitoline deities, Apollo and Diana are marked out for special distinction, thus bringing the revival into close relation with those great deities of the Imperial regime. The opening verses of the "Carmen Saeculare" pay honour to these two deities; twice within the poem are their praises sung, while its closing lines are echoes of their names. Apollo is clothed with many attributes, such as those of the Sun-god, the spreader of pestilence, the god of divination and of healing, all the attributes, in fact, which characterize the great god of Greek mythology. It is interesting, however, to find the poet emphasizing the connection of this deity with the fortunes[4] of Æneas and his band of Tro-

---

[1] For the significance of the number, cf. Diels, op. cit. p. 39 *et seq.*; *ibid.* pp. 90-1.

[2] *Vide infra*, p. 116; cf. Hor. A.P. 198, where the chorus is asked to sing of "leges et salubrem justitiam et apertis otia portis," a passage in which Horace possibly has "Augustan Peace" in mind.

[3] For the method of singing the hymn, see a masterly article by Mr. Warde Fowler in the "Classical Quarterly," July, 1910; cf. "The Religious Experience," p. 444 *et seq.*

[4] Cf. Hor. Odes, IV. vi. 21 *et seq.*

jans, and thus with the origins of Rome itself, an event that may have been insisted upon in order to offer an explanation of the prominence given to the Greek Apollo, beside such a deity as Jupiter, who had hitherto been indissolubly linked in Roman thought with the greatness of Rome. If we survey the deities of the hymn, we find Greek and Latin deities so mingled together, that one is forced to the conclusion that Augustus intended that "the religion of the Romans was henceforward to be a cosmopolitan or Romano-Hellenic one ".[1] The door to cosmopolitanism was further opened when permission was granted, not merely to Roman citizens as heretofore, but to " all free men of every race " to participate in the festival. As we might expect, Horace does not neglect to make a complimentary reference to the ruling prince, sprung from that Trojan line, which Apollo had befriended in days of stress and tribulation. To him, as well as to the gods, is it due that peace reigns throughout Rome's dominions, that so feared is her name that peoples [2] from far distant India send ambassadors to seek the friendship of her ruler. All this has been accomplished by clemency [3] towards fallen foes, and we may presume, judging by the place such deified abstractions have in the hymn, by scrupulous adherence to honour, virtue,[4] and good faith. Augustus has re-accepted the burden of rulership for a further five years, and the poet's prayer is that this " lustrum " may be crowned by a still further increase of happiness and glory for Latium and Rome.

[1] Warde Fowler, " The Religious Experience," p. 444; cf. Carter, op. cit. p. 169.

[2] *Vide supra*, p. 31.

[3] Hor. C.S. 51; Odes, III. iv. 41; cf. Mon. Ancyr. c. 26; Suet. Oct. 21; Strong, op. cit. p. 85, for this theme on one of the Bosco Reale cups.

[4] Mrs. Strong, op. cit. p. 84, takes this as " warlike valour," but it could hardly in that case be called " neglecta ".

CHAPTER III.

HORACE IN RELIGION AND PHILOSOPHY.

It would be a mistake to look in Horace for deep or abiding convictions in either Religion or Philosophy. The poet was essentially a man of many moods, quick-tempered and sensitive, as changing as the hues of an autumn sunset across the Roman Campagna. Our aim should be, not to assign him a complete system of Philosophy, but to catch, and if possible explain those passing moods. It would indeed be as difficult to erect a complete system from the broken fragments of the poet's Philosophy, as to weave into coherent design the scattered fragments of mosaic unearthed by the spade from the ruins of some Roman villa. Even in later life, when Horace evinces a more serious interest in the study of Philosophy than in his earlier years, he proclaims[1] that he will swear allegiance to no single master, much less can we hope to bind him to any definite school of philosophic thought.

The poet's character had first been moulded by a good home training[2] from his father, who, bluff honest freedman that he was, had a healthy contempt[3] for the set rules of the Philosophers, and with shrewd practical good sense was convinced that the best way to train his son to walk in the path of virtue was to point to those in their neighbourhood, who had been failures in life. To him and to those early lessons

---

[1] Ep. I. i. 14.   [2] Hor. Sat. I. iv. 105.
[3] *Ibid.* 113. He was an " abnormis sapiens " like Ofellus; cf. Sat. II. ii. 3.

Horace traces[1] the genesis of his satiric genius.   When the time came to choose a master for the young Horace, his father, though of slender means,[2] refused to send him to the local school at Venusia, and placed him at Rome under Orbilius,[3] one of the most distinguished teachers of his day. Even there, paternal supervision[4] was not wanting.   The father evidently had ambitions for his son, and, when he had pursued his studies in Rome for some years, he sent him to Athens to complete a liberal education.   This was the lot[5] of most of the rich young Romans of the time, and though Horace could not certainly have been as extravagant,[6] and was perhaps not as wayward as Cicero's son, Marcus, during his course at Athens, yet the cost of sending him there must have been a serious strain on his father's modest income.   We do not know how long the poet spent at Athens, nor what his progress[7] was.   The time (c. 43 B.C.) was unfavourable for philosophical studies.   Civil war was in the air.   We may be sure that more politics than Philosophy was then discussed among the Roman colony at Athens.   It was now clear that Cæsar's death had not restored liberty to the Republic, and that the Republican cause would have to be fought again on another field.   Brutus, by the charm of his personality, and his enthusiasm for the cause he espoused, won to his side many of the young Romans who were then in Athens.   The younger Cicero, in spite of his father's ardent wish[8] to make him a philosopher, abandoned such intellectual pursuits for

---

[1] Sat. I. iv. 103.   [2] *Ibid.* vi. 71.

[3] Hor. Ep. II. i. 70 ; cf. Suet. De Grammaticis, ix.

[4] Hor. Sat. I. vi. 81.

[5] Athens was then as always the great centre of " university " life in the Ancient World.   Rhodes was also a favourite centre; cf. Warde Fowler, " Social Life in Rome in the Age of Cicero," p. 199.

[6] We hear a good deal of Marcus' career at Athens, and of his subsequent movements, from Cicero's Correspondence of these years ; cf. Att. xii. 32 ; xiv. 7 ; xv. 15 ; Ad Fam. xii. 14, 16 ; xvi. 21 ; Br. ii. 3.

[7] Cf. Sat. I. x. 31, for his attempts at Greek verse.

[8] Cic. De Off. III. ii. 6.

the more congenial task of soldiering, and won for himself a
high reputation as a cavalry-lieutenant in the army of Brutus.
Horace, too, was seized by the war fever, and set out to join
Brutus, and serve under the Republican banner with rather
inglorious[1] consequences at Philippi. How great were the
fruits of the poet's interrupted studies, or who his masters
were we have no means of definitely establishing. We can
only hope that he was more fortunate in them than the younger
Cicero, who fell, for a time at least, under evil influences. He
may have heard Cratippus, one of the most popular and
highly esteemed[2] philosophers of the time, who expounded the
doctrines of the Peripatetics, or some of the many philosophers,
largely devoid of originality, who in an age which merely
endeavoured to reflect the splendours of the Golden Age
of Greek Philosophy, propounded a system of Eclecticism.[3]
Eclecticism had certainly been the distinguishing[4] mark of
Post-Aristotelian Philosophy in Athens towards the close of
the second century B.C., and we may presume that this characteristic was maintained down to Horace's day. This tendency in Philosophy was one of the results of the growth of
Roman influence in the Greek world. The Roman held
that Philosophy should above all have a practical end in view,
and teach men the secret of happiness. He was concerned
with the differences between schools of philosophic thought
only in so far as they affected this practical end. This attitude
helped to obliterate the sharp lines of cleavage, which had
hitherto divided the various systems. There is no need to
take Horace literally when he tells[5] us that he was a follower
of the Academic school, though, like Brutus,[6] he may have

---

[1] Hor. Odes, II. vii. 9; III. iv. 26; Ep. II. ii. 49.

[2] Cic. De Off. III. ii. 5; xxxiii. 121; De Div. c. 3; Ad Fam. xvi. 21.

[3] Mahaffy, " The Silver Age of the Greek World," p. 98 et seq.; Bevan,
" Stoics and Sceptics," pp. 91-2.

[4] Zeller, " Stoics, Epicureans, and Sceptics," pp. 28-30.

[5] Ep. II. ii. 45.

[6] Plutarch, " Life of Brutus," xxiv.; cf. Prop. III. xxi. 25.

attended the lectures of Theomnestus, who was then at the head of the Academy. We may take him more seriously, when in the same passage he declares that his interest lay in the ethical aspect of Philosophy. The common-sense Roman had little taste for metaphysical speculation, and was inclined to hold suspect those who neglected their duties as citizens to devote themselves to such a pursuit. An occupation of this kind might be worthy of Greeks, but, as I have said, Philosophy appealed to the Roman only in so far as it could subserve some practical end. It is evident that such Roman prejudice was strong, as we find Cicero making elaborate apologies[1] for his devotion to Philosophy, just as we find him, in his impeachment of Verres,[2] endeavouring to guard against another popular prejudice, by professing little knowledge even of the names of the great Greek artists. He devoted himself[3] to Philosophy especially, when the avenues of political activity were closed by the domination of a single man, as a comfort in enforced leisure, as a solace in domestic grief. Moreover, he regarded Philosophy as of the highest importance as an element of general culture, and an effective instrument in the training of an orator.[4] He could thus console himself with the belief that it had a practical value, and he would have had little difficulty in convincing even its bitterest opponents that ethical problems were of deep concern to humanity in general, as being at the basis of that happy life, which all men were in quest of, though all were not agreed as to the means of attaining it.

When Horace then proclaims his interest in such problems, he is at once true to the instincts which he shared with humanity at large, true also to the practical character of the

---

[1] Cic. Acad. II. ii. 6; De Fin. I. ii. 3; De Off. II. i. 2; Tusc. Disp. v. 2; cf. Reid's Introduction to the Academics, p. 23. That the prejudice lingered for many years is clear from Tac. Agr. c. 4. Agricola used to relate "se prima in juventa studium philosophiae acrius, ultra quam concessum Romano ac senatori hausisse".

[2] De Signis, c. 2-3.   [3] De Off. III. i. 2.   [4] Orator, 113-19.

Roman. We cannot, as I have said, estimate with exact precision the fruits of the poet's philosophical training at Athens.
He came home apparently deeply impressed with the value of
one principle—that of the Golden Mean as a criterion of conduct. The practical bearing of this principle he had learnt to
some extent in his father's home, but he could understand its
true inwardness only from the study of Philosophy. It was the
keystone of the ethical teaching of the Peripatetic School, and
the importance, which Horace attaches to it, raises the presumption that he attended the lectures of Cratippus, then its most
brilliant exponent. When poverty[1] drove him to Literature
after the debacle at Philippi, this principle was to serve him in
good stead in his earliest works. To me it seems to furnish
the secret of his outlook upon life, and, as it were, of his own
concept of his mission, when he set himself to write his Satires.
Mr. Gordon, in an interesting study,[2] has shown how this
principle is operative in the "Characters" of Theophrastus,
and the Comedy of Manners, and has pointed out the intimate
connection[3] between the Ethics of Aristotle and the work of
Theophrastus, who was one of his most brilliant pupils, and his
successor as head of the School. Virtue, as Mr. Gordon puts
it, once admitted to be the Mean, it became necessary to
define the Extremes corresponding to it. It was an easy and
natural transition from the definition of such philosophical
terms to the portrayal of the social types, that are their embodiment in the "Characters" and in the Comedy of Manners.
Now, this idea of the Golden Mean is predominant in a
number of the Satires of Horace. His first Satire is a practical
lesson in avoiding extremes. Though he concentrates his
attention on one type of the Extreme, the Avaricious man, he

[1] Hor. Ep. II. ii. 51.

[2] "Theophrastus and his Imitators" in "English Literature and the
Classics," p. 48 et seq.

[3] On this cf. also Jebb's Introduction to the "Characters," p. 10 et
seq.; Butcher, "Aristotle's Theory of Poetry and Fine Art," p. 350.

does not fail to draw the moral of his discourse towards the end of the Satire. When we leave one extreme we are not[1] to rush to another, for there is a mean in all things. The same lesson is inculcated in the following Satire, though Horace here changes his method, and appeals to two examples drawn from the life of his own day, Tigellius typical of prodigality, Fufidius of meanness. Again he draws the moral, the necessity of keeping the middle way.[2] Tigellius reappears in the third Satire, this time not as the typical wastrel, but as an example of inconsistency,[3] one who is ever oscillating between extremes, who one moment speaks of kings and princes and has high ambitions, the next is longing for the simple life. In the following Satire the poet tells us we have only to pick[4] out any one at random from the crowd, and we will find him suffering from some vice, it may be avarice, it may be wretched ambition, all so many aberrations from the Golden Mean. There is a passage in a neighbouring Satire,[5] where Horace tells us that no one can cast in his teeth either the vice of avarice or meanness, implying that he himself has held fast by the principle, which he proclaims with such insistence. Again, Damasippus,[6] while setting out to glorify the Stoic "Sapiens," incidentally preaches a sermon on the Golden Mean. One might trace the working of this principle in many[7] other passages, but I have dealt with examples, that are at once the most obvious and the most important. It is interesting to note that Horace was faithful to this principle all through life,[8] and found its application useful even in his literary

---

[1] Sat. I. i. 103, 106, " est *modus* in rebus ".

[2] *Ibid.* ii. 25, "dum vitant stulti vitia, in contraria currunt".

[3] *Ibid.* iii. 9-19.   [4] *Ibid.* iv. 25.   [5] *Ibid.* vi. 68.

[6] Sat. II. iii.   [7] *Ibid.* ii. 54, 66; iii. 166, 174; vii. 20.

[8] Epode i. 32 *et seq.*; cf. the well-known phrase " aurea mediocritas," Odes, II. x. 5, an Ode addressed to Murena, of which Dr. Verrall made so much, "Studies of Horace," pp. 24, 47. In any study of the Ode, we have to bear in mind what importance Horace attaches to the principle elsewhere in his writings; cf. Ep. I. xviii. 8 *et seq.*; II. ii. 194 *et seq.*

criticism.[1]   But the examples I have quoted from the Satires help us to realize what is the poet's conception of his mission in those early years, and what was the quality of his laughter. Horace himself claims kinship with Lucilius,[2] and, if we push this to its logical issue, he is thus brought into relation,[3] through his predecessor in Satire, with the writers of the Old Comedy.   It is true that the poet at times indulges in personal attack,[4] but even then he claims [5] that there is no malignity in his laughter.   We must remember, too, that many of the names he employs (such as Pantolabus and Nomentanus) had already figured [6] in the Satires of Lucilius.   These names had become typical of certain vices, and for Horace and his contemporaries the individuals had been forgotten, and only the type remembered.   But the importance, which our poet attaches to the principle of the Golden Mean in his Satires, brings him directly into line with the " Characters " and the Comedy of Manners.   As the " Characters " depend for their validity on the principle of the Golden Mean, so the Comedy of Manners was cast in the same mould.   These literary genres could flourish especially in an age when freedom had been extinguished, when the great struggles that raged round political life in the State had ceased, when society was thrown back upon itself, and its members could occupy themselves with analyses of individual emotions.   Society presupposes the Mean, it demands the normal type, which is the embodiment of the Mean in real life.   The abnormal or the eccentric [7] affoids it food for laughter, and furnishes the materials for genuine Comedy.   Much has been written on the nature of the laughter of true Comedy.   Meredith [8] considered Comedy to be the " genius of thoughtful laughter," and for M. Bergson, who has

[1] A.P. 31.   [2] Hor. Sat. I. x. 48 ; II. i. 29, 62.   [3] Ibid. iv. 6.
[4] For instance, Sat. I. ii. 27 ; cf. Sat. I. iv. 72, 91 et seq. ; viii. 95 ; x. 18.
[5] Ibid. I. iv. 70.
[6] Vide Gerlach, " Lucilii Saturarum Reliquiae," Introd. p. 25 et seq.
[7] Gordon, op. cit. p. 85.   [8] In his " Essay on Comedy ".

his thoughts fixed especially on Moliere, it is intelligent laughter, residing in the intellect, not in the emotions.[1] " The function of this laughter is to bring men into line, to keep society broadly true to itself, to restrain its members from wandering outside the beaten path." It is the laughter which restrains men " within the limits of a middle way ".[2] Menander was probably its finest exponent in ancient times, as Moliere has been in modern times. Horace, then, in his Satires wished to render a social service. His laughter was of the nature of the " social gesture," which Bergson describes, and its aim was to bind men down to a life of virtue according to the Golden Mean. It would be interesting to speculate whether Horace was acquainted with the "Characters". He may well have been if he attended the lectures of Cratippus, as the book must have been one of the treasures of the Peripatetic School. It was also a favourite book [3] with teachers of Rhetoric, and even with philosophers other than Peripatetics. There are certainly some passages [4] in the Satires, that seem to follow closely enough in the footsteps of Theophrastus. Again there are many passages [5] in our poet, in which he shows his interest in the New Comedy,

[1] Palmer, " Comedy," p. 12 ; cf. Bergson, Le Rire (édition Alcan), p. 19 et seq., p. 137 et seq. Aristotle made a clear distinction between Comedy proper, which " dramatises the ludicrous," and personal satire, refusing to give the name of Comedy to the Old Comedy with its personal invective ; cf. Poetics, c. iv. 10, v. 3 ; Butcher, op. cit. p. 346 et seq., p. 357. Dryden, " Essay on Dramatic Poesy " (Arnold's ed.), p. 74, says of the laughter of Comedy : " All things, which are deviations from common customs are aptest to produce it ".

[2] Palmer, op. cit. p. 14.   [3] Gordon, op. cit. p. 65.

[4] Cf. Sat. I. iii. 30 et seq., with the " Character " of the ἀγροῖκος, Sat. II. ii. 65, for a definition in the style of Theophrastus. If the name were omitted from the portrait of Avidienus, it might well stand for a " Character " of the Mean Man. Cf. also Sat. I. ii. 12 et seq.; Ep. I. xviii. 9 et seq.

[5] In his analysis of Comedy, Sat. I. iv. 48 et seq., Horace clearly has the New Comedy in mind. Cf. Sat. I. x. 40; II. iii. 11, 261 et seq.; Epode i. 33 ; A.P. 93.

and his acquaintance with one of its great Roman representatives, Terence.

Whatever philosophical opinions Horace may have imbibed at Athens, he leaves us in little doubt as to where his sympathics lay, when he first essayed literature. Speaking broadly, two great systems of philosophy, Stoicism and Epicureanism, had for many years contended, and were still contending in Horace's day, for supremacy at Rome. From what we know of the poet's character, being of a nature rich, sensitive, pleasure-loving, full of the joy of life, he would be as strongly attracted by Epicureanism as he was repelled by the austerity of Stoic teaching. Epicureanism, moreover, had the advantage of being expounded in brilliant and forcible language by a poet, who was one of the most original writers that Rome had ever produced. Epicureanism was decidedly popular[1] towards the close of the Republic, and the work of Lucretius must have contributed in no small degree to its popularity. Though his main arguments often march drearily enough, yet they are interspersed by passages of great imaginative beauty. Virgil in his early days had fallen under the spell of his genius, and for a time at least had toyed with Epicureanism. Lucretius, apart from his philosophical opinions, was a new force[2] in Roman Literature. His was the first great didactic poem in Latin, the first attempt to treat a philosophical subject within the limits of the hexameter. He set himself, too, to supply the defects of the mother-tongue (that "patrii sermonis egestas," which he so often laments), by creating a philosophical terminology, a work which had its counterpart in prose in the splendid achievements of Cicero. Lucretius would thus make a special appeal to one who, like Horace, was for the first time entering the arena of literature.

---

[1] Cic. De Fin. I. vii. 25 ; Tusc. Disp. IV. iii. 7 ; Zeller, op. cit. p. 414, on the question of Epicurean prose-writers at Rome ; cf. Zeller, p. 411 ; Reid, Introduction to the Academics, p. 22.

[2] For his own claims, cf. De Rer. Nat. i. 926 ; v. 336.

There is in the Satires clear evidence of Lucretian influence both in thought and diction.[1]   Horace, in Epicurean fashion,[2] defends the utilitarian origin of justice, law, and society, and that in rather truculent fashion, as a counterblast to the Stoic paradox he has just condemned.   He is here reviving an old [3] controversy, as to whether justice was a law of Nature or a matter of convention.   With Lucretius's treatment [4] of the same problem clearly before his mind, he decides for the theory of the "social contract".   Again, he proclaims,[5] repeating the very words of Lucretius, that he has learned that the gods lead an existence calm and untroubled by the chequered destinies of men, that "no sound of human sorrow mounts to mar their sacred everlasting calm".   He dwells,[6] too, on that fear of the gods, which Lucretius so strongly condemns as vitiating human happiness, and describes the extravagances into which it can lead the superstitious.   In the fable of the city-mouse and the country-mouse, the city-mouse is the exponent [7] of the teaching of Epicureanism on the mortality of the soul, and of its doctrine of pleasure, though at this point Lucretius would part company from all who sought to make mere sensual pleasure the highest end in life.

As Horace was attracted to Epicureanism in those early days, so there is little doubt also of his antagonism to Stoic doctrine.   For this there were many reasons, and temperament

[1] Cf. Hor. Sat. I. i. 19 with Lucr. iii. 938; Sat. I. viii. 46 with Lucr. vi. 130; Sat. II. vii. 28, 111-15 with Lucr. iii. 1058 et seq.   Horace uses the example (Sat. II. iii. 199) of Iphigenia, which Lucretius uses with such effect (i. 84 et seq.), but uses it as an example of madness springing from ambition.

[2] Sat. I. iii. 98 et seq.   [3] Plato, Rep. i. 331 c. et seq.

[4] Lucr. v. 925 et seq.; on the origin of justice, 1020 et seq.; on ancient arms, 1283 et seq.; cf. Cic. De Fin. ii. 16-18; Masson, " Lucretius, Epicurean and Poet," c. vii.; Martha, " Le Poëme de Lucrèce," c. viii.

[5] Sat. I. v. 101; Lucr. v. 83; cf. ii. 646; iii. 18 et seq.; v. 146, 1161; cf. Cic. De Nat. Deorum, i. 16-21; De Fin. ii. 50.

[6] Sat. II. iii. 290-95; Lucr. iii. 81-90; v. 1165 et seq., 1194.

[7] Sat. II. vi. 93 et seq.; cf. Lucr. iii. 417 et seq.

again not the least among them. Strict Stoicism would probably[1] have made a strong appeal to Romans, who were nurtured in the simplicity of the early Republic, but now that the
old simplicity of life had practically vanished, and given way
to reckless luxury, the burden of such a creed would weigh
too heavily on men. The Stoic system, if carried to its logical
issue, meant the exaltation of pure Reason, and a ruthless repression[2] of the emotions. For the Stoics, all emotions were
diseases of the soul, or at least symptoms of a mind that was
suffering from serious maladies. One of their highest ideals
was to reach a condition of Reason, undefiled or unclouded by
passion. If all men were Catos or Tuberos,[3] there would be
little room for the gentler social virtues, for the softening and
refining influences of life. The spirit of independence, advo-
cated by the Stoics, tended, unless strictly guarded, to degenerate into arrogance, while their doctrine of Virtue left no
hope[4] of pardon for the waywardness of mankind. There are
two aspects of Stoicism that especially evoked Horace's ridicule
and hostility—their Paradoxes and their ideal of the Wise Man.
The poet was essentially a moderate man,[5] endowed like most
of his countrymen with a large measure of good sense, and
these seemed to him inherent absurdities of the Stoic system.
The Paradoxes were appropriately so called,[6] because they
ran counter to common opinion. The ethical system of the
Stoics was founded on the paradox that Virtue[7] was the only
good. It is not surprising then to find other paradoxes springing from this fundamental position. Virtue being the only
good, it follows that it is all-sufficient for happiness. Hence,

---

[1] Lecky, " History of European Morals," p. 372.

[2] For the doctrine of ἀπάθεια, cf. Von Arnim, " Fragmenta Stoicorum
Veterum," vol. i. p. 50 ; iii. p. 108; Stock, " Stoicism," p. 37.

[3] Cic. Pro Murena, xxxvi. 75.

[4] *Ibid.* xxix. 61; Seneca, De Clem. ii. c. 7 ; Virg. Georgic, ii. 499.

[5] Hor. Sat. I. iv. 130; vi. 65.   [6] Cic. Introd. to Paradoxa.

[7] Cic. De Off. III. iii. 14; De Fin. III. vii. 25; Zeller, op. cit. p. 231 ;
Von Arnim, vol. iii. p. 10 *et seq.*

the only things that matter in life are Virtue and Vice, while all things else are "indifferent" (ἀδιάφορα), including worldly possessions, usually considered as good. This was a doctrine, as Cicero says,[1] that might suit a community of disembodied spirits, but was hardly suited to men consisting of body and soul. Again, Virtue being, according to the Stoics, a disposition[2] of the soul, it was held to be one and indivisible, and to admit of no degrees. It was possessed by a person either wholly or not at all. The Stoics recognized no mean between Virtue and Vice, between the sinner and the saint. The slightest departure from Virtue was equivalent to its most flagrant violation. Thus we have the paradox[3] that all sins are equal, and worthy of the same punishment.

Now, closely connected with these paradoxes, the embodiment of them in fact, and the crowning paradox of all, was the "Sapiens" or Wise Man. The Sapiens[4] was a sublime but impossible figure, self-sufficing and completely happy, a man of passionless calm, unpitying and unforgiving, a paragon of Virtue, incapable of erring. He alone is free, with the freedom that comes from independence of all external goods, he alone possesses Virtue in its full perfection, he alone is happy, he alone beautiful, he alone rich, though he has none of the world's riches. The Wise Man through Virtue is a king,[5] though his dominion extended apparently over himself alone. The primitive Stoics, in denying the necessity of external goods for happiness, placed the latter in the mind alone, or in Virtue, which is a disposition of the mind. It was a doctrine especially congenial to an age,[6] when men were largely debarred from political activity, and were forced to retire into themselves. From one

---

[1] Cic. De Fin. IV. vii. 17 ; ibid. xi. 28.

[2] Zeller, op. cit. p. 256.   [3] Cic. Paradoxa, iii.

[4] Zeller, op. cit. pp. 253-4, 266 et seq.; Von Arnim, vol. iii. p. 146 et seq.; Stock, op. cit. p. 65 et seq.; cf. Gellius, N.A. I. xxvi.

[5] Cic. De Fin. III. xxii. 75 ; Pro Sulla, viii. 25.

[6] Zeller, op. cit. p. 17.

point of view, it was a splendid dream—this picture of the Sage,
retiring, as it were, within the citadel of his mind, taking his
stand there serene and untroubled, bearing with perfect im-
perturbability the "slings and arrows" of fortune. The Wise
Man, as we saw, possesses Wisdom and Virtue in their fullest
measure, while all who are not "Sapientes" are confirmed [1]
sinners, slaves to vice, fools, and for the Stoics all fools are mad.
As even on their own confession [2] the Sage had hardly ever
been realized among mortals, they were reduced to the absurd
conclusion that mankind at large is hopelessly sinful and cor-
rupt. The doctrines of ἀπάθεια and of Virtue (which are found
in full perfection only in the "Sapiens"), constituted a difficulty, which later Stoics especially endeavoured to solve. It
was one of the antinomies of the Stoic system to have brought
into sharp antagonism the Sage's duties as a member of society,
and his independence of external conditions together with his
freedom from emotion. In the Sage, as described by later
Stoics,[3] we find two apparently conflicting tendencies. The
Wise Man is represented as withdrawn into himself, untouched
by even the emotions of pity and forgiveness for the failings of
mankind. The reverse of the picture shows him taking part in
social and political life as his highest duty, practising towards
his fellow-men the virtues of mercy and forgiveness. Their
doctrine of the Cosmopolis, that world-state in which all men
are brothers and members of one great society, forced them
into the position of depicting the Sage exhibiting boundless
charity and benevolence towards his fellow-creatures. If you
tax the Stoics with inconsistency, they reply that there is none.
For, though the Wise Man practise kindness, gentleness, and
mercy towards brethren in distress, he will do so in a spirit of

---

[1] Cic. Paradoxa, iv. and v.

[2] He was ὥσπερ τι ζῷον σπανιώτερον τοῦ φοίνικος, quoted by Zeller, op.
cit. p. 273.

[3] Zeller, p. 315 et seq.; Stock, op. cit. p. 67 et seq. This attempt at
reconciliation is seen especially in Seneca, Epictetus, and M. Aurelius.

aloofness, without sharing the emotions usually aroused by such actions. All these paradoxes of Stoicism were hard sayings, not relished by Horace or his contemporaries. It is little wonder that the poet directs the keenest shafts [1] of his satire against the "Sapiens," that absurd creation of the Stoic School. Even in later years, when he arrived at a better appreciation of the tenets of the Stoics, he could never be quite reconciled [2] with their Sage. Again, he delivers a trenchant criticism [3] on the paradox that all sins are equal, a doctrine that will never bear the test [4] of reality, that runs counter to our instincts, our habits of life, and even to expediency. He pleads for the common-sense view, that no one is born without faults, while there are certain defects (*haerentia stultis*) clinging to all, who are not Sages, that cannot be eradicated. We must pardon our friends' offences, not be like the Stoic, who shows no pity to erring humanity. Finally, he demands that each vice should be visited by a punishment commensurate with it. In another Satire [5] Horace expounds, through the mouth of his slave Davus, the paradox that none but the Sage are free. The picture of the Sage is there so finely drawn, that some [6] have been inclined to take it as evidence of Horace's [7] awakening sympathy towards Stoicism. Possibly the poet's hostility is not so marked here as in other Satires, but it would be difficult to discover any sign of seriousness of purpose in his treatment of the paradox. We must remember that the picture of the "Sapiens" is drawn by the enthusiasm of a recent convert to Stoicism, nor must we overlook the delicate irony in the setting of the Satire as a whole. Davus takes advantage of the privileges [8] of the Satur-

---

[1] Sat. I. iii. 124 *et seq.* ; II. iii. *passim ;* vii. 83 *et seq.*

[2] Ep. I. i. 106 *et seq.*

[3] Sat. I. iii. 68 *et seq.* ; cf. Cic. De Fin. IV. xxvii.

[4] *Ibid.* Pro Murena, xxix. ; De Fin. IV. xix. 55.   [5] Sat. II. vii.

[6] E.g. Palmer, who finds no ridicule in it.   [7] *Vide infra*, p. 101.

[8] Sat. II. vii. 4 ; cf. Sat. II. iii. 5 ; cf. Kiessling, Introduction to Sat. II. vii.

nalia (*libertas Decembris*) to lecture his master, while he declares[1]
that he has derived his precepts from no higher a personage
than the porter of Crispinus. It is not unlikely that an additional source of Horace's repugnance to Stoicism was to be
found in the Stoic popular teacher,[2] who went about with staff
and flowing beard, and generally unkempt appearance, ex-
pounding the doctrines of the sect. These aggressive propa-
gandists represented, as a rule, the worst features of Stoicism,
in fact its " Cynic "[3] elements, in their contempt for cultured
habits and fine feeling and conventional notions generally.

Horace thus concentrates his attention on those aspects of
Stoic teaching, which were most repugnant to Roman feeling
and to common sense. It was indeed unfortunate, but inevitable, that the minds of many were fixed on the paradoxes,
and distracted from the higher and nobler and more enduring
elements of the system. Moreover, Horace seems quite unconscious at this time of the trend of Roman Stoicism, of that
broadening of the tenets of the school, which had marked the
teaching of Panætius and his pupil Posidonius. Even before
Panætius,[4] efforts had been made to modify Stoic theory
in accordance with the needs of practical life. Stoics like
Cleanthes enunciated the doctrine of "things preferred," dis-
covering a relative value at least in many things, which Stoicism in its pristine rigour would have excluded from the
category of the Good. They discovered intermediate duties
over and above that "perfect duty," which could emanate only
from the Sage. They began to admit degrees of badness, and
consequently the possibility of advance towards perfect virtue.
They allowed the existence of "permitted emotions," which

[1] Sat. II. vii. 45.

[2] *Ibid.* I. iii. 134 *et seq.*; II. iii. 16, 35, 77. Here is probably the secret
of Horace's aversion to Crispinus; cf. Sat. I. i. 120; iii. 139; iv. 14.

[3] Zeller, op. cit. p. 305, 387 *et seq.*; Von Arnim, vol. iii. p. 185; Hor.
Odes, I. xxi. 9; cf. Persius, Sat. i. 133.

[4] Zeller, op. cit. c. xi.

would have been formerly ruled out by the absolutely emotion-
less condition required in the Sage. These concessions to
popular feeling, and to the weaknesses of humanity, were
carried out most systematically by Panætius, who, on coming
to Rome, became a member of the Scipionic circle, and was
the real founder of Roman Stoicism. He helped to bring
Stoicism more into harmony with the Roman character, in
which practical good-sense predominated, and thus did much
to establish its popularity in Rome. This philosopher had
broken with his school at many points, and might really be
considered an Eclectic, though Cicero calls [1] him "gravissimus
Stoicorum". He abandoned [2] the orthodox Stoic teaching on
divination. He modified [3] the doctrine that virtue alone is
sufficient for happiness, and would not reject external goods
as a factor in its attainment, provided they were in harmony
with Virtue. With him ordinary mortals,[4] striving to advance
in goodness, were of more account than the ideal Wise Man.
What his precise attitude was towards the paradoxes of his
school we are nowhere expressly told, unless Cicero's declaration,[5] that he avoided "the bitter dogmas" (*acerbitatem
sententiarum*) of Stoicism, can be taken as an indication.
Cicero himself was profoundly influenced by Panætius, and his
attitude towards the paradoxes might possibly serve as an
index of the attitude of the great philosopher himself. Cicero
had written a special treatise in defence of the paradoxes, but
a phrase [6] in his preface casts some doubt on his earnestness
as their champion. His attitude was possibly more genuinely

---

[1] De Off. II. x. 35. He followed Plato and Aristotle on some questions, though Cicero blames him (Tusc. Disp. I. xxxii. 79) for deserting
Plato on the question of the immortality of the soul.

[2] Cic. De Div. I. iii. 3.

[3] De Off. III. iii. 13.

[4] *Ibid.* iii. 14 ; cf. Arnold, " Roman Stoicism,' p. 100 *et seq.*

[5] De Fin. IV. xxviii. 79.

[6] " Illa ipsa ludens conjeci in communes locos."

revealed in the "Pro Murena". Though the passage,[1] in which he deals with the paradoxes, is a piece of special pleading against the severity of Cato, who was junior counsel in the prosecution of his client, still it served to demonstrate how the intransigent position of extreme Stoicism fails, when brought to the test of real life. His refined and delicate banter of the paradoxes was sure to be an effective weapon when supported by Cicero's matchless eloquence, but this, taken in conjunction with the fact that in the "De Officiis"[2] the paradoxes are of little account, would seem to indicate that they did not figure prominently in the Stoicism of Panætius.

Horace, as far as we can judge, seems quite oblivious of this movement for softening the asperity of primitive Stoicism, and bringing it more into agreement with the needs of the plain man. His study of Stoicism had hitherto probably been only superficial, and he had fixed his gaze especially on those aspects of the system, which seemed to him aberrations from that principle of moderation which he valued so highly. In a later period we find his interest in Stoicism aroused, and a distinct change effected in his philosophical opinions. One reason for this was, in all probability, more extended study,[3] and a consequent appreciation of the value of the Stoic system to all who had regard for high ideals in life, and sought to remedy the evils of the age. Again, advancing years and a more serious outlook upon life would lead to a less rigorous judgment on the merits of a sect, the purity and nobility of whose doctrines no one had ever been able to impugn. To one disposed to study the system dispassionately, beneath a

---

[1] c. xxix. 31. He acknowledges afterwards (De Fin. IV. xxvii. 74), that "he was playing somewhat to the gallery," "aliquid etiam coronae datum".

[2] He follows Panætius in the first two books, while he claims independence in the third, De Off. III. vii. 34; cf. Pro Murena, xxvi. 66.

[3] He can speak now of the "nobiles libros Panæti," Odes, I. xxix. 14.

stern rough exterior, there existed elements of humanitarianism, which among other good effects were exercising a profound influence[1] on that greatest of Roman institutions, Roman Law. Many of the distinguished lawyers towards the close of the Republic were adherents of the Stoic School, and were largely responsible for developing equity in Roman Law, and keeping the administration of justice at a high level. The Stoic insistence upon the existence of a Law of Nature, above all human laws, became the basis of a widening movement in Roman jurisprudence, which began thenceforth to take more account of the spirit than the letter of the Law, and was to bear its richest fruit in later Imperial times. The Stoics insisted, too, on the value of the individual, who in each case possessed within himself a soul that was part of the World-Soul. They spoke much of the brotherhood of Man,[2] and though they accepted the fact of slavery, it is difficult to see how, if they carried such theories to their logical conclusion, they could have made any distinction between slave and freeman. Horace may thus have come to appreciate better the true value of Stoicism, and to realize that, if the obstacles of its paradoxes could be surmounted, there was about it a moral purity and dignity, that must elevate its followers and make them better men and better Romans.

But the change in the poet's attitude seems to me to have been especially occasioned by the movement, inaugurated by Augustus, for the revival of Roman Religion, a movement that influenced not only Horace, but others also of the Augustan poets. There is no need to labour the fact that our poet was won over[3] to the Emperor's programme of reform. Re-

---

[1] *Vide* Heitland, "Roman Republic," iii. p. 474; Warde Fowler, "Social Life in the Age of Cicero," p. 117 *et seq.*; Lecky, op. cit. p. 294 *et seq.*; Lord Cromer, "Ancient and Modern Imperialism," pp. 45-6.

[2] Zeller, op. cit. pp. 216, 326 *et seq.*; Dill, "Roman Society from Nero to Marcus Aurelius," p. 328 *et seq.*; cf. Seneca, De Vita Beata, xxiv. 3; Ep. 95, 33: "Homo res sacra homini".

[3] Cf. especially Odes, III. i.-vi.

publican as he had been, he became convinced that, as
Tacitus phrases it, the vast frame of Empire needed the guidance of a single ruler.   His long and intimate association with
Mæcenas, that was to fructify in intimacy with the Emperor
himself, was sufficient to sap a much more stern republicanism
than Horace could lay claim to.   Now, for all the poet's hostility
to Stoicism in the Satires, it is possible at times, I believe, to
detect a nascent sympathy with its doctrines.   The Satire,[1] in
which he depicts the simple homely life of Ofellus, especially
in its closing lines, may well be reminiscent of Stoic thought.
The poet, when he gathers a few friends together at his festive
board in his Sabine villa, can discuss [2] dispassionately the Stoic
doctrine of Virtue as the Highest Good.   One might argue
from the disastrous [3] ending of the adventure of the city-mouse,
the exponent of Epicureanism, evidence of a reaction against
such a philosophy.   How far Augustus had drawn up or revealed his programme of reform before Actium, it is not easy
to estimate, though it is clear that for some time before his
campaign against Antony he stood forward as the champion [4]
of national and conservative feeling.   Horace has several [5] references to Octavian in the Satires, which show an acquaintance
(second-hand perhaps) with his character.   There is one
passage [6] that, though usually made to bear only a general reference, would gain in point if taken as a defence of Octavian,
especially in view of the slights [7] that were cast upon his
birth by some of his enemies.   But it seems to me particularly
significant that, at a time when he was under the influence
of Epicureanism, Horace should display [8] solicitude for the
ruined temples of the gods.   It looks as if Horace already
knew something of the designs of Augustus for the restoration

---

[1] Sat. II. ii. ; cf. lines 79, 136.   [2] Ibid. vi. 73.

[3] Ibid. iii et seq.

[4] Ferrero, op. cit. vol. iv. p. 31 et seq. ; vide supra, p. 8 et seq.

[5] Sat. I. iii. 4 ; II. i. 18 et seq., 84 ; cf. ibid. II. vi. 55.

[6] Ibid. I. vi. 34 et seq.   [7] Suet. Oct. 2, 4.   [8] Sat. II. ii. 104.

of ancient worship, and was ready to become an advocate in their support.   He was certainly at a later period under the influence of the Augustan Revival, when he announced[1] his conversion from the Epicureanism of former years.   We do not know[2] what precise philosophical opinions were held by Augustus, though like most educated Romans of his time, he was certain to have attached himself to some philosophical system.   For a religious reformer the choice was not difficult to make between the two great rival systems existing then at Rome.   To one, who wished to restore the worship of the gods to its old place of honour, the doctrines of Epicurus were bound to be anathema.   If we admit his teaching that the gods have no share in the government of the universe, we destroy at once the foundations of religion.   As Cicero puts it,[3] if such a position be granted " quid est quod ullos deis im-mortalibus cultus, honores, preces adhibeamus ? "   Whatever were the motives that inspired the Revival, if Augustus, as he undoubtedly did, seriously wished for its accomplishment, devotion to Epicureanism and to its great exponent Lucretius must have been severely discouraged by him amongst all whom his influence could reach.   This will account for the failure[4] of some of the Augustan poets to give Lucretius his due meed of praise, despite his undoubted influence upon them.   It will explain also Virgil's change of front.   He had fallen captive[5] for a time to the glamour of the " De Rerum Natura," but he was essentially of a religious temperament, and one that would not easily cast loose the moorings from the traditional beliefs

---

[1] Odes, I. xxxiv. ; cf. *ibid*. III. v. 1.

[2] For his interest in Philosophy, cf. Suet. Oct. 85.   He wrote a work entitled " Hortationes ad Philosophiam ".

[3] De Nat. Deorum, I. ii. 3.

[4] Ovid, who was not bound to Augustus and his reforms, like Horace and Virgil, pays a tribute to his genius.   Am. I. xv. 23 ; Trist. ii. 425.

[5] Cf. Eclog. vi. 31, 40 ; Duff, Introd. to Lucr. Bk. V., for many of Virgil's imitations of Lucretius.

of his Mantuan home. So we find him,[1] after an enthusiastic
outburst of admiration for the philosophy, that could trample
under foot the fear of "greedy Acheron," proclaiming in the
following lines the happiness of worshipping the deities of
rustic life. If Virgil was ever a whole-hearted adherent of
Epicureanism, his Sixth Æneid furnishes as complete a re-
habilitation as one could wish of those "terrors of the mind,"
which Lucretius regarded as his highest mission in life to
dispel. The Augustan Revival will account, too, as I have said,
for Horace's conversion. He had never probably made a very
profound study of Epicureanism. He gives no indication of
having realized the full import of the message of Lucretius.
This poet had found his contemporaries sunk in superstition,
as he believed,[2] and harassed by fears, which darkened their
whole existence, and "left no pleasure undefiled".[3] There
were fears of the punishments of the gods in this life, fears of
their vengeance in the life to come. Roman religion lent
itself in a peculiar way towards fostering such uneasiness of
spirit. Ritual played an all-important part in Roman worship,
and its exact observance was especially demanded. If a detail
of the ritual was defective, it not only vitiated the sacred ceremony, but it was liable to bring upon the whole community
the vengeance of an outraged deity. Lucretius proclaimed the
great principle of "Law in Nature,"[4] thus precluding the capricious interference of the gods, and by relegating them to a position
of tranquillity and ease, with no share either in the creation or
conservation of the Universe, he freed men at a stroke from
half their terrors. By the equally drastic remedy of denying
the immortality of the soul, he freed them from the terrors of
the life beyond the grave. Horace shows no appreciation of
the fundamental position of Lucretius, the existence of law in

---

[1] Geor. ii. 490 et seq.   [2] Lucr. i. 62 et seq.

[3] Ibid. iii. 40, 978 et seq.; for an ingenious attempt to explain by allegory the punishments of Acheron, ib. v. 1194 et seq.

[4] Ibid. v. 57 et seq.

nature. He had grasped the secondary doctrine that the gods dwell in unalloyed happiness, careless of the destinies of the world and of mankind. This was a principle more easy of comprehension than the former one, but it was one which, as we have said, struck at the roots of religion, and by his denial of it, when his conversion arrives, Horace definitely renounces his allegiance to Lucretius.[1] The explanation in the " De Rerum Natura " of the phenomenon of thunder had broken down for Horace. The poet had heard thunder in a clear sky, and there was no alternative left but to ascribe it to the action of Jupiter himself. The reason seems a paltry one for a change of attitude on such a fundamental question, but it assumes a new aspect in the light of the Augustan Revival. This conversion does not mean for Horace a complete break with Epicureanism. He surrendered only that part of it, that was inimical to a religious revival. He did not feel himself bound to surrender its doctrine of Pleasure, and he frequently interpreted this in a way that would probably have shocked Epicurus, and most certainly would have offended the grim seriousness of Lucretius. To Lucretius the behest to snatch the pleasure of the passing hour seemed a profanation[2] of his master's teaching, and an unworthy device for stifling the thought of death. There is no other doctrine of Epicurus round which the battle has more fiercely raged than this doctrine of Pleasure as the Highest Good, and on it the most violent attacks[3] have been directed by the enemies of his system. It was the source of Cicero's great hostility to Epicureanism, a hostility which he is constantly blazoning forth, and often in the most violent language. Cicero saw that no stable system of ethics could be raised on so insecure a founda-

[1] Cf. Odes, I. xxxiv. 5, and Lucr. vi. 400.

[2] *Ibid.* iii. 912 *et seq.* ; cf. Martha, " Le Poëme de Lucrèce," p. 144.

[3] Cicero says of it (Paradoxa 14) : " mihi vox pecudum videtur, non hominum ",

tion. The master's own life may have been spotless,[1] and his interpretation[2] of the doctrine may have claimed to provide for the exercise of every virtue. His Pleasure may have been merely absence[3] of pain, or a certain tranquillity of mind (ἀταραξία), something akin to the everlasting calm his gods enjoyed. But it is clear from the criticisms[4] of Cicero that, even in the case of Epicurus himself, these were debateable points, and that he was open to the suspicion of having allowed indulgence in bodily pleasure, provided one were a cautious sensualist. There can be little doubt that in the hands of an unscrupulous disciple,[5] Epicurus' theory of Pleasure might be emptied of whatever spirituality and refinement it possessed, and be degraded to mere sensuality.[6] It was this dangerous element in Epicureanism that made Cicero strive to combat the system with all the energies of his talent and eloquence. Horace, at times, leaves us under the impression that he took the doctrine on its lower side. To enjoy to the full the passing hour is again[7] and again the burden of his song, though in this he came nearer perhaps to the position of Aristippus, who taught that the pleasure of the moment was the highest end in life. This philosophy of Hedonism was in harmony with the poet's temperament, while it suited the genius of lyrical composition better than the stern doctrines of the Stoics. It was useful, too, to distract him from the thought of death, which often breaks in upon his enjoyment

[1] For a fine tribute to him, cf. Seneca, De Vita Beata, c. xii.-xiii.

[2] Cic. De Fin. I. xviii. 57.

[3] *Ibid.* xi. 37-8.

[4] De Fin. Bk. ii. *passim*, especially c. vi.-vii., and the fine peroration ; De Nat. Deorum, i. 40; Tusc. Disp. III. xviii., xx. ; V. xxvi. 73-5 ; De Off. III. xxx. 111-16.

[5] Seneca, De Vita Beata, c. xi. ; cf. Friedländer, op. cit. vol. iii. p. 285.

[6] For a picture of the lower side of Epicureanism, cf. Cic. In Pisonem, 28.

[7] Epode xiii. ; Odes, I. iv. 9 *et seq.* ; vii. 17; ix. 13; xviii. ; II. xi. 13 *et seq.* ; III. viii. 27 ; xxi. 13 *et seq.* ; xxix. 42 ; IV. vii. 17.

with a note of sadness, reminding us of the gaiety of Omar, overshadowed by the gloom of the grave :—

> Ah, make the most of what we yet may spend,
> Before we, too, into the dust descend.[1]

We shall find, especially in the Odes, that the flight of years, the hurried passage of youth with its buoyancy, its charms, and its pleasures, the approach of old age, the universality of death are spectres that frequently disturb[2] the poet's mirth and laughter. On the question of life after death,[3] a cardinal point in the system of Epicurus, we find in Horace a strange divergence of views. At times,[4] he seems to proclaim that with death all sensation ends in an eternal sleep. This position is again abandoned, and popular beliefs on the world of shades, its rewards and its punishments, are given[5] a fresh lease of life. One is thus constrained to believe that Horace had never penetrated deeply into Epicureanism, nor had strong convictions with regard to it. As a young man, who had recently enough abandoned his studies at Athens, the brilliancy and scepticism of Lucretius had a certain fascination for him, but it was not easy now, even if he were so inclined, to maintain a sceptical attitude in his poetry, in face of the Emperor's efforts to effect a religious revival. The Epicurean doctrine of Pleasure he might retain, as it was harmless enough, and its effects were likely to go no further than the poet himself.

Just as Epicureanism was the enemy of a Religious Revival, so Stoicism would be in many respects its strongest support. The efforts of Augustus, as we saw, were directed towards restoring the externals of worship, and reviving the conviction that the greatness and prosperity of Rome were intimately

---

[1] Quatrain xxiv. ; cf. Quatrains xxxv., liv.
[2] Odes, I. iv. 13 ; xi. 7 ; II. iii. 25 ; xi. 5 ; xiv. 1 ; IV. vii. 7 ; cf. A.P. 63.
[3] For a fuller treatment of this question, *vide infra*, p. 237 *et seq.*
[4] Odes, I. xxiv. 5 ; II. xi. 11.
[5] *Ibid.* xiii. ; xiv. ; xviii. 34 ; IV. vii. 15 *et seq.*

7 *

bound up with the "Pax Deorum".[1]   Stoic Theology had
endeavoured to make its compromise with Roman beliefs, and
effect a reconciliation between its own deity, and the poly-
theistic system of Rome.   Its one supreme deity was identified
with Jupiter,[2] the great national god of Rome, while the other
members of the Roman Pantheon were considered merely as
his attributes, or as different titles, which he bore.   But over
and above this, its doctrine of a Providence [3] guiding human
destiny was a distinctly valuable asset to a religious reformer.
The interest,[4] which Augustus took in the progress of the
Æneid, was due probably in some measure to the fact, that
Virgil insists so strongly on Rome being a city of destiny,[5] the
foundation of which had been decreed by the will of Heaven,
the fortunes of which were watched over by the gods with
jealous care.   Virgil indeed is so intent upon subjecting Æneas
to the will of the gods, as to endanger [6] his character as an
Epic hero.   The Stoic "Providence" was even more comprehensive than that of the Æneid, and supplied a secure basis for
religion.   We must remember, too, that Roman Stoicism had
not yet time or occasion to develop that spirit of opposition [7]
(based possibly both on moral and political motives) to the
Imperial regime, that was to bring down on its followers the
wrath of succeeding Emperors.   The efforts of Augustus were
directed also to a reform of morals, and here again Stoicism
would prove its value.   The ethics of Stoicism, based as it

[1] Warde Fowler, " Religious Experience," p. 367.

[2] Zeller, op. cit. p. 153; Von Arnim, vol. ii. p. 313.

[3] Von Arnim, vol. ii. p. 322; iii. p. 44; Cic. De Nat. Deorum, ii. 58
(there quoted).

[4] Suet. Life of Virgil, 31-3; cf. Glover, " The Conflict of Religions,"
etc., p. 7.

[5] Vide supra, p. 46.

[6] Boissier, " La Religion Romaine," vol. i. p. 240; Nettleship, " Suggestions Introductory to a Study of the Æneid," pp. 12, 34 et seq.

[7] Tac. Annals, xiv. 57; xvi. 21-35; Agricola, c. 2; Juv. Sat. ii. 8;
Pliny, Ep. iii. 11; Furneaux, Introd. to the Annals, vol. ii. p. 83 et
seq.; Boissier, " L'Opposition sous les Césars," p. 97 et seq.

was on a sure foundation, was the secret of the great charm,[1] which the system had for Cicero in his later years. When the subtleties of its Dialectic were forgotten, that portion of it was bound to endure, and bear rich fruit in purifying and elevating morality. The system, as a whole, had no natural attractions for Horace. His repugnance to it may have been partly overcome, as I have suggested, by more extended study, and a better comprehension of its merits, but the best explanation, I believe, of his awakened sympathy towards it is to be found in the influence upon him of the Augustan Revival. Stoicism, if not professed by the Emperor himself, would probably have been officially encouraged by him, and Horace, who had splendid opportunities of feeling the pulse of Court opinion, would have felt himself bound at least "officially" to exploit it. It is remarkable how largely Stoic views, or views with a Stoic tinge figure in the Odes. There are several Stoic elements in the professedly patriotic Odes. How far these Odes were inspired it is not easy to say, but it shows that Stoic teaching was felt to be in harmony with those reforms of the Emperor, which the poet had set out to glorify. Whether he is exalting the limitation [2] of desires as a source of happiness, or the virtue [3] that knows not defeat, or the steadfastness of purpose [4] that, strong in a sense of justice, is never deflected from the path of duty, or the unflinching courage of a Regulus,[5] who goes to meet torture and death with sublime indifference, it is Stoicism, with its perfect embodiment, the Sage, [6] that is before the mind of the poet. He can now rise to even enthusiastic praise of Cato,[7] who in life had been typical of that rigorous unbending Stoicism, which had excited his disgust at an earlier period. Again, in several

---

[1] Reid, Introd. to the Academica, p. 17.
[2] Odes, III. i. 25; cf. Odes, II. ii. 9; xvi. 13; Cic. Paradoxa, 51.
[3] Odes, III. ii. 17; xxiv. 44; xxix. 55.
[4] *Ibid.* iii. 1; cf. *ibid.* I. xxii. 2. [5] *Ibid.* III. v. 13 *et seq.*
[6] *Ibid.* II. ii. 9; xvi. 15; IV. ix. 38 *et seq.*
[7] *Ibid.* I. xii. 35; II. i. 23.

passages,[1] Horace puts before us what is nothing else than the supreme deity of the Stoics, who rules as a guiding providence over the world. There is one Ode [2] in particular worthy of careful examination. It repeats some of the dominant ideas of the patriotic Odes, and is even more emphatic than they in its demands for reforms. It condemns the prevailing luxury of Roman Society, and sounds a veritable call for " the burning of the vanities ". Horace finds his ideal of the simple life realized among the nomad Scythians,[3] or the Getae, who are content with the gifts of Nature, troubled by no frenzied race for wealth, distinguished by the unsullied purity of their domestic life. His picture of their simple happiness is reminiscent of the Golden Age.[4]

It is remarkable how many of the poets of this period are inclined, in depicting the Golden Age, to lay stress on what might be called its " ascetic elements ". They were in reaction against a complex and decadent civilization, and the cry of " Back to Nature " had for them a charm as potent as it had for Rousseau at a later date. Hesiod [5] rather insists on the perfect happiness of the Golden Age as the outcome of the generosity of Nature, without need of labour on the part of man. The Augustan poets, partly as the result of a reaction against existing conditions, emphasize the necessity, if the blessings of the Golden Age are to be restored, of repressing the lust of war and greed for gold, and they descant on the evils of navigation,[6] which tempt men to the dangers of the

---

[1] Odes, I. iii. 21; xii. 14; III. iv. 45 *et seq.*; xxix. 29; cf. Lucan, Pharsalia, ix. 579 : " Jupiter est quodcumque vides, quodcumque moveris "; Heitland, Introd. p. 43 ; Warde Fowler, " Roman Ideas of Deity," p. 51 *et seq.*; cf. Garrod in " English Literature and the Classics," p. 164 on Virgil's treatment of Jupiter; cf. Æn. i. 229.

[2] III. xxiv.   [3] *Ibid.* 9 *et seq.*

[4] Cf. Hor. Epode xvi. 41 *et seq.*; Virg. Eclog. iv.; Georgic i. 125 *et seq.*; ii. 538; Tib. I. iii. 35 *et seq.*

[5] " Works and Days," 109 *et seq.*

[6] Hor. Odes, I. iii. 21; xxxi. 13; III. xxiv. 36 *et seq.*

deep for commercial gain. The prominence given to such ideas was probably due also, in some measure, to the influence of Stoic thought, which exalted the ideal of the simple life and of indifference to external goods, which it had borrowed from the Cynics. The Stoics[1] held it as unnatural to drag precious metals from the ground, or to sail the seas for "the purpose of bringing the produce of one country to another". Both the Cynics[2] and the later Stoics, in revolt against the degeneracy of the society in which they lived, looked for the realization of their ideals of happiness among rude and barbarous tribes, who were unsophisticated in their ways of life, and unspoilt by the luxury and dissoluteness of an almost effete civilization.

Again we can trace, I believe, the influence of the Augustan Revival upon Horace in the poet's attitude towards the Egyptian deities. Suetonius, in a passage[3] already referred to, sums up the general attitude of Augustus towards foreign cults, telling us, that he showed regard for such rites as were ancient and traditional, but held all others in contempt. When in Greece, he was initiated into the Eleusinian mysteries,[4] but, on a journey through Egypt, he showed his contempt for the god Apis, by refusing to make even a slight detour to visit his shrine. He displayed, in fact, a marked hostility to all Egyptian forms of worship. Rome, as a rule, exhibited a wide toleration for the gods of other peoples, and Roman polytheism could find a place for numberless deities from without its fold. Such

---

[1] Bevan, "Stoics and Sceptics," pp. 61-2 ; cf. Hor. Odes, III. iii. 49.

[2] Wendland, "Die Hellenistisch-Römische Kultur,' p. 40. Tacitus in his "Germania" presents a contrast with the decadent Rome of his day ; cf. especially c. 19 et seq.; Furneaux, Introd. to Germania, p. 7; Virg. Georgic, iii. 349 et seq. (there quoted).

[3] Oct. 93; vide supra, p. 13.

[4] Of Ceres. Possibly Augustus was partial to the worship of the goddess on account of the difficulties of the corn-supply in Italy; cf. Hor. Sat. II. ii. 124 ; Odes, III. ii. 26 ; Cic. De Leg. II. ix. 21.

latitudinarianism [1] aided the assimilation of subject races, and was one of the sources of Rome's successful imperialism. The religious problem did not thus present for the Roman the difficulties it often raises for modern imperialist nations. A restriction was placed by the Romans only on such cults as were believed to be subversive of society.[2] The hostility of Augustus to the gods of the Nile was based in part on political grounds.[3] He wished to keep prominently before the public the significance of Actium, and if no other motive had been present, he would naturally have shrunk from showing favour to the gods of a country, which had lately attempted the over-throw of Roman power. But his hostility was based also on moral grounds, as a religion such as the Egyptian was regarded as corrupting, in its influence, owing to its seductive ritual and its sense of mystery, and was considered unsuited to the gravity of the Roman character. The worship of the Egyptian gods under the forms of animals was especially repugnant [4] to Roman feeling, but for all that, a cult, such as that of Isis, had its spiritual side,[5] that could carry its devotees to the sublimest heights of religious exaltation. The ancient cults of Egypt underwent a serious transformation [6] under the Ptolemies, and were united with elements from the mysteries of Eleusis, and from the worship of Dionysus. There were two great annual festivals of Isis, one in March, the festival of the holy vessel of the goddess,[7] which gave the signal for the opening of navigation for the year, the other in November,

---

[1] Bryce, "The Roman Empire and the British Empire," pp. 48-50; Lord Cromer, op. cit. p. 91.

[2] Cf. Decree against the Bacchic rites, 186 B.C.

[3] Cumont, "Les Religions Orientales," p. 100 *et seq.*

[4] Virg. Æn. viii. 698; Prop. III. xi. 41; Pliny, N.H. viii. 70; Juvenal, Sat. vi. 534; *ibid.* 541; Erman, "Handbook of Egyptian Religion," p. 243; Lucian, Deorum Conc. 10 (there quoted).

[5] Dill, op. cit. p. 574; cf. Apuleius, Met. Bk. XI. *passim.*

[6] Dill, op. cit. p. 560.

[7] Apuleius, Met. Bk. XI. 16 *et seq.* ; cf. Tac. Germania, c. 9.

when for three successive days was enacted the sacred drama[1] of the death of Osiris, and the search for and discovery of his body. The impressive ritual of such a cult had no small share in increasing its popularity, and the liturgical drama exhibiting the despair of Isis in her sorrow for the dead Osiris, and her joy at his return to life, made a strong appeal to the imagination of the worshippers. The resurrection of the god was a symbol of the resurrection after death of those who were initiated into his mysteries. Here, too, was a religion which enhanced the value of the individual soul, and made a definite offer of a happy eternity in the life beyond the grave. Moreover, the idea of human brotherhood was emphasized by the bond of the initiated. Such a religion was democratic in its tendency. Freeman and slave[2] were on the same level, once they had been admitted into the society of the initiated. It is little wonder that the Egyptian cults possessed a powerful fascination[3] for many Romans, who had been nurtured within the comparatively narrow limits of the Roman creed, even as expanded under Greek influence.

These cults came to Italy mostly by way of Puteoli,[4] which was the principal port of call for vessels from Alexandria. A temple was erected there as early as 150 B.C. to that mysterious god Serapis,[5] who, according to the policy of the Ptolemies, had been designed to supplant Osiris, while Isis had her temple at Pompeii, erected probably in the closing years of the second century B.C. The cult of the goddess soon made its way to Rome, and was suppressed by the Senate on four different occasions[6] towards the end of the Republic, but the prohibi-

---

[1] Erman, op. cit. p. 249; Cumont, op. cit. p. 119.

[2] Toutain, "Les Cultes Païens dans l'Empire Romain," vol. ii. p. 26 et seq.

[3] Erman, op. cit. c. xi.

[4] Wissowa, op. cit. p. 351 et seq.; Dill, op. cit. p. 563; L. Ross Taylor, "The Cults of Ostia," p. 66 et seq.

[5] Cf. Tac. Hist. iv. 83 et seq. for some theories about his origin.

[6] 58, 53, 50, 48 B.C.; cf. Glover, "The Conflict of Religion, etc." p. 21.

tions of the Senate did not prevent her worship from being carried on in private.[1] It is not unlikely[2] that the influence of Cleopatra over Julius Cæsar may have helped to win a certain measure of indulgence for this cult. Its popularity, at any rate, continued, and the Triumvirs had to conciliate public feeling by erecting a temple to Isis (42 B.C.). When Augustus became supreme after Actium, he reverted to the policy of repression,[3] and forbade (28 B.C.) the erection of altars to Isis or Serapis within the pomœrium. A few years later (21 B.C.), this prohibition was extended, so as to include all districts within a mile of the city. These repressive measures may have been effective for Rome and Italy, but these cults seem to have spread unchecked in the provinces.[4] Now, it is interesting to see the attitude of the Augustan poets towards these Egyptian cults. We find in Tibullus[5] and Propertius[6] a certain note of complaining against them, but we feel that it is in great measure a personal grievance, because devotion to the deities of the Nile separate them for a time from Delia and Cynthia. The hostility of Virgil[7] is on a different plane, and has its source in the depths of the national consciousness. He looks upon these Egyptian forms of worship as unworthy of the fine traditions of dignity and seriousness, that have so long prevailed among his countrymen. If we can argue so much from silence in the case of one so circumstanced as Horace, his attitude might be described as mostly one of silent contempt.

[1] De Marchi, "Il Culto Privato di Roma Antica," vol. ii. pp. 87-8.

[2] Dill, op. cit. p. 565.

[3] Dio, liii. 2.

[4] Toutain, op. cit. p. 17 et seq. Tiberius continued the hostility of Augustus (Tac. Annals, ii. 85; Suet. Tib. 36). The cult of Isis was formally recognized by Caligula; cf. Cumont, op. cit. p. 68.

[5] Tib. I. iii. 23. However, he (I. vii. 27 et seq.) sounds the praises of Osiris as a leader of civilization.

[6] Prop. II. xxxiii. 1 et seq.; IV. v. 34. For a note of more than personal hostility, cf. Prop. III. xi. 42.

[7] Æn. viii. 698.

He makes but a single reference[1] to an Egyptian god, and that, I believe, in irony—when he describes how the importunate beggar, who has often deceived the public by parading his sham infirmities, can no longer prevail on the passers-by for assistance, though he "swears by holy Osiris," and proclaims his genuineness.

There is another Eastern cult, that of Cybele, which Augustus treated with more respect. I have already spoken[2] of the introduction of the goddess[3] as marking the beginning of the Oriental cults at Rome. Her worship was introduced at the bidding of a Sibylline oracle to rid Italy of the Punic invader, and though many details of it were revolting to Roman notions, still the State felt itself bound in honour to maintain it. However, at all times it endeavoured to emphasize the foreign character[4] of the cult. The great festival[5] of the goddess was not even given a Roman title, while, for many years, Romans were forbidden to enrol themselves among her priesthood. Lucretius[6] gives us an impressive description of the Idaean mother and her ritual, though it was not till the days of the Empire that she attained[7] her greatest glory at Rome. Her provenance, however, from the same region as the Trojan ancestors of the Romans, naturally brought her into relation with the Æneas-legend,[8] and helped to win her a large measure of support. Being thus connected, however

[1] Ep. I. xvii. 60.

[2] *Vide supra*, p. 41.

[3] Wissowa, op. cit. p. 317 *et seq.*; Dill, op. cit. p. 548 *et seq.*; L. Ross Taylor, p. 57 *et seq;* Frazer, "Atlonis Attis Osiris," vol. i. p. 265 *et seq.*, p. 298 *et seq.* For her relation to Rome's Eastern policy at the time, cf. Diels, "Sib. Blätter," pp. 101-2.

[4] Warde Fowler, "Roman Festivals," pp. 69-71.

[5] The Megalesia ; cf. Ovid, Fasti, iv. 143 *et seq.*

[6] De Rer. Nat. ii. 600 *et seq.;* cf. Cat. lxiii.

[7] Especially under Claudius ; cf. Cumont, op. cit. p. 68 *et seq.* For the " taurobolium," cf. Dill, op. cit. p. 555 *et seq.*; Döllinger, " Gentile and Jew," vol. ii. p. 179.

[8] Virg. Æn. iii. 111 ; vii. 139; ix. 82; x. 252 *et seq.*; xi. 768.

remotely, with the Julian house,[1] Augustus was careful to rebuild[2] her temple on the Palatine, which was destroyed, probably at the time that his own house fell a victim to fire.[3]
However prominent the worship of the goddess may have been
at Rome, it does not seem to have appealed strongly to Horace.
He makes a few passing references[4] to the Berecyntian flute
used in her ritual, and these are employed merely for descriptive
colouring, or as a symbol[5] of the unrestrained mirth, that was
to distinguish the banquet to Murena.

Another deity, Bacchus, whose cult in its wild licentious
character breathed much of the spirit of the Orient, is set
before us by Horace[6] with some of the attributes of the Greek
Dionysus, though he appeals to the poet mostly as the god
of wine,[7] or the inspirer of poets,[8] and often with him dwindles
into a mere literary ornament.[9]　In one Ode[10] there are clearly
many reminiscences of the Bacchae of Euripides, but Horace's
use for the god reveals itself when, after he has described
his great exploits, he declares[11] him to be "choreis aptior
et jocis".　He thus endeavours to bring him into harmony
with the needs of his lyric poetry.　The god has not for Horace
the reality or clearness of outline he possessed for Euripides.
There is another Ode[12] to Bacchus, which we feel to be nothing
more than a literary exercise, in which the poet is seeking
to catch the spirit of the Greek dithyramb.　The Greek god,
with his rich warm life, becomes thus attenuated into a mere
literary device in the hands of the Roman poet.

---

[1] For a relief from Sorrento showing the connection of Cybele with the
Julio-Claudian House, cf. Strong, " Roman Sculpture," p. 94.

[2] Mon. Ancyr. c. 19.　　　　　　[3] Suet. Oct. 57 ; Dio, lv. 12.

[4] Epode ix. 5 ; Odes, I. xviii. 13 ; IV. i. 22.

[5] Odes, III. xix. 18.　　　　　　[6] Ibid. I. xviii. 9 et seq.

[7] Ibid. xxvii. 3 ; II. xi. 17 ; III. xxi. 21 ; IV. xv. 26.

[8] Ibid. II. xix. 6 ; cf. III. viii. 7 for Horace's offering to him.

[9] Ibid. II. vi. 19 ; III. xvi. 34 ; IV. xii. 26 ; cf. Æn. i. 215.

[10] Odes, II. xix. ; cf. the Messenger's speech, " Bacchae," 677 et seq.

[11] II. xix. 25.　　　　　　[12] III. xxv.

It is the principal gods of the Græco-Roman Pantheon, that, as we might expect, figure most prominently in Horace. How far these were to him living and breathing realities, it is difficult to say. In reading his poetry, we mostly receive the impression that the gods had ceased to be such vivid and distinct personalities, as could command the poet's unwavering loyalty, and this notwithstanding his vaunted conversion and the influence of the Augustan Revival. He was steeped in the literary traditions of Greece, and his deities are often nothing more than the shadowy creations of the litterateur. What we say of Horace is true of the Augustan poets generally.[1] The Olympian gods had long lost most of their vitality in Greece,[2] but, when transferred to Rome, they were still further emptied of it, and they frequently appear in the Roman poets as mere conventional names,[3] or literary ornaments. This process of decay was naturally hastened[4] as Emperor-worship prevailed, and supplied a new object for human adoration. It is doubtful, indeed, whether even such a masterful personality as Jupiter had much value or significance for Horace. His name is certainly used on several occasions[5] in a merely conventional way for the sky-god, though he is thought[6] of too, as the national god, with whose fortunes the destiny of Rome is bound up, and at times,[7] possibly under the influence of Stoic thought, he stands out in clearer outline with the attributes of the great supreme deity.

Apollo, owing to his place in Augustan policy, is given a position of prominence in the poetry of Horace. The poet is careful to dwell[8] on his connection with Æneas and his Trojan

---

[1] *Vide* Warde Fowler, " Roman Ideas of Deity," p. 135 *et seq.*

[2] Murray, " Four Stages of Greek Religion," p. 107.

[3] Hor. Odes, II. vi. 19 ; xiv. 13 ; III. xvi. 24 ; xxiv. 13 ; IV. xiv. 9.

[4] Strong, " Apotheosis and After Life," p. 74.

[5] Epode xiii. 2 ; Odes, I. i. 25 ; xvi. 12 ; xxxiv. 5 ; II. vi. 18 ; x. 15 ; III. ii. 29 ; x. 7.

[6] Odes, III. v. 12.   [7] *Ibid.* I. xii. 14 *et seq.* ; III. i. 6 *et seq.* ; iv. 45.

[8] Car. Saec. 36 *et seq.* ; Odes IV. vi. 3 *et seq.*

followers, and through them, with the beginnings of Rome itself. Apollo is the friend of the Trojans, who has compassed [1] the death of Achilles, and made it possible, by his intercession with Jupiter, for the fortunes of Æneas to triumph, and win a city "with a fairer omen". Such facts will help to explain, if the Roman public seeks explanation, the position of eminence assigned by Horace to Apollo. Still, it is essentially the Greek Apollo that he paints for us, invested with the many qualities that distinguish the god in Greek literature. Horace is dominated by Greek tradition, and according to his fancy Apollo figures as the god of divination, [2] the god of archery [3] and the spreader of pestilence, the healer, [4] the god of music, [5] and the Sun-god. [6] He probably had special interest for Horace as the inspirer of poetry, [7] as one who had fostered his muse, and given him the gift of song. Moreover, the poet may have been drawn to him as a deity, who had been constituted, as it were, a patron of Roman Letters, through his connection with the library [8] built by Augustus on the Palatine. Of the other deities of Horace there is no need to speak. He might deck out all his gods with the splendid trappings that they wear in Greek poetry, but it was not easy to infuse new life into the decaying forms of the Olympians.

When personal gods lose their sway, there is a tendency [9] among men to worship a mysterious power, that is believed to control human destiny, a power that is conceived at times as Chance, at times as Fate. It is interesting to find traces of this power in Horace, but how it presented itself to his mind it is not always easy to determine. He clearly has

[1] Cf. Soph. Philoctetes, 335.

[2] Sat. II. v. 60 ; Odes, I. ii. 32 ; C.S. 61.

[3] Odes, I. x. 11 ; xii. 23 ; xxi. 13 *et seq* ; III. iv. 60 *et seq.*

[4] C.S. 63.   [5] Odes, I. xxxii. 13 ; II. x. 19.

[6] *Ibid.* III. xxi. 24 ; C.S. 9.

[7] Odes, III. xxx. 15 ; IV. ii. 9 ; vi. 29 ; C.S. 62.

[8] *Vide supra*, p. 67.   [9] Murray, op. cit. pp. 113-15.

at times [1] the conception of a power corresponding to our notion of Destiny, inflexible in its decrees and implacable, from which there is no escape for either the humble or the great. It is probable, as we shall see later,[2] that the spread of Astrology at Rome, with its doctrine of Determinism, helped to focus attention on such a power, and the place it holds in the Universe. But there is another power, Fortuna, that enters also into the poetry of Horace. Mr. Warde Fowler has recently argued,[3] that in the earliest history of Fortuna in Latium, we have not to deal with a power merely indicative of blind chance, but with a "numen" controlling the element of luck or accident (*fors*) [4] in human life. The association of blind chance [5] or caprice with Fortuna was a later development. Such a tendency was almost inevitable in the last period of the Republic, when amidst the wanton cruelty of the Civil Wars, good and bad alike were involved in universal ruin. Whether Fortuna was always regarded as a personal deity or not, is difficult to decide.

When we turn to Horace, we find in him several passages [6] that contain the suggestion of Fortuna as an arbitrary power, that from mere caprice delights in making sport of poor humanity, exalting the humble, and casting down the great from their pride of place. His Ode [7] to the stately queen of Antium seems to me a strange medley of incoherent ideas. In the opening lines he had probably before his mind the ancient Roman conception of Fortuna as a power controlling human destiny, or at least the element of chance in human life. She is worshipped not merely at Antium, but wherever human

---

[1] Odes, II. xvii. 15 ; III. i. 14 ; xxiv. 5.

[2] *Vide infra*, p. 225 *et seq.*

[3] "Roman Ideas of Deity," p. 62 *et seq.* ; cf. Wissowa, op. cit. p. 256 *et seq.* The existence of oracles of "Fortune" at Antium and Preneste supports this contention.

[4] Cf. the cult-title "Fors Fortuna" at Rome.

[5] Pliny, N.H. ii. 5.

[6] Sat. II. ii. 126 ; viii. 61 ; Odes I. xxxiv. 14 ; II. i. 3 ; xxix. 49.

[7] I. xxxv.

beings are found and are subject to the fluctuations of fortune, whether on sea or land. Her decrees are based on a moral purpose, as is clear from the companions in her train. But the goddess, too, as depicted for us by Horace, has her moments of caprice [1] in her dealings with men. Again, so far was the poet from making a clear distinction between Fate and Fortune, that he represents the goddess as preceded by "saeva Neces- sitas," with all the instruments for recording decrees that are fixed and unalterable. He apparently caught up some of the ideas floating in the Roman world of his day, and tried with poor success to weave them into a coherent whole in honour of the goddess of Antium. In all this he was moving on danger- ous ground, if he had only realized it. No one could reprove him for offering his tribute of respect to the deity of Antium, who had been honoured for centuries by his countrymen, but to exalt such powers as capricious Chance or inexorable Destiny, and subject men's lives to their sway, meant the destruction of the value of human effort. It robbed human action of all moral import, and was as inimical to the ideals of a religious revival as the Epicurean doctrine of the gods, which the poet had hastened to abandon. Here as elsewhere, Horace had not looked much below the surface of things, and we need not ex- pect of him any keen or subtle analysis of such ideas.

Whatever feelings the great Græco-Roman deities may have inspired in Horace, it is clear that the gods of the country and the details of rustic worship always retained a deep interest for him. The Augustan poets, even when touched, as Horace and Virgil were, with the prevailing scepticism, never lost their reverence [2] for the gods of the peasant, worshipped, as they were, without imposing or elaborate ritual, in all the sin- cerity of a simple heart. The descriptions of rustic ceremonial preserved for us in Tibullus [3] constitute much of the value and

---

[1] I. xxxv. 13 et seq.; cf. Virg. Æn. viii. 334.

[2] Virg. Georgic i. 10, 338; ii. 473, 493.

[3] Tib. I. i. 19 et seq.; II. i. passim; cf. 37, "rura cano rurisque deos," II. v. 25 et seq.

charm of that poet. Horace, like Virgil, was born in the country, and in his youth must have witnessed, in his home and on the farm, the regular observance of religious practices, and though his education tended to weaken the traditions of those early days, they can never have become wholly obscured. The days he spent on his Sabine farm would have helped to revive their old fascination, while the very simplicity and picturesqueness of these rustic rites must have always held attractions for the best instincts of the poet. In describing life [1] on an Italian farm, with its alternations of labour and sacrifice to its protecting deities, he rises to a high level of enthusiasm. Priapus and Silvanus [2] in due season are offered their share of the harvest fruits, a lamb is slain at the Terminalia [3] to Terminus, the god of the farm-boundaries, while there is a touch of Nature in the poet's description of the band of home-born slaves, that swarm at intervals round the images of the Lares,[4] and bear unmistakable testimony of the prosperity of the house. Though his words are put into the mouth of Alfius, the usurer, we feel that they spring from the poet's own deep affection for such sights and scenes. Again, there are few finer Odes in Horace than his hymn to Faunus,[5] which breathes the very atmosphere of the country. In this Ode Horace knows Faunus as a purely Italian rural god,[6] a spirit of the woodland, to whom he appeals to be propitious to his fields and his little nurslings,

[1] Epode ii.

[2] *Ibid.* 21. For the name as a cult-title of Mars, cf. Warde Fowler, "Roman Festivals," pp. 55, 103.

[3] Epode ii. 59; cf. Ovid, Fasti, 641 *et seq.*; Warde Fowler, op. cit. p. 324 *et seq.*; "The Religious Experience," p. 81.

[4] For the connection of slaves with the Lares, *vide supra*, p. 59.

[5] Odes, III. xviii.; cf. Ovid, Fasti, ii. 155 *et seq.*, 287; iii. 289. For a full discussion of Faunus, cf. Warde Fowler, "Roman Festivals," p. 256 *et seq.*

[6] For his identification with Pan, *vide* Odes, I. xvii. 2; cf. *ibid.* IV. xii. 11; Ovid, Fasti, ii. 227 *et seq.* For Fanio, his modern counterpart in Italy, cf. Leland, "Etruscan-Roman Remains," p. 98 *et seq.*

while the few bold strokes, in which he depicts the hamlet
making holiday in his honour, reveal a depth and tenderness
of feeling not surpassed by Tibullus at his best.   It is in his
treatment of such a festival, that one might look, if anywhere
in Horace, for genuine religious sentiment.   But Faunus appealed to Horace also as a guardian-spirit of poets,[1] and particularly as one who had saved him from the destruction [2]
threatened by a falling tree.   Again, there is a distinctly personal note in the Ode,[3] in which he gives instructions to the
rustic housewife, Phidyle, on the necessity of duly propitiating
the Lares and Penates, if she would secure the prosperity of
her farm and its contents.   She is evidently poor, and the poet
tells her to give from her poverty.   Her humble offerings will
be as acceptable as the costly victims of the wealthy.   This
Ode reveals at once his interest in his neighbours, and in the
details of their religious observances, while it serves also to
bring into relief the simplicity and kindliness of the poet's character.   Whether Horace sings of a sacrifice to Diana,[4] the
guardian goddess of groves and mountains, or of the offerings
he makes [5] to the spring of Bandusia, he lingers with evident
affection and sincerity of feeling on every phase of rustic worship that he celebrates.   I have spoken of the religion of the
country, not to establish a bond between it and the Augustan
Revival, but rather to set up a contrast.   Even when the State-
religion had decayed, the current of religious life in the country
must have flowed largely undisturbed along its old channels,
while the rites observed year by year on an Italian farm
retained their freshness and vitality for the peasant, unaffected

---

[1] Odes, II. xvii. 28.   Nettleship suggested the connection of Faunus
with *fari*, thus making him a god of speech, of poetry, and of prophecy ;
cf. Warde Fowler, " Roman Festivals," p. 259.   For oracles of Faunus,
cf. Virg. Æn. vii. 81.

[2] In Odes, III. viii. 7, his safety is ascribed to Bacchus.

[3] III. xxiii.   [4] *Ibid.* xxii.

[5] *Ibid.* xiii. 1 *et seq.*; cf. also *ibid.* viii. 2 *et seq.*

by the novel theories and strange ideas, that tended to sap the beliefs of his compatriots in the city.

I have spoken of the worship of the Emperor as a religious force destined to be a serious competitor for the honours hitherto enjoyed by the great Græco-Roman deities. We have seen [1] something of the rise of Apotheosis, and of the efforts made by Augustus to keep the homage paid to him within reasonable limits, at least in Rome and in Italy. I have touched upon the various influences, the teaching of Euhemerus and the Astrologers, Greek hero-worship, the deification of kings in the East, which combined to render easier of acceptance at Rome the idea that man could attain to a place among the gods. Throughout all this process of Apotheosis, the conception of the " Euergetes " is a dominant one. Only those who have accomplished deeds almost superhuman, and who have thereby conferred striking benefits on their fellow-men, are marked out for divine honours. Extraordinary honours were lavished on Augustus in his lifetime, and as far as words go, some of the Augustan [2] poets are regarded as the worst offenders in their use of language of extravagant flattery towards the Emperor. Horace, among others, has come in for his share of censure for the want of restraint that characterizes his efforts to honour Augustus in his poetry. He tells us [3] that the gods have never conferred and never will confer a greater boon on men than their present ruler. He goes a step further,[4] and declares that Augustus is to rule as the vicegerent of Jove upon earth, holding wide sway, but still sway not equal to that of the supreme monarch of the universe. He is not content with even these fulsome expressions, but proceeds to proclaim [5] the Emperor a god upon earth, or one who will soon [6] be enrolled in the

---

[1] *Vide supra*, p. 53 *et seq.*
[2] Cf. Virg. Georgics, i. 24 *et seq.*; iii. 16 *et seq.*; Æn. vi. 793.
[3] Hor. Odes, II. ii. 37; Ep. II. i. 17.
[4] Odes, I. xii. 51.   [5] *Ibid.* ii. 41 *et seq.*
[6] *Ibid.* III. v. 2; cf. *ibid.* iii. 12 if " bibet " is read.

ranks of the gods. We shall find, however, that in many passages, in which our poet expresses his homage to his ruler in
such extravagant terms, Augustus stands out pre-eminently as
"Euergetes". He is ranged [1] with Castor and Pollux, Hercules
and Bacchus, who were received among the gods after their
great achievements in advancing civilization, and in bringing
peace and settled life to men. In an interesting passage,[2]
Horace draws a comparison between the homage done to Augustus, when in private worship his "numen" is set among
the images of the Lares, and the honours bestowed by Greece
on Castor and Hercules, showing that, in his glorification of
the Emperor, he had Greek hero-worship particularly before
his mind. If such passages are taken "au pied de la lettre,"
Horace, tested by our modern standards, must stand condemned.
Whether we grant him a certain measure of poetic licence, or
take these passages as merely anticipatory, they conflict with
our notions of propriety, but probably would not have seemed
extravagant to the many who had come to regard the victor
of Actium as the Heaven-sent saviour of his country, who had
rescued it from the anarchy of civil strife, helped to enhance
its prestige, and secure for it the blessings of settled government. I have already spoken [3] of the Fourth Book of the Odes,
as dominated by the spirit of the "Carmen Saeculare". We
might speak of it also as dominated by the idea of " Augustan
peace," or the conception of Augustus as "Euergetes". A
note of triumph runs through many Odes of the book for the
victories won by the Emperor's policy. His measures of reform have begun to have their effect. The purity of domestic
life has been restored,[4] and with it the qualities that had

---

[1] Odes, III. iii. 9 *et seq.*; xiv. 1.; Ep. II. i. 6, "post ingentia facta"; cf.
Odes, III. ii. 21; Virg. Æn. vi. 802 *et seq.*, for a comparison of Augustus
with Hercules and Bacchus. For Hercules, Bacchus, and the Dioscuri on
grave-reliefs representative of Apotheosis, cf. Strong, " Apotheosis," pp.
197, 202.

[2] Odes, IV. v. 34 *et seq.*   [3] *Vide supra*, p. 32.

[4] Odes, IV. v. 21; xv. 10; cf. C.S. 18.

achieved the greatness of Rome in the past.   There is abund-
ance [1] and prosperity at home, while peace [2] reigns throughout
Rome's wide possessions, with her old enemies cowed into
submission, and her name a symbol of power, even for the re-
motest peoples.   It is especially the light of the Emperor's presence that brings joy to his subjects.   As long as he is safe, Italy
need fear no foe, and can enjoy her prosperity undisturbed.
The poet endeavours to create the impression, that the happiness of his countrymen depends upon the actual presence [3] as
well as the benign government of Augustus.   He is sorely
missed, when some tangle in the provinces compels his absence
from Rome.   All this is interesting in view of the honours [4]
showered upon Augustus, whenever he returned to the capital
from abroad, and especially in view of the reception [5] given to
him on his return from Spain and Gaul (13 B.C.), when he had
successfully arranged the affairs of these provinces.   The Senate ·
decreed that in his honour an altar of "Augustan Peace"
should be consecrated in the Campus Martius, and sacrifices
offered there annually.[6]   The altar was erected on the site of
the modern Palazzo Ottoboni-Fiano, near the Corso.   We are
fortunate in having a number of fragments of the reliefs that
decorated it, though these are now scattered in various museums.

A good deal of attention has been devoted to the study [7]
of these fragments in recent years, and their subjects have been
reconstructed with comparative accuracy.   I have already [8]

---

[1] Odes, IV. v. 15 et seq.; xv. 4; cf. Ep. I. xii. 28.

[2] Odes, IV. v. 25 et seq.; xiv. 41 et seq.; xv. 9, 21 et seq.; C.S. 53; Ep. II.
i. 255; cf. Mon. Ancyr. c. 13; Suet. Oct. 22; Dio, li. 20; liii. 26.

[3] Odes, IV. ii. 43; v. 2, 15; III. xiv. 14; cf. the story told by Suetonius
(Oct. 98) of the sailors at Puteoli, who declared in Augustus' presence,
"per illum se vivere, per illum navigare libertate atque fortunis per illum
frui"; cf. also Homer's picture of the good king, Odyss. xix. 107 et seq.

[4] Suet. Oct. 57.   [5] Mon. Ancyr. c. 12.

[6] Rushforth, op. cit. p. 52; C.I.L. i. 395; Ovid, Fasti, i. 649 et seq.

[7] For an account of her own and other recent studies of the Ara Pacis,
cf. A. Strong, "Roman Sculpture," p. 39 et seq.

[8] Vide supra, p. 73.

referred to the beautiful relief of Tellus, one of the best-pre-
served of all.   She is depicted as the fruitful and kindly mother,
the giver of plenty.[1]   She presides over a scene of perfect
happiness and contentment, in which there is everywhere
tangible evidence of the bounty of the Earth to man.   We have
depicted for us also in these reliefs a scene of sacrifice, and a
sacred procession, in which the Emperor, wearing the head-
dress of the Pontifex Maximus,[2] is the chief figure, while other
figures have been identified (with probability) as those of
Agrippa and Livia, and various other members of the Imperial
family.   In the subsidiary ornamentation of the altar,[3] the
flowers and fruits of the earth are extensively represented.   The
later Odes of Horace, and many of the monuments of contemporary Art, are thus at one in their endeavour to celebrate the
glories of the Pax Augusta, and the blessings it had conferred
upon Italy.   They are born of the same feelings of gratitude
and admiration for the great Emperor, who, by his unceasing
efforts and watchful care, had made possible the life of security,
happiness, and prosperity, which the Romans, after many
tribulations, were at length able to enjoy.   Horace, extravagant
as is the language he sometimes employs, is but re-echoing
the sentiments of many of his countrymen, when he proceeds
to confer even divine honour on Augustus, the Euergetes.   Before leaving this subject, I must direct attention to another
passage,[4] which may help to throw some light on Horace's own
conception of the part he was playing in raising Augustus to
a place among the gods.   The passage is so worded as to point

---

[1] For similar ideas of Peace and Prosperity in other specimens of contemporary Art, cf. Furtwängler and Urlichs, op. cit. p. 234; Strong,
" Apotheosis," p. 72 *et seq.*   For column erected to Nero at Mayence,
in which the Emperor, Pax, Tellus, and Victory are united, cf. pp. 81, 105-6.

[2] The altar, though decreed in 13 B.C., was thus apparently not completed till Aug. had become P.M. 12 B.C.

[3] Strong, " Roman Sculpture," p. 65.

[4] Odes, III. xxv. 4 : " Cæsaris . . . meditans decus stellis inserere et
consilio Jovis ".

to a merely literary Apotheosis.   Horace elsewhere proclaims [1] the power of poetry to confer immortality, and declares [2] that it is potent to exalt men even to Heaven.   In connection with this latter aspect of poetry, it is interesting to find him mentioning the names of those very heroes, whom he had coupled in a former passage with Augustus as typical examples of deified mortals, as if he would suggest that they owe their privilege of deification to poetry alone.   It is thus possible that the poet may have wished a passage such as this to serve as a key to the interpretation of other passages, in which he had practised less restraint.

I have spoken of the material part of the Augustan Revival as the easiest of all to accomplish.   At no other point can we realize better the ravages of the Civil Wars, and their devastating effect upon Roman religion, than in the neglect and decay into which the temples of the gods had fallen.   Here again, Horace faithfully reflects the conditions of his time.   We meet in him many expressions of complaint that the temples of the gods have been allowed to sink into ruin.   As we saw,[3] a note of this kind is first struck in one of his Satires,[4] composed probably before Actium.   There he appeals to the rich to spend their superfluous wealth on worthy objects, that will bring some benefit to their country, and suggests that the restoration of the temples of the gods might well be one of these.   We know that Augustus himself,[5] in later years, encouraged such enterprise on the part of leading citizens.   Horace's solicitude for the honour of the gods, in that period of pronounced scepticism, may have sprung, as I have said, from an acquaintance with Octavian's designs for a revival of their worship.

[1] Odes, IV. ix. 26-8 ; cf. Tib. I. iv. 63 *et seq.*

[2] Odes, IV. viii. 29, " Caelo Musa beat " ; cf. the expressions used by him in Odes, I. i. 6, 30.

[3] *Vide supra*, p. 94.

[4] Sat. II. 2, 103 ; cf. Sat. I. vi. 35 ; Prop. III. xi. 47 ; Suet. Oct. 30 ; Tac. Annals, ii. 49.

[5] Cf. Suet. Oct. 29, for several examples of private munificence.

In one of the Odes,[1] Horace connects the ruin of the altars
of the gods with the demoralization of society that accompanied
the Civil Wars.   Though that was a leading cause of their
decay, still it was but a contributory cause, for the loss of faith
in Roman religion, signs of which had appeared long before
the Empire was established, must have led to a general indifference towards the maintenance of the worship of the gods.
The poet again tells [2] the Romans of his day, that they will
continue to pay the penalty of their forefathers' guilt, until they
have repaired the ruined or decaying temples and shrines, and
replaced in them their disfigured statues.   He looks back [3]
with regret, too, to "the brave days of old," when the State
flourished, and when care was taken to build and adorn the
temples of the gods with a magnificence impressive for the
time, and one that contrasted strongly with the simplicity of
the citizens' own private dwellings.

Augustus had revived many of the old priesthoods, and
much of the splendid pageantry of ancient ritual.   This
aspect of Roman religion had appealed to the imagination of
Virgil, in whose eyes every vestige of early Rome was invested
with a sacred character.   The Æneid is a storehouse of details
of ceremonial, many of which were believed to have been
handed down from a remote past.   Virgil considered it in-
cumbent on himself to study these, as one who wished to
link together Past and Present, and cast a halo of romance
round the origins of Rome.   Horace did not possess the antiquarian [4] cast of mind, and the ceremonial revived by Augustus
had not for him any hallowed associations.   In this he seems
to have escaped the influence of an age, which had fixed its
attention steadfastly on the beginnings of Rome, and had endeavoured to reconstruct its past.   He seldom shows interest [5]

---

[1] Odes, I. xxxv. 37.   [2] *Ibid.* III. vi. 2.   [3] *Ibid.* II. xv. 13 *et seq.*
[4] He has no patience with the " antiquarians," who are ready to enthuse
over the Salian Hymn, Ep. II. i. 86.   He is interested, however, in the
origin of Roman drama, *ibid.* 139 *et seq.*
[5] Cf. Odes, I. xii. 32 *et seq.*; III. v. 9 *et seq.*; IV. vi. 23; C.S. 37.

in the history of early Rome, preferring to dwell on the glories
of the actual Rome, and sing the praises of the reigning house
of Cæsar.   He was drawn, as we saw, towards the details of
rustic worship, but the more elaborate ceremonial of State-
worship seems to have had little attraction for him.   If he
refers[1] to it at all, it is only in the most perfunctory way.
With a rather cynical outlook upon life he directed his attention to the splendour of the Pontiffs' feasts, to which he refers[2]
with a touch of irony.   He is interested, too, in the Hymn[3] as
part of the sacred ritual, especially in honour of Apollo and
Diana, and in the sacred dance[4] in honour of the same
goddess.   These, however, like that most venerable of Roman
institutions, the cult of Vesta, which for Horace was a symbol[5]
of the everlasting power of Rome, appealed primarily to the
instincts of the poet, and not of the antiquarian.

Closely bound up with the revival of religion was, as we
have seen,[6] Augustus's attempt to effect a reform of morals.
Here again Horace is a faithful guide.   In the first three
books of his Odes, what strikes one forcibly is his insistence
on the need of, and his repeated demands for reform.   The
cataclysm of the Civil Wars ended inevitably in social anarchy,
and in a degeneracy of morals,[7] that tended to expand in ever-
widening circles.[8]   Motives of self-interest as well as patriotism
must have impressed upon the Emperor the necessity of re-
establishing social order, and of curbing the prevailing licentiousness.   It was comparatively easy to rebuild temples, and
revive the externals of worship, but it was a far more difficult
task to wean men from dissolute ways, and make religion a
living force issuing in true morality.   Here, as elsewhere in

[1] Odes, I. xxxvii. 2 et seq.
[2] Ibid. II. xiv. 28 ; cf. ibid. I. xxxvii. 2.
[3] Ibid. xxi. ; IV. vi. 35 ; Car. Saec.   [4] Odes, II. ii. 17 et seq.
[5] Odes, III. v. 11 ; xxx. 8 ; cf. Odes, I. ii. 27.
[6] Vide supra, p. 68 et seq.
[7] Odes, I. ii. 23 ; xxxv. 33 et seq.; III. vi. 17 et seq.; Suet. Oct. 32.
[8] Odes, III. vi. 45.

his statecraft, Augustus seems to have proceeded warily.   It
is probable that in virtue of the censorial power, which he
received in 29 B.C., that he endeavoured,[1] soon after Actium,
to effect a reform of the most flagrant abuses in the State.
His efforts apparently did not meet with much success.   It
was only, however, after some years (18 B.C.), that he ventured
to introduce his great measures of reform, the Leges Juliæ.
The ground was being prepared for their reception, partly
through his religious revival.   It was necessary above all to
impress the public mind with the need of reform, as such a
programme as Augustus contemplated, would inevitably en-
counter the fiercest opposition[2] from many quarters.   In
modern times a government will often carry on a lengthened
propaganda before the actual introduction of a revolutionary
measure.   The poets under Augustus were able to influence
public opinion, not of course to the same extent, but in a
measure like the Press of our own day.   Whether Horace was
inspired from official quarters or not, he dwells repeatedly on
the decadence of his Age, and in particular in the well-known
opening Odes of the Third Book, he selects for commendation
many of the reforms, the accomplishment of which Augustus
regarded as one of the chief tasks of his Principate.   The poet
descants[3] on the blessings of order and contentment, is enthusiastic in his praise of patriotism and of the military virtues,
glorifies national ideals, purity in public life, and loyalty in
religion.   He condemns[4] the subversion of domestic purity
and the growing licence of the young, which were undermining
the fabric of Roman society, and implies that, if such vice is
allowed to range unchecked, generations yet unborn will reap
a harvest of disaster.   Now, all this points to, not reforms
already achieved, but efforts towards reform.   It is clearly

[1] Pelham, "Essays in Roman History," p. 118; Prop. II. vii. 1 (there
quoted); cf. Hor. Odes, I. ii. 47.
[2] Suet. Oct. 34.   [3] Odes, III. i.-vi.
[4] *Ibid.* vi. 17 *et seq.*; cf. Prop. II. vi. 25 *et seq.*; xxxii. 47; III. xiii. 23.

Augustus the poet has in mind, when he speaks[1] of the just
man, who keeps on "the even tenor of his way" in spite, it is
implied, of unprincipled attempts to thwart his designs, while
the various allegories of Jove[2] struggling with the giants are
intended to suggest the battle of the Emperor against the
forces of disorder.   There is another Ode,[3] to which I have
already referred, closely allied in thought, and evidently springing from the same inspiration as these patriotic Odes.   Here
again, the crying need of reforms as yet unaccomplished is
insisted upon, while the poet calls in emphatic tones for
the strong man to come forward, and remedy the prevailing
evils in the State.   Whoever wishes to have the title "Pater
Urbium" inscribed upon his statues, "indomitam[4] audeat
refrenare licentiam".

The attempt at reform is to proceed upon national lines, and
is to concentrate especially upon the young, who are to be
trained in manly exercises suited to a Roman rather than be
allowed to waste their days in gambling, and in disporting
themselves with the Greek hoop.   Such an appeal points to
one alone in Rome, but it suggests that many obstacles have
been encountered in the path of reform, while it calls for
generous sacrifices from the citizens as a body, if they seriously
wish for the regeneration of their country.   Legislation can
effect little, if men are not ready for a true reform in themselves of character and disposition.   We saw that Augustus
introduced among other measures a sumptuary law to restrain
the extravagance of his subjects.   We shall see later[5] what
light Horace throws on the question of Roman luxury in his
day.   There are many passages, in which he condemns his
countrymen for their luxurious mode of living, and their reckless expenditure in villas and their equipment, while he points
to the simple life as containing the secret of genuine happiness

---

[1] Odes, III. iii. 1.   [2] Ibid. i. 5 et seq.; iv. 42.
[3] Ibid. xxiv.   [4] Ibid. xxiv. 28.
[5] Vide infra, p. 167 et seq.

and contentment, and the secret, too, of Roman greatness.
While in the earlier books of his Odes Horace thus fore-
shadows reforms sorely needed, but as yet unaccomplished, in
his Fourth Book he speaks of reforms,[1] which are already an
accomplished fact.   The poet centres high hopes in the Leges
Juliae, but it was not easy to remedy by legislation evils already
deep-seated, of which some were fostered by the Imperial position of Rome, others were rooted in the perversity of human
nature, while all in a greater or less degree were to contribute
their share to the final disintegration [2] of the Empire.

[1] Odes, IV. v. 22; xv. 10; C.S. 18; cf. Ep. II. i. 3; A.P. 199.
[2] Cf. Balfour, " Decadence," p. 21 *et seq.*

CHAPTER IV.

THE PERIOD OF THE EPISTLES.

"Non eadem est aetas, non mens."—Ep. I. i. 4.

WHEN we turn from the Odes of Horace to his Epistles, we are
struck at once by his change of tone and outlook. This was
due no doubt, in part, to the influence of a different poetic
medium. The lyrical metres of the Odes were a suitable
medium for those occasional playful trifles [1] on love and wine,
so much in harmony with the spirit of the poet and the genius
of lyric poetry. Many of the Odes are merely passing fancies
born of some momentary mood, but many more, as we have
seen, are impregnated with deeper feeling, and coloured by the
movements of contemporary history. When Horace had completed the Third Book of the Odes, and had raised a "monument more lasting than bronze," he delivered, as it were, in the
closing Ode [2] a valedictory address to lyrical composition. At
the opening of the Epistles, we find Mæcenas [3] endeavouring
to turn his thoughts back into the old groove, in which he had
won such striking success, but Horace resists the call of his
friend and patron, and it was only some years later, at the
bidding of Augustus himself,[4] that he turned again to lyrical
composition.

In the meantime he addresses himself to the more serious
work of the study of Philosophy, but in announcing his change
of life it is strange to find him with a certain note of dis-

---

[1] Hor. Odes, I. vi. 17; II. i. 37; III. iii. 69.   [2] *Ibid.* III. xxx.
[3] Ep. I. i. 3.   [4] Suet. Life of Horace; cf. Odes, IV. i. 1.

paragement comprehending in the phrase[1] "versus et cetera ludicra," not only the Odes that were mere playful sallies, but the Odes of high ideals and serious purpose, in which he had summoned his countrymen to repentance and reform. He found it difficult apparently to dissociate the mood of trifling from the lighter metres of the Odes. Hence, with a change of poetic medium we may expect a change of tone, but one has to look deeper, and raise the question, why in the first instance he elected with deliberate choice to abandon lyrical composition, which in his own and succeeding generations constituted his chief glory. If one had to account for a similar phenomenon at the present day, one might ascribe it to some spiritual development, some crisis of the inner life, which made him view the world from a different standpoint from heretofore, but this explanation will not apply to Horace, at least in the modern sense of such terms. He realizes now that there is a higher purpose in life than in spending his years in lyrical effusions, however exquisitely conceived and brilliantly executed.[2] "Nec lusisse pudet, sed non incidere ludum." He feels that there are serious problems in human existence that call for an answer, and that he must not trifle to the end. He thinks, too, that he has a message of import to deliver, which the wayward metres of the Odes cannot adequately convey. There was development then in Horace, but it was a development due mainly, I believe, to his advance in years. He can no longer[3] lay claim to the same buoyancy of spirit, the same spontaneous gaiety, the same joy of life, the unrestrained mirth, that characterized him in former days. The glow of youth has departed, and the old fires have burnt out. The years have brought the "philosophic mind".[4] His outlook upon the world is more steady and more serene. Rich with the maturity of experience, he can with a certain air of aloof-

---

[1] Ep. I. i. 10.   [2] *Ibid.* xiv. 36.
[3] *Ibid.* vii. 25; xiv. 32 *et seq.*; cf. Odes, III. xiv. 25 *et seq.*; IV. i. 3.
[4] Ep. I. iii. 27; II. ii. 55 *et seq.*, 141 *et seq.*

ness sit in judgment on the follies of his generation, laying aside the bitter invective of the Satirist, and passing the calmer and more reasoned judgment of the Philosopher. He can tell his contemporaries what is wrong with the world, lay bare the maladies that afflict society, pass in review the various panaceas for happiness prescribed by the leaders of Philosophy, and add many a piece of golden advice drawn from the treasures of ripened experience.

Horace, since his days at Athens, had always been a student of Philosophy. We have seen the influence of his early education upon his mind, and the moral vein that runs through his Satires. He tells us in one interesting passage[1] in those early years, that when he retired to the country and gathered his friends round the festive board, it was not the merits of the latest theatrical dancer they discussed, but loftier questions, such as the sufficiency of virtue for happiness and the nature of the Highest Good. We have seen, too, how in the Odes his allegiance shifted in a measure from Epicureanism to Stoicism, and what were the influences that effected the change. Still, through all these years, he was never more than a dilettante in Philosophy, never penetrating much below the surface, at no time possessed of whole-hearted convictions. When we come to the Epistles, he seems to promise something different. He has laid aside the trifling of former years, and is now wholly absorbed[2] in wrestling especially with the problems of Moral Philosophy. We have here no longer the spirit of the dilettante, but of the serious student of Philosophy. He has returned to the old problems of the Schools, which had formerly exercised him, but he has returned with an added zest. They are no longer for him mere academic questions, for now, after all the intervening years, he can bring them to the test of experience, and judge of their practical application to the life around him. It is possible, too, that this reborn zeal for Philosophy was in part

---

[1] Sat. II. vi. 73 *et seq.*   [2] Hor. Ep. I. i. 11.

a concession to the spirit of the Age. We find then prevailing, especially among the poets, a keen interest in Philosophy,
particularly in the questions of physical science, an interest
that was probably heightened, if not awakened by the master-
piece of Lucretius. Virgil proclaims[1] his interest in such
questions, and tradition tells us that he intended to devote
the evening of his life to the study of Philosophy. In a fine
passage,[2] manifestly influenced by Lucretius, Propertius lays
aside the solution of such problems as the task of his old age.
Tibullus,[3] in revol tagainst the prevailing fashion, declares that
Love alone will be his theme, and leaves to others the work of
prying into the secrets of Nature. Horace himself depicts [4] his
friend Iccius as engaged, amidst the cares of wealth, in searching
out the answers to some of Nature's enigmas, so that the poet,
when he announces that he will once again seriously occupy himself with the old problems is following in the footsteps of many
of his contemporaries.

Signor Ferrero would have us believe [5] that Horace's abandonment of lyric poetry and the altered tone of his writings
at this period are due to the pressure of the Puritan party.
There is no need to have recourse to such an hypothesis. The
reasons I have advanced will, I believe, sufficiently account
for the change, without postulating any such pressure from outside. Ferrero seems to me to attach excessive importance to
the " Puritan movement," as he terms it. Even in the decadent Rome of the time, there were doubtless many whose moral
fibre had not been unstrung, many possessed of high ideals and
serious views of life. Periods characterized by the deepest

[1] Georgic ii. 475 *et seq.*; cf. Æn. i. 742 *et seq.*; vi. 724 *et seq.*, a
passage, which shows the influence of various philosophical systems;
Catalepton vii. Ite hinc; cf. Norden's Introduction to the Sixth Æneid;
Garrod in " English Literature and the Classics," p. 164.

[2] Prop. III. v. 23 *et seq.*; cf. II. xxxiv. 51 *et seq.*; Lucr. iii. 978 *et
seq.*; v. 509 *et seq.*

[3] Tib. II. iv. 17-8; Panegyricus Messallae, 18 *et seq.*

[4] Ep. I. xii. 15; cf. Ep. I. vi. 3 *et seq.*   [5] Op. cit. vol. v. p. 39.

depravity are never lacking in strongly-marked contrasts[1] of virtue and vice, but there is no proof adduced by Ferrero that the Puritan party was then as strong, or as insistent in its demands as he would have us believe. Augustus had undertaken a revival of religion, not always, it is true, with disinterested motives. His Revival was assuredly not meant to be mere empty show, or a formula devoid of meaning, and if it had any reality behind it, it was designed to serve as the basis for a revival of morality as well. That such a revival had always been in the mind of the Emperor seems clear from those Odes of Horace, which reflect the policy and ideals of Augustus. We cannot then represent him, as Ferrero does,[2] as submitting to the mandate of the Puritan party, when he introduced the "Leges Juliae". These were the necessary pendant to his Religious Revival. Neither is there need to conceive Horace as yielding to the same power, when he elected to turn from the Odes to the Epistles with their pervading note of gravity and earnestness not unmixed with irony.

Now, even when the poet has definitely decided to direct all his energies to the study of Philosophy, it is not easy to apprize his philosophic standpoint. For one thing, we may note that his interests are now purely philosophical. His intellectual centre · of gravity has shifted. There is scarcely, if we except one or two passing allusions,[3] a genuine religious touch in the Epistles. One can with difficulty imagine him to be the poet, who under the spell of the Augustan Revival had proclaimed his conversion from the scepticism of his early years, and had made such apparently sincere and eloquent appeals on behalf of the decaying worship and ruined temples of the gods. With the temper of the philosopher, he is rather interested[4] in the growth of certain depraved forms of worship, that were excrescences upon the popular religion. Again, the difficulty of estimating his

---

[1] *Vide* Tacitus, Introduction to the Histories.
[2] Op. cit. vol. v. p. 52.
[3] Hor. Ep. I. xvi. 28 ; xviii. 111.   [4] *Ibid.* 58.

position in Philosophy at this period is increased by his declaration [1] of independence of any settled system, or rather by his determination to take shelter under the roof of each system in turn, according as it could offer him attractions.

When Horace refuses to swear complete allegiance to any master, he is true to the spirit of Philosophy in its later developments. When the great leaders of Philosophic thought had passed away, reverence for their memory for a time kept their disciples true to the tenets of their school. They had laid broad and deep the foundations of their system, and generally speaking, there was thenceforth little scope for originality, except in comparatively unimportant details. When loyalty to traditional principles began to wane, and a broader sympathy towards the teaching of other schools prevailed, a spirit of compromise arose, which fostered an Eclecticism, in which men could attain at least a semblance of originality. With the old inspiration of genius gone, in new combinations of old doctrines drawn from different sources men found the fairest field for their efforts. We have already seen something of this tendency to Eclecticism in Roman Stoicism. A teacher like Posidonius [2] could so dazzle his contemporaries by the freshness of his presentation of old truths illumined with a wealth of illustration (of which only one of his encyclopædic learning was capable), as to stand out from contemporary Philosophers with a distinctive personality of his own. But whatever system Horace chooses to adhere to, it is clear that, within the domain of Philosophy, his supreme interest lies in Ethical problems. Here again, he is true to the spirit [3] of Post-Aristotelian Philosophy. With the decline of political freedom in Greece, Ethics and Politics became divorced, and the whole outlook of the people narrowed. The broader

---

[1] Hor. Ep. I. i. 13 *et seq.*

[2] *Vide* Bevan, " Stoics and Sceptics," p. 85 *et seq.*

[3] *Vide* Zeller, " Stoics, Epicureans, and Sceptics," pp. 16, 29; cf. Wendland, " Die Hellenistisch-Römische Kultur," p. 47.

questions of Philosophy were gradually neglected, and the individual, his interests, his happiness, his destiny became of
paramount importance. It was at such a time, and in such
an environment that the Comedy of Manners could flourish,
while the Old Comedy, the very breath of whose existence
was political Satire, passed from the stage. It was in such an
atmosphere, too, that a literary genre like the "Characters"[1]
of Theophrastus could attain popularity. However, Horace's
interest in Ethical questions was undoubtedly accentuated by
the evils of his Age, to which he was keenly alive. He describes[2] for us the mad race for wealth, the unscrupulous
legacy-hunting, the fruitless search for happiness in large villas
and constant change of scene, which characterized the society
of his day. His patron Mæcenas, he tells us,[3] is more concerned about certain laxities of dress than about looseness of
moral principles. We should almost expect this from a confirmed dandy like Mæcenas, but it was probably not an uncommon feature of the Age. Horace would find in Philosophy[4]
a specific for all these ills. Again, in showing a predilection
for Ethical questions, the poet is following the bent of the
national character. The Roman was nothing if not practical,[5]
and showed little zeal for the solution of the merely specu-
lative problems of Philosophy. Seneca expresses well this
attitude of his countrymen, when he says[6] that "Philosophia
nihil aliud est quam recte vivendi ratio". And in fact, with
Stoic and Epicurean alike, the supreme question in life was to
discover the secret of happiness, and the nature of the Highest
Good, though each gave a different answer to the riddle. We

---

[1] *Vide supra*, p. 80 *et seq.*

[2] Hor. Ep. I. i. 53, 77 ; ii. 44 : xi. 27.

[3] *Ibid.* i. 94 ; cf. Sat. I. iii. 30 *et seq.*

[4] Ep. I. i. 34 ; cf. *ibid.* ii. 36.

[5] *Vide* Hor. A.P. 325 *et seq.*; cf. Wilkins, " Roman Education," p. 9
et seq.

[6] Fragment quoted by Zeller, op. cit. p. 56.

shall find numerous passages [1] in the Epistles, in which Horace
shows his interest in the secret of the "bene vivere," or the
"recte vivere" as he sometimes puts it. He is fond,[2] too, as I
have said, of passing in review the various panaceas for happiness suggested by opposing schools. His moral prepossessions
are nowhere more evident than in his attitude to Literature at
this period. He contemplates [3] a union of Philosophy with
Literature, and applies the principle [4] of the Golden Mean in
his literary criticism. As a compensating advantage for the
indiscriminate poetising of his day, he proclaims [5] the moral
mission of the poet, and its value to society. He is clearly, at
this period at all events, no believer in the doctrine of " Art
for Art's sake," but is conscious that his art has a high moral
aim, that its greatest task is that of fashioning the character of
the young, and eradicating vicious habits from their minds.
While at other times [6] he dwells on the immortality, which
poetry can confer on the subject of its song, here he is
especially interested in the poet as a teacher of morals. He
regards Literature not so much as an end in itself as a medium
for the inculcation [7] of moral lessons. In this he was but
following a tendency,[8] that was prominent in Roman literary
criticism generally. When he resumes [9] once more his reading
of Homer, it is not the glow and vigour and freshness of the
poet's imagination, not the beauty of his imagery, not the
fury of his battle-scenes, not the gorgeous pageantry of his
kings and heroes, that attract him, but his value in providing
useful precepts for the conduct of life. The wanderings of
Ulysses, and the wild romance of his adventures are merged in

[1] Ep. I. ii. 41 ; vi 29 ; xi. 28 ; xvi. 17 ; II. ii. 213.

[2] *Ibid.* I. vi. *passim ;* xviii. 96 *et seq.*

[3] Hor. A.P. 309 *et seq. ; vide* Wickham, Introduction to the Ars
Poetica, p. 335.

[4] A.P. 31.   [5] Ep. II. i. 118 *et seq.*

[6] *Vide* Odes, IV. viii. 28 ; ix. 26.

[7] Hor. A.P. 319, 343 ; Ep. II. i. 124.

[8] *Vide infra,* p. 251.   [9] Ep. I. ii. 1 *et seq.*

his interest in the hero as a splendid example of endurance and self-control. He is re-reading Homer in the light of mature experience and of his altered mood, and the elements in the poet, that appealed to his boyish imagination,[1] have no longer a powerful attraction for him. We find Quintilian in later days inclined to view Homer from the same moral standpoint. It is not impossible that Horace, in thus viewing Homer, was influenced by the Stoic Allegorists.[2] Homer was interpreted by them as giving a complete picture of human life, with all its trials and vicissitudes, just as in later times mediæval scholars [3] discovered an allegory of the varying fortunes of man's existence in the wanderings of Æneas.

Now, though Horace declares in his opening Epistle that he will not bind himself to any master, still it seems to me that the change from Epicureanism to Stoicism, which we have already noticed, is maintained, and that in this period he is predominantly under the influence of Stoic thought. His language in the Epistles is frequently interwoven with Stoic phraseology. One phrase, "vivere convenienter naturae,"[4] springs at once to our attention. This, though borrowed by the Stoics from the Old Academy, was made one of the corner-stones of their own system. They leave us frequently in doubt [5] as to what was for them the full significance of the phrase. It is not easy to determine whether "life according to nature" meant life according to individual nature (the nature of each thing being

[1] Ep. II. ii. 41.

[2] *Vide* Zeller, op. cit. pp. 354-6; Murray, "Four Stages of Greek Religion," p. 146; Wendland, op. cit. p. 49. Ulysses was regarded by the Stoics as approaching their ideal of the "Sapiens". This practice of allegorical interpretation was, however, anterior to the Stoics; cf. Diog. Laert. ii. 3; Dio, Chrys. ed. Arnim, vol. ii. p. 118.

[3] Comparetti, "Virgil in the Middle Ages," p. 107; *vide* Strong, "Apotheosis and After Life," p. 202, for allegories of Æneas on graves in the Rhine and Danube districts.

[4] Hor. Ep. I. x. 12; cf. Sat. I. i. 50.

[5] Zeller, op. cit. pp. 227, 399; Stock, "Stoicism," p. 8; Murray, "Conway Lecture," p. 34; Von Arnim, op. cit. vol. i. p. 45; *vide* Cornford, "From Religion to Philosophy," p. 127 *et seq.*, for conception of "Physis" among the Ionian Philosophers.

the end of its becoming), or life according to universal nature, which for the Stoics was identical, from their particular viewpoint, with Reason, or Soul, or God. Horace's use of the phrase is practically colourless, but this, and many other phrases,[1] which, though not so obvious, are still, I believe, derived from the study of Stoic authors, help to show that at this time he was steeped in Stoic phraseology. Again, we find that in the Epistles the doctrine that Virtue is the source of happiness[2] figures prominently. Horace was not at any time ready to subscribe to the extreme Stoic doctrine that Virtue is the *only* good, but we find that with him now Virtue gets a foremost place as a constituent of happiness, and, as with the moderate Stoics of the Roman School, external[3] goods, though necessary, are relegated to a subordinate position. Again, he recommends, as the Stoics do, simplicity and frugality of life[4] as one of the great means for the attainment of happiness. Closely bound up with this doctrine of Virtue is another Stoic idea, which appears frequently in the Epistles, that Virtue and its consequent, happiness, are largely a thing of the mind.[5] The rich man, on whom pall the pleasures of wealth, seeks relief by change of scene, but, as Horace puts it,[6] " coelum non animum mutant, qui trans mare currunt ". Milton is but re-echoing the doctrine, when he says that—

> The mind is its own place, and in itself
> Can make a heaven of hell, a hell of heaven.

---

[1] *Vide* Ep. I. x. 8, " vivo et regno," a reminiscence of the Stoic doctrine that the Wise Man is a king; cf. Ep. I. i. 59; xi. 30, " animus si te non deficit aequus," a re-echo of the Stoic doctrine of ἀπαθεία; Ep. I. xviii. 99, " rerum mediocriter utilium," suggested by the Stoic teaching on " things indifferent " (ἀδιάφορα). Ep. I. xvi. is saturated with Stoic thought. For other reminiscences of it, *vide* Ep. I. ii. 40; iii. 26; x. 44; II. ii. 128.

[2] *Ibid.* I. i. 17; vi. 30; xii. 11; xvi. 52.

[3] *Ibid.* i. 52; xvii. 9.   [4] *Ibid.* x. 33; xii. 7.

[5] *Ibid.* xi. 25, 30; xiv. 13; xviii. 12.

[6] *Ibid.* xi. 27; cf. Odes, II. xvi. 19; Lucr. iii. 1059.

Contentment of mind and purity of conscience [1] will enable a man to boldly [2] confront every assault of Fortune.   This whole doctrine of Virtue as the source of happiness, a Virtue whose seat was mainly in the mind, was intimately associated with the Stoic doctrine of ἀπαθεία.   Virtue for the Stoics was little more than a negation, and for the primitive Stoics at any rate, its finest flower consisted in that state of passionless calm, in which alone perfect happiness could be attained.   We have already seen that, sublime as this doctrine was in theory, it could not be rigorously applied in ordinary life, and could only issue in such an absurdity as the "Wise Man".   But having taken ἀπαθεία as the great essential for happiness, the Stoics were naturally led to deal carefully with the question of the Passions, and to enter into that minute analysis [3] of them, which is such a striking feature of their system.   Now, we find in Horace an echo of the doctrine of ἀπαθεία in the well-known phrase [4] "nil admirari".   Horace moreover, in true Stoic fashion, gives us in several passages [5] a catalogue of the passions, and at times goes into a rather minute analysis [6] of them.   The Stoics regarded [7] the passions as diseases of the soul, and we find in Horace [8] also a reflection of the same idea.   Again he tells [9] us himself, that he expressly followed the lead of the Stoics in one point, when in accordance with Stoic teaching [10] he decided to take an active part in political life.   If the Stoics followed out their own theories to their logical issue, the perfect Stoic would live in splendid isolation, untouched by

---

[1] Ep. I. i. 61.   [2] Ibid. 68.

[3] Vide Von Arnim, op. cit. vol. iii. pp. 92 et seq., 108, 163; Diog. Laertius, vii. 123 (there quoted); Cic. Tusc. Disp. iv. 7, 14; Zeller, op. cit. p. 244.

[4] Ep. I. vi. 1, 10.

[5] Ibid. i. 33 et seq.; ii. 51; vi. 12; xviii. 98 et seq.

[6] Ibid. ii. 62; vi. 10; xvi. 63; II. ii. 205 et seq.

[7] Vide Von Arnim, op. cit. vol. i. p. 50 et seq.; vol. iii. p. 108.

[8] Ep. I. i. 33 et seq.; viii. 6; cf. Sat. II. iii. 80, 120.

[9] Ep. I. i. 16.

[10] Vide Zeller, op. cit. p. 323; Von Arnim, op. cit. vol. iii. p. 163.

the current of political events, but for all their theory he was never allowed to forget his duty as a citizen. Many later Stoics,[1] with regard to this tenet, diverged from the original teaching of their school, and advised abstention from political life, though under an Emperor such as Nero, at a time when Roman Stoicism was linked so closely with the Republican party, the grounds for such abstention were partly moral, partly political.

We cannot of course be sure what Stoic authors Horace studied, though it is not improbable that Cicero, who, in Ethics [2] at least, adhered closely to Stoic teaching, had no little influence in moulding his opinions. In many passages of his Satires he shows himself a close student of Cicero's Letters, and he may have studied his philosophical works with equal care. At times, it looks as if he had before him some popular collection of Stoic maxims,[3] some of which he embodied in his Epistles. These he may intend by the " Verba et voces,"[4] which are to " minister to a mind diseased," though in this phrase [5] he clearly also has in view those magical formulæ, that were considered so potent in the opinion of the vulgar. The succession of short crisp sentences, each containing a moral maxim, to which he treats us,[6] may well be drawn from some popular handbook of Stoicism. Though he claims absolute freedom in the choice of a philosophic system, and though he cannot refrain [7] from having a thrust at the old object of his aversion, the Stoic Sapiens, still, I think, we may conclude that his philosophic thought in the Epistles is predominantly Stoic.

Here [8] and there he returns to his old allegiance, and pro-

---

[1] Tac. Annals, xvi. 21-35 ; cf. Furneaux, Introduction to the Annals, vol. ii. pp. 83-4 ; Boissier, " L'Opposition sous les Césars," p. 99 *et seq.*

[2] *Vide* Reid, Introduction to the Academics, p. 17.

[3] Such as the " Sayings " of Epictetus or Marcus Aurelius in later times.

[4] Ep. I. i. 34.   [5] *Ibid.* 37.

[6] *Ibid.* ii. 54 *et seq.*   [7] *Ibid.* i. 106.

[8] *Ibid.* i. 18 ; iv. 12 *et seq.*; xvii. 16.

fesses Hedonism, and that joy of life (with the shadow of death
not far distant), which is so marked a feature of the Odes.
He weighs Cynicism [1] in the balance against the more human
Philosophy of Aristippus, and finds it wanting, but this need
cause us no surprise, when we remember [2] how repugnant to
his nature were the Cynic elements in Stoicism.   Again, in an
invitation to Torquatus, on Cæsar's birthday, he celebrates [3]
the glories of wine and revelling with his old abandon.   It
was probably the man more than the day that prompted this
epistle.   More than likely Torquatus was a confirmed bon-
vivant, [4] to whom a sober mood would have been repulsive, and
Horace is consciously adapting himself to the temperament of
the guest he is inviting.   But speaking generally, the old careless gaiety · of the Odes is absent from the Epistles, and is
replaced by a solemn seriousness, which concerns itself with
the moral upheaval of the Age, and the deeper problems of
human existence.   Once, [5] the poet proclaims himself an op-
portunist, and once, [6] he has to announce the breakdown of
all his philosophy, when he is ill at mind, and afflicted with
the same spirit of inconstancy he so often condemns in others.

In the period of the Epistles there seems to me also apparent in Horace an ever-increasing love of the country.   He
was born, [7] it is true, in the country, but the time he spent at
Athens, and the campaign at Philippi may have unfitted him,
temporarily at least, for its quiet uneventful existence.   Cer-

---

[1] Ep. I. xvii. 13 *et seq.*   [2] *Vide supra*, p. 90.
[3] Ep. I. v. 14 *et seq.*   .
[4] Compare the Epicurean tone of Ode IV. vii. addressed to the same
Torquatus, an Ode which seems to many commentators singularly out
of place.   But one must note that not in this Ode alone (cf. Odes, IV.
x.-xiii.) does the old mood of levity return to Horace, when he again essays
lyrical composition after what we might call the " period of purgation "
in the Epistles.   The Epistle seems to me even more out of place, unless
we conceive Torquatus as I have done.
·   [5] Ep. I. xv. 42.   [6] *Ibid.* viii. 4 *et seq.*
[7] Hor. Sat. II. i. 34; cf. Odes, III. xxx. 10.

tainly, in early life, the city had powerful attractions for
him.   He tells us[1] how he spent his days there, when he loved
to wander round the market-place, and ask the price of vege-
tables, and stop to listen to the charlatans of the Forum.   This
was probably before Mæcenas had given him the gift of the
Sabine farm (c. 34 B.C.),[2] which was to exercise so powerful an
influence on his genius, and so largely colour his poetry.   But
even after the gift had been made, the city seems to have held
its spell over him, though he is fully conscious[3] of the restraints
and annoyances of city-life, and at times can display genuine enthusiasm[4] for the country.   He retires[5] there from the
licence of the Saturnalia, with the Greek Comic poets for his
companions, and it is clear that he regards this journey to his
retreat among the Sabine hills (*in montes et in arcem*),[6] as one
to a citadel of peace from "the smoke and wealth and din of
Rome".   He spent his time in the country, either amidst his
books, or in gathering in his neighbours to help to create and
share in those "noctes coenaeque deum,"[7] which he describes
for us with such loving detail.   In this period, he puts[8] into
the mouth of the usurer Alfius, with a note of irony it is true,
an ideal picture of an Italian farmstead with its rustic worship,
in which the peace and happiness of the country are brought
into sharp contrast with the extravagance, ostentation, and
frenzied ambition of the Capital.   Still Horace, as his slave
Davus reproaches[9] him, sometimes felt the call of the city
too powerful for him, though the allurements[10] and disil-
lusionments of city-life for the country-mouse may have been
intended as a picture of the poet's own condition.   But in the
period under consideration, it seems to me that there is a

---

[1] Sat. I. vi. iii *et seq.*

[2] *Ibid.* II. vi. 3; Epode i. 31, seems a clear allusion to the Sabine
farm, and if so, its opening lines refer to the Actian war, not, as some
have conjectured, to the campaign against Sextus Pompey (36 B.C.).

[3] Sat. II. vi. 23 *et seq.*   [4] *Ibid.* 60 *et seq.*   [5] *Ibid.* iii. 10.

[6] *Ibid.* vi. 16.   [7] *Ibid.* 65.   [8] Epode ii.

[9] Sat. II. vii. 28.   [10] *Ibid.* vi. 79 *et seq.*

decided change noticeable in his attitude towards the country. Occasionally[1] of course, in a fit of despondency, when ill at ease, he begins to weary of the beauty of the Sabine hills, and to long for the bustle and excitement of the city. But his attachment to the country has become more secure, and his affection for it increases as the " fleeting years roll on ". It is not now merely a retreat from the ennui of existence at Rome. The poet has become definitely enrolled[2] among the lovers of the country, and grows fervidly eloquent in descanting on its charms. He shows, too, a keen appreciation of the beauty of its natural scenery, its groves and streams and moss-grown rocks, and has come to see[3] how superior are the generous gifts of Nature to the artificial creations in the rich dwellings of the city, how much finer is a carpet of green grass than the splendour of Libyan mosaic. He has come to recognize that the country is the only secure place of happiness,[4] that it is only in the country he can find his true self.[5] He is filled with sadness, when some " hateful business "[6] drags him off to Rome, and his thoughts are ever wandering back to his beloved Sabine retreat. He has a sort of contemptuous pity for his bailiff, who thinks to find happiness in the sordid joys of city-life, though the memory of his own youthful follies prompts the poet to extend indulgence to an erring brother. Horace has taken to gardening, though the sight of his fat stunted figure[7] wielding the hoe, with all the awkwardness of a novice, must well have moved the laughter of his neighbours.[8]

Of course, in speaking of the country, Horace has particularly in mind his Sabine farm. He had longed for a little farm,[9] with a garden and a spring of fresh water, and some trees to shade him from the summer suns. His wishes had been

---

[1] Ep. I. viii. 12.　　　[2] *Ibid.* x. 1 *et seq.*; xiv. 16.
[3] Ep. I. x. 19; cf. Odes, III. x. 5; Virg. Georgic ii. 460 *et seq.*
[4] Ep. I. xiv. 10.　　　[5] *Ibid.* 1.　　　[6] *Ibid.* xiv. 17.
[7] Sat. II. iii. 307; Ep. I. iv. 15; xx. 24; *vide* Suet. Life of Horace.
[8] Ep. I. xiv. 39.　　　[9] Sat. II. vi. 1 *et seq.*

more than realized, and it is clear from many passages [1] that he
regarded the farm as his most precious possession, as a haven of
peace and contentment, where, with few needs and these satisfied, he can afford to despise wealth, and the anxiety that
follows in its train.   He had already shown [2] his appreciation
for the natural beauty of its surroundings, but it seems as if his
feeling for its charms was growing with the years.   He gives [3]
us now a detailed description of its position and productiveness.
Life in the country, which went on in even flow, undisturbed
by jealousy and hatred, was becoming part of his being.   His
"nature is subdued to what it works in, like the dyer's hand,"
and we find him,[4] when driving home some moral lesson, inclined to take his metaphors from the conditions and occupations of the country.   He had become convinced too,[5] that
the quiet of the country was one of the essentials for success
in poetical composition.

He thus, with advancing years, set a higher value on the
delights of rural life, but it is possible that his health played
no little part in shaping his predilections in this period.   As
one who had once occasion to spend some part of August in
Rome, I can thoroughly sympathize with his reluctance [6] to
accept the invitation of Mæcenas to come to the city during
that month.   Its sweltering heat at such a season would have
tried the endurance of a more robust constitution than Horace
could lay claim to.   But his health in fact, from early years,
seems to have caused him no little solicitude.   It is evident
from the diary of the journey to Brundusium that his digestion was a serious trouble.   At Forum Appii,[7] owing to the

---

[1] Odes, I. xvii.; II. xviii. 14; III. i. 47; xvi. 29.

[2] *Ibid.* III. xiii.; cf. *ibid.* I. vii. 12.

[3] Ep. I. xvi. 1 *et seq.*; cf. Odes, I. xvii., where the description is not so
detailed; cf. also Ep. I. xviii. 104 *et seq.*

[4] Ep. I. xiv. 4; II. ii. 212; cf. Sat. I. iii. 36.

[5] Ep. II. ii. 65; cf. Sat. II. vi. 23.

[6] Ep. I. vii. 1, 44; cf. Sat. II. vi. 18; Odes, III. xxix. 16; Juvenal,
iii. 9.

[7] Sat. I. v. 7.

wretched quality of the water, he performs an enforced fast, rendered all the more exasperating from his being compelled to await his companions, who were apparently enjoying a hearty meal. He tells us too [1] of a weakness of the eyes from which he suffered, and for which he carried an ointment. But his digestion was his main anxiety, and it caused him to inquire carefully into the quality of the bread and water at various stages of his journey.[2] At the little town, whose name will not allow it to be included in his verse, he found water scarce, but splendid bread. At Canusium the bread was gritty, and the problem of good water recurred once more at Egnatia. Other indications [3] are not wanting that, even in those early years, he was compelled to be continually careful of his diet, which seems to have ordinarily been of the simplest kind. In the person of Ofellus, he sounds the praises of the simple life,[4] taught, we may be sure by bitter experience, the danger of venturing on rich viands and varied fare. As the years went by, his malady was not apparently lessened, and it may have, in part at least, accounted for his greyness, and that quickness of temper, which he confesses [5] to have been a feature of his character. We find him [6] in this period under the care of the famous Court physician, Antonius Musa, who had won his reputation by curing the Emperor,[7] through his cold-water treatment, of a serious illness contracted while in Spain. Musa forbade Horace to go to Baiae, as he was accustomed to do. Possibly the poet may have been in the habit of plunging too eagerly into the pleasures of that gay watering-place,[8] or it may be, as he says, that its sulphur-baths were found to be no longer suitable for his ailment. The

---

[1] Sat. I. v. 29, 49.　　　[2] *Ibid.* 88 *et seq.*

[3] *Ibid.* vi. 127; Odes, I. xxi. 15. For a later date, *vide* Ep. I. v. 2; xii. 7; xiv. 35.

[4] Sat. II. ii. 70 *et seq.*

[5] Ep. I. xx. 25; cf. Sat. II. iii. 323; vii. 35.

[6] Ep. I. xv.　　　[7] Suet. Oct. lxxxi.　　　[8] *Vide infra,* p. 176.

popularity of Baiae indeed [1] seems to have at this time
suffered somewhat of an eclipse through the cold-water cure
of Musa, while towns, like Clusium and Gabii, were in the
ascendant.   Horace is to winter at Velia, or Salernum, and
he writes to a friend asking for an account of their climate.
The old solicitude was ever present, and we find him [2] again
anxiously inquiring about the quality of the bread and water
in those towns, though he seems determined to be as oblivious
as possible of his malady, and to make his trip in thorough
holiday mood.   It is this same digestive weakness that makes
him, when describing his Sabine farm, dwell on the detail of
its spring, [3] the water of which "infirmo capiti fluit utilis, utilis
alvo".   But this was not the only ailment with which he was
afflicted during these years.   He clearly insinuates, [4] in his
reply to the invitation of Mæcenas to come to Rome in mid-
summer, that his chest was not as strong as in former days,
and in another passage [5] we can discern the tone of the confirmed invalid, who is constantly inclined to test his health
barometer.   From all these indications it is clear that, during
those years, Horace was not over-robust, and this fact will
partly account for the desire he betrays to cling more than
formerly to the country.

Even a casual reader of the Epistles will not fail to notice
the large amount of genuine worldly wisdom they contain,
often crystallized in lines and expressions, [6] that might easily
pass into proverbs, or at least are suitable for quotation.   It is
the wisdom of a man who has lived with keen observation of
the world around him, and who has not omitted to profit by its
lessons.   The poet has often been praised for his independence,
and the stock example of it quoted is his refusal to accept the
post of secretary [7] offered him by Augustus.   He undoubtedly

---

[1] Hor. Ep. I. xv. 5 *et seq.*   [2] *Ibid.* 14 *et seq.*

[3] *Ibid.* xvi. 14; cf. Sat. II. vi. 2; Odes, III. xvi. 29.

[4] Ep. I. vii. 25.   [5] *Ibid.* xii. 5.

[6] *Vide* Ep. I. vi. 38; vii. 20; x. 30; xi. 27; xiv. 13; xvii. 10; xviii. 71.

[7] Suet. Life of Horace.

valued his freedom[1] above all things else, and hated the irk-someness of rank and wealth.[2] When he had won the favour of Mæcenas and Augustus, he never showed the least disposition to belittle his old comrades of the Republican party, as a weaker man might have been tempted to do, but on the contrary makes many flattering references to them. He shows indifference,[3] if not contempt, for the esteem of the Roman mob, which he believed unstable and capricious, and in his writings makes no appeal[4] for its sympathy or support. But the years of association with Court circles had their inevitable influence upon him, and Horace had learnt well how to play the courtier. We have already seen his connection with the Augustan Revival, and the lengths he was prepared to go to second the efforts of his Imperial master. His intimacy with Court circles may well have helped to endow him with that splendid tact, which he so frequently exhibits. His short letter to Tiberius,[5] recommending a friend to his favour, is a marvel of tact, especially when we remember the naturally morose and reserved character[6] of the future Emperor. His tact is again shown at the opening of his long Epistle[7] to Augustus, and in another passage[8] he makes a passing reference to Philippi with the skill of a trained diplomatist. But nowhere is the temper of the courtier more clearly displayed than in the two Epistles,[9] in which he gives advice to friends of different station how to live with the Great. Though he professes himself incompetent to proffer such advice, still he shows how thoroughly he has mastered the art of the courtier. His instructions[10] could hardly be surpassed for acuteness of observation, and for appreciation (indelicate if we wish) of the difficulties of such a task. The precepts in these two letters

---

[1] Ep. I. vii. 35. The whole Epistle is a plea for freedom.
[2] Sat. I. vi. 99 et seq.; Odes, III. i. 48.
[3] Sat. I. vi. 17; Odes, I. i. 7; II. xvi. 40; III. ii. 20; Ep. I. i. 76.
[4] Ep. I. xix. 37. [5] Ibid. ix. [6] Suet. Tib. li., lvii.
[7] Ep. II. i. [8] Ibid. ii. 47 et seq. [9] Ibid. I. xvii., xviii.
[10] Ep. I. xvii. 43 et seq.; xviii. 37 et seq.

might form a "complete manual for the successful courtier".
They are apparently given in all sincerity, with no admixture
of irony, and show little trace of that independent spirit that
is one of the poet's chief charms at other times.   "Placuisse
principibus non ultima laus est,"[1] and he himself glories[2] in the
fact that he "has found favour with the chief men of the State
in peace and war".[3]

[1] Ep. I. xvii. 35.   [2] *Ibid.* xx. 23.
[3] Professor Phillimore reminds me that this is an echo of Terence,
Adelphi, Prol. 18.

CHAPTER V.

HORACE AND SOCIAL PROBLEMS.

IF there was one economic question more than another, that exercised the minds of Roman statesmen, it was the land-question. The evil associated with it in Roman territory took the form of the growth of "latifundia" or large estates, with all the fatal consequences that naturally followed in its train, especially the decline of the small farmer and the free labourer, and the rise of slave labour. The problem of the growth of large estates is not unknown in modern times, and it is interesting to see the remedies that were proposed for the evil in Ancient Italy.

The fact, that most obviously strikes the student of this question, is the number of agrarian laws that were passed in Rome from time to time. It is, however, often forgotten that these laws dealt solely with the Ager Publicus,[1] that is the land which had come into possession of the Roman community as a corporate body, generally as the result of a victorious war. The State dealt with the Ager Publicus in different ways,[2] either by assignation of land to a colony or to individuals, or by sale to individuals, who could rent the land on certain terms, or come into its use by what is known as "possessio". This latter did not confer property-rights,

[1] Appian, B.C. i. 8; cf. Daremberg and Saglio, "Dictionnaire des Antiquités," Art. "Agrariae Leges," p. 156.

[2] Cardanali, "Studi Graccani," p. 96 *et seq*. This is an excellent special treatise dealing fully with the historical aspect of the Roman land-question.

but, in exchange for a certain proportion of the produce of the land, the State guaranteed to "possessores" protection against the usurpations of a third party.

The series of land-laws began early, but the first law of real importance was the well-known Lex Licinio-Sextia (367 B.C.),[1] which provided that no one should possess more than 500 jugera of the public land, or maintain upon the public pastures more than 500 sheep or 100 oxen. An attempt was made[2] some years ago by Niese to impugn the usually accepted date of the law, and to place it somewhere in the period 202-167 B.C. Niese's chief reason for casting doubt on the traditional date was that the law presupposes a wide extent of public land within the Roman State. Rome had comparatively little territory in 367 B.C. Hence it is probable, Niese contends, that some chronicler has simply cast back to an earlier date a condition of things, which obtained only after many conquests on the part of Rome. Cardanali discusses[3] the arguments of Niese at great length, and seems to me successful in upholding the commonly received date. Of course the patricians, who till then had monopolized political power, were responsible for usurping the Ager Publicus, and the agitation which led to the Lex Licinio-Sextia, was part a general agitation on the part of the plebeians to secure equality of rights within the State. Next we find Flaminius bringing in a bill (232 B.C.) for the distribution of the Ager Gallicus and the Ager Picenus. This bill was designed especially to assist the plebeians, but the nobles, who were probably already in possession of these lands,[4] vehemently opposed it. Flaminius got the bill passed in the Popular Assembly, though its operation was delayed for some time through the intrigues of his political opponents.

---

[1] Livy, v. 30; Appian, B.C. i. 8; Plutarch, Tib. Gracchus, 8; Mommsen, "History of Rome," vol. i. p. 294 ("Everyman" edition).

[2] In Hermes, 1888. His view has been supported by Pais and E. Meyer; vide Cardanali, op. cit. p. 129.

[3] Op. cit. p. 134 et seq.   [4] Polybius, ii. 21, 7.

Some further light is thrown[1] on the abuses connected with the Ager Publicus, by the action of the Senate in 172 B.C. It was discovered that many of those, who occupied the Ager Campanus, had for some time evaded the payment of their quota to the State, and had treated the land as their own. This territory had become State property after the conquest[2] of Capua in the Second Punic War, and at all times was regarded[3] as the fairest portion of the Roman domain. The Senate now ordered a revision of the land and its holders. Those in possession had recourse to various subterfuges, so that finally (165 B.C.) the Senate determined to redeem for the State the whole of the land in that district. Laelius,[4] the friend of Scipio Africanus Minor, possibly when tribune, formed a plan for securing more even justice in the distribution of the public land, but in face of the opposition of the rich his design never matured. Some years afterwards came the great effort[5] of the Gracchi to settle the question of the Ager Publicus. The effort was to cost them their lives, but the opposition it provoked, proved clearly the alarming extent of the evil they had undertaken to remedy. Tiberius Gracchus, when tribune (134 B.C.), proposed a law, by which the State should resume from all possessors such lands as had been held without remuneration. The Lex Sempronia was practically a revival[6] of the old Lex Licinio-Sextia. The land so resumed was to be divided into lots of 30 jugera each, and distributed among the Roman burgesses and Italian allies, as " inalienable heritable leaseholds ". The holders bound themselves to till the land, and pay a small rent to the State. The clause mak-

---

[1] Cardanali, op. cit. p. 116.   [2] Livy, xxvi. 16.

[3] Cicero, De Lege Agr. ii. 29, 31 ; Suet. J. Cæsar, 20.

[4] Plutarch, Tib. Gracchus, 8 ; cf. Cardanali, op. cit. p. 113 *et seq.*

[5] Cicero, De Lege Agr. II. v. 10 ; xii. 31.   For ancient sources generally, *vide* Greenidge and Clay, " Sources of Roman History," p. 1 *et seq.* ; cf. Mommsen, Hist. vol. iii. p. 85 ; Heitland, " The Roman Republic," vol. ii. p. 270 *et seq.*

[6] Appian, B.C. i. 9.

ing the land inalienable was the very core of the bill.   Its aim
was to create and foster a class of small farmers, arrest the decay of Italian agriculture, and check that decline in population,
which had been causing grave concern to all who had at
heart the interests and position of Rome.   As Appian puts it,[1]
the object of Tiberius was more εὐανδρία than εὐπορία.   The
death of Gracchus did not end the good effects of his law,[2]
but still the work of the Commission appointed by the Lex Sempronia for the recovery and distribution of land was largely
nullified, when a decree was passed (129 B.C.) giving the consuls power to determine what was domain-land and what was
not.   When Caius Gracchus was elected tribune (123 B.C.), he
restored[3] their former powers to the Commissioners, thus en-
abling them to proceed once more unhampered in the distribution of land.   To help further to relieve distress among the
Roman burgesses, he proposed a far-reaching scheme[4] for
establishing colonies in Italy, and more revolutionary still was
his proposal for the establishment of colonies beyond the seas.
With the murder of Caius Gracchus, most of the great fabric
of reform he had raised, collapsed.   His scheme of colonization
was set aside, practically in every detail.   The Senate, the better
to undermine his popularity, had already, through M. Drusus,
made counter-proposals, which released those who had received
land under the Lex Sempronia from the rent imposed on them,
and declared their allotments free and alienable.   The Lex
Thoria[5] (119 B.C.) abolished the Commission, but imposed a
fixed rent on the occupants of domain-land for the benefit of
that needy city-proletariate, that was ever growing more needy
and more importunate in its demands.   A decree of the
Senate some years afterwards (111 B.C.), declared that the
domain-land then occupied was to become the private property

---

[1] B.C. i. 11.   [2] Mommsen, Hist. vol. iii. p. 96.
[3] *Ibid.* p. 103; Velleius, ii. 6.
[4] Greenidge and Clay, op. cit. pp. 29-30; Velleius, ii. 7 (there quoted).
[5] Mommsen, vol. iii. p. 126; Appian, B.C. i. 27.

of the present holders, free of rent. In future, however, the domain-lands were to be merely leased, or open as public pasture. This latter provision came too late, as most of the domain-land was already disposed of. Post-Gracchan legislation generally, was in favour of the nobility and the rich. Not only did they actually possess a goodly share of the public land, but by revoking the clause in the Lex Sempronia, which declared allotments inalienable, the aristocracy, as Mommsen puts it,[1] "had given itself legal permission to buy out the small holders, and, in its new arrogance, allowed itself with growing frequency to drive them out". The growth of the latifundia began once more.[2]

During the last century of the Republic there were numerous agrarian laws proposed, and some passed. It was unfortunately a century remarkable for an almost unbroken series of Civil Wars, and these agrarian laws were usually proposed by party leaders to reward loyal adherents, or to serve some political purpose. This was the century, too, when individual commanders began to assume greater importance than the Republic itself, when a class of professional soldiers was created, which yielded allegiance rather to a Marius, a Sulla, or a Cæsar than to the State. Each commander regarded himself as obliged to reward liberally those who had served under him. After a civil war, the reward was almost invariably conferred by the victors at the expense of political opponents, through the confiscation of their lands. The law of Saturninus [3] (100 B.C.) had as its main object the settlement of the veterans of Marius, who had served in the campaigns against the Cimbri and the Teutones. Cæsar proposed [4] an agrarian law (59 B.C.) for the purchase of land in Italy, and its distribution among the heads of poor families. Among the land so distributed was the plain

---

[1] Hist. vol. iii. p. 130; cf. Appian, B.C. i. 27.

[2] This is clear from a number of allusions in Cicero's speech " De Lege Agraria," ii. 26, 28, 78 ; iii. 2, 9.

[3] Mommsen, Hist. iii. p. 196.   [4] Suet. J. Cæsar, 20.

of Stellas, part of the Ager Campanus. A Lex Antonia[1] was proposed (44 B.C.) for the distribution of the Ager Publicus in Sicily and Campania among Cæsar's veterans, but this was abrogated in the following year by the Lex Vibia. A series of confiscations[2] followed the battle of Philippi. The second triumvirate of Bologna had promised the veterans eighteen cities in Italy. When Octavian led back the veterans after the battle, "he could," says Suetonius, "satisfy neither the veterans nor the landholders". We certainly could hardly expect the latter to be satisfied when driven from their homes. It was in the commotion of these years that Virgil[3] and Propertius[4] lost their ancestral farms.

Now, as I have said, the agrarian laws, properly so called, deal with the Ager Publicus and its distribution. The authors,[5] who speak of the growth of the latifundia, have the Ager Publicus in mind, but we may be sure that, what Cato calls the "ingens cupido agros continuandi,"[6] was operative also in the case of private holdings. The rich continued to buy out the poorer tenants, or drive them out by force. This question is, however, bound up with the larger question of the decay of Italian agriculture and its causes.

From a very early time in the history of Rome the small farmer had laboured under serious disadvantages. He had in the nature of things frequently to borrow money[7] (at a high rate of interest in the early period), and, if unable to repay, the Roman laws on debt put him absolutely at the mercy[8] of

---

[1] Cicero, Phil. ii. 39, 100; v. 2, 4; vi. 5; xi. 5.

[2] Suet. Oct. 13, 15; Dio, xlvii. 13; Appian, B.C. v. 2. 14.

[3] Eclog. i. 71; ix. 29; Georgic, ii. 198.

[4] Prop. IV. i. 127 *et seq.*

[5] Sallust, Jugurtha, 41; Plutarch, Tib. Gracchus, 8; Appian, B.C. i. 7-11, gives an excellent sketch of the Roman land-question, and the economic problems involved in it.

[6] Livy, xxxiv. 4-9.

[7] Mommsen, Hist. vol. ii. c. xii.; vol. iii. c. ii.; Bloch, "La République Romaine," p. 41.

[8] *Vide* Varro, "Res Rusticæ," I. xvii. 2, on "obærati".

his creditor.   Under such conditions, many a small farmer must have disappeared.   With the Punic Wars, however, came the first serious symptoms [1] of the decline of Italian agriculture, and the growth of latifundia.   Especially after the Second Punic War, the depopulation of many districts gave a number of rich nobles the opportunity of extending their estates.   Besides, as the result of Roman conquest, there were large tracts of land in Southern Italy for distribution, and, as always, the nobles were highly favoured, when the spoils were being shared.   But what helped more than any other circumstance to compass the ruin of the small farmer was the importation of cheap corn into Italy.   Sicily had become, even in Cato's time, the granary of Rome.   The Carthaginians had at an early date perfected the slave system [2] in that island, and its land was worked almost wholly by slave-labour.   The corn grown under such conditions could be sold in the Italian market at a price far below that at which the native farmers could afford to sell their produce.   The inequality became still more marked, as the Roman possessions increased and Rome was able to draw upon Sardinia and Africa (and in later times Egypt) for her supplies of corn. The Italian farmer was handicapped, too, by the difficulties of transport [3] in his own land, and thus succumbed before unequal competition, while Rome became dependent for her existence on imported corn. [4]   Knights, and Senators [5] (for whom trading was unlawful), often enriched by the spoils of conquered provinces, invested their money in land, and from every point of view were in a position to buy out the small holders.   With the influx of foreign corn, and the growth of

[1] Frank, "Roman Imperialism," p. 130.
[2] Mommsen, Hist. vol. iii. p. 74.
[3] *Vide* Varro, R.R. I. xvi. 1, on the selection of a site for a farm.
[4] Livy, xxvi. 40; xxvii. 8.
[5] Daremberg and Saglio, Art. "Res Rusticae," p. 916; Mommsen, Hist. vol. ii. p. 354.

large estates, came a change in the character of Italian agriculture. It was found no longer profitable to grow corn, and those rich landholders [1] set themselves either to the cultivation of the olive and the vine, which required substantial capital to start with, or to the rearing of sheep and cattle. The large grazing tracts were particularly attractive to the capitalists, and were to be found especially in Southern Italy, which was in many respects an ideal grazing country. It had been severely devastated in the long struggle between Hannibal and Rome, and, even in Cato's time, pastoral husbandry was preponderant there. The flocks and herds could spend [2] the summer in the upland pastures of the Central and Southern Apennines, and be driven, in the winter, down to the plains of Apulia and Calabria, as is the custom even at the present day. Those large tracts of pasture land were tended by only a few slaves. Varro [3] gives an interesting account of the choice of shepherds to look after these pastures, and of their mode of life. He [4] prefers Gauls for the work. They were armed as a rule, and were usually a wild and lawless body, that often provided material [5] for political incendiaries. The master had but to visit his estate a few times a year, and was sure of an easy return for his outlay. It is little wonder that, under such conditions, agriculture (particularly the growth of cereals) continued to decline, and that the small farmer went down in the struggle for existence.

Again, the ravages of the Civil Wars, with the unrest and confusion that followed in their train, as well as the rise of the professional soldier, must have aided considerably in bringing

---

[1] Stuart Jones, "Companion to Roman History," p. 305 *et seq.*; Mommsen, vol. iii. c. ii. *passim.*

[2] Varro, R.R. II. i. 16; ii. 9; III. xvii. 9.   [3] *Ibid.* x.

[4] *Ibid.* 4. The treatises of Varro and Cato were written primarily for the capitalist; cf. Gummerus, "Der Römische Gutsbetrieb," p. 20.

[5] Pelham, "Essays on Roman History," p. 306; Warde Fowler, "Social Life in the Age of Cicero," p. 221.

about the decay of agricultural life in Italy. A soldier, who had spent years in campaigning, even if he wished to return to his farm, often found[1] that he had no farm to return to. Still, a number of veteran soldiers were settled at different times upon the land, but the experiment was not always attended with the happiest results. Their minds were usually unsettled for the pursuits of husbandry, and men, who had spent the best portion of their lives in active warfare, often in distant lands, did not readily settle down to the uneventful existence of the farmer. If the theory[2] be true, which suggests that the "Georgics" was written to make attractive the life of the husbandman to the veterans of Octavian, we may be sure that not even Virgil's idyllic pictures[3] of the peace and happiness of country life were sufficient to make some of them contented on the land. The case was probably not rare, in which a soldier settled on the land, oppressed by the monotony of the existence, soon surrendered his farm, and drifted to one of the towns or cities to enjoy the excitements it afforded. Here was again an opportunity for the rich landholder to increase his already broad estates.

But another evil arose in connection with the latifundia, the notice of which must not be omitted. According to the laws of ancient warfare, with every conquest of Rome, the number of slaves at its disposal increased.[4] Especially after the Asiatic wars of Rome foreign slaves poured into Italy in great numbers, and were gradually employed[5] for almost every labour. It was an irresistible temptation to the capitalist landowner to employ slaves upon his estate to replace the

---

[1] Sallust, Jugurtha, 41.   [2] *Vide* Sellar, "Virgil," p. 176.
[3] Virg. Georgic, ii. 458 *et seq.*, 523 *et seq.*
[4] For some interesting estimates of slaves sold after various campaigns, *vide* Warde Fowler, op. cit. p. 207 (with references).
[5] Heitland, op. cit. vol. ii. p. 235 *et seq.*; Davis, " Influence of Wealth in Imperial Rome," p. 238 *et seq.*; cf. Lecky, "History of European Morals," p. 262, for the effect of slavery on the economic condition of Italy.

free labourer,[1] who had hitherto, for the most part, done his
work.   Of course, it is clear from Varro [2] that the free labourer
was never wholly excluded from the work of the farm, especially the harvesting of the vine and the olive.   Still the
temptation was strong to employ slaves, whenever possible, and
their employment seems to have been the invariable rule [3] in
the large pastoral tracts in Southern Italy.   The free labourer
thus fell upon evil days, and had no alternative left to him
but to become a soldier, or join the ranks of the needy in the
Capital.   Varro,[4] speaking presumably of his own day, dwells
in very clear and forcible language on the general decay of
agricultural life.   "And now that nearly all heads of families
have deserted scythe and plough, and have sneaked (correp-
serunt) within the city-walls, preferring to keep their hands
astir in the theatre and circus rather than amidst corn-crops
and vineyards, we contract with people to bring us corn from
Africa and Sardinia, whereby we may grow fat, and get in the
vintage by ship from the islands of Cos and Chios."   Later
in the same Preface, he says that his countrymen "have
turned corn-land into meadow, not knowing the difference
between agriculture and grazing".   From the days of the
Gracchi you had in process of formation that city proletariate,
which grew in demoralization as the years went on, and became increasingly restive and insistent in its demands.   It
would be a difficult but engrossing subject to estimate its
influence on Roman politics.   It was courted by all who
aspired to office, and was ever ready [5] to sell its votes to the

---

[1] The problem of slave versus free labour had appeared as early as the
days of the Licinian Rogation.   *Vide* Appian, B.C. i. 8; Bloch, op. cit.
p. 44.

[2] R.R. I. xvii. 2; Warde Fowler, op. cit. p. 218.

[3] Cæsar enacted that one-third of the "pastores" should be freemen.
Vide Suet. J. Cæsar, 42.

[4] Preface to Book II.   I quote from Storr-Best's translation with one
small change in the order of the words.

[5] Cf. the various trials for "ambitus," in which Cicero took part.

highest bidder.   It evolved finally into that turbulent throng, that under the Empire often threatened the peace of Rome in its cry for "Bread and Games".   It was an evil day for Rome, when Caius Gracchus, with no higher motive than political expediency, introduced his law [1] for the distribution of cheap corn to the city populace.   Mommsen styles him "the true founder of the urban proletariate".   His was an unfortunate precedent, for the largesses of corn helped to attract large numbers into the city, and were the first fatal step in the degradation of the poorer classes in Rome.   The decline of agricultural life was unhappily accompanied by a serious shrinkage in the population.   This was an evil which, as we have seen, was apparent even in the days of the Gracchi,[2] and which the Gracchan legislation had set itself to obviate.   It was an evil so intensified [3] by the Civil Wars, that it had reached alarming proportions in the time of Julius Cæsar, who in part at least of his legislation [4] sought to apply a remedy.

Such were the evils that the Elder Pliny had before his mind, when he delivered [5] his famous judgment—"Latifundia perdidere Italiam".   It is a sweeping assertion, but he is undoubtedly right in associating the ills of rural life with the growth of the latifundia.   It is difficult, however, to decide how far the evil of the latifundia itself extended.   There can be little doubt that a number of small holdings [6] continued to exist up to very late times.   The evil of the latifundia showed varying intensity according to the district.   In the period following the Second Punic War, Mommsen maintains [7] that there

---

[1] Plutarch, C. Gracchus, 5; Appian, B.C. i. 21; Velleius, ii. 6; cf. Greenidge and Clay, op. cit. p. 24, for further references; Mommsen, Hist. vol. iii. p. 114.

[2] Appian, B.C. i. 7, 11.

[3] Dio, xliii. 25; Furneaux, Introduction to Annals of Tacitus, vol. i. p. 108; Livy, vi. 12, 5 (there quoted).

[4] Suet. J. Cæsar, 20.   [5] N.H. xviii. 6, 35.

[6] Stuart Jones, op. cit. p. 305.

[7] Mommsen, vol. ii. c. xii. ; cf. Varro, R.R. I. xxix. for Apulia in his day; Hor. Odes, III. xvi. 26.

were a number of flourishing small farms between the Po and
the Apennines. Umbria and Etruria, which had been the first
to introduce the Sicilian slave-system into Italy,[1] were not so
favourable to their continuance. Southern Italy had been
devastated in the Hannibalic War, and with the decline of its
population came the inevitable tendency to the growth of large
estates. As time went on, the ravages of war would have been
at work to change the character of other districts in the same
way. We must remember, however, that there were influences
at work which helped to counteract, in some degree at least,
the growth of the latifundia. In every period of Roman history
colonies were founded, which must have secured the establishment of a certain number of small holders on the land. If the
schemes of the Gracchi for the distribution of land and for
extensive colonization had succeeded according to the wishes
of their originators, the balance might have been restored in
favour of the small farms. Even as it was, their efforts were
not in vain. Again, during the period of the Civil Wars, we
witness the spectacle of individual commanders, when victorious,
settling many of those who had served under them, either on
a portion of the public land, or on the lands of their political
opponents. These soldiers, as I have said, did not make ideal
farmers, and, as in the case of the old veterans of Sulla, who
had been planted round Faesulae (Fiesole), they were often a
source of serious disturbance in times of political unrest. It
was from these that Catiline,[2] in his efforts at revolution, drew
a number of his supporters. Still, many of them must have
settled down, however disinclined, to what must have seemed
to them after the excitements of a campaign the dreary round
of duties that year by year fall to the lot of the husbandman.
Such then were some of the influences that tended to lessen the
evil of the latifundia. Still, even when all these considerations
have been taken into account, this evil must have been a serious

---

[1] For slave prisons in Italy, *vide* Suet. Oct. 32; Tib. 8.
[2] Mommsen, vol. iv. p. 162.

one, with its concomitant evils of the decline of the small farmer and the free labourer, the growth of slave labour, the decrease in population, the decay of Italy as a corn-growing country, and its dependence for its supplies on corn imported from abroad.   I have thought it necessary to give this sketch, in order to show the problems, social and economic, that confronted statesmen, and called for a solution at the end of the Republic.   It will enable us to estimate the atmosphere, as it were, in which Horace lived, and to appreciate more fully the many scattered references to such problems that reveal themselves in his works.

Horace, in many pictures of large estates, clearly has the latifundia in mind.[1]   Occasionally, in referring to them, he uses the very word (*continuare*) which Livy [2] puts into the mouth of the elder Cato, in denunciation of the desire of wealthy Romans for broadening their estates.   It looks as if Horace desired to rouse invidiousness by the very suggestion of the word.   In one passage,[3] he strikingly puts before us the idea of a large estate, by imagining a union of Libya with distant Gades.   It is an image that gains in point from the fact that, possibly in Horace's day, and certainly in later times, Africa [4] was "the classic land of large estates".   In another passage [5] the poet describes for us the rich upstart, who ploughs a thousand acres of Falernian land, part of that rich Campanian plain, which the Romans had so long reserved from the scope of every Agrarian law.   He frequently [6] has before his mind the upland pastures (saltus) of Southern Italy, especially Lucania and Apulia, those rich pasture lands,[7] that were the delight

[1] Sat. I. i. 50 ; Odes, III. xvi. 4.

[2] Livy, XXXIV. iv. 9 ; cf. Cic. De Lege Agr. II. xxvi.

[3] Odes, II. ii. 9.

[4] Daremberg and Saglio, Art. "Res Rusticae," pp. 956-63 ; cf. Hor. Odes, I. i. 10.

[5] Epode iv. 13 ; cf. Prop. III. v. 5.

[6] Odes, I. xxxi. 5 ; II. iii. 17 ; III. iv. 15 ; Ep. II. ii. 177.

[7] For the history of the Pascua, *vide* Pelham, "Essays," p. 300 *et seq.*

of the capitalist landowner.   Here large herds of cattle could be pastured with little trouble to the owners.   Southern Italy too (Calabria in particular),[1] was noted for its breed of sheep, while Tarentum [2] was remarkable for the splendid quality of its wool.   Luceria [3] in Apulia was also noted for its wool, and outside Italy, the rich land of Gaul [4] was in this respect a serious rival to Southern Italy.   Horace has one interesting reference [5] to the change of the flocks and herds from the plains of Calabria to the uplands of Lucania before the burning summer heat intervened.   Sicily also was in Horace's day, as it always had been, a country containing many large estates. Agrippa, we know,[6] had extensive possessions there, and his steward Iccius is warned to beware of the contagion of the lucre that he gathers from the estates.   All this would go to show that the evil of the latifundia was felt in Horace's time, but it is not easy to determine how widespread the evil was. There were rich men, who extended the estates they already possessed, by buying out their poorer neighbours.[7]   But worse still, there were rich who went to the length of driving them from their lands.   Horace surely has contemporary conditions in mind, when he describes,[8] in few but impressive words, the eviction scene, in which the poor man with his wife and children and household gods are cast out to give broader acres to the rich.   The poet, too, complains [9] that the encroachments of the rich upon the lands of their neighbours have often as their motive merely the creation of pleasure-parks.

[1] Odes, I. xxxi. 5 ; Ep. I. viii. 6.

[2] Odes, II. ii. 18 ; cf. Virg. Georgic, ii. 197; Varro, R.R. II. ii. 18 (on " oves pelliti ") ; Pliny, N.H. viii. 73.

[3] Odes, III. xv. 13.   [4] *Ibid.* xvi. 35.

[5] Epode i. 27 ; cf. Varro, R.R. II. ii. 9 ; III. xvii. 9.

[6] Hor. Ep. I. xii. 1 ; cf. Odes, II. xvi. 33 ; Cic. In Verrem, II. iii.

[7] Odes, II. iii. 17.

[8] *Ibid.* xviii. 23 *et seq.* ; cf. Sallust, Jug. 41 ; Cic. Paradoxa, vi. 46, " expulsiones vicinorum ".

[9] Odes, II. xv. 1 *et seq.*

Between the encroachments of the rich and the confiscations, that followed the Civil Wars, the tenure of property must have been regarded by many as insecure.[1] Twice at least, Horace raises the question of property-rights, and seems to express in these passages the general feeling of insecurity among his contemporaries.[2] Ofellus had lost his farm, probably after the conflict at Philippi. The farm may have formed part of the Ager Publicus, Ofellus being originally only a "possessor"[3] in the technical sense of the word, enjoying usufruct, but not strict property-rights. After a civil conflict, when victorious commanders made an effort to settle their veterans, many private owners, as well as those holding part of the State land, would almost inevitably be disturbed. Hence we can appreciate the anxiety[4] of the public to know whether Augustus after the battle of Actium would settle[5] his veterans in Italy or Sicily. Ofellus, who has been driven from his farm, still works the land, paying rent to the new owner, but he makes it clear that even the new master has no fixity of tenure, and that through his own vice, or ignorance of some legal point, he may yet have to yield up his property to another. Horace raises the whole question of property-rights again,[6] some years later, in the Epistles. He does so with the object of pointing the moral that Nature gives no man full dominion over a thing that may, if not through human agency, at least through Death, the great arbiter, pass at any moment into the possession of another. But it is the various aspects of human agency[7] (*nunc prece, nunc pretio, nunc vi*), that are the real point of

---

[1] Sat. II. ii. 129, 133; Ep. II. ii. 173. [2] Sat. II. ii. 114

[3] For the concept of "possessio," *vide* Cardanali, op. cit. p. 101.

[4] Sat. II. vi. 55.

[5] For the restlessness of Octavian's soldiers after Actium, cf. Suet. Oct. 17; Dio, li. 3. For the various colonies of soldiers founded by Augustus, cf. Mon. Ancyr. c. 15-16, 28. He claims to have been the first, "within the memory of his own age," to pay for the Italian farms, in which he settled his soldiers.

[6] Ep. II. ii. 158 *et seq.* [7] *Ibid.* 173.

interest. Horace has probably here in mind a clause in the interdict [1] "uti possidetis," which guaranteed possession of property, into which one had come "nec vi, nec clam, nec precario". The passage as a whole reflects for us the feeling of insecurity of possession, that weighed on the minds of many of the poet's contemporaries.

Returning for a moment to the question of the latifundia, we can discover easily on which side the poet's sympathies lay. His ideal is Ofellus the "fortis colonus," [2] the small farmer and sturdy tiller of the soil, a man of homely simple habits, who is generous but not wasteful of his substance. The ideal would be complete, if we could imagine Ofellus, as in the days before the stranger came, master of the soil he tills. Horace dwells on the details of the picture with evident satisfaction, and must have felt convinced that such were the men, that formed the sinews of Italy in the days of its greatest prosperity. His ideal, too, is revealed for us in his second Epode, which in eloquent language draws for us a charming picture of the happiness pure and unalloyed of life on an Italian farm. It is not the rich landowner [3] that the poet here portrays, but a prosperous farmer of moderate means, who is lord of his land which has been in his family, [4] possibly for generations. It is a blessed existence, in which the protecting deities of the farm are duly honoured. The land is worked so as to yield the fullest return, and its produce is varied enough to satisfy even the most fastidious tastes. Horace, I am sure, wishes to emphasize the fact that the farm is self-supporting, and that, when the master of the house returns home weary after the labours of the day, the repast set before him is purely home-grown [5] (*dapes inemptae*). The

---

[1] For an interesting discussion of its application to the "possessores" of the Ager Publicus, *vide* Cardanali, op. cit. p. 103; Ulpian Dig. 43, 17, 1; Festus, p. 233 (there quoted); cf. Cic. De Lege Agr. III. iii. 14.

[2] Sat. II. ii. 112 *et seq.*; cf. Odes, I. xii. 43.

[3] Ep. II. 4.　　　　[4] *Ibid.* 3, " paterna rura ".

[5] *Ibid.* 48; cf. Varro, R.R., Introd. to Bk. II.; II. iv. 3; Virg. Georgic, ii. 514.

poet must have looked back with regret to the days, when most Italian farms were in a similar condition, and above all when Italy was independent of supplies of corn from Sicily and Sardinia,[1] and the more distant provinces of Africa and Egypt. The economic condition of Italy had, as we saw, changed considerably since the Hannibalic war, and the change must have been a source of serious anxiety to all interested in the welfare of Rome, and particularly to Augustus, who had now control of its destinies. The Emperors especially had to pay the penalty for the decline of Italian agriculture, for the safety of the Imperial throne was often in jeopardy, when the Capital was threatened by famine. Their difficulties had increased with the growth of the city-proletariate, and the custom of distributing cheap or free corn. The city-proletariate had by now become a very motley crew, among whom were to be found numerous foreigners, for the most part adventurers, from every province of the Empire. The decay of agriculture had forced many to drift into the city, while the number of the needy there had been swelled by discharged soldiers. As Appian so forcibly puts it : [2] "the distribution of corn to the poor, which takes place at Rome, only draws thither the idle, the beggars, the vagrants of all Italy ". These were a restless multitude, the " mobilium turba Quiritium,"[3] for which Horace has such profound contempt.[4] They courted the favour of the rich, they were wheedled by intriguing politicians, but fickle as the wind (*ventosa plebs*)[5] they were ever ready to exalt some popular favourite, or, if he opposed their caprices, to as quickly degrade him. It was no easy task to keep under restraint such an unruly crowd, in which for the most part the

---

[1] Hor. Odes, I. xxxi. 3.

[2] B.C. II. xvii. 120; cf. Lecky, " History of European Morals," p. 267 *et seq.*

[3] Odes, I. i. 7.

[4] Sat. I. vi. 17 ; x. 74 ; II. iii. 182 ; Odes, II. xvi. 39.

[5] Ep. I. xix. 37 ; cf. Odes, III. ii. 20 ; Ep. I. vi. 7 ; xvi. 33.

spirit of patriotism, or if we wish to so style it, loyalty to the Imperial idea, was dead beyond recall. They were kept in good humour by frequent gifts of corn and money, and by a continuous round of festivals and games. Augustus, as Suetonius tells us,[1] " surpassed all his predecessors in the frequency, variety, and splendour of his public shows ". He added further to the demoralization of the city populace by giving it frequent largesses of money.[2] He at one time thought of abolishing the distributions of corn,[3] " because, through dependence on them, agriculture had fallen into abeyance," but he did not persevere in his design, " feeling convinced that one day they would be renewed, through desire for popular favour (*per ambitionem*) ". The Emperor himself made frequent distributions of grain,[4] often at his own expense, and when Italy was afflicted with famine (22 B.C.), he was persuaded to undertake the administration [5] of the food supply, and " in a few days he freed the people from the fear and danger, in which they found themselves ". But the burden was a serious one for even Augustus to shoulder, because, with Italy in the condition in which it was, dependent on imported corn, its supplies were largely at the mercy [6] of the winds and waves. Over and above this uncertainty, another serious danger had frequently to be confronted. In a time of civil war, a favourite method [7] adopted by the leader of a party to bring his adversary to his knees, was to lock up the corn supply or part of it in the provinces, or blockade the Italian

---

[1] Suet. Oct. 43 ; cf. Mon. Ancyr. c. 22-3, where Augustus recounts these gâmes and spectacles as one of the great glories of his reign ; Vell. ii. 100 ; Dio, li. 22 ; liii. 1 ; liv. 19 ; Hor. Ep. I. vi. 7 ; vii. 59.

[2] Mon. Ancyr. c. 15 ; Suet. Oct. 41 ; Dio, li. 21 ; liv. 29.

[3] Suet. Oct. 42.   [4] Mon. Ancyr. c. 15.

[5] *Ibid.* c. 5 ; cf. Dio, liv. 1. Possibly Hor. Odes, I. xxi. refers to this year, cf. Kukula, Römische Säcularpoesie, p. 3. Suet. Oct. 18, tells of the efforts of Augustus to make Egypt more fruitful, and better adapted to supply corn to Rome.

[6] For a letter of Tiberius to the Senate on this subject, cf. Tac. Annals, iii. 54.

[7] Appian, B.C. V. viii. 67 ; Tac. Hist. ii. 82 ; iii. 8.

coast to prevent grain reaching Rome.   In the year 22 B.C.,
Augustus appointed two commissioners to superintend the corn
supply, and towards the end of his reign the whole management
of the supply was centred in the hands of a new official[1] called
"praefectus annonae," appointed by the Emperor himself.
Still, in spite of every precaution, the supply at times broke
down, and the capital was faced with famine, so that Augustus
on one occasion,[2] to relieve distress, expelled from Rome all
slaves who were for sale, the schools of gladiators, all foreigners
except physicians and teachers, and a certain proportion of
the household slaves.   It is little wonder that he showed solicitude for the revival of Italian agriculture.   Among the religious
associations restored by him to its old place of honour, were the
Fratres Arvales, one of whose chief functions was to conduct
each year the festival of the Ambarvalia,[3] a solemn lustration
of the fields to insure a fruitful harvest.   We saw the importance [4] assigned to Tellus in the Saecular Games, and the prominence she receives in the Art of the Augustan Age associated
with the name of the Emperor.   How far the solicitude of
Augustus was rewarded it is not easy to determine, though
Horace, availing probably of the licence of the poet in his
glowing eulogy of the Pax Augusta, represents a flourishing
countryside as one of the great glories of the Emperor's reign.

The institution of slavery existed in Italy from very early
times, though it did not reach its full development till the great
Roman wars of conquest.   The growth of the number of slaves,
and of slave labour had become a very serious problem since
the Second Punic War, and had largely helped to revolutionize
the economic life of Italy.   Slaves and slave-labour occupy a
prominent place in the treatises of Cato and Varro upon agri-

---

[1] Suet. Oct. 37 ; cf. Greenidge, "Roman Public Life," p. 411.

[2] Suet. Oct. 42 ; Dio, lv. 26.

[3] Carter, "The Religion of Ruma," p. 157 ; Warde Fowler, "Roman
Festivals," p. 124 *et seq.*

[4] *Vide supra*, pp. 73, 117 *et seq.*

culture.   Varro [1] gives elaborate details on the number of slaves
necessary for a farm such as he contemplated, and on the amount
of work to be expected from them.   But slavery exercised a profound influence too, on the life of the city.   In the great man-
sions of the rich, particularly under the Empire, the number of
slaves [2] in the "familia urbana" must have been always very
considerable, as their functions were highly specialized.   Sepulchral inscriptions [3] of slaves of both sexes, and of others who had
won their way from slavery to freedom, setting forth, as they
frequently do, the position these occupied in life, help us to
appreciate the number and variety of their duties.   Rich ladies
were especially well provided with attendants of every description.   Among a host of other functionaries, we find mention of
a lady's maid (*ornatrix*), a maid-in-waiting (*pedisequa*), a keeper
of the jewels (*ad margaritas*), a weaver (*textrix*), a slave whose
duty it was to fold her mistress's clothes (*vestiplica*), and one
who was commissioned to look after her work-basket (*quasil-
laria*).   The inscriptions in memory of male slaves reveal an even
greater diversity of duties, as limited in scope.   What with conquest and an ever active slave-trade,[4] the supply of slaves from
almost every quarter of the globe, but especially the East,[5] must
have been never-failing.   Varro, too,[6] recommends that the
slaves in the "familia rustica" be encouraged to have children,
for thus, he adds, "they become steadier and more attached to
the estate".   The union of slaves (*contubernium*) was not regarded as a legal one, but the slaves born in the household

---

[1] R.R. I. xvii.-xviii. ; II. x. ; Warde Fowler, "Social Life in Rome,"
c. vii.

[2] *Ibid.* p. 216 ; Friedländer, "Roman Life and Manners," vol. ii. p. 218
et seq. ; Wallon, "Histoire de l'Esclavage dans l'Antiquité," vol. ii. c. 3.

[3] Dessau, "Inscriptiones Selectae," ii. 2, p. 771 *et seq.* ; Wallon, op.
cit. vol. ii. p. 104 *et seq.* ; cf. Hor. Sat. I. ii. 98 ; Plautus, Trin. II. i. 23
et seq.

[4] Hor. Sat. II. iii. 285 ; vii. 43 ; Ep. I. xvi. 69 ; II. ii. 13 *et seq.*

[5] Hor. Sat. I. vi. 38 ; II. viii. 14 ; cf. Tib. II. iii. 5.

[6] R.R. I. xvii. 5.

apparently enjoyed a greater measure of freedom [1] than the rest, and were looked upon as the sign of a flourishing house.[2]   It is not easy to determine the number of slaves ordinarily attached to a rich household, and probably the number fluctuated considerably.   Horace has one interesting reference,[3] that may help us to fix an estimate.   He describes for us Tigellius of Sardinia as a man who was never consistent, but was always oscillating between extremes, having now only ten slaves, now two hundred.   Tigellius was wealthy, and, if he can be regarded as typical of his class, Horace seems to suggest that for one in his position either of these numbers would be an extreme.   He again censures [4] the meanness of the praetor Tillius, who is often seen on the road to Tibur with only five slaves to attend him.

The whole institution of slavery, apart from its economic aspect, was demoralizing [5] in its effects upon the community at large.   The slave had no legal rights, and was absolutely at the mercy of his master,[6] who had the power of life and death over him, unhindered by any external authority.   Cato, who in spite of his unbending severity, may be taken as typical of the Roman of an earlier period, and Varro, in a later age, simply regard the slave as an instrument, from which the greatest amount of wealth should be extracted.   In particular, the slaves of the "familia rustica" had little to alleviate the hardship [7] of their lot.   The numerous slave risings are a clear indication of the intolerable treatment to which slaves were subjected.   But these insurrections had usually the effect of inflaming popular resentment against them, while the growing frequency of gladiatorial shows,

[1] Hor. Sat. II. vi. 66 ; cf. Tib. I. v. 26.   [2] Hor. Epode ii. 65.
[3] Sat. I. iii. 11 ; cf. Pliny, N.H. xxxiii. 10 ; Petronius, Sat. 37 ; Tac. Annals, xiv. 43.
[4] Sat. I. vi. 108.   Horace himself has three slaves to wait at table (Sat. I. vi. 116) ; eight slaves on his Sabine farm (Sat. II. vii. 117).
[5] Warde Fowler, op. cit. p. 222 et seq.; Lecky, op. cit. p. 300 et seq.
[6] Juvenal, Sat. vi. 221.
[7] Hor. Sat. II. vii. 117; Plautus, Most. I. i. 17; Captivi, II. ii. 107; Becker, Gallus (Eng. Trans.), p. 220 et seq.

as time went on, helped to deaden in the hearts of many any
sensitiveness they might have entertained towards the sufferings of the slave.   Still there were some noble exceptions to
this prevailing attitude, and men like Cicero, Seneca,[1] and the
younger Pliny [2] could be found, who felt that slaves should be
treated as human beings.   Here and there one finds references [3]
in Roman authors to unwavering loyalty and devotion on
the part of slaves towards their masters, a loyalty that could
hardly have been rendered to cruel or selfish masters.   Plautus
for the most part keeps close to his Greek originals, and for
that reason evidence drawn from him may be suspect, but
the character of the slave in the Captivi and Menaechmi is drawn
with no unsympathetic hand.   There were, moreover, at all
times in Rome, slaves of distinct value, physicians, copyists,
slaves versed in Greek literature,[4] and many endowed with
skill in music and singing, whom it was the interest of the
master to treat with consideration.   In many households the
slave could look forward to freedom as the reward of devoted
service.   Still, when all these facts have been taken into account, the truth remains that the vast majority of the Roman
public were indifferent to the helpless misery of the slave's condition.   On this point Horace was the child of his Age.   Just
as he acquiesces without protest [5] in the brutal institution of the
gladiatorial show, so with regard to slaves he never rises above
the prevailing sentiment.   He, though a freedman's [6] son himself, does not show a glimpse of humanitarianism in speaking
of the slave, and never wonders at the abjectness of his condition or his utter dependence on his master's caprice.   He

----

[1] Ep. 47.   [2] Ep. v. 19.; viii. 16.
[3] Val. Max. vi. 8 ; Seneca, De Benef. III. xix. *et seq.* ; Tac. Hist. i. 3 ;
cf. the plea of Pretextatus on behalf of the slave, Macrob. Sat. I. xi. 2 *et
seq.* ; Dill, op. cit. p. 328.
[4] Hor. Ep. II. ii. 7 *et seq.*
[5] Sat. II. iii. 85, 310 ; vi. 44 ; vii. 96 ; Ep. I. i. 4 ; xviii. 19 ; II. ii. 98.
[6] Sat. I. vi. 6, 45 ; Ep. I. xx. 20.

speaks without comment of the punishment[1] and of the[2] exe-
cution of slaves. They must[3] not, however, be crucified for
venial offence:. He refers[4] to the daily distribution of bread
among them, which seems at times to have been so meagre as
to compel them to run away.[5] He tells of the work,[6] to which
slaves were put, without any touch of sympathy for their lot.
He takes it for granted[7] that slaves can be used as instruments
of lust. It is little wonder that a feeling of insecurity[8] obsessed the minds of many in Italy, who naturally expected
treachery instead of loyalty from the victims they treated with
such heartless cruelty. Once only does Horace seem to extend a large measure of indulgence to a slave, but that was
during the Saturnalia, when Davus took advantage[9] of the
liberty granted to all slaves as long as the festival lasted. Many
years were to elapse before any real amelioration of the slave's
lot was to be effected. The humanitarian elements latent in
Stoicism, with their softening influence upon Roman Law,[10] and
the Mystery religions, with their recognition of the dignity of
human personality, contributed something towards lightening
the burden of the slave, while Christianity, when its spirit
began to prevail, helped still further to ameliorate his condition.

Now we come to the important question of Roman luxury.
Friedländer[11] warns us to walk warily in dealing with it. He
says that there is an excessive tendency to generalize from iso-

---

[1] Sat. I. v. 65 ; II. vii. 105 ; Epode iv. 3.

[2] Ep. I. xvi. 48.   [3] Sat. I. iii. 82, 119.

[4] Ep. I. xiv. 40; xvi. 48 ; cf. Sat. I. i. 47.

[5] Sat. I. v. 68 ; II. v. 16 ; Ep. II. i. 121; ii. 16.

[6] Ep. I. xvi. 70 *et seq.* ; cf. *ibid.* xiv. 14 ; Sat. II. vii. 79.

[7] Sat. I. ii. 117; Odes, II. iv. 1 ; Ep. I. xviii. 72.

[8] Sat. I. i. 77; Epode iv. 19 ; ix. 10 ; xvi. 5.

[9] Sat. II. vii. 4.

[10] Cf. Lecky, op. cit. p. 306 *et seq.*, for an account of legislation favourable to slaves ; Lord Cromer, op. cit. p. 46.

[11] Op. cit. vol. ii. p. 130.

lated instances, and that moreover our three principal authorities on Roman luxury, Varro, Seneca, and the Elder Pliny, were men of peculiarly simple habits, and therefore inclined to exaggerate the evil. But Friedländer himself is so often intent upon instituting comparisons between Roman luxury and the luxury of modern times, that he in turn tends to minimize the undoubted facts of Roman luxury. Luxury is, of course, a very relative term, and we have to remember that many authors, who condemn luxury at Rome, judge by the standard of the simplicity of early Republican days, or of the period before Roman power had expanded. There is a tendency [1] in some, possibly based largely on individual taste, to glorify the Past at the expense of the Present, and to look back with regret to old times with their character of homely simplicity. Still, when we find the luxury of their contemporaries drawing expressions [2] of disapproval from such poets as Ovid and Propertius, we begin to feel that the evil must have developed into a serious one in the Augustan age. Compared with the days before the Second Punic War, the Romans had undoubtedly made an extraordinary advance in luxury. This advance was an almost inevitable consequence of the expansion of Roman power. The campaigns of the Roman armies in the East had familiarized [3] the soldiers with Oriental luxury, and this knowledge could not fail to react, on their return, upon life at home.

Again, the spread of Greek culture helped indeed to refine Roman society, but, as Cato anticipated, it also, while broadening the vision of the Roman, made him discontented with prevailing conditions, and shook the fabric of his old simple way of living. With the spread of Roman power, and the increase in the number of Roman provinces, wealth began to

---

[1] Hor. Odes, II. xv. 10 *et seq.*; Livy's Preface; Sallust, Cat. 9-13; Juvenal, Sat. iii. 168, 182; xi. 108.

[2] Prop. III. xii. 18; xiii. 4, 60; Ovid, Fasti, i. 209 *et seq.*

[3] Livy, xxxix. 6, on the beginnings of Asiatic luxury in Rome; cf. Sallust, Cat. 13; Pliny, N.H. xxxiii. 53; xxxvii. 6.

pour rapidly into Rome.   I need not dwell on the government
of the provinces under the Republic.   A system of provincial administration,[1] in which the governor enjoyed authority
practically uncontrolled, and in most cases lasting only for a
year, combined with the Roman custom of farming the taxes,
left the provinces an easy prey to rapacious governors and unscrupulous tax-gatherers.   The provinces were, for the most
part,[2] exploited in the interests of the governing classes, and
many a ruined noble left Rome, either as the governor of a
province or as a member of the governor's staff, with the intention of repairing his shattered fortunes during his term
of office.   How far the wealth, that reached Rome from the
provinces, was distributed, it would be difficult to say.   It did
not fall to every one's lot to amass such huge fortunes as
Lucullus or Crassus.   But many must have been enriched by
the spoils of the provinces, and with increase of wealth luxury
inevitably increased.   By the close of the Republic, Rome had
definitely become a great imperial city.   Her imperial mission
had become stereotyped,[3] not only in the mind of a poet like
Virgil, but in the mind of the public at large, and it was felt
to be fitting that the Empire, to its farthest boundaries, should
contribute to her glory, her opulence, and her ease.   It was
partly under the influence of this new vision that Virgil sur-
veyed mankind,[4] as it were, and told in poetic strains of distant
lands and their products, but his picture must owe not a little
to the activities of Roman or Italian merchants in his day.
With the improvement of communications, commercial enterprise had increased, and was now bringing the produce of the
most distant provinces, and of lands beyond the sway of Rome

---

[1] Greenidge, op. cit. c. viii.; Lord Cromer, op. cit. p. 50 *et seq.*;
Boissier, " Cicero and his Friends," p. 312 *et seq.*; Lucas, " Greater Rome
and Greater Britain," p. 75.

[2] Catullus, x.; Cic. Ad Fam. viii. 14; Heitland, op. cit. vol. iii. p. 499.

[3] Virg. Æn. vi. 852; Ovid, Ars. Am. iii. 95; Hor. Ep. II. i. 193 *et seq.*

[4] Georgic, ii. 114 *et seq.*

into the great imperial city.   Horace reflects in many passages
the commercial activity of his time.   One has to be careful
in dealing with such references as he gives, and endeavour to
extricate fact from what is mere poetic ornament.   Roman
commercial activity had begun early in the Republic,[1] and it
was natural to expect that, as Rome extended her conquests,
new fields would be opened to the enterprise of the Roman
merchant.   Trade may in some cases have preceded the flag,
but increase of trade [2] was certain to follow in its wake.   Some
idea of the activities of the Roman merchant [3] may be formed
from the finds of Roman coins in places widely separated.
Late Republican and early Imperial coins have been discovered
in the Punjab, in Further India, and in Ceylon.   The principal
trade route to the East lay through Alexandria, along the Nile,
and through the Red Sea ports of Berenice and Myoshormus.
But the produce of India found its way to the West also, " by
the port of Charax on the Persian Gulf, thence by the
Euphrates, and across the desert by the caravan route, passing
through Palmyra to Damascus ".   India [4] furnished gold-dust,
pepper, tortoise-shell, and pearls, while from South Arabia
came spices, perfumes, and precious stones.   Syria [5] gave the
purple dye of Tyre, its fine linen, and the glass of Sidon.
Roman merchants made their way also to the Black Sea,[6] and
the Sea of Azov.   The silk trade was developed with the island
of Cos, with Assyria, and with distant China.   In the West,
the Romans traded for amber with Northern Europe.   Roman

---

[1] Frank, " Roman Imperialism," c. xiv., gives an account of Roman commerce under the Republic.   The Italians of S. Italy, and freedmen of
Greek and Oriental stock were especially prominent in commercial life ;
cf. Hor. Ep. I. xvi. 71, for slaves in commerce.

[2] Lucas, op. cit. p. 74.

[3] Friedländer, op. cit. vol. i. p. 308 *et seq.* ; Stuart Jones, " Companion
to Roman History," p. 316 *et seq.*   Much of the material these two authors
have collected relates to the period of the Empire.

[4] Prop. III. xiii. 5 *et seq.* ; Tib. III. ii. 23 ; Ovid, Fasti, i. 341.

[5] Friedländer, op. cit. vol. ii. p. 175.   [6] Persius, Sat. v. 135.

coins have been discovered all over North Germany. Coins of Republican date have been discovered in Silesia, while Roman merchants had early penetrated into Bohemia. A brisk trade, especially in oil and wine, had been carried on with Gaul even before Cæsar's conquest, the Gauls giving in return warm woollen garments and pottery. Naturally, extensive trade had been carried on with Spain [1] since the time of its conquest. Its possession was a valuable asset to the Romans on account of its mines, as copper, lead, gold, tin, and other minerals were found in various parts of the country. But the monopoly of trade was not left to the Roman or Italian merchant.

The spread of foreign cults in Italy and throughout the Empire,[2] coming as they did especially through the ports,[3] is a clear indication of the enterprise of the foreign merchant, who was generally loyal to his national gods. The Egyptians and Syrians were particularly active, and carried their religion as well as their wares to the farthest frontiers of the Empire. Traces of the Syrian have been discovered [4] through inscriptions in almost every province, and his activity continued till quite late times. St. Jerome, speaking of his own time, says: "To the present day commerce is the genius of the Syrians, compelling them to wander through the whole world, and even now, when the Empire is held by barbarians, driving them to seek wealth amidst armed camps".[5] The Spanish ship,[6] too, was to be found in Italian ports. It is, however, the com-

---

[1] Bouchier, "Spain under the Empire," c. vi.

[2] Toutain, "Les Cultes Païens," vol. ii. *passim*; Cumont, "Les Rel. Or." p. 29 *et seq.*

[3] For Puteoli, cf. Stuart Jones, op. cit. p. 316; Dill, op. cit. p. 563; Suet. Oct. 98. For Ostia, cf. L. Ross Taylor, "The Cults of Ostia," p. 8 *et seq.*, 57 *et seq.*

[4] Stuart Jones, op. cit. p. 319; Bouchier, op. cit. p. 84; "Syria as a Roman Province," c. vii.

[5] Quoted by Friedländer, op. cit. vol. i. p. 313.

[6] Hor. Odes, III. vi. 31.

mercial enterprise of his own countrymen, especially in over-
seas trade, that Horace depicts for us most of all.   At times[1]
he deprecates all such navigation as a tempting of Providence.
Though he has been storm-tossed,[2] the merchant, unschooled
to endure poverty, is ever ready to refit his ships, and essay
the deep once more.   The Roman merchant,[3] the poet tells
us, is to be found in every quarter of the globe.   That man is
surely a favourite of Heaven,[4] who three or four times a year
can voyage in safety to the Atlantic, and whose lot it is to
drink from golden cups the wine he has got in exchange for
Syrian merchandise.   Here he may possibly have in mind a
Syrian merchant, just as in another passage [5] he may have in
mind a merchant from Bithynia.   Again, he pictures for us [6] a
young merchant, who has gone trading to Bithynia, and
starting too late on his return journey is forced by stress of
weather to winter at Oricum in Epirus.   Another brings back
goods from Bithynia,[7] and from Cibyra in Phygia, a place noted
for the excellence of its ironwork.   He speaks,[8] too, of merchandise coming from Cyprus and from Tyre.   He tells us [9]
that, as a proof of fidelity to a friend, he is ready to go with
him to distant Gades, or again,[10] if the Muses are propitious,
he will sail to the raging Bosporus, both places probably well
known through the voyages of Roman merchants.   The poet
also can look forward [11] to the prospect of his Epistles reaching
Utica or Ilerda.   From these many scattered indications in
Horace it is clear that commercial activity was very great in
his day.   The expansion of Roman commerce must have been
especially marked after the battle of Actium, as the result of
the peace established by Augustus.   One cannot, of course,

---

[1] Odes, I. iii. 21 ; xxxv. 7.   [2] *Ibid.* i. 15 *et seq.*
[3] Sat. I. i. 38 ; iv. 29 ; Odes, III. xxiv. 36 *et seq.*; cf. Odes, II. xvi. 2 ;
I. iv. 2 ; Ep. I. i. 45.
[4] Odes, I. xxxi. 10 *et seq.*   [5] *Ibid.* xxxv. 7.
[6] *Ibid.* III. vii. 3 *et seq.*   [7] Ep. I. vi. 33.
[8] Odes, III. xxix. 60.   [9] *Ibid.* II. vi. 1.   [10] *Ibid.* III. iv. 30.
[11] Ep. I. xx. 13 ; cf. Odes, II. xx. 14 *et seq.*

conclude that all this traffic was in luxuries alone, but making due allowance for trade in the necessaries of life, it is probable that the stream of luxuries flowing into Italy, and especially into the Capital, was ever increasing in volume. It is significant that some years previously Julius Cæsar found[1] it necessary to impose a duty on foreign wares, not as a protective tariff, but solely for the purpose of lessening the influx of luxuries.

Now, with the growth of commerce, the wealth of Italy naturally increased. Here again, we do not know how it was distributed, but for the most part it probably remained within a small but ever-widening circle. Horace, in his moralizing moods, throws some light for us on the influence of wealth in his day. Poverty,[2] or a small income was the great evil and the great reproach, and a man's worth[3] was calculated precisely by the money he possessed. "Mistress Cash" was the arbiter[4] of a man's destinies, and he who could boast of a well-lined purse was assured of success in life. Hence sprang the universal greed for gain, a greed[5] not to be discouraged by the most serious obstacles. The lesson[6] most generally taught, and most willingly learned was the need of making money, honestly, if one could, but, if that were impossible, by whatever means necessary to attain the desired end. Horace pictures[7] for us the usurer who is especially on the watch for minors, to whom he is ready to lend money at an exorbitant interest. The avarice[8] of his contemporaries comes also under the poet's lash. In Horace's age the art of legacy-hunting

---

[1] Suet. J. Cæsar, 43.

[2] Odes, III. xxiv. 62; Ep. I. i. 43; cf. Sallust, Cat. 12; Ovid, Fasti, i. 218.

[3] Sat. I. i. 62; II. v. 8.

[4] Ep. I. vi. 37; cf. Sat. II. iii. 94; Ep. I. x. 47.

[5] Sat. I. i. 38 *et seq.*

[6] Ep. I. i. 53 *et seq.*; ii. 44 *et seq.*; cf. Prop. III. xiii. 48.

[7] Sat. I. ii. 12 *et seq.*; Ep. I. i. 80.

[8] Sat. I. iv. 26; II. iii. 82 *et seq.*; Ep. I. ii. 44.

was already perfected, and one[1] of the most brilliant and wittiest of his Satires was directed against its practice. The increase of wealth in the community was bound also to produce a crop of parvenus such as Horace portrays in his description of Nasidienus,[2] who endeavoured to make vulgar display a substitute for noble lineage. But wealth and its concomitant luxury had the inevitable effect of giving rise to a certain ennui and restlessness,[3] that are commonly characteristic of a society which, departing from its old simplicity, has become over-refined and fastidious in its tastes, and already holds within itself the germs of decay. Change of scene and climate are sought by the rich to relieve their weariness of life, and this longing for change has penetrated[4] even to the poor. Men do not seem to realize, says Horace,[5] that wealth alone does not confer happiness, that, when they fly to other lands, they do not escape their own wretched selves, and that they hold in reality the key to happiness within their own minds. When the rich man goes on board his brazen trireme,[6] he has Care as a fellow-passenger, and wealth, as it grows, brings with it the inevitable burden of solicitude.[7] The poet himself on his Sabine farm, untroubled by the pinch of poverty, is happier than if he possessed broad domains and endless riches.

Now, when Horace descends to detail on the matter of luxury, he singles out especially for reprobation the craze that

---

[1] Sat. II. v.; cf. Ep. I. i. 77; Cic. Paradoxa, v. 39; vi. 49; Ovid, Ars Am. ii. 267; Pliny, Ep. ii. 20; Tac. Ger. 20; Friedländer, op. cit. vol. i. p. 213.

[2] Sat. II. viii.; cf. Epode iv.

[3] Sat. I. i. 3 *et seq.*; Ep. I. i. 82 *et seq.*; Sat. II. vii. 9.

[4] Ep. I. i. 91 *et seq.* For the poet's own restlessness, cf. Sat. II. vii. 29; Ep. I. viii. 12.

[5] *Ibid.* xi. 27; Odes, II. xvi. 19; cf. Lucr. iii. 1057 *et seq.*; Seneca, Ep. 69.

[6] Odes, II. xvi. 21; III. i. 39.

[7] *Ibid.* III. i. 48; xvi. 17; cf. Prop. III. vii. 1 *et seq.*

was prevalent in his day among the rich for building large villas. The evil was no new one, for already Sallust could speak[1] in his own time of "houses and villas built like cities ". In a later age Tiberius was compelled to protest[2] against "villas infinite in extent ". Horace speaks[3] of the "regal piles" erected by some of his contemporaries, and laments that the pleasure parks of the rich, with their artificial ponds, their groves of plane-trees, and their mass of fragrant flowers and shrubs, will soon leave few acres for tillage. It was the sea-coast especially that they chose for the site of their villas, and the Mediterranean coast by predilection. The sea seems to have possessed a special attraction for the Romans.[4] Among them love of Nature was strong, but they had not the modern taste for wild mountain-scenery,[5] though hill-scenery made some appeal to them. They were attracted[6] rather by a quiet country-scene, cool verdant valleys, or a large expanse of rich fertile plain, well watered and well wooded. They found a charm not only in the songs of the birds but in the music of the streams, while beneath the shade of trees they could sleep, sheltered from the summer heats. The sea, however, in all its moods seems to have filled them with especial delight. Many villas must have been built, like Pliny's Laurentine villa,[7] so as to command a good view of the sea. The oppressiveness of the summer at Rome made it an imperative necessity for all, who could afford it, to leave the city during the summer months. But apart from this, the rich, who could indulge in such luxuries, built villas that would afford them at various times of the year a welcome retreat from

---

[1] Cat. 12 ; cf. Cic. Paradoxa, v. 37.   [2] Tac. Annals, iii. 53.

[3] Odes, II. xv. 1; cf. however, Ep. I. xv. 46.

[4] *Ibid.* vii. 11 ; xi. 10, 26 ; Suet. Oct. 72.

[5] Geikie, "The Love of Nature among the Romans," c. xiii.

[6] Hor. Epode ii. 23 *et seq.*; Odes, I. i. 21 ; II. iii. 9 *et seq.*; III. xiii. 13; Ep. I. x. 19 *et seq.*; xiv. 35 ; xvi. 5 *et seq.*; xviii. 104; Virg. Georgic, ii. 198 *et seq.*, 469 *et seq.*; iii. 520; cf. Pliny, Ep. viii. 8 ; Macrob. Sat. VI. ii. 5 ; Friedländer, op. cit. vol. i. p. 380 *et seq.*

[7] Pliny, Ep. ii. 17 ; vi. 31.

the smoke and din of Rome, and the wearisome round[1] of formalities, which social prestige in the Capital entailed. The number of such villas must have been large, if one can judge from those possessed by Cicero,[2] who had no less than eight in all, as well as some temporary stopping-places (*deversoria*) to be used in journeys off the beaten track. But it is significant of Roman taste that six of Cicero's villas were on the sea-coast, and of these six, three[3] were on or near the coast of Campania. On that lovely stretch of coast from Cumae to the Gulf of Salernum (Salerno), which is one of the great attractions for travellers in modern Italy, many Romans[4] were induced to build their villas, and pass at least the season there. Horace pictures[5] the rich man building his stately mansion on the coast, sometimes out into the very sea. Baiae,[6] in particular, seems to have been a favourite spot for the villas of the wealthy. It was believed that no bay in the world could vie with it in beauty. Its baths[7] and its clear air drew many invalids to it, but possibly for many others the Greek refinement of the district, and a certain laxity of manners[8] in the town proved an additional attraction. But the Romans frequented

---

[1] Hor. Sat. II. vi. 23 *et seq.*; Ep. I. vii. 8; II. ii. 67; Pliny, Ep. I. 9.

[2] For a good account of Cicero's villas, *vide* Warde Fowler, " Social Life," p. 251 *et seq.*; cf. Friedländer, op. cit. vol. i. p. 329 *et seq.*; Heitland, op. cit. vol. iii. p. 499.

[3] At Cumae, Puteoli, and Pompeii.

[4] Hor. Ep. I. i. 84; Pliny, Ep. VI. xvi. 9; cf. Cic. Pro Plancio, xxvi. 65. The orator once came to Puteoli at " the height of the season," when a crowd of the élite (*plurimi et lautissimi*) was gathered there.

[5] Hor. Odes, III. i. 33; xxiv. 2; Sallust, Cat. 13; Ovid, Ars Am. iii. 108.

[6] Hor. Ep. I. i. 83; Odes, II. xviii. 17.

[7] Hor. Ep. I. xv. 2; Odes, III. iv. 24; Tib. III. v. 3; Pliny, N.H. xxxi. 2.

[8] Prop. I. xi. 1, 27; III. xviii. 2; Cic. Pro Coelio, 48; Ad Att. I. xvi. 10; Varro Fragments, Riese, p. 105; Livy, xxiii. 4; Pliny, Ep. VI. 4. For the history of Baiae as a pleasure resort, cf. Friedländer, vol. i. p. 336 *et seq.*; Becker, " Gallus," Scene vii.

many other towns [1] along that coast, while further south, Tarentum [2] was a favourite resort on account of its mild climate. They went inland also, especially among the hills, for their *villegiatura*.[3]   Praeneste (Palestrina) had a special attraction [4] for Horace, while, in that age when foreign travel [5] was becoming common among the Romans, the poet declares [6] his predilection for Tibur (Tivoli) over many places of interest abroad.   There were also numerous little towns not far from Rome, among the Alban or Sabine hills, to which the Romans were fond of escaping from the heat and oppression of the Capital.

Horace, too, can be our guide with regard to various forms of extravagance within the villa.   In two passages [7] at least he mentions the use of mosaic flooring.   Mosaic pavements had been in fashion since the days of Lucilius, who refers to such work as "emblema vermiculatum," [8] a name believed to be derived from the fact that the appearance of the mosaic suggested the writhing of worms.   Suetonius mentions [9] as a proof of the luxurious tastes of Julius Cæsar, that he carried tessellated and mosaic flooring (*tessellata et sectilia pavimenta*) about with him in his campaigns.   The Elder Pliny is our best ancient authority [10] for the history of mosaic-work, which had its origin, he tells us, among the Greeks, who used it to imitate painting.

---

[1] Such as Surrentum, Hor. Ep. I. xvii. 52; xviii. 20; Velia and Salernum, Ep. I. xv. 1.

[2] Hor. Odes, II. vi. 9 *et seq.*; III. v. 56; Ep. I. xvi. 11.

[3] Friedländer, op. cit. vol. i. p. 329.

[4] Odes, III. iv. 22; Ep. I. ii. 2.

[5] Friedländer, op. cit. vol. i. c. vii.

[6] Odes, I. vii. 12 *et seq.*; II. vi. 5; III. xxix. 6; cf. Suet. Oct. 72.

[7] Sat. II. iv. 83; Ep. I. x. 19; cf. Varro, R.R. III. i. 10 (*emblema aut lithostratum*); ii. 4; Fragments, Riese, p. 226; Pliny, N.H. xxxvi. 25 (Weis's edition).

[8] Cic. Or. 149; De Or. iii. 171.

[9] J. Cæsar, 46.

[10] N.H. xxxvi. 60-4; cf. Stuart Jones, op. cit. p. 411 *et seq.*; Becker, "Gallus," p. 270.

He distinguishes mosaic from "lithostrata," pavements[1] consisting of small slabs of marble not exhibiting any design, which were introduced into Rome in the time of Sulla. Some idea of the beauty of the mosaic used in the flooring of Roman villas may be formed from the "Mosaic of the Doves" in the Capitoline museum at Rome, or the splendid specimen of mosaic-work preserved in the Palazzo Barberini at Palestrina, or from the Woodchester pavement.[2]

Horace speaks at times of the splendour of the ceilings in Roman houses, done in lacquered work,[3] in gilded panels sometimes inlaid with ivory. He has numerous references, too, to the use of marble in the adornment of the Roman house. Supporting columns of marble, especially in the peristyle, were common by Horace's time. The Censor, L. Crassus, had been the first (92 B.C.)[4] to adorn a private house with marble, using four columns from Hymettus, and had irritated public opinion by his action. But the custom, once introduced, spread rapidly. Some years later the Knight Mamurra, the object of Catullus' bitter invective,[5] introduced the practice[6] of covering the walls of the house with slabs of marble. Horace refers[7] to the use of marble of various colours in the peristyle of the house, where a miniature garden with trees was planted, surrounded by a colonnade. He mentions by name some of the marbles that were used, and it is significant that they are foreign marbles. The Phrygian,[8] which was a white marble with purple veins (*pavonazzetto*), came from Synnada

[1] Cic. Paradoxa, vi. 49; Tib. III. iii. 16.
[2] Walters, " The Art of the Romans," p. 111.
[3] Odes, II. xvi. 11; xviii. 2; I. xxxvi. 6; cf. Lucr. ii. 28; Pliny, N.H. xxxiii. 18 (on *laquearia*).
[4] Friedländer, op. cit. vol. ii. p. 185; Stuart Jones, op. cit. p. 58.
[5] Cat. xxix., lvii.
[6] Becker, "Gallus," p. 272; Pliny, N.H. xxxvi. 6, 7 (there quoted).
[7] Odes, III. x. 5; Ep. I. x. 22; cf. Tib. III. iii. 15.
[8] Hor. Odes, III. i. 41; cf. Tib. III. iii. 13; Stuart Jones, op. cit. p. 58.

in Phrygia, and was highly prized.   Horace speaks also [1] of beams of white marble from Hymettus pressing down on columns of marble quarried in distant Africa.   This latter was the Numidian marble (*giallo antico*), yellow in colour and showing veins of red, which was first introduced [2] by M. Lepidus, the colleague of Catulus.   We hear, too, of marble from Carystus in Euboea,[3] and of marble from Taenarum (*verde antico*).   Lucullus in his day had introduced a black marble, which bore his name.   With the conquest of Egypt, the Romans had new fields opened up for extravagance in decoration, and were able to obtain porphyry from the Arabian desert, and alabaster from Jebel Urakan.   Pliny speaks [4] of a marble from Egypt called ophite, so named because it was "serpentium maculis simile," while two other Egyptian marbles discovered, one in the reign of Augustus, the second under Tiberius, were named respectively after these Emperors.   It is interesting to find [5] that the Romans had begun to use the marble from the Luna quarries as early as the days of Mamurra, who employed both it and Carystian marble in the decoration of his house.

Now, when we come to the furniture of the Roman house, we find again the same evidence of extravagance.   The artistic taste of the Romans, as we know, was not high.   Virgil [6] proclaimed that their mission in the world was an imperialist one, and apparently thought it impossible to reconcile Art and Imperialism.   We cannot imagine a Roman giving expression to the sentiments of Pericles [7] when he announced the ideal, which Athens had set before herself, of aiming above all at being a lover of the Beautiful.   The Romans were essentially utili-

---

[1] Odes, II. xviii. 3.

[2] Pliny, N.H. xxxvi. 8.   On the general question of marbles used by the Ancients, *vide* Pliny, N.H. xxxvi. 5 *et seq.*; cf. Friedländer, vol. ii. p. 186-90; Becker, " Gallus," p. 16.

[3] Tib. II. iii. 43; III. iii. 14.   [4] N.H. xxxvi. 10.

[5] *Ibid.* 7; cf. Suet. Nero, 50.   [6] Æn. vi. 848 *et seq.*   [7] Thucydides, ii. 41.

tarian in their interests, caring little for the graces and refinements of life. The man who took an interest in Art for its own
sake was looked upon with suspicion, just as he was who devoted
himself to the study of Philosophy without some practical end
in view. The Elder Cato, typical of the conservative Roman,[1]
considered that the art treasures, brought to Rome from Syracuse by Marcellus after the sack of that city, were destined
to prove the bane of the Romans. His excessive hostility to
Greek culture was not general with his countrymen in after
years, but the popular prejudice against Art seems to have long
continued, and its continuance explains the apologetic tone
which Cicero adopted, in his impeachment of Verres, for his
knowledge of the names and works of the great Greek artists.
This, however, was not Cicero's invariable mood, and at times
he displays at least an amateur's interest in works of Art. He is
fond of using the works of the great Greek masters,[2] both in
painting and in sculpture, as illustrations in his treatment of
a subject like oratory, and at times speaks of such works in
the language of extravagant enthusiasm. He frequently, too,
gives commissions [3] to his friends to buy him *objets d'art*, but,
generally speaking, he betrays the fact that in all this his enthusiasm is not that of the genuine Art connoisseur. For him
the dominant interest in procuring such objects is not their
artistic value, but their utility in furnishing his villa. He wants
something that will be suitable for his "gymnasium" or his
"Academia," or, as he puts it in his letter to Fadius Gallus,
"something that will suit his library, and be in harmony with
his studies". Cicero's attitude on such matters was probably
typical of many of the educated Romans of his day.[4] The
numerous works of Art, which had found their way to Rome,
after the conquest of such cities as Syracuse and Corinth, could

---

[1] Livy, xxxiv. 4.   [2] Cic. Or. 5, 74, 234; Brutus, 70, 75.
[3] Ad Att. I. i.; vi. 2; ix. 2; x. 3; Ad Fam. vii. 23. On Cicero's taste in
Art, cf. Sandys, Introd. to Orator, p. 71 *et seq.*
[4] Friedländer, op. cit. vol. ii. p. 325 *et seq.*

hardly fail to have their effect on even the most Philistine of nations.   Moreover, the custom of foreign travel, especially through the Greek world, had become prevalent during the last century of the Republic, and the great artistic creations of the Greeks were bound to awaken some enthusiasm in the minds of the Romans who saw them.   But in spite of all this, the vast majority of educated Romans showed little intelligent appreciation of Art.   If they sought for works of Art, they did so, actuated for the most part like Cicero by a desire to furnish their villas, or from mere love of display.   Horace refers [1] to the anxiety of some of his contemporaries to procure silver and bronze plate, especially antiques.   It is not likely that there were many art dealers at Rome like Damasippus,[2] who was apparently a keen connoisseur.   Horace's description of him is intended to be a satire on the prevailing passion for antiques, particularly those to which an historical or supposed historical interest was believed to attach.   Damasippus is represented [3] as searching for the bronze vessel in which "Sisyphus had washed his feet," an object to be paralleled for its associations only by the dish [4] that had been handled by Evander.   The extravagant length to which such a craze could go is well illustrated by Petronius, who represents [5] Trimalchio as claiming to possess the bowl which Prometheus had bequeathed to Patroklos.   Damasippus was an expert in judging bronze by the roughness or smoothness of its casting. Vessels of Corinthian bronze,[6] the secret of which was lost by Horace's time, were those most highly prized.   Trimalchio [7] claimed to be the only one in his own day who possessed

[1] Ep. I. vi. 17 *et seq.*; II. ii. 180.

[2] Sat. II. iii. 20 *et seq.*; cf. Cic. Ad Fam. vii. 23, 2; Ad Att. xii. 29, 2.

[3] Sat. II. iii. 21.   [4] *Ibid.* I. iii. 90.

[5] Satyr. 52; cf. Suet. J. Cæsar, 81; Martial, VIII. vi. 4 *et seq.*; VII. xix.; Friedländer, vol. ii. p. 331.

[6] Hor. Sat. I. iv. 27; Cic. De Signis. I. i.; Paradoxa, v. 37; Virg. Georgic, ii. 464; Prop. III. v. 6; Pliny, N.H. xxxiv. 6; Pliny, Ep. III. i.

[7] Petron. Satyr. 50.

genuine "Corinthian bronzes," because they were made for him by a metal-worker named Corinthus. Martial[1] tells us that connoisseurs could detect the genuineness of such vessels by the peculiar odour they emitted. Augustus was criticized[2] by some of his contemporaries for his fondness for Corinthian bronzes, and it was believed that he had caused some men to be proscribed, in order to obtain such specimens as they possessed. Tiberius during his own reign had to complain[3] that the prices of Corinthian bronzes had risen to an enormous figure.

The Romans also had a leaning towards silver-plate,[4] whether plain or ornamented.[5] This latter was either chased (the *argentum caelatum* properly so called), or showed repoussé work, or was adorned with separately attached reliefs (*emblemata* or *crustae*). Here again, Roman predilection would naturally be for antiques, especially the work of such distinguished artists as Mentor and Boethus.[6] But even in Imperial times excellent silver-work was executed, as may be seen from the wonderful Bosco Reale[7] treasure discovered near Pompeii (1895), most of the pieces of which are now in the Louvre, or the Hildesheim treasure now in Berlin. The Bosco Reale cups were made probably during the reign of Augustus, or shortly after his death. On one of them that Emperor is seen receiving the submission of a group of barbarians, while on another Tiberius appears wearing the "corona civica," and riding in a triumphal car adorned with reliefs of Victories. Most of the

---

[1] Ep. ix. 59, 11.   [2] Suet. Oct. 70.   [3] *Ibid.* Tib. 34.

[4] Hor. Sat. I. iv. 27; II. vii. 47; Ep. I. vi. 17; II. ii. 181; cf. Cic. Paradoxa, v. 37; De Signis. xxiv. 54; Walters, op. cit. p. 125 *et seq.*; Friedländer, vol. ii. p. 205 *et seq.*

[5] *Leve* or *purum*, cf. Cic. De Signis. xxii. 49; Pliny, Ep. III. i.; Juv. Sat. xiv. 62.

[6] Cic. De Signis. xviii. 38; xiv. 32; Prop. I. xiv. 2. For a list of famous metal-workers among the Ancients, cf. Pliny, N.H. xxxiii. 55.

[7] *Vide* Walters, op. cit. p. 126 *et seq.*; Stuart Jones, op. cit. p. 430 for illustrations.

ornamental metal-work among the Romans was in bronze or silver, but their extravagance sometimes went the length of using vessels of gold.[1] We find a proposal made,[2] early in the reign of Tiberius by Q. Haterius, "that vessels of solid gold be not used to serve up food". The reply of Asinius Gallus on the occasion is interesting. The condition of the State, he said, had changed since ancient times, and one could no longer expect the simplicity of life of a Fabricius ; wealth had increased, and private luxury should keep pace with it.

There is no need to dwell on the taste of the well-to-do Romans for statuary, and for plastic art generally. That predilection of theirs is, as we saw, well illustrated by Cicero. Even in Sulla's time [3] statuary was an almost indispensable element in the adornment of a rich Roman house. Horace speaks [4] of the craze of Damasippus for purchasing old statues. Naturally the works of the great Greek artists appealed most, even to those who had no very high appreciation of their excellence. The desire to possess a statue by Polycletus or Praxiteles,[5] or a bronze figure from the hands of Myron might be paralleled by the desire of some of the rich in our own day for a Raphael, a Titian, or a Corot. The price of originals would be prohibitive to the ordinary man, so that their possession can have been the privilege of only a select few. We may remember the astonishment expressed by Cicero [6] at the ridiculously small price (1600 sesterces) paid by Verres for a Cupid by Praxiteles. Horace on one occasion [7] laments that he is not rich enough to send some work by Scopas as a present to a friend. The occasion was probably the Saturnalia, when it was customary [8] at Rome for friends to exchange presents, which often took the form of

---

[1] Hor. Sat. I. ii. 114 ; Odes I. xxxi. 10.
[2] Tac. Annals, ii. 33 ; cf. iii. 53.
[3] Friedländer, vol. ii. p. 263.   [4] Sat. II. iii. 64.
[5] Cic. Paradoxa, v. 37 ; De Signis. ii. 4 ; vi. 12 ; Varro, R.R. III. ii. 5 ; Suet. J. Cæsar, 47.
[6] De Signis. vi. 12.   [7] Odes, IV. viii. 5.
[8] Suet. Oct. 75 ; Claudius, 5 ; Friedländer, vol. ii. p. 270.

little statues. These, we may presume, would frequently be copies of great originals. There is abundant evidence [1] of the great artistic industry that prevailed at Rome, especially under the Empire, an industry, which diffused its influence over the vast world under Roman sway. It was natural enough for people to desire copies [2] of such works as the Discobolus of Myron, the Diadumenos of Polycletus, or the Cnidian Venus of Praxiteles. The smaller copies at least of such works would probably be cheap, as there were numerous associations [3] in Rome, composed for the most part of slaves, engaged in their production.

The poet has but few references [4] to Painting, but the elaborate comparison he institutes between Poetry and Painting at the opening [5] of the Ars Poetica shows his acquaintance with the art. His slave Davus reproves him [6] for losing himself in admiration of a picture by Pausias,[7] a native of Sicyon, who (c. 370 B.C.) first became distinguished as a painter of encaustic [8] pictures, executed, according to Pliny, on either wood or ivory. The Romans had early manifested [9] an interest in the art of Painting, and as far back as 304 B.C. Fabius, who in consequence had received the cognomen " Pictor," had adorned with frescoes the walls of the temple of Salus. They were especially fond of historical paintings,[10]

[1] Friedländer, vol. ii. pp. 301 *et seq.*, 314 ; cf. Hor. A.P. 32.

[2] For the larger copies of these works, cf. Gardner, " Six Greek Sculptors," pp. 63, 124, 152.

[3] Inscriptions afford evidence of artistic industry at Rome and elsewhere in the Empire; cf. Dessau, " Inscriptiones Selectae," vol. ii. pt. 2, pp. 758, 809-15.

[4] Odes, IV. viii. 6 ; Ep. I. ii. 52 ; II. i. 239 ; ii. 180.

[5] Cf. A.P. 361.   [6] Sat. II. vii. 95.

[7] Pliny, N.H. xxxv. 40-1 ; cf. Varro, R.R. III. xvii. 4.

[8] Martial, Ep. iv. 47.

[9] For the history of Painting in Italy, *vide* Pliny, N.H. xxxv. 7 *et seq.* ; Stuart Jones, op. cit. p. 398 *et seq.* ; Friedländer, vol. ii. pp. 267 *et seq.*, 323 ; Walters, op. cit. c. v.

[10] Livy, xxiv. xvi. 19.

and had many pictures painted to celebrate their triumphs. But a taste for other subjects soon developed, and we find Augustus [1] dedicating a picture of Venus Anadyomene in the temple of Divus Julius, and two scenes from the life of Alexander in his own Forum. Paintings, too, became an almost necessary adjunct in the decoration of a rich private dwelling, and we find provision made by Vitruvius [2] for a Pinacotheca in his plan of the Roman house. Wall-painting was already well developed in Italy by the end of the Republic. The discoveries at Pompeii have made it possible to trace its development [3] from the beginning of the first century B.C. to the Flavian period. This form of Painting became only gradually perfected. It was first employed to imitate [4] various kinds of marbles, then to execute figure-subjects, most frequently taken from Greek mythology, and also landscape scenes. Pliny speaks [5] of a certain Ludius, who in the reign of Augustus, was the first to adorn walls with elaborate landscape scenes, and scenes representing many of the occupations of rustic life. The paintings [6] at Pompeii, as well as those in the house of Livia on the Palatine, are living monuments of the excellence attained in Italy in the art of wall-painting. We know, too, that it was not uncommon [7] at Rome for one who had escaped shipwreck to have the scene of his escape painted (generally on wood), and hung up as an ex-voto offering at the shrine of some deity.

Horace touches on several other points in the furniture of the house, which are indications of the extravagance of his contemporaries. In describing the dinner at the house of

---

[1] Pliny, N.H. xxxv. 36.

[2] Vitruvius, De Archit. VI. iii. 8 (Scheider's ed.) ; cf. Becker, " Gallus," p. 263 ; Pliny, N.H. xxxv. 2 (there quoted).

[3] Cf. Stuart Jones, p. 399 *et seq.* for the various styles of decoration.

[4] Vitruvius, vii.   [5] N.H. xxxv. 37.

[6] *Vide* Stuart Jones, p. 402 ; Walters, op. cit. p. 94, for illustrations.

[7] Hor. Sat. II. i. 33 ; Odes, I. v. 13 ; A.P. 20 ; cf. Juv. Sat. xii. 27.

Nasidienus, Horace speaks [1] of his table of maple-wood, a
material that was highly prized by the Ancients, and in fine-
ness [2] (*subtilitas*) ranked next in their eyes to citrus-wood.[3]
In tables of citrus-wood the leaf consisted of a single piece,
and rested frequently on a single column of ivory. Cicero
paid a million sesterces for a table of this kind, and in general
the extravagance [4] of the Ancients in their tables was very
remarkable.   Our poet speaks [5] also of ivory couches being
used in the houses of the rich, by which he apparently means
couches not wholly of ivory but inlaid with that material.   On
the couches were spread coverlets [6] dyed in various rich colours,
especially purple and saffron.   Cicero describes [7] for us how
the simplicity of Tubero, who had his couches covered only
with the skins of kids, caused annoyance among the guests he
had invited to his house.   Horace refers [8] also to the hangings
(*aulaea*), probably often of tapestry,[9] which covered the walls
of the triclinium, and were regarded as a sign of wealth in the
owner of the house.   It is possible that the *aulaea*, mentioned
in his description of the dinner given by Nasidienus, may have
hung from the ceiling of the triclinium as a kind of awning.
At any rate these hangings had gathered a quantity of dust in
their folds, and their fall was attended with disastrous consequences.

Horace has many references that throw some light on the
question of personal luxury in his day.   He speaks [10] of the

[1] Sat. II. viii. 10.   [2] Pliny, N.H. xvi. 26.

[3] Cic. De Signis. xvii. 37 ; Varro, R.R. III. ii. 4.

[4] *Vide* Becker, " Gallus," p. 294, for numerous examples.

[5] Sat. II. vi. 103 ; Odes, I. xxxi. 6 ; cf. Macrob. Sat. III. xiii. 11 ; Apul.
Met. x. 34.

[6] Hor. Sat. II. iv. 84 ; vi. 103 ; Odes, III. xxix. 15 ; Ep. I. v. 21 ; cf.
Cic. De Signis. xxvi. 58 ; Catullus, lxi. 168 ; Virg. Georgic, ii. 506.

[7] Pro Mur. 36.

[8] Sat. II. viii. 54 ; Odes, III. xxix. 15.

[9] Prop. II. xxxii. 12, " aulaea Attalica " ; cf. Cic. De Signis. xii. 27.

[10] Odes, II. xvi. 35 ; cf. Epode II. ii. 181 ; Epode xii. 21 ; Odes, III. i. 42 ;
Tib. II. iii. 58.

rich man, who is clothed in woollen garments dyed (twice) with African purple, a dye produced[1] in the island of Meninx, and derived from the African murex.   He refers also to purple garments from Laconia,[2] and to purple dyes from Tarentum[3] and Aquinum.[4]   But none of these was so highly prized in antiquity as the purple of Tyre or Sidon,[5] one pound of Tyrian purple wool, stained twice through, costing over a thousand denarii.[6]   The privilege of wearing genuine purple had been confined originally to magistrates, senators, and knights, but the practice in course of time became so common that Julius Cæsar found it necessary to forbid[7] the use of purple garments to all except persons of a certain age and position, and even for these their use was restricted to certain days.   The Romans seem to have been as fond of bright colours as many of the Italians are at the present day.   The toga of the men was white,[8] but the women seem to have contracted[9] early a taste for brilliant colours.   We hear of purple, green, violet, scarlet, saffron, and hyacinth being worn by them, and these fashions became prevalent also in course of time among Roman dandies.

Horace speaks, too,[10] of the use of "Coae vestes," garments of silk from the island of Cos, which were commonly worn by

---

[1] *Vide* Pliny, N.H. ix. 60 *et seq.* for the history of the use of purple at Rome, cf. Stuart Jones, op. cit. p. 231.

[2] Odes, II. xviii. 7.   [3] Ep. II. i. 207.   [4] *Ibid.* I. x. 27.

[5] *Ibid.* vi. 18; x. 26; cf. Prop. II. xvi. 55; III. xiv. 27; Tib. II. iv. 28; III. viii. 17; Ovid, Ars Am. ii. 293; iii. 152; Macrob. Sat. II. iv. 14.

[6] Pliny, N.H. ix. 63; cf. Friedländer, op. cit. vol. ii. p. 175.

[7] Suet. J. Cæsar, 43; Dio, xlix. 16. Possibly the prohibition applied only to the genuine (Tyrian) purple; cf. Becker, "Gallus," p. 447; Cic. Pro Coelio, 30 (there quoted).

[8] The colour usually worn, too, by matrons; cf. Hor. Sat. I. ii. 36.

[9] Ovid, Ars Am. iii. 155 *et seq.*; Petron. Satyr, 67; Becker, "Gallus," p. 444; Friedländer, vol. ii. p. 175.

[10] Sat. I. ii. 101; Odes, IV. xiii. 13; Prop. I. ii. 2; II. i. 5; IV. ii. 23; Tib. II. iii. 53; iv. 29; Ovid, Ars Am. ii. 294; Martial, viii. 68, 7.

courtesans. The Coan silk was distinguished by a certain gloss [1] and transparency of its own, but it, as well as the silk which the Romans imported from Assyria, was considered inferior [2] to the true "Serica vestis" which came from China, though the secret of its origin from the silk-worm was for long unknown to the Romans. Silk garments were at first worn [3] only by women, but here again, we find men in course of time succumbing to the fashion. Tiberius was forced to forbid [4] their use to men during his reign, while a feature of the extravagance of Caligula [5] was the silk garments which he wore. It is probable that men wore not whole-silk garments (*holoserica*), but a mixture of silk and linen (*subserica*), as Heliogabalus is mentioned by his biographer [6] as having been the first among Roman men to wear a garment of pure silk.

The taste for precious stones was already well developed among the Romans in the time of Augustus. According to Pliny,[7] the diamond (*adamas*) ranked highest of all in antiquity, while pearls came next in value, and were especially worn in ear-rings by the Roman ladies. Julius Cæsar, when in power, had to restrict [8] the use of pearls, though Suetonius [9] tells us that the belief was held by some that his chief motive in invading Britain was the hope of getting pearls there. He once [10] bought a pearl costing six million sesterces for Servilia, the mother of Marcus Brutus. Horace [11] tells the story of the

---

[1] Persius, v. 135, " lubrica Coa ".

[2] Stuart Jones, op. cit. p. 319; Friedländer, vol. ii. p. 173; Ovid, Am. I. xii. 6.

[3] Becker, " Gallus," p. 442; Dio, xliii. 24 (there quoted).

[4] Tac. Annals, iii. 53.   [5] Suet. Gaius, 52.

[6] Becker, " Gallus," p. 442; Lampridius, Sev. Alex. 26 (there quoted).

[7] N.H. xxxvii. 15.   [8] Suet. J. Cæsar, 43.

[9] *Ibid.* 47. The British pearls (see Pliny) were " parvae et decolores," N.H. ix. 57; cf. Tac. Agric. 12.

[10] Suet. J. Cæsar, 50.

[11] Sat. II. iii. 239; cf. Pliny, N.H. ix. 59. A similar story is told of Cleopatra, Macrob. Sat. III. xvii.

son of the tragic actor Æsopus, who took a pearl from the ear of Metella, and dissolving it in vinegar, drank it in order to swallow a million sesterces at a draught.   It is probable that the use of pearls [1] spread rapidly after the conquest of Alexandria, when the pearl fisheries of the Persian Gulf and the Indian Ocean could be exploited in the Roman interest.   Besides the pearl, Horace [2] mentions by name only the emerald, which Pliny [3] ranks highest after the diamond and the pearl. Pliny mentions as many as twelve different species of emerald, but assigns the palm to those found in Scythia.   Next in value came the beryl and the opal.   Pliny [4] says that the hierarchy of stones, as arranged by him, was based principally on the authority of the ladies (*mulierum maxime senatusconsulto*). Horace at times [5] makes but a general reference to such forms of extravagance.   When he is condemning Roman luxury, he appeals [6] to his countrymen to send their " gems and precious stones " as a gift to the Capitol, or to cast them into the nearest sea, here making a distinction between stones that were graven, and those that were ungraven.   The gem or engraved stone was either an *intaglio*, in which the design was engraved below the surface, or a *cameo*, in which the design was in low relief. The former was often used in signet rings by the Romans, who had at first used iron rings and later gold rings for their seals.[7] The sardonyx was the stone most commonly used in signets of Republican date.   Portraiture on signet gems became common

---

[1] Hor. Ep. I. vi. 6; Ovid, Ars Am. iii. 112; cf. Tib. II. ii. 15 ; III. ix. 20.   Pliny, N.H. ix. 54, deals fully with the history of the pearl in ancient times ; cf. Macrob. Sat. II. iv. 12 ; Friedländer, vol. ii. p. 180 ; Stuart Jones, op. cit. p. 319 ; Dessau, op. cit. vol. ii. 2, p. 802 (7603).

[2] Sat. I. ii. 80 ; cf. Tib. II. iv. 27 ; Prop. II. xvi. 43.

[3] N.H. xxxvii. 16.   [4] *Ibid.* 23.

[5] Odes, III. xvi. 7 ; IV. xiii. 13 ; Ep. I. vi. 17 ; II. ii. 180 ; cf. Prop. I. xv. 7 ; Ovid, Ars Am. I. 237 ; Am. I. viii. 27 ; Martial, xi. 50, 4.

[6] Odes, III. xxiv. 48.

[7] On the Roman use of seals, *vide* Pliny, N.H. xxxvii. 4 ; on rings, *ibid.* xxxiii. 6 ; cf. Macrob. Sat. VII. xiii. 11 *et seq.* ; Stuart Jones, op. cit. p. 420.

from the time of Alexander the Great, and this art was increasingly developed with the invention of the cameo. Some of
the extant specimens like the Vienna cameo,[1] or the "Grande
Camée de France " help us to realize the perfection, which the
art of gem-engraving had reached among the Ancients. The
Romans displayed a passion for gem-collecting as early as the
last century of the Republic. Pompey [2] carried off the fine
collection (*dactyliotheca*) of Mithridates of Pontus, and Julius
Cæsar, who was an enthusiastic collector,[3] dedicated no less
than six collections of gems in the temple of Venus Genetrix.

Horace has a few references [4] to the use of scents and
cosmetics among his contemporaries, but other Augustan poets,
like Propertius and Ovid, make it clear that these articles were
in high favour, especially among the Roman ladies. Ovid [5]
gives a vivid picture of the various devices (*medicamina formae*),
which the ladies of his time employed to assist the shortcom-
ings of Nature. The East [6] was constantly pouring its treasures
into Rome, and innumerable articles of personal luxury could
be purchased in the shops along the Via Sacra,[7] and in the
Vicus Tuscus.[8] Propertius speaks of the myrrh of Orontes,[9] and
the scents that come from Arabia.[10] Horace refers to the use of
Syrian ointment [11] and Persian nard [12] as a sign of extravagance,

---

[1] *Vide* Stuart Jones, op. cit. p. 418 *et seq.*; Walters, op. cit. p. 115 *et
seq.* for illustrations.

[2] Pliny, N.H. xxxvii. 5.   [3] Suet. J. Cæsar, 47.

[4] Odes, I. v. 2 ; II. iii. 13 ; vii. 23 ; Ep. II. ii. 183 ; cf. Friedländer, op.
cit. vol. ii. p. 183 ; Becker, "Gallus," p. 378.

[5] Ars Am. iii. 145 *et seq.*, 181 *et seq.*; cf. Prop. II. xviii. 23.

[6] Hor. Odes, I. xxxi. 6 ; Tib. III. ii. 24 ; ix. 17 *et seq.* ; Prop. III. xiii. 4
et seq. ; Ovid, Fasti, i. 341 ; Pliny, N.H. xii. 41.

[7] Prop. II. xxiv. 14 ; Ovid, Ars Am. ii. 262 ; cf. Buecheler, " Carmina
Epigraphica," 74 ; Dessau, op. cit. vol. ii. 2, p. 803 (7610).

[8] Hor. Sat. II. iii. 228 ; Ep. II. i. 269 ; cf. Dessau, op. cit. vol. ii. 2, p.
801 (7597).

[9] Prop. I. ii. 3 ; cf. Pliny, N.H. xii. 46.

[10] II. xxix. 17 ; Tib. II. ii. 4 ; Pliny, N.H. xii. 30-3 ; xiii. 2.

[11] Odes, II. vii. 8 ; on *malobathrum* cf. Pliny, N.H. xii. 59 ; xiii. 2. Found
in Syria and Egypt, but the best quality came from India.

[12] Odes, III. i. 44 ; cf. Epode xiii. 8 ; Ovid, Fasti, i. 341.

and again he invites a friend to a carousal, in which they are to drink with their locks anointed with Assyrian nard.[1] Pliny[2] regards the use of unguents as having first originated among the Persians. The custom of using them probably became fashionable in Rome about the time of the Roman wars in the East, and their use was forbidden (188 B.C.) after the war with Antiochus. Pliny condemns the folly of their indiscriminate use in his own day. Pearls and gems you can leave to your heirs, he says, but the value of unguents is purely fleeting (*suis moriuntur horis*).

It is only natural to expect that, with the growth of wealth and extravagance at Rome, luxury would make itself felt especially as regards the table. This was, long before Horace's time, a characteristic of Roman life. One cannot of course base an argument on the many references[3] in Plautus to such a form of luxury, as the dramatist was probably following close upon his Greek originals, not reflecting Roman conditions. There is a satire by Ennius, entitled Phagetica,[4] which seems to have dealt with some phases of this extravagance. However, in this department again, the Romans learnt their lesson most thoroughly in the East. The professional cook[5] began to be held in honour among the Romans, and, though many sumptuary laws[6] were passed to restrain this, as well as other kinds of extravagance, it seems to have grown to an enormous

---

[1] Odes, II. xi. 16 (Assyrian = Syrian); cf. Odes, IV. xii. 17; Pliny, N.H. xii. 26; Petron. Satyr. 78.

[2] N.H. xiii. 1; on their use in Rome, xiii. 4. For their use on the dead, cf. Tib. III. ii. 23 *et seq.*; Ovid, Tristia, III. iii. 69; Petron. Satyr. 78.

[3] Menæchmi, I. iii. 26 *et seq.*; Capt. IV. ii. 67 *et seq.*; Trin. II. iv. 6; cf. Ter. Eun. 256 *et seq.*

[4] Or "Hedyphagetica"; cf. Apuleius, Apologia, xxxix. 6, and Butler and Owen, ad loc.

[5] Livy, xxix. 6; Pliny, N.H. ix. 31; xviii. 28; Friedländer, op. cit. vol. ii. p. 14.

[6] *Vide* Macrob. Sat. III. xvii. for a list of sumptuary laws beginning with the Lex Orchia in the time of Cato the Censor; cf. Gellius, N.A. II. xxiv.; Livy, xxxiv. 1; Suet. J. Cæsar, 43.

extent by the middle of the last century of the Republic. The
strictures of Sallust on Metellus Pius,[1] and the menu of the
pontifical dinner preserved by Macrobius,[2] show what that
age was capable of in the luxury of the table. Varro, who so
strongly condemns[3] the departure of his countrymen from
the old Roman simplicity, still, practical man that he was,
shows how profitable is the cultivation of dainties for the table.
The Third Book in particular of the "Res Rusticae" is a useful
commentary on the various passages in Horace dealing with
the tastes of the Roman epicures. Varro tells us[4] of a villa
in which the aviary brought its owner 60,000 sesterces in
a single year, while M. Aufidius Lurco[5] made more than
that sum annually in the fattening of peacocks alone. By
the end of the Republic, many dainties from foreign lands had
become acclimatized in Italy.[6] The peacock first made its
appearance at a dinner[7] given by the orator Hortensius to
celebrate his election as augur. Varro gives instructions[8] for
the rearing of the guinea-hen (*gallina Numidica*), and of
special breeds of hares[9] from Spain and Gaul, and also for
the cultivation of snails[10] from Illyricum and Africa. In the
fragment of a satire "Περὶ ἐδεσμάτων," preserved by Gellius,[11]
he speaks of the Phrygian heathcock, cranes from Melos, kid
from Ambracia as among the delicacies of the Roman table.
Fish seems to have formed part of every dinner[12] at Rome
with any pretensions to elegance, and here again the wealthy

[1] Quoted by Macrob. Sat. III. xiii. 6.
[2] *Ibid.* xiii. 11.   [3] R.R. III. ii. 16.
[4] *Ibid.* 14; cf. iv. 2; Pliny, N.H. x. 72 on aviaries.
[5] R.R. III. vi. 1; Pliny, N.H. x. 23.
[6] Friedländer, op. cit. vol. ii. p. 165 *et seq.*
[7] Varro, R.R. III. vi. 6, 3; cf. Pliny, N.H. x. 23; Hor. Sat. I. ii. 116;
II. ii. 23.
[8] R.R. III. ix. 17; Pliny, N.H. x. 67.   [9] R.R. III. xii. 6.
[10] *Ibid.* xiv. 4; cf. Pliny, N.H. x. 82.
[11] N.A. VII. xvi.; cf. Martial, x. 48, 14; Juv. Sat. xi. 66; Petr. Satyr. 119.
[12] Hor. Sat. II. ii.; Ep. I. xv. 23; cf. Pliny, N.H. ix. 53.

Romans went far afield to satisfy their tastes. Varro has an interesting chapter,[1] in which he gives elaborate instructions for the construction and care of fish-ponds, both of fresh and salt-water, though those of salt-water are expensive to stock and maintain. The size of these fish-ponds, often "more extensive than the Lucrine Lake,"[2] is regarded by Horace as one of the scandals of his time. Sergius Orata derived[3] his cognomen from the cultivation of gold-fish, and had also the distinction of being the first to lay down oyster-beds[4] at Baiae. He was a connoisseur in the matter of fish, and gave it as his judgment that the best oysters were the Lucrine, that the best turbot were to be found at Ravenna, the best sturgeon at Rhodes, and the best lampreys in the waters round Sicily. Licinius Murena received his cognomen from his success in cultivating lampreys,[5] always a favourite dish with the Romans. Varro, in the fragment already referred to, mentions various kinds of fish which appealed to Roman epicures, among them the sturgeon from Rhodes, the scallop from Chios, and the scar from Cilicia. Pliny[6] gives us a vast amount of miscellaneous information about the fish in use among the Romans, and tells us[7] that in his own day the scar was the most highly prized of all, but among the *Ancients* the sturgeon.[8] The mullet[9] was also in high favour, especially the bearded mullet, and we hear of three mullets being sold[10] in the reign of Tiberius for the enormous sum of 30,000

[1] R.R. III. xvii.

[2] Odes, II. xv. 2; cf. Sat. II. v. 44; Tib. II. iii. 45; Varro, R.R. III. iii. 10; xvii. 5; Macrob. Sat. III. xv.; Stuart Jones, op. cit. p. 314.

[3] Varro, R.R. III. iii. 10; Pliny, N.H. ix. 79.

[4] Macrob. Sat. II. xi.

[5] Pliny, N.H. ix. 39, 81; cf. Cic. Paradoxa, v. 37; Hor. Sat. II. viii. 42; Martial, x. 30, 23; Macrob. Sat. III. xv.

[6] N.H. ix. *passim*.   [7] *Ibid.* 29.

[8] *Ibid.* 27-8; cf. Hor. Sat. II. ii. 47; Macrob. Sat. III. xvi.

[9] Varro, R.R. III. xvii. 7; Hor. Sat. II. ii. 33; Pliny, N.H. ix. 30; Juv. Sat. iv. 15; Macrob. Sat. III. xvi. 9.

[10] Suet. Tib. 34.

sesterces. The Romans, in their quest for novelties, went as far as the Black Sea,[1] which was then a well-known fishing centre, and was especially noted for its tunny-fish.

By the time of Horace many fruits from other lands were naturalized in Italy.[2]   The pomegranate[3] (*malum puni-cum*) was known in Cato's time, while the cherry[4] was introduced by Lucullus from Cerasus in Pontus (73 B.C.).   The quince-apple[5] (*cotonea*, which came from Crete), the date[6] and the fig were common in Varro's day.   The best dates were derived originally from Syria[7] and Egypt, while Varro mentions[8] several species of figs, the Chian, Chalcidian, Lydian, and African, that were grown successfully in his time.   The chestnut, which the Romans got from Sardinia,[9] was known to Virgil, while the plum,[10] which found its way to Italy from Damascus, was acclimatized when Pliny was writing his "Natural History".   It is from him[11] we can derive most information about the various fruits which the Romans received from foreign lands, and gave a home to in their own.

When we come to estimate the strictures of Horace upon the luxury of the table in his day, we must remember that the poet was perforce given to a simple diet for reasons of health, and it is from that point of view especially that he sets forth its advantages.[12]   Moreover, he is at times inclined to contrast[13] the

---

[1] Persius, Sat. v. 134 ; Pliny, N.H. ix. 18 *et seq.*

[2] Friedländer, op. cit. vol. ii. pp. 166-7.

[3] Pliny, N.H. xv. 11 ; cf. Varro, R.R. i. 59, 3.

[4] Pliny, N.H. xii. 7 ; xv. 30 ; cf. Keightley, "Flora Vergiliana".

[5] Varro, R.R. i. 59, 1 ; cf. Prop. III. xiii. 27 ; Pliny, N.H. xv. 10 ; Martial, xiii. 24 ; Macrob. Sat. III. xix. 2.

[6] Varro, i. 67.

[7] Pliny, xv. 34 ; Martial, xiii. 27.

[8] R.R. i. 41, 6 ; Pliny, N.H. xv. 19 ; Martial, xiii. 23 ; Macrob. Sat. III. xx.

[9] Pliny, N.H. xv. 25.   [10] *Ibid.* xv. 12 ; Martial, xiii. 29.

[11] N.H. xv. *passim.*

[12] Sat. II. ii. 1 *et seq.*, 70 *et seq.* ; Odes, I. xxxi. 15 ; Ep. I. v. 2.

[13] Sat. II. vii. 23.

growing luxury of his own age with the simplicity of an earlier
Rome, to the great disadvantage of the former.   Again, in the
picture he draws for us of the dinner of Nasidienus,[1] it is as
much the vulgarity of the host, a *nouveau riche*, as the luxury
of the meal that he satirizes.   Nasidienus insisted on pointing
out the merits of each dish, and was assisted in this by Nomentanus, whose function it was to call the attention of the guests
to any hidden excellence that might have escaped their notice.
It is probable that such acts of extravagance as that of the sons
of Q. Arrius, who dined on nightingales' tongues,[2] were very
rare.   Still, for all this, the luxury of the table, which Horace
depicts for us, was a big advance on the Roman standard of living of even the previous century, and was wholly unknown to the
Romans of the early Republic.   The poet directs his attacks
especially on certain refinements of luxury, that characterized
the tastes of the epicures of his day.   The material, however,
for most of the dishes which Horace mentions, came from
Italy itself, though, with all that Italy could then produce [3] for
the service of the table, there was ample room for the indulgence of luxurious tastes.   Horace mentions comparatively few
specifically foreign delicacies in the pictures of extravagance
that he gives us in his Satires, though many such delicacies
must have been in favour [4] with the choice livers of that time.
Many, of course, of the dainties enumerated by the poet were
originally alien to Italy, but had become naturalized before the
Augustan Age.   He mentions only a few Greek wines [5] as in
use among his countrymen.   The Chian was especially highly
prized,[6] though Nasidienus served up Chian that was "maris
expers," [7] probably an Italian wine similar in flavour to the

[1] Sat. II. viii.   [2] *Ibid.* iii. 243.
[3] Varro, R.R. I. ii. 6; Hor. Odes, II. vi. 13 *et seq.*; Macrob. Sat. III.
xvi. 12.
[4] Hor. Epode ii. 50 *et seq.*; Sat. II. ii. 22.
[5] Sat. I. iv. 29; II. viii. 9; Epode ix. 34; Odes, I. xvii. 21; cf. Odes, I.
xxxvii. 14; cf. Macrob. Sat. III. xvi. 16.
[6] Hor. Sat. I. x. 24; II. iii. 115.   [7] *Ibid.* viii. 15.

genuine Chian.   A wine from Methymna was used [1] as an ingredient in a sauce served up at the dinner of Nasidienus.
Virgil knows [2] of a much greater variety of foreign wines, and
is able to tell of their effects, but he is speaking as a student of
the subject, and we cannot argue from him that all the wines
he mentions were then finding their way to Italy.   Horace
tells us [3] of the use of honey from Hymettus, which with old
Falernian wine was believed to make the best mead.[4]   He
mentions [5] snails from Africa as a special delicacy designed to
refresh the flagging drinker.   He speaks also of a fish-pickle [6]
that came from Byzantium, and of saffron from Cilicia,[7] that
was used for flavouring.   He refers [8] to several kinds of foreign birds and fish that appealed to the tastes of the Roman
epicures.   If the use of delicacies from other lands were the
only criterion of extravagance, Horace would leave the impression that the luxury of the table was not so very extraordinary
in his day.   As far as this phase of Roman extravagance
is concerned, if we were to judge by Horace alone, it would
appear to be merely in its infancy in the Augustan Age, as
compared with the succeeding ages depicted for us by such
authors as the Elder Pliny, Martial, and Columella.   It is
probable, indeed, that the development of Roman commerce
under the Empire, which began after the peace insured by Actium,
led to a constantly increasing inflow of foreign delicacies into
Italy.   Evidence, however, such as Pliny supplies must be
handled with care, as he is a historian, with an eye not merely on
contemporary conditions, but also retrospective in view.   Much
of the material he has gathered would be valid for the reign of

[1] Sat. II. viii. 50.

[2] Georgic, ii. 89 et seq.   Suet. Oct. 77 tells us that Augustus liked
Rhaetian wine best; cf. Pliny, N.H. Bk. xiv. passim.

[3] Sat. II. ii. 15.   [4] Macrob. Sat. VII. xii. 10.   [5] Sat. II. iv. 58.

[6] Sat. II. iv. 66 et seq., used as an ingredient in a sauce; cf. Ibid. viii.
28, 45; Pliny, N.H. ix. 19; Martial, xiii. 102-3.

[7] Sat. II. iv. 68; Pliny, N.H. xxi. 17.

[8] Epode ii. 50 et seq.; Sat. II. ii. 22.

Augustus. How far the importation of foreign delicacies had advanced, when Horace wrote his Satires, we have no means of accurately estimating. If these had been written towards the end of the reign of Augustus instead of in the years round Actium, the poet might possibly have dwelt more on this aspect of Roman luxury. As it is, he directs comparatively little attention to it. His aim was not to give a complete picture of the luxury of the table in his time, but to inveigh against the excessive refinements and fastidiousness of Roman gastronomy, and ridicule the vulgarity of a parvenu like Nasidienus. Even if we were to conclude that the Augustan Age contrasts favourably with later times in the luxury of the table, we shall still have to admit that the extravagance depicted for us by Horace was a very marked advance on the simplicity that characterized Roman life in the days before Asiatic luxury followed in the wake of the victorious armies from the East.

CHAPTER VI.

HORACE AND POPULAR BELIEFS.

WHEN we examine the works of Horace for traces of folk-lore, we must at first confess to a feeling of disappointment. Though he furnishes fairly abundant material, we would naturally expect to find in him a larger element of popular belief and superstition. He was sprung from the common people, and lived among them for many years.[1] He despised, it is true, the Roman mob, and possibly kept aloof from it, but, in strolling[2] nonchalantly through the Roman Forum, the Circus, and the market-place, he must inevitably, with his inquiring mind, have come across many vestiges[3] of strange popular customs and beliefs. When he retired to his Sabine farm, the poet was in still closer touch with the people, as he listened[4] to the "old wives' tales" of Cervius, showed an interest[5] in the details of rustic worship as practised by Phidyle, or joined,[6] as he probably did from the vividness of his description, in the village festival of the Faunalia.

No matter how advanced in culture a community is, one must expect in it survivals of primitive superstitions,[7] and such were not lacking in Ancient Rome. It is clear from many sources[8] that magical practices prevailed in Italy from

---

[1] Odes, III. iv. 6.   [2] Sat. I. vi. 111 *et seq.*   [3] Ep. II. ii. 208 *et seq.*
[4] Sat. II. vi. 77.   [5] Odes, III. xxiii.   [6] *Ibid.* xviii.
[7] Jevons, "The Idea of God," p. 56 *et seq.*; Gomme, "Ethnology in Folk-Lore," c. i.; Bailey, "The Religion of Ancient Rome," pp. 5-6; Murray, "Four Stages of Greek Religion," p. 25 *et seq.*
[8] Cato, De Re R. 70-1; Pliny, N.H. XXX. i. 3-4; Apuleius, Apol. 47; Abt, "Die Antike Zauberei," pp. 83, 266; Toutain, "Les Cultes Païens," vol. ii. pp. 210-12.

very early times, and certain of them, which aimed at the injury of a neighbour, were actually forbidden by the Laws of the Twelve Tables. It is proved[1] also, that at a primitive period, many rites purely magical in their origin became embedded in Roman Religion. There was, however, no coherent system of magic in Italy.[2] It was the Magi of the East (the Persian Empire), that first developed a complete system of magic, based on their ideas of a dualism of the powers of Good and Evil. Their system subsequently became fused[3] with much of the lore of the Chaldæan astrologers. Some of these magical beliefs and practices may have followed in the train of the Eastern Religions, and reached Rome soon after the Roman campaigns in the East. The professional magician naturally arrived in the course of time, and it is against him as well as the "Chaldaei," with whom he is often confounded, that we find a number of repressive laws directed,[4] punishing offenders with death or exile. We may be sure, however, that at all times in Italy many harmless magical practices[5] were in vogue, of which the law took no cognisance.

Horace has left us a few valuable pictures of magic,[6] as practised by Canidia and her sister-witches. The pictures that he draws for us, may be based in some measure upon actual fact, but it is probable that they are highly coloured by the manifest enmity of the poet for Canidia. In ancient times, magicians were credited with the most extraordinary powers,[7] and it was believed that for some of them nothing was im-

[1] Warde Fowler, " The Religious Experience," c. iii.
[2] Cumont, " Les Religions Orientales," p. 225.
[3] *Ibid.* p. 228. On the origin of magic, cf. the opening chapters of Pliny, N.H. xxx.; cf. Theoc. ii. 162, on the Assyrian stranger as teacher of magic.
[4] Tac. Annals, ii. 27, 32; xvi. 30.1.
[5] Toutain, loc. cit. p. 211; Cod. Theod. Lib. ix., Tit. 16, Lex 3 (there quoted).
[6] Sat. I. viii. ; Epodes v., xvii.
[7] Apul. Met. ix. 29 ; Apol. 26.

possible of accomplishment. Their powers[1] extended to
Nature in all its aspects, and by their charms they could sus-
pend its laws, and change its course to subserve their evil
designs. They were able, it was thought, to draw down the
moon from the heavens to render their magic more potent
through its influence, and could compel the stars to descend at
their bidding. Their spells could stay the flow of rivers, make
the sun linger in its course, veil the world in darkness, prolong
night, change the order of the seasons, chain the ocean tides,
or render the sea impassable. At their command rain will fall,
or the earth will be afflicted with a drought, the crops may be
drawn from a neighbour's field, or his land reduced to barren-
ness. They had power over the souls of the dead,[2] whom
they could send as ministers of vengeance against their enemies.
Their power was especially great over their own bodies, which
they could render invisible, or transform, according to their
fancy, into the shape of any animal, or even inanimate object.
They were believed, too, to be able to shorten or extend the
span of human life. But most interesting of all was the belief
in their power to constrain supernatural beings,[3] whether the
gods above or the deities of the under-world, to do their
bidding. They could do violence to them by their charms,
or magic potions, or even by their threats.[4] This aspect of
magic, like so many others, is well illustrated for us by Lucan,[5]
who represents the dread witch Erictho bringing her heaviest
batteries to bear on both supernal and infernal powers, especi-

---

[1] Hor. Epode v. 45; xvii. 4; Tib. I. ü. 41 *et seq.*; viii. 17 *et seq.*; Virg.
Eclog. viii. 71; Ovid, Met. vii. 203; Am. II. i. 23 *et seq.* Seneca, Medea,
753 *et seq.*; Lucan, vi. 443 *et seq.*, 461 *et seq.*; Apul. Met. i. 8-9; ii. 5;
cf. Abt, op. cit. p. 124 *et seq.*, and an interesting passage from Hippo-
crates on the power of the magician there quoted.

[2] Abt, op. cit. p. 133.

[3] *Ibid.* p. 122; cf. Fahz, " De Poetarum Romanorum Doctrina Magica,"
pp. 142, 158 *et seq.*

[4] Fahz, op. cit. p. 160; Papyr Paris, 2902 *et seq.* (there quoted).

[5] Pharsalia, vi. 496, 607, 730 *et seq.*

ally Hecate, whose most cherished secrets she threatens to reveal unless she be subservient to her wishes. Cumont has shown[1] how in circumstances of this kind there is a point of contact between magic and religion. He believes that a magical element can be discovered in primitive Egyptian religion, where the aim of a sacred rite is not so much the supplication of a deity as his constraint. The sacred words of the liturgy are thus a species of incantation, which compel the power to which they are addressed to obey the officiating minister. Sometimes the contrary phenomenon takes place, when the magic formula becomes a prayer of supplication[2] to some supernatural being.

The witches in Horace[3] do not rely merely on the potency of their witchcraft, but invoke those powers of the under-world that are likely to be propitious to them in their dread rites. The magician may at times trust to his own unaided powers, or to the use of instruments that were believed to possess innate magic of their own,[4] but often he calls to his aid certain deities,[5] that were considered to be intimately associated with the working of magic. These were almost invariably chthonic deities,[6] such as Hades, Pluto, Demeter, Persephone, and Hermes Chthonios, though occasionally we find figuring in the Papyri the names of Egyptian deities[7] such as Isis and Osiris, while again mysterious and unintelligible names are often applied to the gods invoked in magic. The magician has power, as I have said, to compel a deity to his service,[8] especially if he is in possession of his name. One

[1] Op. cit. pp. 114, 226. [2] Cumont, op. cit. p. 224.
[3] Sat. I. viii. 33.
[4] Cf. the theory of " Mana," so much discussed by modern writers on magic.
[5] Tib. I. ii. 62; Lucan, vi. 577; Tac. Annals, xvi. 31; Apul. Met. i. 10.
[6] Daremberg and Saglio, Art. " Magia," p. 1512; Abt, op. cit. p. 190; Fahz, op. cit. p. 169.
[7] Toutain, op. cit. vol. ii. p. 216.
[8] Abt, op. cit. p. 119 *et seq.*; Papyr Paris, 185 (there quoted).

of the witches in Horace has recourse merely to an *invocation* [1] of Hecate, who was pre-eminently the favourite deity [2] with workers in magic. She was invoked as the goddess of ghosts [3] (Apuleius calls her "manium potens"), as one who was considered to have special power over the spirits of the dead, [4] whom she could send abroad as ministers of vengeance. In this capacity also, she was naturally believed to have an intimate connection with graveyards. [5] As Trivia she was worshipped as the goddess of cross-roads, [6] where it was thought the spirits of the dead were accustomed to assemble. She was invoked, however, under various titles, and in her case a process of syncretism with other deities went steadily on. Seneca calls her "triformis," [7] as the same goddess was believed to be Luna in heaven, Diana or Trivia upon earth, and Proserpine in the realms of the dead. Abt [8] quotes from the Paris Papyrus a "Εὐχὴ πρὸς Σελήνην," which very clearly illustrates the various forms and titles, under which the goddess was invoked by workers of magic. There she is styled "τριπρόσωπε" and "πολυώνυμε," and, as we know from Theocritus, Simaetha in her distress invokes indifferently [9] Selene, Hecate, or Artemis. The moon was considered to be the abode of spirits, and its influence [10] was regarded as powerful in magic of every kind. In answer to the invocation of the witches in Horace, Hecate

---

[1] Sat. I. viii. 33 ; cf. Apul. Apol. 31. The Greek expression ἐπικαλεῖν occurs frequently in the Papyri.

[2] Seneca, Medea, 840 ; Lucan, vi. 737 ; Eur. Medea, 397 ; Theoph. Char. xvi. ; cf. Fahz, op. cit. pp. 116, 129.

[3] Virg. Æn. vi. 118 ; Seneca, Oed. 569.

[4] Especially the "ἄωροι" and "Βιαιοθάνατοι". Hermes Chthonios held similar sway ; cf. Abt, op. cit. p. 193.

[5] Theoc. ii. 13.

[6] Daremberg and Saglio, p. 1512 ; Papyr Paris, 2722 (there quoted) ; Theoc. ii. 36 ; Tib. I. v. 16.

[7] Medea, 7 ; cf. Hor. Odes, III. xxii. 4 ; Virg. Æn. iv. 511 ; vi. 13 ; Lucan, vi. 700 ; Apul. Met. xi. 2 ; Cat. xxxiv.

[8] Op. cit. p. 200.   [9] Cf. Hor. Epode v. 51 ; xvii. 2-3.

[10] Abt, op. cit. p. 23 ; Norden, Introd. to Æn. vi. p. 22 *et seq.*

comes accompanied by her hounds. The hound[1] and the wolf were animals sacred to this goddess, and at times she herself appears[2] under the form of a hound. The hounds were believed to be the souls of the departed, which accompanied Hecate on her visit to earth. Horace[3] makes the second witch Sagana call the Fury Tisiphone to her aid, which raises the presumption that the images used on the occasion were intended to wreak vengeance on some enemy, or some faithless lover. The Furies were frequently invoked in magic, especially in connection with necromancy.[4]

The names of some of those renowned for magic in antiquity are preserved for us in literature, but among them Medea[5] stands out as a pre-eminently awe-inspiring figure who had fathomed every secret of witchcraft, and as one to whose magic power nothing was impossible. Euripides, in drawing the character of Medea, is rather intent upon depicting the dread anger of the injured wife, but through the atmosphere of tragedy, that hangs over the play from its very opening, he occasionally[6] allows us to catch a glimpse of the witch behind the woman, and leaves us in no doubt about the strange, oriental, uncanny character of that forcible personality. Seneca,[7] on the contrary, is more interested in the witch in Medea, and to heighten the effect, he piles extravagance on extravagance, exhibiting to the full the violence and exaggeration of the rhetorician. There is hardly a species of witchcraft ever known or imagined, which he does not lay to her charge. Medea thus stands out as one of the most clearly defined types of magician, which antiquity could reveal. Her home

[1] Tib. I. ii. 52 ; Theoc. ii. 12 ; Abt, op. cit. p. 202. In Papyr Paris, 2722, she is called " σκυλακάγεια ".

[2] Abt, p. 126 ; Papyr Paris, 1434 (there quoted).

[3] Sat. I. viii. 34; cf. Lucan, vi. 730.   [4] Fahz, op. cit. p. 120.

[5] Hor. Epode iii. 10 ; v. 61 ; Tib. I. ii. 51 ; II. iv. 55 ; Ovid, Ars Am. ii. 101 ; Met. vii. 182 ; Pliny, N.H. xxv. 5 ; Apul. Met. i. 10.

[6] Medea, 385, 395, 717.

[7] Ibid. especially 670 et seq. ; cf. Hor. A.P. 118.

in Colchis[1] became proverbial as a centre of witchcraft, and was believed to possess the most potent herbs that could enter as ingredients into a magic potion. Circe, whose fame had been celebrated by Homer,[2] also figures[3] in Roman literature as another typical worker of magic. Pliny gives[4] us the names of many others, such as Zoroaster, Democritus, Orpheus, and Pythagoras, who were famed among the Ancients for their magical powers.

It is interesting to find, that not only individuals but whole peoples enjoyed a reputation for witchcraft in antiquity. Thessaly was par excellence the land of marvels, and is pictured for us by Apuleius[5] as a country which, by common consent, was regarded as the "birthplace of sorceries and enchantments," where so prevalent was enchantment that the most bizarre and extravagant happenings would not excite wonder. It was famous for its herbs,[6] which were believed to be of special efficacy in magic, and its inhabitants were considered to be skilled botanists,[7] and very expert in their use. The Thessalian[8] witch was renowned for her magical powers, and the aid of her charms and philtres was invoked,[9] particularly in love-magic, both to loose and bind a victim. Greek literature had already done much to spread the fame of Thessalian witchcraft,

---

[1] Hor. Epode v. 24; xvii. 35; Odes, II. xiii. 8; Prop. I. i. 23; II. i. 54; Lucan, vi. 441. The "'Ριζοτόμοι" of Sophocles also dealt with Medea as magician; cf. Abt, p. 172; Macrob. Sat. V. xix. 9.

[2] Odyss. x. 213 et seq.

[3] Hor. Epode xvii. 17; Ep. I. ii. 23; Tib. II. iv. 55; III. vii. 61; Prop. II. i. 53; Ovid, Met. xiv. 405.

[4] N.H. xxx. 7 et seq.; cf. Abt, p. 318; Daremberg and Saglio, p. 1499.

[5] Met. II. i.; cf. Hor. Ep. II. ii. 209; J. E. Harrison, "Themis," p. 81.

[6] Tib. II. iv. 54; Lucan, vi. 438 et seq.

[7] Cumont, op. cit. p. 225.

[8] Hor. Epode v. 45; Prop. III. xxiv. 10; Plautus, Amphit. IV. iii. 9; Pliny, N.H. xxx. 7; cf. Θετταλη of Menander, of which some fragments remain, Abt, p. 171.

[9] Hor. Odes, I. xxvii. 21; Prop. I. v. 6; Lucan, vi. 452; Seneca, Hippolytus, 421; Juv. Sat. vi. 610.

and Horace was evidently following in its footsteps in his reference to the magic of that country. But the poet has a few allusions to his own land, that throw some light on Roman ideas of the magical powers of their neighbours. The idea that other tribes and peoples possess magical powers often lingers among a nation far advanced in religious belief. " In any country, an isolated and outlying race, the lingering survivor of an older nationality, is liable to a reputation for magic." [1] We know that a highly civilised people will often attribute the most extraordinary qualities to their more backward neighbours, and through the mist of legend, that springs up around them, these may often be transformed into the strangest shapes.[2] Horace attributes magical powers to many of the Italian tribes. It is hardly credible that such a belief continued to exist among educated Romans, when the more intimate fusion of the Italian peoples had been effected after the Social War, but it may have lingered in Horace's day among the unenlightened, and at any rate it was picturesque enough to appeal to the imagination of a poet. Horace's own future had been foretold [3] in his boyhood by a Sabellian fortune-teller, and, in after years, Sabellian charms [4] were powerful enough to harass his soul. The Pelignians,[5] too, enjoyed a reputation for witchcraft, but it was the Marsi [6] especially, that stood in greatest repute as workers of magic. These hardy mountaineers [7] had been prominent in resisting the extension of Roman power, and probably lived in comparative isolation from Roman influence. Their isolation in part, and in part a certain tribal hatred would account for the persistent belief in their magical powers. Cicero refers [8] to them as diviners of the future. In their land also, herbs [9]

---

[1] Jevons, " Introduction to the History of Religion," p. 36; Gomme, op. cit. c. iii. ; Daremberg and Saglio, p. 1495.

[2] Ridgeway, " The Origin of Tragedy," p. 15, on Sileni and Centaurs.

[3] Sat. I. ix. 29.   [4] Epode xvii. 28.   [5] *Ibid.* 60.

[6] Granger, " The Worship of the Romans," p. 162.

[7] Hor. Epode xvi. 3; Odes, II. xx. 17; Virg. Georgic, ii. 167.

[8] De Div. i. 58.   [9] Virg. Æn. vii. 758.

of wonderful potency were believed to grow, and their spells [1]
were famed for their efficacy in procuring the injury of an
enemy, as well as in love-magic. The Marsi were considered
moreover to be endowed with a strange power against serpents,[2]
whose bite they could render innocuous, or whose bodies they
could burst asunder by the force of their charms.

When Horace describes for us the witchcraft of Canidia and
her companions, his first account [3] is put into the mouth of the
god Priapus, who claims to have witnessed their nocturnal
rites. The poet places the witches on fitting ground, in laying
the scene of their activities on the Esquiline,[4] a spot which
had formerly been a burial-place for the poor, but had now
been transformed into a public garden, through the munificence
of Mæcenas. Graveyards [5] have always been the favourite
hunting-ground of witches. They, as well as cross-roads, were
regarded as the abode of spirits and as impure, and magic has
to do essentially with the impure and the unnatural.[6] In
graveyards especially, witches believe that they can count on
the secrecy [7] indispensable to their impious rites. They come
there in the darkness of night,[8] as the light of day, and the
Powers [9] of light can counteract their evil designs. Sometimes,
workers of magic go the length of creating artificial darkness.[10]

---

[1] Hor. Epode v. 76; cf. Epode xvii. 29; Ovid, Ars Am. ii. 102 on
"Marsa nenia"; Virg. Æn. vii. 750 et seq.

[2] Pliny, N.H. xxviii. 4; Lucilius, xx. 5 (Gerlach).

[3] Sat. I. viii.

[4] Vide Stuart Jones, "Classical Rome," p. 221; cf. Lanciani, "Ancient
Rome," p. 64 et seq. on the "puticuli" discovered on the Esquiline; cf.
Hor. Epode v. 100.

[5] Ibid. 17; xvii. 47; Prop. III. vi. 29; Lucan, vi. 511; Apul. Met. i.
10; ibid. ii. 5.

[6] Daremberg and Saglio, p. 1514.

[7] Hor. Epode v. 52; xvii. 56; Pliny, N.H. xxx. 7; Abt, op. cit. p. 286.

[8] Hor. Sat. I. viii. 21; Epode v. 51; Tib. I. v. 16; Ovid, Met. vii. 192;
Apul. Met. iii. 16; cf. Abt, p. 269, for many references to the Magic
Papyri.

[9] Lucan, vi. 645, 743.　　　　　　　　　[10] Abt, p. 270.

Canidia is represented as coming to the Esquiline to gather the bones of the dead. She and her companions must have had to dig for them, as Horace dwells upon the change, wrought by the improvements of Mæcenas, from the old days, when the whitening bones of many of the poor, that had been carelessly interred, lay strewn around and disfigured the whole area. Human remains were a favourite instrument of witch-craft, particularly such as was designed to inflict injury on another. What had once been in contact with death [1] was potent, on the principle underlying sympathetic magic, to pro-duce death in others, so that even a brand [2] snatched from the pyre, on which a dead body had been burnt, was prized by workers of magic. Much more efficacious, of course, were the actual remains of the dead, [3] especially those who had perished by suicide, or by any other form of violent death. [4] From the remains of the dead, certain figures [5] used in vengeance-magic, as we might call it, were sometimes fashioned, and, as we shall see, portions of a dead body were often employed in concocting a love-potion.

Canidia and her companions came to the Esquiline, not only to procure the remains of the dead, but also to gather herbs, [6] which have always figured largely [7] in the stock and trade of witchcraft. The herbs of certain countries were celebrated, in literature at least, as endowed with special potency in magic, but in every country herbs could be discovered, that

[1] Hor. Epode v. 17; Pliny, N.H. xxviii. 4-6; Daremberg and Saglio, p. 1507.

[2] Apul. Apol. 8; Fahz, op. cit. p. 148; Seneca, Oed. 550 *et seq.* (there quoted); Abt, p. 203.

[3] Ovid, Heroides, vi. 90; Lucan, vi. 533; Apul. Met. ii. 20, iii. 17.

[4] Lucan, vi. 561; Apul. Apol. 34; Tac. Annals, ii. 69: Daremberg and Saglio, p. 1512; Fahz, op. cit. pp. 132, 167; Abt, p. 215; Papyr Paris, 1877 (there quoted).

[5] Cf. the German "Rachepuppe".   [6] Hor. Sat. l. viii. 22.

[7] Hor. Epode v. 67; Ovid, Ars Am. ii. 101; Met. vii. 226; Virg. Georgic, ii. 129; Tib. I. viii. 7; Prop. I. xii. 10; IV. v. 11; Apul. Apol. 30; Leland, " Etruscan Roman Remains," p. 58.

would serve the purpose of the magician. They were usually cut with a bronze knife,[1] as bronze was looked upon as prophylactic, and as efficacious in frightening away any evil spirits that might be likely to confound the task of the magician. Horace adds an interesting touch when he describes Canidia as coming to gather herbs by the light of the moon, as the moon was believed to increase the magic power[2] of plants. Even in modern times,[3] the healing power of plants is regarded by the superstitious as dependent on the time at which they are gathered, and herein lies a point of contact between magic and popular medicine, which Pliny[4] was not slow to notice. But, in all ages,[5] the influence of the moon on magical operations has been considered as almost impossible to exaggerate. We have seen how the aid of the Moon-Goddess is frequently invoked by the magician. We find, too, frequent references[6] in Ancient Literature to the power of witches to draw the moon down from the heavens to render its influence still more potent in their impious work. The Moon was the great ally of the magician, who could let loose her vengeance on one whom he sought to injure, by merely proclaiming him an enemy of the goddess.[7] The influence of certain of the planets[8] also had its importance for the magician, and thus Astrology and Magic were able to join

---

[1] Virg. Æn. iv. 513; Tib. I. viii. 23; Macrob. Sat. V. xix. 9 et seq.; Abt, pp. 159-60, on the use of bronze in magic; Theoc. ii. 36 (there quoted).

[2] Lucan, vi. 505, 669; Apul. Apol. 30; Abt, p. 161; Papyr Paris, 2967 et seq. (there quoted); Fahz, op. cit. p. 153.

[3] Burne, "The Handbook of Folk-lore," p. 158.

[4] N.H. XXX. i. 2.

[5] Frazer, "The Golden Bough" (3rd ed.), vol. i. p. 165.

[6] Hor. Epode v. 45; xvii. 78; Virg. Eclog. viii. 69; Tib. I. viii. 21; Prop. I. i. 19; II. xxviii. 37; Ovid, Am. II. i. 23; Apul. Met. i. 3, 8; Theoc. vii. 106; Arist. Clouds, 749 et seq.

[7] For a "διαβολὴ πρὸς Σελήνην," cf. Abt, p. 123; Griffith-Thompson Papyri, p. 145 (there quoted).

[8] Seneca, Medea, 695 et seq.; Daremberg and Saglio, p. 1507.

hands. This will account for the frequent use of astrological
signs in the magical formulæ that have been preserved to us.

From poetic literature at least, we can derive very few names
of plants employed in magic, as, naturally, these would have
been carefully guarded from the knowledge of the uninitiated.
The poets usually refer to such plants by the generic name of
"herbae". Writers like Pliny[1] and Theophrastus preserve
the names of many plants so employed, while the names of
many more are to be found in the magical papyri. Some of
these plants were used in distilling magic draughts, especially
love-potions. Some were believed to possess specific properties
for healing, while others, like the olive and laurel, were regarded
as prophylactic[2] in nature. Sulphur[3] and certain spices were
believed, too, to share this latter property, which was attributed
also to several stones and metals.[4] The amethyst was so
called by the Greeks as being a charm against intoxication, while
in modern times amber beads are often worn, not only as a cure
for weak eyes, but as a protection against the evil eye. The
Bulla[5] worn by the Roman boy was carried as an amulet to
ward off from him evil influences of every kind, and hence we
find Canidia and her comrades,[6] before proceeding to their
sacrifice, stripping their boy-victim of the insignia of his boyhood, the Bulla, and the toga praetexta[7] which had probably a
sacred meaning, and was emblematic of the purity and sanctity
of boyhood. These had served to shield him previously
against the machinations of the witches. But many other
things were considered by the Ancients to be apotropaic in

---

[1] N.H., especially Books XXVII., XXX. ; cf. Abt, pp. 163-5.

[2] Virg. Eclog. iv. 62 ; viii. 83 ; Theoc. ii. 23 ; Theop. Char. xvi. ;
Abt, pp. 145, 151 ; Diels, " Sib. Blätter," p. 120; Leland, op. cit. p. 23.

[3] Tib. I. v. 11.

[4] Daremberg and Saglio, p. 1507; Haddon, "Magic and Fetishism,"
pp. 30-1 ; cf. Pliny, N.H. xxxii. 11.

[5] Warde Fowler, "The Religious Experience," p. 60; cf. Haddon,
op. cit. p. 33.

[6] Hor. Epode v. 12.

[7] Warde Fowler, "Classical Review," 1896, pp. 317-19.

their nature, and, among others, the wolf's muzzle. When Canidia and Sagana,[1] at the time they summoned back the shades of the dead, buried in the earth a wolf's beard and a serpent's tooth, their action was probably apotropaic,[2] and designed to prevent their work being brought to nought by hostile spirits, or by the charms of another enchantress. For we meet at times [3] with the conception of a contest of charms and magicians. The charm of a witch is often unable to prevail because its effect is counteracted by the charm of some more powerful worker of magic. Canidia complains that her intended victim has been freed from her own spell by the spell of one more potent than herself, and threatens to prepare a charm, against which no force can countervail. She warns Horace [4] himself that it is useless for him to have consulted "Pelignian hags," and procured a magic-potion from them, as he cannot escape the fate she has destined for him. The "vincula in-cantata,"[5] that fell from the witches' arms in their panic, when their labours were disturbed by the sportive Priapus, were also intended to serve as a prophylactic. I take them to have been strands of wool, possibly parti-coloured, and not unlike the "licia discolora" mentioned by Apuleius.[6] Wool [7] was in itself a prophylactic, but certain colours [8] also (notably red, purple, and blue) were believed to possess this property, and the com-bination of both would constitute a very powerful protective influence. These "licia diverso colore," [9] usually knotted to-

[1] Sat. I. viii. 42.

[2] Kiessling, ad loc.; Fahz, op. cit. p. 147; Pliny, N.H. xxviii. 157 (there quoted).

[3] Hor. Epode v. 71, 75 et seq.; xvii. 60; Odes, I. xxvii. 21; Abt, p. 133.

[4] Epode xvii. 60.　　　　　　[5] Sat. I. viii. 49.

[6] Apol. 30; cf. Abt, p. 148; Ovid, Fasti, ii. 451-7.

[7] Virg. Eclog. viii. 65.

[8] Theoc. ii. 2; Haddon, op. cit. p. 31; Abt, p. 149; Griffith-Thomp-son Papyri, col. iii. p. 39 (there quoted).

[9] Virg. Eclog. viii. 74; Ovid, Am. I. viii. 7; cf. "magicus nodus,' Tib. I. viii. 5; Daremberg and Saglio, p. 1507; Fahz, op. cit. p. 126.

· gether, were also employed in love-magic to symbolize the bonds of love, and on the sympathetic principle to bind to one's self the object of affection.

The witches in Horace are said to harass men's minds[1] with "brewed enchantments" (*carminibus atque venenis*). The poet here uses a phrase, that occurs frequently in Roman Literature, where reference is made to magical practices. "Carmen," from being originally a harmless word,[2] came gradually to have the meaning of incantation. This meaning it can bear even when unqualified,[3] though occasionally[4] one finds it united with the epithet "magicum". It was naturally one of the favourite instruments of the magician's art, and the power of these incantations is often celebrated in literature.[5] Apuleius speaks[6] of the "incredibilis vis cantaminum". The "carmen" was sometimes used to effect a cure from illness, but more often for the distinctly harmful purpose of laying an enemy under a spell. As is clear from Theocritus and Virgil, it was also largely employed in love-magic. It is probable that in Horace's day a number of magic formulæ were current at Rome. He seems to have such in mind in the phrase "sunt verba et voces,"[7] which he applies to the precepts of philosophy. Naturally the most powerful of these incantations would be known only to the magicians themselves, or to those who shared their secrets. For a fuller knowledge of such formulæ one must have recourse to the Papyri,[8] which

---

[1] Sat. I. viii. 19.

[2] *Vide* Abt, p. 96, for the evolution of its meaning; Apul. Apol. 9 plays on the two meanings; cf. Hor. Ep. II. i. 138.

[3] Virg. Eclog. viii. 67; Æn. iv. 487; Tib. i. H. 53; Ovid, Am. I. viii. 5.

[4] Tib. I. v. 12; Prop. IV. iv. 51; Lucan, vi. 822; Juv. Sat. vi. 610.

[5] Hor. Epode xvii. 4; Virg. Eclog. viii. 70 *et seq.*; Tib. I. viii. 19; Ovid, Heroides, vi. 83-8; Am. II. i. 23 *et seq.*

[6] Apol. 26.

[7] Ep. I. i. 34, 37; cf. Epode xvii. 4; Virg. Georgic, ii. 129; Tib. I. v. 43.

[8] Fahz, op. cit. p. 167; Abt, op. cit. pp. 129, 226-8, 245; cf. Burne, op. cit. p. 148.

however generally belong to a period[1] later than the Augustan
Age.   These form strange reading.   Elaborate instructions
are given for the working of the spell, but the magical formulæ
proper are, as a rule, an unintelligible jumble of words without meaning to the ordinary reader, but possibly fraught with
significance for the magician, and for the initiated.   Words of
Egyptian and Babylonian origin[2] frequently figure in them,
pointing possibly to the original home of these formulæ, or at
least indicating that they were modelled upon those of Egypt
and Babylon, as likely to be the most efficacious.

The word "venenum" passed through a similar evolution[3]
to that of "carmen," from being comparatively harmless in its
origin, till it arrived at the meaning of a magic potion.   Hence
the Digest orders it,[4] when used, to be qualified by the word
"bonum" or "malum".   Standing by itself, it can bear the
meaning of a poisoned drink,[5] but, in the Latin poets generally, even when unqualified, it almost invariably connotes a
draught prepared by a magician.   A magic potion could be
employed[6] for the purpose of wreaking vengeance on an
enemy, but it was employed most extensively in love-magic,
both to loose and bind the affections.   The winning of
another's affections could be achieved by a mere charm,[7]
and the power of the word alone was considered sufficient
to overcome all rivals, but the love-philtre[8] (*desiderii poculum*)
seems to have been the favourite instrument resorted to for
such a purpose.   It was sometimes an ordinary drink,[9] over

---

[1] Daremberg and Saglio, p. 1503.

[2] *Vide* Apul. Apol. 38 for an interesting passage imitative of a magic
formula ; cf. Abt, p. 226 ; Daremberg and Saglio, p. 1519.

[3] Cf. the Greek Φάρμακον ; Homer, Odyss. iv. 230.

[4] L. 16, 236, quoted by Abt, p. 186.

[5] Hor. Sat. II. i. 48; Tib. III. v. 10; cf. Tac. Annals, xii. 52, 67.

[6] Hor. Epode iii., v., xvii. 35.

[7] Lucan, vi. 452 ; Apul. Apol. 67 ; Abt, p. 309 *et seq.*

[8] Hor. Epode v. 38; xvii. 80; Prop. I. v. 6 ; Tib. II. iv. 55 ; Ovid, Ars
Am. ii. 100 *et seq.* ; Juv. vi. 611 ; cf. Livy, xxxix. 11 ; Apul. Met. ix. 29 ;
Theoc. ii. 1.

[9] Abt, p 312.

which a magic name had been recited. It was frequently concocted from herbs alone,[1] and it was probably with that end principally in view that Canidia and her companions went to gather herbs upon the Esquiline. We find, however, that the love-philtre was at times compounded[2] from a large number of ingredients of the most diverse kind. Horace in his gruesome picture of the witches starving their young victim to death in order to concoct a love-potion, tells us[3] that their aim was especially to procure the marrow and liver of the boy. The liver was considered particularly valuable, as it was believed by the Ancients to be the "sedes libidinis".[4] Besides portions of the human body, we find parts of animals employed in the love-philtre. Horace relates[5] that among the other ingredients used by Canidia in the potion she was brewing, were a screech-owl's feathers, and eggs smeared with a toad's blood. Certain animals were closely associated with magic. The owl[6] as a night-bird, and so symbolic of the powers of darkness, was probably the commonest of all, and even in our own day it is regarded by many as a bird of evil omen. We find also[7] figuring the bat, toad, lizard, hare, ibis, and snake. Pliny gives us a most bewildering collection of cures,[8] in which the parts of animals form the main ingredients. It is clear, however, from the employment of the mystic numbers, three and nine, in connection with them, that in the vast majority of them, magic was in close touch with popular medicine. Certain fish[9] also, such as the anchovy, which

[1] Hor. Epode v. 67; Tib. I. viii. 17; Prop. III. vi. 25; Ovid, Ars Am. ii. 101.

[2] Fahz, pp. 132-4.   [3] Epode v. 37.

[4] Hor. Odes, I. xxv. 15; IV. i. 12; Ep. I. xviii. 72.

[5] Hor. Epode, v. 19 et seq.; cf. Prop. III. vi. 27 et seq.

[6] Tib. I. v. 52; Prop. II. xxviii. 38; Ovid, Am. I. xii. 19; Fasti, vi. 119; Lucan, vi. 689; Seneca, Medea, 733; cf. ibid. 670-739 for materials used in magic; Lucan, vi. 667 et seq.; Pliny, N.H. xi. 35.

[7] Abt, p. 183; Fahz, p. 128; Papyr Paris, 2943 et seq. (there quoted); Daremberg and Saglio, p. 1506.

[8] N.H. especially Bks. XXVIII.-XXX.

[9] Apul. Apol. c. 30; cf. Abt, pp. 140 et seq., 209 et seq.

was considered sacred to Venus, were commonly used in brewing a love-philtre. The best illustrations of the many and varied ingredients that entered into it, are preserved, in the Papyri,[1] and serve to throw light on a number of passages in the Roman poets. Among other things we find prescribed the body of a shrew-mouse, a little shaving from the head of a man who has died a violent death, nine apple-seeds, the blood of a worm, the blood from the second finger, and the blood of a black dog.

Horace refers[2] to another common characteristic of magic, the use of an image to affect its original in some way desired by the worker of magic. Such a practice was based on the idea of extended[3] personality, which had very wide ramifications in magical practices. It is easy enough to see how the belief could arise that what had once been in contact with a person, such as his hair, nail-clippings, and even his clothes, shared his personality. Another, who came into the possession of these, could act through them by magic[4] (" contagious magic" such writers as Frazer and Haddon would call it) on their original possessor. A mysterious affinity[5] was believed to exist between many things in Nature, and things, related as I have described, were considered to vary together. Hence springs the anxiety of people in a primitive stage of civilization to destroy the clippings of their hair or nails, lest they should come into the possession of an enemy, and be employed to

[1] Abt, pp. 312-13; Griffith-Thompson Papyri (there quoted), Col. xiii. p. 97, Col. xv. p. 105. For that strange ingredient, the "hippomanes," and the different meanings attached to the word, cf. Virg. Æn. iv. 515; Lucan, vi. 456; Juv. vi. 616; Tib. II. iv. 58; Prop. IV. v. 18; Ovid, Am. I. viii. 8; Theoc. ii. 48; Abt, p. 166; Fahz, p. 134.

[2] Sat. I. viii. 30.

[3] Jevons, op. cit. p. 29; Burne, op. cit. pp. 46 et seq., 141; Harrison, "Themis," p. 87.

[4] Frazer, "G.B." (3rd ed.), vol. i. pp. 66, 206, 213. A person's footprints also were considered to share his personality; cf. Haddon, op. cit. p. 3; Abt, p. 153.

[5] Cumont, "Les Religions Orientales," p. 223.

their detriment.   The hair was looked upon as particularly important, as being the seat of a person's strength.[1]   An offering[2] of one's hair to the dead was supposed to be a substitute for the sacrifice of the whole person.   The burial of the hair of an enemy was believed to cause his death, and through the hair or the nail-clippings[3] sickness also might be communicated to him.   In love-magic the burning of the hair was believed to draw its original owner to the place where it was burnt.   We know from Theocritus[4] that Simætha believed she was able to influence the object of her affection, through the fringe of the cloak he had once worn.   There is an interesting quotation given by Abt[5] from a Christian writer, Thos. Ebendorfer von Haselbach (c. 1439), which shows the prevalence of such practices in the Middle Ages.   His work dealt with the Decalogue, and in it he lays down the following rule: "Item gravissime peccant, qui per vestes hominis, vel crines, vel ungues vel herbas procurare volunt alios ad sui amorem".   But the idea of personality was still further extended, and it was believed to be shared[6] by one's name, effigy, or shadow.   The knowledge of one's name, considered as it was an inseparable part of one's personality, was particularly important for the worker of magic.   It was used especially in connection with the "Tabellae Defixionum,"[7] which were designed to injure an enemy, often fatally.   These were usually tablets of bronze or lead,[8] on which the name or the

---

[1] Abt, p. 181.   [2] Sophocles, Ajax, 1173, with Jebb's note.
[3] Apul. Met. iii. 16.
[4] II. 53 ; cf. Virg. Eclog. viii. 92 ; Eurip. Hippol. 513 et seq.
[5] Abt, p. 180.
[6] Haddon, op. cit. p. 22 ; Gomme, op. cit. p. 51 ; Fahz, pp. 127-30 ; Abt, pp. 98, 118-19.
[7] Dessau, "Inscriptiones Selectae," vol. ii. pt. ii. p. 996 et seq. ; Toutain, op. cit. vol. ii. p. 217 ; Friedländer, op. cit. vol. iii. p. 308.   For some further specimens, cf. "American Journal of Philology," xxxiv. p. 74 et seq.
[8] Tac. Annals, ii. 30, 69 ; Toutain, op. cit. vol. ii. p. 217.

image of the victim was inscribed, and contained as a rule imprecations to the Powers of the under-world, to whom the victim was vowed, or delivered over for vengeance. The tablets were sometimes placed under water, or in graves,[1] that the death of the victim might be compassed. A magician by the mere possession of a spirit's name can compel it to work in his interests. It has been noticed that members of savage races are usually reluctant to reveal their names to strangers, lest they should thereby place themselves in their power.

In connection, however, with this idea of extended personality, we find the use of images in magic perhaps most frequently referred to in the Latin poets, and their use in such circumstances has been not unknown even in modern times. They are often employed for the purpose of wreaking vengeance[2] on an enemy. A likeness of him is fashioned usually from wax or clay, and whatever ill-treatment the image is subjected to, the original is believed to suffer in a similar way.[3] "The practice of making a Corp Chredh (a clay body) to injure an enemy lingered in the Hebrides within recent years." The image was sometimes pierced with pins[4] to cause pain to the intended victim, and if his death was decreed, the heart or its neighbourhood was transfixed. But the image was employed extensively also in love-magic.[5] As the image of wax, for instance, was melted in the fire, so the heart of the beloved would melt for the one who desired to gain his or her affections. Here we have in operation the principle of Sympathetic Magic, or Mimetic Magic, as Dr. Haddon would call it.[6] Sometimes

---

[1] "American Journal of Philology," 1912, p. 301 *et seq.*

[2] Haddon, op. cit. p. 20; Abt, p. 133.

[3] Burne, "Handbook of Folk-Lore," p. 147.

[4] Ovid, Her. vi. 91 *et seq.*; Am. III. vii. 29; cf. Fahz, p. 133.

[5] Hor. Sat. I. viii. 30 *et seq.*; cf. Epode xvii. 76; v. 82 (on burning of bitumen). It is doubtful whether the "limus" and "cera" of Virgil, Eclog. viii. 80, refer to images or merely to pieces of clay and wax. Cf. Theoc. ii. 28; Apul. Apol. 30; Abt, p. 153 *et seq.*

[6] Op. cit. p. 15; cf. Frazer, "G.B." vol. i. p. 55 *et seq.*

the magic effect of the image was strengthened, by binding it with strands of wool,[1] which were symbolic of the bonds of love.   In the Canidia Satire, Horace describes the witches [2] as manipulating two images, one of wool, the other of wax.   It is not improbable that the image of wool was intended to represent Canidia herself, or the spirit, whose aid she invoked. The image of wool stood for the superior power, and wool was suitably used for its prophylactic properties, as being capable, by its own intrinsic virtue, of counteracting the machinations of a rival power.   The waxen image probably represented some faithless lover, whom Canidia first wished to punish for his defection.   Later, the image of wax is burned in the flames, as if the witch, in spite of her anger, desired to regain the affections that had been lost to her.

There is another device in love-magic, the magic wheel, that is frequently alluded to in Latin literature.[3]   The wheel was usually of bronze, a material that, as we saw, was commonly used in magic on account of its apotropaic powers.   The wheel is to be identified with the ἴυγξ [4] of the Greek poets, a word which originally signified a bird, that attracted its mate by means of a rotatory motion of the neck.   The motion of the wheel was in itself magical in its effect, and proceeded on the sympathetic principle that the beloved could be compelled to move by a similar motion towards the door of the lover.   At times, the bird was tied to the wheel, and a double charm was thus set in operation.

In his picture of Canidia and her comrades on the Esquiline, Horace describes for us a weird scene,[5] in which the

---

[1] Virg. Eclog. viii. 74; cf. Tib. I. viii. 5; Fahz, op. cit. p. 128; Daremberg and Saglio, p. 1507.

[2] Sat. I. viii. 30; Abt, p. 155; Papyr Paris, 295 *et seq.* (there quoted).

[3] Hor. Epode xvii. 7; Prop. II. xxviii. 35; III. vi. 26; Ovid, Am. I. viii. 7; Lucan, vi. 460; cf. Theoc. ii. 30; Abt, p. 160.

[4] Theoc. ii. 17; Arist. Lysis. 1110; Pindar, Nem. iv. 35; cf. Abt, p. 178; Daremberg and Saglio, p. 1517.

[5] Sat. I. viii. 26 *et seq.*; cf. Epode xvii. 79.

witches call forth the spirits of the dead, that they may foretell
the future. There is frequent mention of necromancy[1] in the
Roman poets, and, though in their case we may make some
allowance for poetic licence, references to the practice by sober
prose writers[2] make it clear that it was not uncommon. The
dead were recalled, as a rule, to foretell the future. They
seem to have been recalled, at times by the force of a simple
incantation,[3] at times by the use of magic herbs,[4] and again by
libations of milk, honey, wine, or even water,[5] or by the sacrifice
of animals of dark colour. Cicero is hardly exaggerating,[6]
when he goes a step further, and charges Vatinius with the
sacrifice of a boy-victim, in order to recall the spirits of the
departed, and, if Servius is to be believed, the sacrifice of a
human victim was essential for success in necromancy. At
times[7] the raising of the ghost takes place at some reputed
entrance to the under-world. Thither Ulysses travels in his
desire to discourse with the souls of the dead. Horace fitly
enough places his necromantic scene in the now transformed
cemetery on the Esquiline, beneath whose soil lay the bones of
many of the Roman poor. It is on the corpse-strewn plains
of Emathia that Lucan,[8] with unrivalled power and accumulat-
ing horror of detail, depicts the witch Erictho making choice
of a body, into which its spirit is to return by her magic power.
It is interesting to find her in quest of the body of one who has

[1] Virg. Eclog. viii. 99; Æn. iv. 490; Tib. I. ii. 45; Ovid, Met. vii.
206; Lucan, vi. 752 *et seq.*

[2] Cic. In Vat. c. 14; Tusc. Disp. I. xvi. 37; Tac. Annals, ii. 28; Suet.
Nero, 34; Aug. De Civ. Dei, vii. 35 (on Varro). Apuleius is, of course,
among the "Romantics"; cf. Met. ii. 28.

[3] Tib. I. ii. 45; Ovid, Am. I. viii. 17.   [4] Virg. Eclog. viii. 96 *et seq.*

[5] *Vide* Fahz, p. 110 *et seq.*, where the whole question of necromancy is
profusely illustrated; cf. Odyss. xi. 26 *et seq.*

[6] In Vat. 14; cf. Halliday, "Greek Divination," p. 242; Servius on
Æn. vi. 107 (there quoted); Lucan, vi. 560; Fahz, p. 111.

[7] Halliday, op. cit. p. 238; Cic. Tusc. Disp. I. xvi. 37; cf. Norden, op.
cit. p. 200.

[8] Lucan, vi. 620 *et seq.*, 752 *et seq.*

quite recently departed, as it was believed [1] that one, whose spirit was still hovering, as it were, between the realms of the living and the dead, was best suited to reveal the secrets of the future. To judge by the title of Æschylus' lost play, the ψυχαγωγοί, there were in some communities special ministers set apart to practise divination through the dead, and at times they were able to determine, [2] by the behaviour of the sheep they sacrificed on such occasions, the exact spot at which the divination should take place. The magician, however, though doubtlessly he often exercised this art, as Canidia and her companions did, near the burial-places of the dead, was not constrained to a choice of place, but could raise, wherever he wished, the souls of the departed. Horace in describing the scene upon the Esquiline, gives details, which must have been familiar enough in many ceremonies of the kind. [3] A trench was first dug, a lamb of dark colour was slain, and its blood poured into the trench. These details are familiar from the ghost-raising of Ulysses. The ghosts, as in Homer, [4] are conceived as mere unsubstantial shadows, that require a draught of blood to increase their vital force, before they come into contact with living beings. Horace is here probably following closely on Greek tradition, and incidentally his description reveals a belief in the condition of the dead, that is in harmony with the Homeric conception. As we shall see, Horace at times exhibits other beliefs on the state of the dead in the life beyond the grave. At times [5] the spirits of the dead, like their mistress Hecate, are invoked not to return to earth, but to send dreams from which the future can be read.

[1] Cic. De Div. i. 63; Halliday, op. cit. p. 243; Norden, Introd. to Æn. vi. p. 42; Abt, p. 193.

[2] Halliday, op. cit. p. 241; cf. passage from Suidas, περὶ ψυχαγωγίας (there quoted).

[3] Fahz, p. 112.

[4] Odyss. x. 495; xi. 35; cf. Cornford, "From Religion to Philosophy," p. 109; Eurip. Hec. 536 (νεκρῶν ἀγωγούς); Lucian, Necr. c. 9; Frazer, "G.B." vol. i. p. 90 et seq.

[5] Abt, p. 244; Papyr Paris, 2501 (there quoted).

Now the question may be raised as to where we are to look for the sources of the descriptions of the various magical operations, that Horace depicts for us. It is not likely that the poet himself witnessed Canidia and her companions engaged at their impious work, though he may have heard something of their activities from others. But his description of their magic-working is so elaborate and detailed, that it is probable that it was drawn in some measure at least from literary sources. Many of the details in Horace's descriptions of magical practices can be paralleled from Greek Literature.[1] In addition to authors like Homer, the dramatists of the Old and New Comedy, and Theocritus, an extensive literature in magic grew up in the Hellenistic period,[2] which our poet may have laid under contribution. Pliny enumerates[3] the various schools of magic in antiquity, Persian, Jewish, and Cypriote. In each of these a system of magic was perfected, and possibly a treatise issued, embodying the system, which may in time have become popularized. It is not unlikely that works on magic, like the Book of Hermes Trismegistus may have become current in Rome before the Augustan Age. In one passage[4] Horace seems to have in mind works of a still more popular character, which contained charms and magic formulæ of various kinds, and possibly, too, prescriptions for love-philtres. It would not be easy to determine, however, the exact extent, to which Horace was indebted to such sources for the many details of magic which he recounts for us. Comparative folk-lore has made one thing plain that many superstitions and magical practices are common to every country. There is no need to have recourse to a theory of borrowing to account for some at least of the elements in Horace's descriptions of magical opera-

---

[1] On the possible literary sources of magic in Greek, *vide* Apul. Apol. 30; Abt, p. 168 *et seq.*

[2] Norden, op. cit. p. 199; Fahz, p. 144 *et seq.*

[3] N.H. xxx. 2 *et seq.*

[4] Epode xvii. 4, " Per libros carminum valentium," etc., *vide supra*, p. 211.

tions. He refers himself to the magical powers believed to
have been possessed by some of his countrymen, and the traditions, that prevailed about them, would have furnished him
with some material. He would thus have interwoven native
and foreign tradition to give greater vividness to the picture
which he draws of Canidia and her sister-witches.

The fortunes of Magic and Astrology were often closely
bound-up at Rome, and it is clear from Horace, that a belief
in astrology was not uncommon in his day. To moderns, who
are accustomed to regard the universe from the scientific point
of view, such a belief must seem one of the strangest aberrations of the human mind. Yet it existed in England up to
comparatively recent times, and apparently not even Swift's
famous satire on the Astrologers (1708) succeeded in giving it
its death-blow. It has left its impress on the English language
in various epithets, such as jovial, mercurial, saturnine, which
are expressive of qualities believed to be engendered in men
through the influence of the planets.

Astrology had its origin in Babylonia, but it soon began its
march from the country of its birth, and reached Syria,[1] where
the speculations of the " Chaldæi " became fused with the cults
of the Syrian Baals and of Mithras. Through the Syrian cults
it was introduced into Rome[2] after the war with Antiochus.
It had already attained a certain measure of popularity before
the death of the Elder Cato, for he gives special instructions[3] to
farm-bailiffs to refrain from consulting Astrologers. It seems
to have spread rapidly, and caused some anxiety to the governing authorities, as the prætors (139 B.C.) expelled from Rome[4]
the Jews and the " Chaldæi," as the Astrologers were commonly called.   It was considered an exact science,[5] and

[1] Cumont, "Les Religions Orientales," p. 211; Bouché-Leclercq,
"L'Astrologie Grecque," p. 605.

[2] Cumont, op. cit. pp. 149-50.   [3] De Re Rus. v. 4.

[4] Cumont, op. cit. p. 198; Carter, " The Religion of Numa," p. 119.

[5] Cumont, op. cit. p. 197; " Astrology and Religion among the Greeks
and Romans," p. 137.

through its scientific appeal it gradually ousted from popular favour other means of divination. But the spread of astrology was aided immeasurably, when some of its doctrines became incorporated in the Stoic system. Stoicism, whose founder and many of whose leading members were Orientals,[1] had always a leaning towards the mystical speculations of the East. The fusion of Stoicism and Astrology was advanced especially through the agency of the Syrian,[2] Posidonius, the greatest light in Roman Stoicism, a man of encyclopædic learning, whose philosophic thought was permeated with mysticism. This philosopher was in many respects the heir of the ages, who had gathered together into his system the various threads of speculation of his predecessors, had introduced many strands of mystical thought, and woven all this diverse material into a new, brilliant, and harmonious texture. There is nowadays perhaps a tendency to exaggerate the influence of Posidonius, and with regard to a good deal of the philosophic thought of Cicero, Virgil, Manilius, Seneca, to see in him the power behind the throne. We may witness a reaction against this tendency, but it cannot be denied that he was primarily responsible for perfecting the alliance between Stoicism and Astrology.

The lore of the "mathematici" was still further popularized by that strange figure, Nigidius Figulus, who was profoundly versed in mysticism,[3] especially that of the Neo-Pythagoreans. These had propounded a theory of the eternity of the Universe, and of the influence of the stars on all that takes place on

---

[1] Bouché-Leclercq, op. cit. p. 544 *et seq.*; Toutain, op. cit. vol. ii. p. 182; Cumont, "Les Rel. Or." p. 202.

[2] Bouché-Leclercq, p. 545; Cumont, "Astrology and Religion," p. 178; Bevan, "Stoics and Sceptics," Lecture iii.; Warde Fowler, "The Religious Experience," p. 382; Norden, op. cit. pp. 21, 24.

[3] Lucan, i. 639 *et seq.*; cf. Cumont, "Les Rel. Or." p. 198; "Astrology and Religion,' p. 88; Bouché-Leclercq, op. cit. p. 548; Heitland, "The Roman Republic," vol. iii. p. 485; Th. Breiter, Manilius, Astronomica, vol. ii. Introd. p. 6.

earth. They developed also a mystical doctrine of numbers, to which they ascribed mysterious powers, thus revealing an affinity with the beliefs of the "mathematici". Nigidius displayed an interest in occultism of every kind. He had the distinction also of being the first to expound the "barbaric sphere,"[1] a series of constellations not recognized by the Greeks. Both he and Varro[2] endeavoured to reconcile Astrology with Etruscan divination. The comet, that appeared on the death of Julius Cæsar, gave the Astrologers a splendid opportunity of entering the lists with their speculations, and of competing with the sooth-sayers. Moreover, the dark days of civil strife, that followed the dictator's murder, tended to send men adrift from traditional beliefs, and made easier the acceptance of the doctrine of Fatalism, which was fundamental in Chaldæan theology. Cicero had already[3] given a glimpse of the popularity of Astrology in his day, and told us of the frequency with which the Astrologers were consulted. In spite of the repressive measures of Agrippa[4] (33 B.C.), the popularity of the Astrologers was not impaired. Astrology was in fashion in the Augustan Age, and lent its colour to some of the poetic literature of the period.[5] The Emperor himself consulted[6] the astrologer Theogenes at Apollonia, and such was his confidence in the destiny predicted for him, that he published his horoscope, and had a silver coin struck, bearing the stamp of Capricorn, under which he was born. But the great monument erected in this period to the astrological creed was the poem of Manilius, which was begun under Augustus,[7] and may have reached its present form before his death. The work

---

[1] Swoboda, P.N. Figuli Reliquiae, Quaestiones Nigidianae, pp. 43 *et seq.*, 35.

[2] Aug. De Civ. Dei, vii. 35 ; xxii. 28.

[3] Pro. Mur. xi. 25; Tusc. Disp. i. 40-96 ; De Div. I. xix. ; cf. Lucr. v. 727.

[4] Dio, xlix. 43.

[5] Virg. Georgic, i. 33, 336 ; Prop. II. xxvii. 3 ; IV. i. 76 *et seq.*

[6] Suet. Oct. 94.   [7] Breiter, op. cit. vol. ii. p. 11.

is highly technical in character, and for that reason often difficult and intricate, but the Prefaces are valuable, as setting forth
the author's philosophical views, which, as one might expect,
are deeply tinged with Stoicism. I need not follow further the
fortunes of Astrology at Rome,[1] though it was in the period
subsequent to the Augustan Age that it perhaps enjoyed
greatest vogue, and could reckon Emperors, such as Tiberius,
Nero, Otho, and even the sober Vespasian among its votaries.
In spite of severe enactments and frequent expulsions of the
Astrologers, Tacitus' famous judgment[2] continued to be true,
that "this class of men will ever be forbidden in the State, and
ever retained".

When we come to examine the philosophical basis of Astrology, we find that its real point of contact with Stoicism
lay in the doctrine of the "sympathy of the whole,"[3] i.e. the
sympathy, that was believed to exist between the various parts
of the Universe. The Stoics argued back from this principle
to the unity of the Power which created the world, and this
principle too, served as a basis for their belief in Divination.
Originally, the Stoic principle of "sympathy" seems to have
meant nothing more than a coincidence of phenomena in the
various parts of the Universe, but it was an easy step to transform this conception of "sympathy" into one of active influence
between the different parts, and so join hands with the Astrologers,[4] who also preached a doctrine of the solidarity of

---

[1] On this point *vide* Bouché-Leclercq, op. cit. p. 552 *et seq.*; Cumont,
"Les Rel. Or." p. 197 *et seq.*; "Astrology and Religion," p. 85 *et seq.*;
Lecky, "History of European Morals," p. 171; Friedländer, op. cit. vol.
i. pp. 69, 185-8.

[2] Tac. Hist. I. xxii. 1; ii. 62-3; Annals, ii. 32; vi. 20·1; xii. 22, 52;
cf. Suet. Tib. 14; Lucan, i. 639 *et seq.*; Juv. vi. 533 *et seq.*; x. 93; xiv.
248. For the influence of Astrology on Art, cf. Strong, "Apotheosis and
After Life," p. 72; Cumont, "Astrology and Religion," p. 111.

[3] Zeller, "Stoics, Epicureans, and Sceptics," pp. 375, 183; Epic. Diss,
I. xiv. 2 (there quoted).

[4] Cumont, "Les Rel. Or." p. 207 *et seq.*; Bouché-Leclercq, op. cit.
p. 572.

the Universe, but gave pre-eminence in it to the stars, which they regarded as inexhaustible fountains of energy acting incessantly upon the earth, and upon human destiny.   It is especially on the microcosm, man, that the influence of the stars is felt, and, according to the Astrologers, every act of his is regulated by their movements.   It is this theory in particular, that is most associated in the popular mind with Astrology, and it is this too, that has left the deepest impress upon literature.   From the star that was in the ascendant at one's birth, the whole of one's future could be divined.[1]   Horace does not profess exact knowledge of his own horoscope, but he proclaims that the star of his destiny agrees in a marvellous way with that of his patron, Mæcenas.   The casting of a horoscope was always a serious undertaking, as the Astrologers (*mathematici*) had to enter into the most elaborate calculations.[2]   As usual some cynics were discovered, who questioned the validity of their findings, and who advanced serious objections [3] to the whole science of Astrology.   How, it was said, can the beneficent or maleficent influence of a star be determined?   How comes it that twins have for the most part very different destinies in store for them, while people born at different times, and under different stars, perish in a single catastrophe, such as an earthquake or a shipwreck?   These and similar objections put the professors of Astrology on their defence, and their replies, though specious and plausible enough, must still have been unconvincing to many even in that credulous age.

Now, if life as a whole upon the Universe is controlled by the movement of the stars, we reach as an immediate consequence the idea of Determinism [4] in human conduct.   The

[1] Hor. Odes, II. xvii. 17 *et seq.* ; cf. Ep. II. ii. 187, where he has at least the language of Astrology in mind ; cf. an imitation in Persius, v. 51.

[2] Hor. Odes, I. xi. 2 : " Babylonii numeri ".

[3] Cic. De Div. II. xliii. 90 ; Bouché-Leclercq, op. cit. p. 573 *et seq.*

[4] Cumont, " Les Rel. Or." pp. 216-18 ; " Astrology and Religion," p. 153 ; Murray, " Four Stages of Greek Religion," pp. 125, 199.

"Chaldæi" pushed this fundamental doctrine of theirs to its logical conclusion, and conceived the idea of Necessity do-minating the Universe.   Here again, they were brought into close contact with Stoicism, which, among the prominent tenets of its school, held by the notion of Fate [1] (εἱμαρμένη) controlling the world as a whole.   This theory, if followed out to its logical issue, could only result in a feeling of despair. It destroyed Free Will, and the value of human endeavour. It destroyed the basis of morality, and in religion it removed the necessity of prayer and sacrifice.   Augustus, when he de-voted himself to Astrology, did not perhaps realize to the full the nature of the instrument, with which he was dealing.   He did not perceive that Astrology, bound up as it was with such a doctrine of Determinism, was irreconcilably opposed to a Religious Revival such as he was contemplating, or if he did realize the full import of Astrology, his adherence to it would raise the presumption that his Revival, though outwardly religious, was essentially political in character.

The Stoics had already felt the difficulty of reconciling Free Will with their doctrine of Fate, and Chrysippus [2] especially, had laboured to effect a reconciliation.   The Stoic idea of Fate was a complex one.   According to the angle from which it was viewed, it might be regarded as the Reason of the World, as Universal Law, as Providence or as Zeus, its living embodiment, but, whatever way it was regarded, it seemed to always imply the unchangeable connection of cause and effect throughout the Universe.   There were some, who crudely cut the knot by removing the human will, and it alone, from the sphere of Destiny.   Chrysippus,

---

[1] Cic. De Div. I. lv. 125; cf. Von Arnim, op. cit. vol. i. p. 44; vol. ii. p. 264 et seq.; Zeller, op. cit. p. 170.   For the Stoic idea of Fate in Lucan, cf. Heitland, Introd. p. 44.   For the concept of Moira in Greek thought, cf. Cornford, "From Religion to Philosophy," pp. 12, 189.

[2] Von Arnim, vol. ii. p. 282 et seq.; cf. Cic. De Fato, 39; Gellius, N.A. VII. ii.; Aug. De Civ. Dei, v. 10; Zeller, op. cit. p. 170.

arguing with greater subtlety, endeavoured to escape from the difficulty, by making a distinction between perfect and principal causes, and merely assisting causes. The will may be set in motion from outside, but the cause is merely an assisting one, and the motion of the will is in the last resort determined by itself. His answer was considered unsatisfactory by many, and starting, as it did, from the idea of Fate (*sempiterna quaedam et indeclinabilis series rerum et catena*), it left the real problem untouched. The Astrologers, in after years, had to face a similar difficulty,[1] which was vigorously pressed against them by their opponents.

As we have already seen,[2] when the personal deities of Polytheism lose the allegiance of men, there is a tendency to pay homage, either to Fate, conceived as an inexorable, unchangeable power, or to Fortune, regarded as mere capricious chance. The two notions, though widely disparate, were often confounded, and both alike tended to destroy the moral value of human effort. Belief in such Powers is especially rife when society is enveloped in some great catastrophe, or in a period of revolution and anarchy, when men's best efforts are set at nought, and the virtuous succumb to the machinations of the wicked. Such conditions were characteristic of Roman society[3] during the period of civil strife with its attendant chaos, that followed the revolution of the Gracchi. Both the ideas of Fate and Fortune are found frequently in Horace. His poetic activity was cast, for the most part, under the stable government of Augustus, but his personal experience enabled him also to look back to dread periods of fratricidal strife, when the worst passions of Romans were unloosed in the interests of political parties. He draws for us pictures of inexorable Destiny in passages,[4] where he is possibly under the influence of astrological beliefs. He also

---

[1] Bouché-Leclercq, op. cit. p. 572.   [2] *Vide supra*, p. 110 *et seq.*
[3] Bouché-Leclercq, op. cit. p. 547.
[4] Odes, III. i. 14 ; xxiv. 5 ; cf. Odes, II. xvii. 16, 24 (where astrological ideas are clearly marked) ; IV. ii. 38.

recognizes [1] a capricious deity, Fortuna, that makes sport of frail mortality, humbling the proud and exalting the lowly. But so far was Horace at times from clearly distinguishing the two concepts of Fate and Fortune, that he mingles both in his Ode [2] in honour of the Queen of Antium. Elsewhere he reaches a conception [3] akin to the Stoic εἱμαρμένη, or that rather, as it had developed into the idea of Providence.

We must consider briefly astrological beliefs on the nature of the soul, and its fate in the world beyond the grave. Here again, Astrology comes into close relation with Stoicism. The Stoics [4] taught that the soul was composed of fiery breath, which was an emanation [5] from the World-Soul, conceived at times by the Stoics as God who created and sustains the Universe. The primitive Stoics, as a rule, believed that the majority of individual souls were reabsorbed at death into the Universal Soul. A similar doctrine [6] had been common in early Greece, and Heracleitus [7] had taught that the one living soul substance, of the nature of fiery breath or ether, revolves in an endless cycle of birth, death, and rebirth of individual souls. One result of all this speculation was the development of a belief that the home of the soul (whether its fate was *personal* immortality or not) was no longer in the tomb or in the under-world, but in the upper spaces of the firmament. Here we get in touch with the beliefs of Astrology. The Astrologers held the stars to be divine, [8] a doctrine that was shared by Pythagoras, Plato, his pupil Aristotle, and the early Stoics. The mutual harmony and

---

[1] Odes, I. xxxiv. 15; II. i. 3; III. xxix. 49; cf. Sat. II. viii. 61.

[2] Odes, I. xxxv.   [3] *Ibid.* III. xxix. 29.

[4] Cic. Tusc. Disp. I. ix. 19; xviii. 42; Virg. Georgic, iv. 229 *et seq.*; Æn. vi. 730, 747; Von Arnim, vol. i. p. 37 *et seq.*; vol. ii. p. 235 *et seq.*

[5] Hor. Sat. II. ii. 79, " divinae particula aurae ".

[6] Cumont, "Astrology and Religion," p. 38 *et seq.*

[7] Cornford, op. cit. p. 184 *et seq.*

[8] Cumont, "Astrology and Religion," pp. 39 *et seq.*, 175; Von Arnim, op. cit. vol. ii. p. 200; Cic. De Nat. Deorum, II. xv. 39 (there quoted).

eternal movement of the stars, in orbits fixed and unchangeable, easily led to the belief that they were swayed in their
motion by some divine Reason.   Special powers were attributed to the planetary gods,[1] as they were called, and to the
sun and moon.   The soul of man, according to the Astrologers,[2] was of the same material as the stars.   After its
separation from the body, the soul ascends to the region of
the stars, and dwells there as their companion.   Similar ideas
were propagated by the Orphics,[3] who held that the human
soul had fallen from the stars into the prison-house of the
body.   A dualism of soul and body was thus set up, and,
according to Orphic teaching, the union of the soul with the
body was in reality a punishment for some sin committed,[4]
which the soul had to expiate either by its life on earth, or by
a process of purgation in the under-world.   After a series of
incarnations, at the end of the Great Year it might ascend
once more to the fiery ether from which it sprang, and there
regain its divinity.   Pythagoras had propounded similar
doctrines,[5] with certain modifications, and Plato has made
them familiar in the Phaedo.   The idea that the soul was
defiled by contact with the body, and needed purification
before it could attain perfect happiness, was taken over later
by Virgil.[6]   How far these ideas were borrowed from Babylonia
is a disputed point,[7] but there seems little doubt that its
Astral Theology had considerable influence in directing Greek
thought along such channels.

The abode of the Blest was placed sometimes near the

---

[1] Cumont, op. cit. p. 124 *et seq.*

[2] Cic. Tusc. Disp. I. xvii. 40 ; *ibid.* xix. 43.

[3] Cornford, op. cit. p. 178 *et seq.*

[4] Echoes of this doctrine are found in Cicero's Consolatio ; cf. Warde
Fowler, " The Religious Experience," p. 389 ; Norden, op. cit. Introd.
p. 18.

[5] Cornford, op. cit. pp. 198 *et seq.*, 246.

[6] Æn. vi. 720 *et seq.*; cf. Norden, Introd. p. 21.

[7] Cumont, " Astrology and Religion," p. 42.

sun,[1] sometimes between the sun and moon, at times in the
Milky Way, or again in the region of the fixed stars.   The
question was also discussed,[2] how the soul could reach its
final abode of happiness.   It was thought that at times various
means of locomotion were employed, such as a winged horse
or an eagle, and these animals appear [3] in the grave reliefs of
Imperial Rome as symbolic of the soul's apotheosis.   The
soul might also be raised by solar attraction, or ascend by its
own nature.[4]   Again, we meet with the idea that the soul,
which, pure essence as it is, has been infected by its union
with the body, must go through a process of purgation in the
air, before it can finally reach its home among the stars, there
to dwell, with its vision unimpaired by human passion, in
ecstatic contemplation of their beauty.

From all this we can see how readily Stoic thought could be
reconciled with the teachings of the Astrologers.   Cicero, who
had been a pupil of Posidonius, was the first to give clear expression [5] in Latin literature to such ideas of the after-life.
Who was to share in such happiness was never very fully
defined.   The privilege was probably accorded in the East [6]
originally only to those monarchs, who for their services were
raised, even in their life-time, by the worship of their subjects
to an equality with the star-gods.   The Greeks worshipped
heroes, and also held a belief in "catasterism," [7] i.e. that men,
for their great exploits and services to mankind, are transferred to the heavens as constellations.   All these influences

---

[1] Cumont, "Astrology and Religion," p. 195 *et seq.*; "Les Rel. Or."
pp. 151-3 ; Norden, op. cit. Introd. p. 24.

[2] Cumont, "Astrology and Religion," p. 183 *et seq.*

[3] Strong, "Apotheosis and After Life," pp. 62, 68, 126.

[4] Cic. Tusc. Disp. I. xix. 43.

[5] Somnium Scipionis, especially c. 3; cf. Warde Fowler, "The Religious Experience," p. 383 *et seq.*

[6] Cumont, "Astrology and Religion," p. 180 *et seq.*

[7] Bouché-Leclercq, op. cit. p. 551 ; Cumont, op. cit. pp. 117, 176 ; "Les
Rel. Or." p. 209 ; Cic. Tusc. Disp. I. xii. 28 ; Virg. Æn. vi. 130.

combined to widen the circle[1] of those who were to enjoy the exalted privilege of apotheosis among the stars, and such beliefs had their share[2] in the development of Imperial Deification at Rome. There can be little doubt that Horace was influenced by such beliefs in the many passages, in which he proclaims the deification of Augustus.[3] He ranges the Emperor among the great heroes, such as Castor and Pollux, Hercules and Bacchus, who were raised to the rank of gods, or had gained a place among the stars for their great achievements, and for the benefits they had conferred on their fellowmen. He plainly, too, has the doctrine of "catasterism" in mind, when he refers to the "Julium sidus,"[4] and to Ariadne's elevation to a place among the stars.[5] Again, in his mock recantation of his bitter invective against Canidia,[6] he promises that she will one day range as a golden constellation among the stars. At other times,[7] whether he meant to subscribe to the doctrine of "catasterism" or not, his mode of expression was undoubtedly influenced by it.

The question might be raised, how far was Astrology in vogue among the common people at Rome. The poem of Manilius is sufficient proof of the great popularity it enjoyed among the educated, and the Emperor's leanings towards it would have helped to set the fashion in court circles. It is clear, too, that it had attained a certain measure of popularity among the common people. There must have been at Rome, and in the larger towns of Italy, a number of charlatans (those whom

---

[1] Cic. Tusc. Disp. I. xii. 27; Somnium, iii. 13; Virg. Æn. vi. 660 *et seq.*; Norden, op. cit. pp. 36-7; cf. Tac. Agric. 46.

[2] Strong, op. cit. p. 60 *et seq.*; *vide supra*, p. 53 *et seq.*

[3] *Vide supra*, p. *et* 115 *seq.*; cf. Odes, III. iii. 9; ii. 21; Strong, op. cit. p. 197.

[4] Odes, I. 12, 47; cf. Virg. Eclog. ix. 47.

[5] Odes, II. xix. 13; cf. *ibid.* I. iii. 2; Virg. Æn. ix. 641.

[6] Epode xvii. 41.

[7] Odes, I. i. 36; III. xxv. 6; IV. ii. 23; viii. 31; cf. Virg. Georgic, i. 31.

Cicero would style "de circo astrologi"[1]), who claimed to be versed in the science of Astrology, and plied their trade at the street-corners, or in the public places of the city before an admiring and curious crowd. The precepts of Cato[2] to his farm-bailiff point to the fact that Astrology, from its earliest arrival in Italy, had found favour with the less educated. Astrology itself claimed to be scientific in character, and would naturally make its strongest appeal to men of cultured minds. There were many, however, of the less cultured, who were content with its conclusions, without seeking to pry into the processes by which they had been arrived at, and who exhibited unquestioning faith in the professed masters of the science. The poem of Manilius was intended primarily for the more educated classes of the community, but he finds a place[3] in it too for artisans, labourers, and men engaged in the most diverse trades. Here, as in the case of magic, we may be sure that a number of popular handbooks were compiled to meet the demands of those who were unable to follow Astrology in its more abstruse aspects. The people often consulted[4] the Astrologers for the most trivial reasons, to know, for instance, the issue of some comparatively unimportant law-suit, or to ascertain the most propitious times for the various processes of agriculture.

Now we pass to another aspect of popular belief, that which concerned itself with the condition of the dead in the life beyond the grave. The ancient Italian belief[5] was that

---

[1] De Div. I. lviii. 132 ; cf. De Fato, viii. 15 ; Hor. Sat. I. vi. 114 "adsisto divinis ".

[2] Vide supra, p. 221.   [3] Astronomica, iii. 96 et seq.

[4] Gellius, N.A. XIII. i. 4 ; cf. Toutain, op. cit. vol. ii. p. 184 ; Aug. De Civ. Dei, v. 7 (there quoted).

[5] Cumont, " Les Idées du Paganisme Romain sur la Vie Future," p. 8 ; Fustel de Coulanges, " La Cité Antique," pp. 8 et seq., 13 ; Bailey, " Ancient Rome," p. 52 ; Boissier, " La Religion Romaine," vol. i. p. 266 ; cf. the phrases "animam sepulchro condimus," Æn. iii. 67 ; " sit terra tibi levis" ; Buecheler, " Carmina Epigraphica," Nos. 128, 197, 429 ; Tib.

the soul of the dead person lived an obscure existence with the body in the tomb. On certain fixed days, his friends came year by year to make offerings of food and drink at the grave, to refresh the spirit of the departed, who was subject to much the same needs as during his earthly life. Salt cakes, milk, wine, and sometimes blood were offered at the tomb. The Sepulcretum[1] discovered by Boni some years ago in the Roman Forum (where both inhumation and cremation had been practised), contained many relics of such offerings. The early tombs generally reveal a desire[2] for the protection and well-being of the dead modelled on their earthly life, but exhibit "no clear vision of a life beyond the grave". The belief, that I have mentioned, was especially associated with inhumation,[3] and its influence persisted[4] on into the Empire, when it was still the practice with many to have their tombs built beside the great highways, where a prayer for the dead might be procured from the passers-by. There was another very ancient belief in Italy with regard to the dead,[5] in which the spirits of the departed were hardly regarded as individualized. The soul of the dead person was believed to join the mass of Manes in some dim abode in the centre of the earth. Such ideas may well have arisen with the practice of cremation, by which the earthly tenement of the soul was destroyed, and the spirit left to lead an independent existence. Still, the spirit or

---

II. iv. 50. The tomb is called "domus aeterna"; cf. Buecheler, Nos. 57, 59, 71, 72.

[1] Huelsen, "Le Forum Romain," p. 224; Strong, op. cit. p. 163 et seq.

[2] Ibid. p. 165.

[3] Warde Fowler, "The Religious Experience," p. 382; Strong, op. cit. p. 125; cf. Ridgeway, "The Origin of Tragedy," p. 125. Mr. Bailey, "Some Greek and Roman Ideas of a Future Life," p. 9 et seq., associates such a belief with the animistic stage in religion.

[4] Boissier, op. cit. vol. i. pp. 306-7.

[5] Warde Fowler, op. cit. pp. 381-86; Strong, op. cit. p. 162; Boissier, op. cit. vol. i. p. 269; Carter, "The Religion of Numa," p. 14 et seq.

shade was always imagined under bodily form.[1] It is doubtful [2] if the Romans, at this period at least, worshipped their
dead, though the phrase " Di Manes" seems to point to some
vague form of worship.

Now came a further development in belief concerning
the soul's condition after death, in which Greek influence was
at work.   Homer had pictured [3] " the dank house of Hades " as
a vague shadowy realm, on the confines of the ocean stream,
where dwelt the shades of the dead, unsubstantial phantoms,
that yet enjoyed bodily shape.   The dead dwelt there with the
faintest ray of consciousness, leading a cheerless existence [4]
almost akin to a mere negation.   Towards the end [5] of the
Homeric picture we come upon an idea, that was to be fruitful
in the development of the Under-world.   Minos is enthroned
as judge, wielding a golden sceptre.   While the great mass
of the dead lead a pale colourless existence, we are suddenly
introduced to the figures of the great sinners, Tityos, Tantalus,
and Sisyphus, expiating the crimes they had committed upon
earth.   A moral tone [6] is thus imparted to the picture, and
the suggestion is that men must make expiation in the world
beyond for the sins of their former life.   There is a faint
suggestion, too, in the case of Hercules, that a man's good
deeds will win him a reward.   These ideas of judgment
delivered, of reward and punishment, were to be enlarged and
reach their highest development in Roman Literature in
Virgil's picture of the Under-world, with its strange mixture of
philosophy, mysticism, and popular tradition.   In this a more
vivid consciousness is attributed to the dead, and a clear distinction is made between the places of reward and punishment
in the Under-world.   But for long, men fixed their gaze rather

---

[1] Cic. Tusc. Disp. I. xvi. 37.

[2] Bailey, " Ancient Rome," p. 49 et seq.

[3] Odyss. x. 51 et seq. ; xi. 13.

[4] Ibid. xi. 476, 489 et seq.   [5] Ibid. 568 et seq.

[6] Bailey, " Some Greek and Roman Ideas," p. 11.

on the punishments of the world below, than on its rewards. The terrors of Tartarus and Acheron were increased and intensified [1] by the pictures of poets and painters, and by the brooding of the popular imagination. Certain details must have been especially impressive, and we may be sure that the figure of Charon, the ferryman, had become a grim reality to many minds. He was taken over by the Christian poet Dante, [2] who in his "Inferno" follows closely, in many details, in the footsteps of his guide Virgil. Charon, too, was to figure in Michelangelo's great fresco of the Last Judgment, and has even lived [3] on in the folk-lore of modern Greece. Lucretius clearly considered that such beliefs were widespread, and that the thought of death and of the terrors, which were to follow, had a blighting effect on human life. The poet is at all times serious and conscious of a high mission, but at no point is his seriousness more intense and sustained than when he is combating the "fear of Acheron," [4] which must be driven headlong from the thoughts of men. However, the alternative of annihilation, which he proposed as a solution, must have seemed to many a poor substitute for some form of conscious existence after death, even though attended with a certain element of fear. The study of philosophy, whether Stoic or Epicurean, must have helped largely to exorcise, at least from the minds of the educated, all these imagined terrors of the Under-world. Cicero, possibly in a burst of enthusiasm for the new mystical doctrines, which he had imbibed from Posidonius, proclaims [5] that no old woman is mad enough to believe in them, and ridicules the Epicurean attack upon them

---

[1] Plautus Captivi, 998 et seq. (cf. Lindsay, ad loc.); Cic. Tusc. Disp. I. vi. 10; xvi. 37; Lucr. III. 629 et seq.; Virg. Æn. vi. 295 et seq., 567 et seq.

[2] "Inferno," Canto iii. 28 et seq.; cf. Virg. Æn. vi. 298 et seq.

[3] Friedländer, op. cit. vol. iii. p. 298.

[4] Lucr. iii. 25, 37, 86; cf. Virg. Georgic, ii. 491.

[5] Cic. Tusc. Disp. I. xxi. 48; cf. ibid. vi. 10, 11; De Nat. Deorum, II. ii. 5.

as mere tilting against groundless fears. The Greeks themselves, from whom these beliefs ultimately sprang, were more
inclined to dwell on the delights of Elysium than on the
horrors of Tartarus. Virgil, too, though he depicts for us the
punishments of Tartarus, yet seems more at home[1] in painting
the joys of the Blessed in the Elysian fields. The poet had
felt the breath of the new spirit of mysticism, which had begun
to pervade Roman thought[2] towards the close of the Republic.
Indeed, as time went on, belief in Elysium[3] came into greater
prominence, and the world beyond the grave was looked on
as a place, where the inequalities of the present life might be
redressed. Under the influence of the Mystery religions, and
those views of the soul which I have already described,[4] we
find also making its appearance a belief in some process of
purgation, by which the soul, defiled by contact with the body,
is purified before it reaches its destined happiness. The
Mystery religions in particular had various specifics[5] for the
initiated, by which they were assured of reaching a blessed
immortality. There were rites of purification (often indeed
merely ceremonial, without exacting a corresponding moral
purity), and formulæ of instruction to guide the soul in its
journey through the lower world to its final haven of happiness. But gradually the localisation of Elysium became
shifted, and the ultimate destiny of the soul was the starry
heavens. Here again, various religions professed to give instructions[6] that would insure the soul after death a safe passage through the perils, that beset its path, till it reached its

[1] Compare the spirit of Fra Angelico's " Last Judgment " with that of
Michelangelo's.

[2] Warde Fowler, " The Religious Experience," Lecture xvii.

[3] Buecheler, op. cit. Nos. 492, 498, 525, 588.

[4] *Vide supra*, p. 228 *et seq.*

[5] Bailey, " Some Greek and Roman Ideas," pp. 18, 19; cf. Harrison,
" Prolegomena to the Study of Greek Religion," Appendix, p. 660 *et seq*,
on the Orphic tablets; Boissier, op. cit. vol. i. p. 308.

[6] Cumont, " Astrology and Religion," p. 193.

home among the stars, there to dwell for ever in contemplation of their beauty and enjoy the music of the spheres. These mystical beliefs find echoes in many grave-inscriptions [1] in Imperial times. They were to exercise a profound influence [2] also on the sepulchral Art of the Empire, and were to issue in an elaborate symbolism of the soul's journey to its final resting-place.

When we turn to Horace, we find a strange medley of ideas concerning the condition of the soul after death. We have seen [3] that the poet is frequently obsessed with the fear of death, and that this fear finds expression mostly in passages distinctly Epicurean in tone. It is not, we may be sure, the fear of Tartarus or its punishments that oppressed his spirit, but rather the dread of being separated from all the pleasant things, that life held in store for him. It is the passage [4] of youth, and its fleeting joys, that casts a shadow of gloom over his merrier moments, and as a consequence he is filled with a renewed resolve to enjoy the passing hour. He insists [5] frequently on the universality of death, from which neither rich nor poor can escape. Life is short, and, when we go to the shadowy house of Pluto, we can no longer hope to enjoy [6] such pleasures as we enjoyed in our earthly life. The Emperor Hadrian, in his famous address to his soul, assures it that, when death comes, " nec, ut soles, dabis joca ". We find the same sentiment expressed in a number of sepulchral inscriptions.[7] The suggestion is that our destiny is completed

---

[1] Buecheler, op. cit. Nos. 590, 591, 603, 611.

[2] Strong, op. cit. pp. 175 *et seq.*, 199, on the monument from Pettau, showing clear traces of Orphic beliefs.

[3] *Vide supra*, p. 99.

[4] Odes, I. xi. 7 ; II. iii. 14 *et seq.* ; III. viii. 27.

[5] *Ibid.* I. iv. 13 ; xxviii. 15 ; II. iii. 25 ; xiv. 9 ; xviii. 32 ; Ep. I. vi. 27.

[6] Odes, I. iv. 16 *et seq.*

[7] Buecheler, op. cit. Nos. 76, 77, 85, 185, 186, 190, 243 ; Dessau, " Inscriptiones Selectae," vol. ii. 2, p. 883, 8163 *et seq.* ; Friedländer, op. cit. vol. iii. p. 283 ; Boissier, op. cit. vol. i. p. 302.

here, and that our duty is to enjoy to the full all the pleasures that the present life affords. It is not easy to determine if the passages in Horace, that are so redolent of Epicureanism, point to a definite belief regarding the After-life. We can infer this much at least from them that death could not be lɔked forward to with pleasure. If it involves existence at all, it is a cheerless one, and our best alternative is to seize the " gifts of the passing hour ". Once,[1] Horace seems to suggest definitely that our destiny is measured by the present life, but later in the same Ode he clearly intimates that the soul is not destroyed by death, for the judgment of Minos is to follow its separation from the body, and will determine what its fate is to be in the life beyond the grave. The poet, in several passages,[2] seems to be dominated by the Homeric view that the soul in the Under-world is an unsubstantial phantom, leading a colourless existence, and unable to participate in pleasure. Death is again for Horace [3] an " eternal exile," whither the shade is transported in Charon's bark. Occasionally,[4] he conceives death as night coming to oppress the soul with darkness. If such an idea were found by itself in a sepulchral inscription, we might regard it as referring to the complete extinction of the soul, but in the one passage,[5] the poet supposes the soul to exist, even though with the pale existence of the shade, while in the other it is clear from the context, in which the spirit of Archytas is one of the speakers, that existence does not end with death. Horace evidently, in calling death " night " or " eternal exile," wished merely to convey an idea of its cheerlessness, and of the isolation of the soul from all the joys of life. There is one passage,[6] in which we might plume ourselves on convicting the poet of pure

---

[1] Odes, IV. vii. 7.

[2] Ibid. I. iv. 16; x. 18; IV. vii. 16; cf. Sat. I. viii. 28 et seq.

[3] Odes, II. iii. 27.

[4] Ibid. I. iv. 16; xxviii. 15; cf. Cat. v. 6; Buecheler, op. cit. No. 545.

[5] Odes, I. iv. 16.   [6] Ibid. xxiv. 5.

Epicureanism, when he laments that his friend Varus sinks on death into "perpetual sleep ".[1]   Here again he baffles us, for he speaks of his friend's soul as a "vana imago," which Mercury [2] has gathered into the herd of Manes in the world below, and is thus far from the Lucretian idea of death as involving complete annihilation.   We sometimes meet in sepulchral inscriptions with the same lack of a clearly defined view on the life beyond.   On the tomb of a certain Petronius Antigenides, we find described in elegant verse [3] the dead man's accomplishments in life, and his journey after death to the lower world; then in reference to the tomb itself we come upon the phrase, "haec domus aeterna est, hic sum situs, hic ero semper ".   We are thus left in doubt, as to whether the soul was supposed, according to primitive Italian belief, to reside with the body in the tomb, or was believed to join the Manes in the Under-world.   Horace was an adherent of Epicureanism in his early years, but, as we saw, his philosophical convictions were never very profound.   He never at any time gives a clear indication that, like Lucretius, he believed that the soul was composed of fine atoms and dissolved on its separation from the body.   Lucretius had laboured to destroy belief in Tartarus and its terrors, but we find Horace on many occasions [4] setting forth, with every "pomp and circumstance," the dread realities of the Under-world, thus helping, perhaps unconsciously, to perpetuate the fears, which Lucretius had sought to allay.   All this diversity of view gives no indication of settled convictions on a subject of vital importance.   Horace, at certain points, is probably in touch with popular opinion, for it is clear from inscriptions what great variety of beliefs regarding the dead continued to prevail at Rome, and in the

---

[1] *Vide* Buecheler, op. cit. No. 481 ; cf. Nos. 90, 507.

[2] Odes, I. xxiv. 18 ; cf. *ibid*. x. 17 ; Prop. IV. vii. 1.

[3] Buecheler, op. cit. No. 434 ; Orelli, 1174.

[4] Epode xvii. 65 *et seq*. ; Odes, I. xxxiv. 10 ; II. xiii. 21 ; xiv. 17 *et seq*. ; xviii. 34 *et seq*. ; III. iv. 75 *et seq*. ; xi. 16 ; cf. Prop. III. xviii. 23.

territory under her sway, till comparatively late times.   In
other passages, he is clearly dominated by literary tradition,
and especially by the Homeric description of the Under-world.
It is strange that he came hardly, if at all, under the influence
of the new mystical spirit that was stirring at Rome.   One
would expect him to have caught some echoes of it from
Pindar,[1] whose poetry he so much admires, and who was impregnated with Orphic and Pythagorean thought.   As we have
seen, he shows traces of the influence of Astrological doctrines,
and of a belief in "catasterism," but these are almost invariably
subordinated to the purpose of deifying the Emperor.   He exhibits, once at least,[2] some conception of happiness beyond
the grave, while in another Ode[3] he describes the Elysian
fields, the "sedes discriptas piorum," where Sappho and
Alcaeus still sing their songs as in their earthly life, and are
the centre of an admiring throng of shades.   It is possible
that the Sixth Æneid was published, when the Ode was
written, and that Horace was following in the wake of Virgil.[4]
Still, this is only a passing phase, and never at any time does
he reach the splendid vision of the Under-world, and of the
abode of the Blest, that is enshrined in Virgil's immortal verse.

Closely connected with the various beliefs, that postulated
the survival of the soul after death, was the belief in the necessity of giving the dead due burial.   This conviction can be
traced back to the earliest period, when the idea still prevailed that the soul on death remained united to the body in
the tomb.   The necessary rites were few and simple, and consisted of casting a little earth (Horace says[5] "injecto ter
pulvere") on the corpse, and of uttering the last words of
farewell to the dead.[6]   If the due rites were not performed, it

[1] Ol. ii., especially 64 et seq.   [2] Odes, I. x. 17.
[3] Ibid. II. xiii. ; cf. Virg. Æn. vi. 638 et seq.
[4] Ibid. 661 et seq.
[5] Odes I. xxviii. 36; cf. Prop. I. xxii. 8.
[6] Cat. ci., Ode at his brother's tomb; cf. Virg. Æn. vi. 231.

was believed that the soul would wander from the body,[1] and come to torment the living.   Even when belief in an Underworld developed, the necessity of giving due burial none the less existed ; for if these last rites were not paid to the soul, it could never hope to reach its proper resting-place[2] in the world below.   It was the interest alike of the living and the dead to have due burial given.   People took the most elaborate precautions to insure that their heirs would perform the due ceremonies (*justa facere*) over their remains.   If an heir failed in this duty, he had to atone for his neglect[3] by the annual sacrifice of a sow to the Earth deities, Ceres and Tellus.   If affection was not a sufficient incentive, the fear of the wandering ghost was in most cases sufficient to prevent the omission of this debt to the departed.   The Romans, as we know,[4] took precautions against the return of the dead to their former home.   They carried the corpse from the house feet foremost, that it might not be able to find its way back, and, when they returned from the grave, they took care to purify the house, which they regarded as defiled by contact with the dead. Many modern scholars trace the origin of gravestones[5] back to this fear of the return of the dead, and contend that primitive man set up "his first rough tombstone with a magical intention in order to provide the ghost of the inhabitant of the tomb with a shrine or dwelling-place ".   All the exquisite care,

---

[1] Pliny, Ep. vii. 27; cf. Fustel de Coulanges, op. cit. p. 10; Warde Fowler, "The Religious Experience," p. 82; Boissier, op. cit. vol. i. p. 267; Ridgeway, op. cit. p. 153; Burne, "The Handbook of Folk-Lore," p. 82.

[2] Virg. Æn. vi. 325 *et seq.*, 365; Odyss. xi. 72.

[3] Warde Fowler, op. cit. p. 121; Bailey, "Ancient Rome," p. 51; cf. Buecheler, op. cit. p. 385.

[4] Plutarch, Roman Questions, 5; cf. Jevons, Introd., p. 35 *et seq.*; Burne, op. cit. p. 214, for precautions taken in some modern communities against the dead returning.

[5] Strong, op. cit. p. 115 *et seq.*, 119, on the sarcophagus from Hagia Triada; cf. Burne, op. cit. p. 215.

16

shown by the living for the dead, was designed, originally at least, to keep the dead contented in its new home. The living were especially anxious to keep the dead at a distance from them. If they were to return, as they might naturally wish to do, from a desire to revisit their former haunts, provision was made for them to return only at certain specified times. Hence the custom [1] obtained at Rome of opening the Mundus (a round pit on the Palatine, popularly believed to be an entrance to the Under-world), on three days of the year, Aug. 24, Oct. 5, and Nov. 8, that the dead might come forth to revisit their friends, though, as Mr. Warde Fowler suggests, the Mundus was in origin probably nothing more than the *penus* of the new city, where grain was stored.

Now the same fear of the ghost is apparent in one of the Roman festivals of the dead, the Lemuria.[2] The Lemures were regarded as hostile spirits,[3] and it was a characteristic feature of the Lemuria, as described by Ovid, that the head of the household rose at midnight, and, after various preliminary rites through the house, beat bronze vessels, and called out nine times "Manes exite paterni," in his efforts to expel the ghosts. In February there was a festival of the dead, the Parentalia,[4] of a totally different character, in which, during the celebrations, the most friendly relations existed between the living and the departed. The festival was essentially a cheerful one, and concluded (Feb. 22) with the Caristia,[5] a "kind of love-feast of the whole family," when the Lares shared in the sacred meal. Ovid clearly intimates,[6] that the Lemuria was the

---

[1] Warde Fowler, "Roman Festivals," pp. 211, 212, on "Mundus Patet"; Macrob. Sat. I. xvi. 18 (there quoted); Boissier, op. cit. vol. i. p. 269; Bailey, op. cit. p. 50.

[2] In May; cf. Ovid, Fasti, v. 371 *et seq.*; Warde Fowler, op. cit. p. 106 *et seq.*; "The Religious Experience," pp. 393-5.

[3] Hor. Ep. II. ii. 209.

[4] Ovid, Fasti, ii. 227 *et seq.*; cf. Warde Fowler, "Roman Festivals," pp. 306-10.

[5] Ovid, Fasti, ii. 459 *et seq.*; cf. Bailey, "Ancient Rome," p. 53.

[6] Ovid, Fasti, v. 431 *et seq.*

older festival of the two. He derives the name from Remuria, and traces the institution of the festival to an endeavour to expiate the violent death of Remus. Ovid's explanation of the origin of the festival is purely fanciful, but his suggestion of its antiquity is of some value. If it is true[1] that we have to recognize at Rome the existence of two distinct races, the Lemuria may go back to the more primitive of the two. But it is possible, too, that the Lemures were, at least when the Lemuria was first instituted, not the whole body of the dead, but only the unburied dead, and that the element of fear associated with the festival was akin to the general fear of the wandering ghost, the spirit of one, to whom the due funeral rites had not been paid. This double attitude to the dead, exhibited in the Roman festivals, has its parallels[2] in many communities in modern times. Bearing in mind this fear of the unburied dead, that was prevalent in antiquity, we can make allowance for the strength of the indignation manifested at Athens after Arginusae, when it was discovered that the Athenian generals had neglected to search for and give due burial to those, who had been lost in the battle. We can understand, too, the prominent place the necessity for burial gets in Classical Literature. In the *Antigone* the mainspring of the action is the conflict between divine and human law. Antigone maintains that, in performing for her dead brother the due burial rites, she is but obeying a divine ordinance, which cannot be overridden by the decree of a human ruler. Euripides has employed this same idea of the need of burial in one of the most effective passages of the *Troades*.[3] In Latin

---

[1] Warde Fowler, " The Religious Experience," p. 393 ; Ridgeway in " Companion to Roman Studies," p. 27 *et seq.* ; cf. Peet, " The Stone and Bronze Age in Italy," c. xviii.

[2] *Vide* Burne, " Handbook of Folk-Lore," p. 82 *et seq.*, for examples from India and New Guinea ; *ibid.* p. 216 for Prussian festival (16th cent.), which resembles the Lemuria in many details.

[3] Troades, 380 *et seq.* ; cf. Soph. Ajax, 1177.

Literature we find a similar prominence given to this idea.[1]
The greatest fear, that could beset one was that his body would
lie unburied, while almost equally poignant were men's fears
lest those, who were dear to them, should not receive the last
debt of respect from the living.[2]   The direst curse,[3] that could
be uttered against an enemy, was that his bones might remain
unburied.   As the "Tabellae Defixionum" phrase it[4] at
times—"ultimus suorum moriatur"—may no friend survive to
pay him the last rites at death!   Horace turns to account in
his Archytas Ode[5] this need of receiving due burial.   The Ode
has many difficulties, but its effect is considerably heightened
if we imagine the shade to be that of Archytas, who, great
philosopher that he was, had fathomed during life the secrets
of Nature, and now is reduced to begging for a little dust for
his unburied corpse.   Again, the poet is close to popular feeling, when prominent among the punishments marked out for
the witches by their boy-victim, he declares[6] that their bones
will lie unburied, the prey of birds and wolves.

We find another popular belief reflected in Horace, the importance of omens, especially omens of departure.   The poet
mentions several unfavourable omens,[7] which he hopes may
happen to the impious on their journey.   Among them is the
passage of a snake across their path, and the hooting of the
screech-owl, a bird which, as we saw, was closely associated
with magic, and was always regarded as of evil omen.   Primitive man inclined to look upon the cries and flight of birds
as ominous.[8]   Moreover, in every age, the occurrence of the

---

[1] Prop. III. xvi. 21; Ovid, Heroides, x. 123 *et seq.*

[2] Hor. Sat. II. iii. 195; Virg. Æn. ix. 485 *et seq.*; Prop. I. xxii. 8; III.
vii. 9; Suet. Oct. 13.

[3] Hor. Epode x. 21; Æn. iv. 620; Tib. II. iv. 44.

[4] Dessau, "Inscr. Selectae," vol. ii. 2, p. 885, 8185a, 8185b.

[5] Odes, I. xxviii.   [6] Epode v. 99.

[7] Odes, III. xxvii. 1 *et seq.*; Epode x. 1; Ep. I. xvii. 30.

[8] Halliday, "Greek Divination," p. 247; Tylor, "Primitive Culture,"
i. pp. 119, 120 (there quoted).

abnormal[1] is sufficient to constitute an omen, and frequently "anxiety on important occasions" will succeed in creating one. If one is setting out on a journey, on which important interests depend, an omen of success or failure may in such moments of tense excitement be drawn from the most trival happenings, even from the uttering of a chance word. Hence we can understand the importance attached to "ἐνόδιοι σύμβολοι"[2] even in a comparatively enlightened age, which had left behind it many superstitious beliefs. Having its origin largely in solicitude of mind, it is clear that the creation of omens is capable of endless development,[3] and if the omen is a vague one, as it often is, it necessitates recourse to a professional interpreter. Cicero ridicules[4] his contemporaries for their belief in such omens, and makes capital especially out of the want of agreement between the professors of the science of augury. "Ita nobis sinistra videntur, Graiis et barbaris dextra meliora." A raven on the right or a crow on the left was to be regarded as a credible omen![5] Still, in spite of such disagreement, and notwithstanding the apparent absurdity of drawing omens from mere chance occurrences, it is interesting to find[6] that Augustus was particularly influenced by them, and his attitude may be taken as an index of the prevalence of such beliefs in his day. Horace tells us[7] also of birds being taken as omens of impending rain. This phenomenon, however, is common in every age, for the habits of birds, especially

---

[1] Halliday, op. cit. p. 165 et seq.

[2] Æschylus, P.V. 487; cf. Arist. Frogs, 196; Eccles. 792; Plutus 41; Theop. Char. xvi.; Tib. I. iii. 17 et seq.; Burne, "Handbook of Folk-Lore," p. 124 et seq. for modern examples.

[3] Cf. Prop. IV. iii. 60.

[4] De Div. II. xxxix. 81 et seq.

[5] Ibid. xxxviii. 80; Hor. Odes, III. xxvii. 15; Virg. Eclog. ix. 15; Plutarch, Roman Questions, 25, 78.

[6] Suet. Oct. 92.

[7] Hor. Odes, III. xvii. 12; xxvii. 10; Virg. Georgic, i. 388; Lucr. v. 1084 et seq.

of migratory birds, are often conditioned by a change of seasons and of the weather. By many primitive peoples the birds were believed[1] not merely to furnish signs of coming changes of weather, but to be actually the authors of such changes.

One of the best known Odes of Horace is that in praise of the Fons Bandusiae.[2] It is, however, the natural beauty of the spring and its setting that rises spontaneously to our memory, and we are apt to forget its sacred character, evidenced by the offerings, that are made to it of wine and flowers, and by the sacrifice of a kid. The sacrifice was evidently an annual one, made on an appointed day, possibly on the festival of the Fontanalia[3] (13 Oct.). Such a sacrifice probably had its origin in an animistic age, and was offered to the spirit of the spring, that the supply of fresh water would not fail. The Romans commonly regarded wells and springs as sacred in character.[4] The Younger Pliny gives us an elaborate description of the source of the Clitumnus,[5] of the temple of the river-god, and of the votive offerings, that were cast into the stream. In the middle of the last century, when the mouth of one of the sulphur springs (*Aquae Apollinares*) near Lake Bracciano was being cleared, a valuable find was made of many such votive offerings.[6]

Horace preserves for us another piece of popular superstition, in reference to the efficacy of certain numbers. "There is a divinity in odd numbers," and odd numbers especially

---

[1] Halliday, op. cit. p. 259; Frazer, "G.B." vol. i. p. 261.

[2] Odes, III. xiii.

[3] Warde Fowler, " Roman Festivals," p. 240; cf. quotation there given from Varro, L.L. 6, 21.

[4] Hor. Sat. I. v. 24; Odes, I. i. 22; cf. Odes, I. xxvi. 6; Ovid, Fasti, iii. 281 *et seq.*

[5] Ep. viii. 8.

[6] Lanciani, " Ancient Rome," pp. 46-7; cf. Burne, op. cit. p. 27 *et seq.*; Gomme, " Ethnology in Folk-Lore," p. 71 *et seq.*, for such beliefs in modern times.

were regarded as possessing extraordinary powers. This belief in the efficacy of certain numbers was intimately related to the religious ideas of the Chaldæans. They believed Time and the divisions of Time to be divine,[1] and hence the numbers, corresponding to the divisions of Time which they recognized, were also regarded as divine. Numbers were first revealed to men by Uranus,[2] through the movements of the stars. As the result of such speculations, numbers such as nine, correspond- ing to the third part of the month, seven and twelve, correspond- ing to the number of the planets and the signs of the Zodiac, were believed to be endowed with a potency peculiar to them- selves. At this point Astrology and Magic are again in close contact. We find numbers such as three, seven, nine, figuring prominently in magical incantations, and magical formulæ have to be pronounced a certain number of times [3] before they pro- duce the desired effect. Three has always been regarded as a number of very marked efficacy. It was intimately bound up with the cult of the dead,[4] and both itself and its multiples, nine and twenty-seven, were considered to be sacred numbers. We find " three " occurring repeatedly [5] in connection with magic formulæ, and the old belief in its power still finds an echo in our modern phrase " the third time is the charm ". Its multiple, nine, was likewise used in magic, in prayers addressed to the deities of magic,[6] and in rites for the ex- pulsion of ghosts.[7] We know how frequently another multiple, twenty-seven, figured in sacred ceremonies.[8] To the number

---

[1] Cumont, " Astrology and Religion," p. 111.

[2] *Ibid.* p. 50.   [3] Hor. Ep. I. i. 37.

[4] Diels, " Sib. Blätter," p. 40 *et seq.*, quotes examples from Roman and modern times ; cf. Hor. Odes, I. xxviii. 36.

[5] Abt, op. cit. p. 241 ; Papyr Paris, 850 *et seq.* (there quoted) ; Hor. Odes, III. xxii. 3 ; Sat. II. i. 7 ; Virg. Eclog. viii. 74 ; Tib. I. ii. 54 ; Ovid, Fasti, ii. 449 ; Met. vii. 190 ; Seneca, Medea, 840 ; Pliny, N.H. xxx. 44.

[6] Tib. I. v. 16.   [7] Ovid, Fasti, v. 395.

[8] Diels, " Sib. Blätter," p. 41 ; Horace's " Carmen Saeculare " was sung by a choir of twenty-seven youths and twenty-seven maidens ; cf. Warde Fowler, " The Religious Experience," p. 441.

seven [1] also, a special potency was attributed in magical operations. Gellius, following a work of Varro entitled "Heb-
domades," treats us [2] to a long description of the many and
varied powers of this number, largely based on its connection
with Astrology.

There are a few other points of lesser importance, where
Horace is in touch with popular usage and belief. He speaks
of the "triste bidental," [3] a name given to a place, that had
been struck by lightning, or where a thunderbolt had fallen.
The lightning or thunder was believed to be buried there, so
that all such places were surrounded by a low wall, and became "loca religiosa," invested, as it were, with taboo, and
preserved from human contact. Again, he refers [4] to the
custom of making *ex-voto* offerings at the shrine of some
deity. It was customary after shipwreck for one, who had
been saved, to have a painting of the scene executed and
hung up in the temple of some god, to whom he believed
he was indebted for his safety. Such votive tablets were frequently hung up, too, in honour of Isis, [5] by patients after their
recovery from illness. It was not unfrequent either for a
warrior, as the result of a vow, to dedicate his arms [6] to some
deity on the completion of a successful campaign. Finally,
Horace mentions a belief, [7] which may have prevailed among
his countrymen, that the dreams, that come to us towards
morning, bear the stamp of truth. In this case, however, as

[1] Ovid, Fasti, ii. 452.

[2] N.A. III. x.

[3] A.P. 471 ; cf. Persius, ii. 27 ; Warde Fowler, op. cit. pp. 37, 52, 309 ;
Wissowa, " Religion und Kultus," p. 122 (on *puteal*) ; *ibid.* pp. 477-9.

[4] Sat. II. i. 33 ; Odes, I. v. 13 ; A.P. 20.

[5] Tib. I. iii. 27 ; Juv. xii. 27 ; cf. F. Richter, " Lateinische Sacralin-
schriften," pp. 251, 252.

[6] Cf. Horace's application of the custom, Odes, III. xxvi. 4 ; cf. Ep. I.
i. 4.

[7] Sat. I. x. 33.

the same belief is referred to by Moschus,[1] we are faced with the same doubt, that confronts us with regard to many points in the poet's treatment of magic, whether he is merely following Greek literary tradition, or reproducing a popular belief of his own-day.

[1] I. 2-5 (quoted by Lejay and Kiessling, ad loc.); cf. Imitation in Ovid, Her. xix. 195.

CHAPTER VII.

LITERARY CRITICISM.

HORACE entered early into the arena of literary criticism. When he returned from Philippi, and was compelled by poverty to take to literature, he essayed a species of poetry, that was invested with an element of danger for a young man aspiring to win an honourable place in Roman Letters. In his Satires, he offended the susceptibilities of certain of his contemporaries by his freedom of attack, and he incurred the wrath of the admirers of Lucilius by his strictures on their favourite poet. He was placed on his defence, and had to justify the position he had assumed.[1]   At a later period, when his reputation among Roman poets was securely established, he did battle for the school of Virgil and Varius,[2] to which he belonged, against those who wished to exalt the Ancients over the Moderns. Thus, a goodly portion of Horace's literary criticism was delivered by way of polemic, but it was not all born amidst the din of battle. In later life, when his own fame was secure, he felt he had a message to impart, especially to his younger contemporaries who wished to accomplish something in the realms of poetry. He was then less exposed than formerly to the tooth of envy,[3] and on the strength of the position he had won [4] he could speak with an air of authority. He had made many successful experiments in the Greek metres. His mind was now matured, and he had pondered

[1] Sat. I. x.; II. i.   [2] Ep. II. i. 20 *et seq.*; A.P. 53 *et seq.*
[3] Odes, IV. iii. 16; cf. Sat. II. vi. 47.
[4] Odes, II. xx. 13; III. xxx.; Ep. I. xx. 13 *et seq.*

on the theory of poetry. Though he had never quite probed its depths, still he could give the benefit of a ripe experience, and say many things of value to those, who wished to walk in the same path as he himself had trodden. He lacked the broad sympathy, and the power of deep penetration into the principles underlying his art, that go to make a great critic, but he has the merit that, within his limitations, he gives us, as a rule, genuine literary criticism, and was uninfluenced by those extra-literary considerations,[1] which often governed appreciation for literature among the Ancients. There never was a time, when an able ciitic was more needed, when there was a more urgent call for a clear enunciation of the essentials of great literature than in the Augustan Age. It was an age of extraordinary literary activity, which ranged from the worthless effusions of poetasters,[2] like Bavius and Mævius, to the greatest monument of Roman poetry, the Æneid. Such activity is reflected in Horace and his brother poets.[3] Horace often directs his satire against the worthless poets of his day,[4] while he refers on many occasions [5] to the indiscriminate desire for poetic composition, that prevailed among his contemporaries, especially among the rich, who were always able to gather an admiring audience for the recitation of their poems. On a higher plane than these poetasters were the amateur poets on the staff of Tiberius [6] during his mission to the East, young men, who found relief in literature from the labours of

---

[1] Hor. Ep. I. ii. 1 et seq.; Quintilian, In. Or. X. i. 42, 87 ; cf. Saintsbury, " History of Criticism," p. 355 ; Nettleship, " Lectures and Essays " (Series II.), p. 45; Butcher, "Aristotle's Theory of Poetry and Fine Art," c. v.

[2] Virg. Eclog. iii. 90; ix. 36 ; Hor. Epode x. ; Prop. II. xxxiv. 84.

[3] Ibid. I. iv. 1 ; Ovid, Am. I. xv. 25 et seq.; III. vii. 60 et seq.; Tristia, IV. x. 44 et seq.; Ex Ponto, II. x. 13 ; IV. ii. 2 ; xii., xvi.; cf. Patin, " Études sur la Poesie Latine," vol. i. pp. 140, 184 et seq. ; Wight Duff, " A Literary History of Rome," p. 612 et seq.

[4] Sat. I. iv. 14, 21 ; x. 35, 80 ; II. v. 41.

[5] Ibid. I. iv. 141 ; Ep. I. xviii. 40; II. i. 117 ; A.P. 241 et seq., 382, 416.

[6] Ep. I. iii.

the camp. Horace would place still higher those literary friends,[1] including Virgil and Varius, whose approbation for his work he wished to win. But, of many of the writers, that figure in the pages of Horace and Ovid, all but their names have passed into oblivion, and we are left without material for judging if literature is the poorer for the loss. There can be little doubt that much undeserved praise[2] was lavished on poets at Rome during the Augustan Age. The obscurity, for instance, that in after years seems to have enshrouded the name of Valgius leaves' little ground for supposing that he possessed the Homeric qualities attributed to him.[3] Here lay one of the fatal defects of Roman literary criticism. The Romans, even in their criticism, kept their eyes fixed too steadfastly on the "exemplaria Graeca," and the tendency was to institute a comparison [4] between a Roman writer and his Greek or supposed Greek original, without consideration of differences of language, of epoch, and of general outlook. Again, that type of criticism had little value which coupled together the names of Virgil and Rabirius.[5]

From all this it is clear that Horace had a great field open to him, if he wished to lay down clearly the principles of great literature, and teach men to distinguish base coin from all that had the ring of genuine poetry about it. Possibly, he was too much distracted by the literary quarrels of his time to devote himself whole-heartedly to the task, even if he had the will and capacity to do so. It is difficult, too, for the great poet and the great critic to be ever united in the same person. A poet's criticism is in danger of being bounded by the limitations

---

[1] Sat. I. x. 81 et seq.; cf. Odes, I. vi. 1 et seq.; xxxiii. 2; II. i., ix. 9 et seq.; IV. ii. 33 et seq.

[2] Cf. Hor. Sat. I. x. 2; Ep. II. i. 73 et seq.; A.P. 263 et seq., for instances of defective criticism in his own and previous ages.

[3] Panegyr. Mess. 180; cf. Hor. Odes, I. vi. 2 on Varius.

[4] Hor. Ep. II. i. 57, 58; cf. Quintilian, X. i. 86 on Virgil; ibid. 101, 105; Prop. II. xxxiv. 61; Nettleship, op. cit. p. 53.

[5] Velleius, ii. 36.

of the poetic art as expounded in his own verse. He is thus likely to lack that wide sympathy essential for successful criticism. If by chance a critic were also a great creative poet, and wished to lay bare the secret of his art, it is doubtful if he could reveal the whole secret. This would demand a revelation of his soul, of all the convolutions of his genius, of those flashes of insight into realities not revealed to the "profanum vulgus," those visions of eternal verities not granted to meaner mortals. Horace cannot lay claim to be a great creative poet, but he has some useful lessons to impart on the technique of his art. In this he was almost flawless. The verse of his lyrics in particular came near perfection in polish and symmetry. He could thus teach the lesson of careful workmanship to a generation given to indiscriminate poetising.

It is not easy to determine with precision how far Horace wished to play the rôle of critic. The aim of the "Ars Poetica" especially has been the subject of much discussion,[1] some professing to find in it a complete didactic poem, while for others it possesses merely the casual and desultory character of the "Epistle". Norden, with a vast show of erudition, has endeavoured to prove that it was a treatise belonging to what he styles "Isagogic" literature,[2] a class of treatises, which were introductory to a subject, and professed to expound the results of scientific research in a manner intelligent to beginners. This theory, interesting as it is, is unconvincing. The "Ars Poetica" was certainly never meant to be a complete treatise on the art of poetry, or, for one thing, Horace would have felt himself bound to devote as much space to the

---

[1] *Vide* Kiessling, Introd. to Ars Poetica, pp. 279-80; Norden, "Hermes," vol. xl. p. 481 *et seq.*; Hack, "The Doctrine of Literary Forms," p. 5 *et seq.*, in "Harvard Studies in Classical Philology," vol. xxvii.; Boissier, "Révue de Philologie," vol. xxii. 1898; "L'Art Poétique d'Horace et la Tragédie Romaine," p. 2 *et seq.*

[2] Norden, op. cit. pp. 512, 516, 527.

other forms of poetry as he does to the dramatic genres.   In it, moreover, Horace says many things that have a direct bearing on the literary efforts of the Pisos [1] and of other contemporaries.   The work, too, shows traces of Horace's own literary creed, and of the limitations from which he suffered as a critic. He was trammelled by the restraints imposed by his predecessors.   Many of his precepts are purely mechanical and conventional.   His criticism is case-hardened in the "doctrine of literary forms," [2] which dominated ancient critics generally. Hence springs his clear distinction between Tragedy, Comedy, and Satyric drama, his rules for the employment of various metres, his law of the five acts and three actors in Tragedy, his rules for the chorus, his encouragement of traditional subjects.   He often insists [3] on the need of preserving propriety in depicting the characters of a drama, and with some at least of his precepts no one can quarrel.   But his plea for sanity in literature, for the need of rigorous self-criticism or the guidance of a competent and fearless judge, his appeal for a fuller consciousness of the poet's mission, his insistence on the "unimpeachable doctrine of style" have still their value, and were particularly suited to an age when there were so many aspirants to literary fame,[4] and when flattery was often made a substitute for candid criticism.

As we have seen, Horace, generally speaking, was uninfluenced by the antiquarian tendencies of his time, but

---

[1] A.P. 38, 128, 154, 278.

[2] Hack, op. cit. pp. 27, 38, 41, 43 *et seq.*   The whole Essay is suggestive, though his strictures on the doctrine of literary forms often resemble the revolt of the Romanticist against the Classical school.   One might deplore the doctrine, as exhibiting the limitations of ancient criticism, just as one might rail at Classical architecture for not possessing the freedom of the Gothic.   One of its worst effects, however, in poetry was to distract attention from the spirit, and direct it to mere externals.

[3] A.P. 110, 156 *et seq.*, 316.

[4] This was a not uncommon characteristic of Imperial times ; cf. Persius, i. 69, 105 ; Petron. Satyr, 118 ; Pliny, Ep. i. 13 ; Juv. iii. 9.

possibly it was under the influence of such tendencies that he set himself to describe [1] the development of drama at Rome from its first faint beginnings. The passage is especially interesting in the light of a passage in his contemporary Livy,[2] which bears some analogies to it. It was certainly Livy's intention to trace the origin and development of drama [3] at Rome, but his account has given rise to a storm of criticism.[4] He begins his account with the introduction, on the occasion of a pestilence at Rome (365 B.C.), of dancers from Etruria, who danced their national dances, "in not ungraceful fashion," to the music of the flute. He next proceeds to sketch a development among the Romans themselves, as the result of the example set by the Etruscans. The free-born youth [5] of the city began to *imitate* [6] the Etruscans in a kind of rude dialogue ("inconditis inter se jocularia fundentes versibus "), accompanied by appropriate gestures. As is clear from Livy's subsequent statement,[7] this first stage of purely Roman development centred in the Fescennine verses. Livy now advances to a further stage, in which no longer the free-born youth but professional actors "saturas modis impletas, descripto jam ad tibicinem cantu, motuque congruenti peragebant". This stage, with its variety of melodies, its flute accompaniment, and the appropriate gestures of the actors, was an advance upon the crude improvisations of the Fescennine verses, and it is this stage of "dramatic satire" that has

---

[1] Ep. II. i. 139 *et seq.*

[2] Livy, VII. ii. 4 *et seq.*; cf. Val. Max. II. iv. 4.

[3] I.e. of Comedy. Livy does not concern himself with Tragedy.

[4] *Vide* Michaut, "Sur les Trétaux latins," p. 88 *et seq.*; cf. Lejay, Horace Satires, Introduction, p. 83 *et seq.*

[5] For "juventus," cf. Cic. Pro Sulla, xii. 34, and phrase "princeps juventutis ".

[6] "Imitari " is used probably in a very general way to denote that the Roman youth was stirred to native effort by the example of the Etruscans.

[7] " Non sicut antea Fescennino versu similem, etc."

especially provoked the attacks of modern critics.[1]   Livy now
takes us a step further, and introduces Livius Andronicus as
the first to give these dramatic pieces a regular plot,[2] in the
sense of giving unity to pieces before disconnected in character,
and loosely strung together.   The development, which Livy
puts to the credit of Andronicus, is an organic development
from the older saturae.   Thus the stage of regular artistic
drama was reached, with the result that "res a risu et soluto
joco avocabatur".

Hendrickson and those who think with him maintain that
this whole account is neither Livy's own nor based on
actual fact, but is due to some critic, who, in endeavouring
to trace the development of Comedy at Rome, was influenced
by Aristotle's history of Greek Comedy.   Aristotle exhibits
three stages of development in the Comedy of Greece, its
beginnings [3] in the Phallic hymns, which were followed by
the Old Comedy [4] (ἡ ἰαμβικὴ ἰδεά), to which he denies the
name of Comedy proper.   Finally came the New Comedy, the
founder of which was Crates,[5] who abandoned personal invective, and *generalised* his plots and themes.   Hendrickson maintains that there are three corresponding stages in Livy—the
Fescennine verses, which, like the Phallic hymns, were designed to promote fertility, the "Saturae," the stage of personal invective (*solutus jocus*) corresponding to the Old Comedy,
and finally the great innovation of Livius, in constructing, as
Crates did, a regular plot, and thus giving Rome a drama akin
to the New Comedy in Greece.

---

[1] Hendrickson, "Am. Jour. of Phil." vol. xv. 1894, p. 1 *et seq.*; *ibid.*
vol. xix. p. 285 *et seq.*; Leo, "Hermes," 1904, vol. xxxix. p. 63; Kiessling,
Introduction to Horace Satires, p. 10.   On the conservative side, cf. Knapp,
"Am. Jour. of Phil." vol. xxxiii. p. 175 *et seq.*; Webb, "Classical Philology," vol. vii. p. 177 *et seq.*, "On the Origin of Roman Satire".

[2] "Ab saturis ausus est primus argumento fabulam serere."

[3] Arist. Poet. iv. 1449a.

[4] *Ibid.*; cf. ix. 1451b; Butcher, op. cit. p. 349 *et seq.*

[5] Arist. Poet. v. 1449b.

Hendrickson now advances a step further, and finds a parallel to Livy's account in Horace,[1] to whom he applies a similar criticism. In Horace we meet first with the Fescennine verses, rude improvisations, which were harmless enough as long as they were associated with the old harvest festivals, but gradually the second stage is reached, when personal invective became the dominant note in such performances ("jam saevus apertam in rabiem coepit verti jocus"), which so wounded reputations and so spread uneasiness, that the law was compelled to intervene to suppress such unrestrained licence. With this a change was wrought, when the New Comedy was introduced, the characteristics of which Hendrickson claims to find in Horace's words, "ad bene dicendum et delectandum redacti," the distinctive marks, according to Aristotle,[2] of the New Comedy. With this stage Horace, Hendrickson says, associates the introduction of the Greek drama, when the "grave virus" of the old performances passed away, though some traces of rusticity still lingered.

Now, let us return to Livy, and see how far Hendrickson's statement is true that Livy's account is ultimately derived from Aristotle. Hendrickson concentrates his attention especially on Livy's second stage of "dramatic satire," and it is against it in particular that he directs his destructive criticism. But, if Livy's account is merely a pendant to Aristotle's history of Greek Comedy, the first stage of the Fescennine verses will be involved in similar destruction to the second. At first sight, there seems a clear analogy between the Phallica and the Fescennine verses, especially if we adopt the second etymology suggested by Festus, which derives the name " Fescenninus " not from the Etruscan town of Fescennia,[3] but from "fascinum," though the difficulties of the derivation are obvious. One thing, however, is clear that

---

[1] Ep. II. i. 139 et seq.
[2] Nic. Ethics, iv. 14, 7, τῷ μὴ λύπειν τόν ἀκουόντα τὲ και τέρπειν.
[3] Michaut, op. cit. p. 40 ; Servius ad Æn. vii. 695 (there quoted).

17

the idea of the promotion of fertility was associated with these verses, and, with this end in view, they were sung at marriage feasts,[1] and were employed for the same purpose in harvest festivals.　The same idea was dominant in the Phallic hymns, but, as students of anthropology know, in such primitive material as these two, one cannot argue from analogy to identity.　The performance of certain rites [2] accompanied by song and dance at the time of harvest or vintage, either to insure fertility, or to offer thanks for fruitful crops already obtained, is a custom, the existence of which in primitive Italy need cause no surprise.　To explain it, recourse need not be had to an hypothesis of borrowing.　Virgil describes [3] a native and primitive country festival, as a pendant indeed to a Greek one, in which the old inhabitants of Italy disported themselves in rude song and unrestrained mirth in honour of Bacchus to promote the fertility of the vine.　A purely dramatic element entered into the festival, as those, who took part in it, wore masks and apparently acted in character. Virgil says nothing of dialogue, but the very use of the mask seems to suggest some kind of dialogue between the actors. The "versus incompti" employed on the occasion may well be the crude improvisations of the Fescennine verses.　Again, Tibullus traces [4] the origin of song and dance to rustic festivals.　Here also, there are traces of a dramatic element.　The countryman winds through the dance with his face dyed in red vermilion, thus apparently dancing in character.　In such festivals one can find the first faint beginnings of drama.　Such vintage and harvest festivals were characterized by a certain rude banter and looseness of language, in which the "Italum acetum"[5] found expression.　It might be argued that Virgil

[1] Pliny, N.H. xv. 24 ; cf. Catullus, lxi. 122.

[2] Michaut, p. 35 *et seq.*

[3] Virg. Georgics, ii. 385 *et seq.*; cf. "Ausonii" and "carmina patria "; cf. Hor. A.P. 405.

[4] Tib. II. i. 50-6.

[5] Hor. Sat. I. vii. 32 ; cf. Michaut, op. cit. p. 19 ; Gerlach, " C. Lucilii Reliquiae," Introd. p. 89.

and Tibullus both show traces of Greek influence in their descriptions, but, even if that is conceded, it is difficult to believe that such descriptions were written without some well-established tradition to support them. Virgil's description in particular seems to point to the Fescennine verses, and to involve the rudiments of drama in connection with them. From what we know of other peoples, it is not un-natural to expect that the Romans, for long a purely agricultural community, would have developed such hymns at their vintage and harvest festivals, to secure the fertility of the crops.

It is interesting to note that Livy takes up the Fescennine verses, and follows their fortunes in a second series of developments. Some time after the establishment of the regular drama at Rome, they were revived [1] as "exodia" by the "juventus," who left the acting of the regular plays to professional actors. These "exodia" were played as epilogues [2] to larger pieces, generally, we may presume, as a relief after the strain of a serious play, thus serving the same purpose as the Satyric drama in Greece. The "Fabulae Atellanae" played a similar rôle,[3] and in process of time these revived Fescennine performances commonly became fused with them,[4] probably, as Michaut suggests, because the Atellan play was an Italian product, and these "exodia" were exhibited as a reaction against the drama imported from Greece. If Hendrickson's criticism is followed out to its logical conclusion, one would have to sweep away not merely the Fescennine verses in their original form, but all this elaborate structure of their revival and their fusion with the Atellan plays. It is difficult to believe that this is all mere invention on the part of Livy, or of the critic to whom he was indebted for his account.

[1] " Inter se *more antiquo* ridicula intexta versibus jactitare coepit."
[2] Michaut, op. cit. p. 76.
[3] *Ibid.* p. 82 *et seq.* for a good deal of evidence; *cf.* Cic. Ad Fam. IX. xvi. 7.
[4] " Consertaque fabellis potissimum Atellanis."

Now let us pass to Livy's second stage of "dramatic satire," which Hendrickson maintains was invented purely as an analogue to the Old Comedy in Greece. He depends especially on the phrase [1] which Livy uses to describe his "saturae "—" res a risu et soluto joco avocabatur". He declares that in the phrase "solutus jocus" you have the characteristics of the Old Comedy, with its violence of personal invective. There is no proof that the phrase can express all that Hendrickson wishes it to express. Lejay takes it to mean [2] something that passes the limits of good taste. We might even go further, and admit that it can mean rude banter,[3] such as was common at Roman triumphs and harvest festivals, but it would still be a long way from expressing the bitter spirit of invective, that characterized the Old Comedy. It cannot be proved that Livy's "solutus jocus" has a parallel in Horace's "saevus jocus". Livy mentions not a word about the intervention of the law to restrain the "saturae," while such intervention took place in the case of the Old Comedy,[4] and is given great prominence in the corresponding stage in Horace.[5] Again, the flute accompaniment,[6] to which Livy attaches importance in his account of the "saturae," is a purely Italian element. Moreover, the plays of the Old Comedy have a continuous coherent plot, while Livy denies such to his "saturae". Hendrickson suggests that the employment of the name "saturae" in Livy's passage was due to some one, who identified [7] the Satires of Lucilius with the

---

[1] This, of course, is not the whole of Hendrickson's case. He relies too, on a passage from Evanthius, and on the tradition of Saturae written by Nævius; cf. Art. 1894, pp. 14, 19; Lejay, pp. 88, 93. I am concerned here only with the argument drawn from the text of Livy.

[2] Op. cit. p. 87.

[3] Cf. Virgil's "risus solutus," Georgic, ii. 386; Livy, iv. 53, "ab risu solutisque jocis non abstinerent"; Hor. Sat. I. iv. 82.

[4] Hor. A.P. 281 et seq.   [5] Hor. Ep. II. i. 152.

[6] This is a point emphasized by Lejay, op. cit. p. 86.

[7] Michaut, op. cit. p. 58; Diomede, iii. (Keil, i. 485); Evanthius, De Fabula, ii. 5 (there quoted).

Old Comedy. The same characteristics being discovered in the dramatic pieces described by Livy, the name "saturae" was transferred to them. All this, however, is irrelevant in a criticism of Livy's passage, unless it can be shown that Livy's "saturae" possess the characteristics of the Old Comedy. It is precisely in proving this, that Hendrickson seems to me to have failed. I would be inclined to think that the name "saturae" was transferred to the dramatic pieces in Livy, not from the Satires of Lucilius, but from those of Ennius. The dominant note in "satura," as handled by the predecessors of Lucilius, was that of a mixture or medley, without any suggestion of a spirit of invective. The dramatic pieces sketched by Livy were discursive and disconnected, and Andronicus is represented as effecting an improvement in them, by giving them a certain unity of plot. It is possible, then, that some critic after Ennius transferred the name "satura" from his Satires, which had no relation with the stage, to the dramatic medley sketched for us by Livy. We may quarrel with the name as misleading and inappropriate, but it is not possible, I believe, to deny the existence of the performances so circumstantially described by Livy, on the ground that they are a mere fancied analogue to the Old Comedy.

When we proceed to Livy's third stage, and the rôle played by Livius Andronicus in the development of the drama, here again we may question whether the historian or the critic he follows is treading closely in the footsteps of Aristotle. Andronicus is said to play the same part in Livy's account as Crates does in Aristotle's history of Greek Comedy. Livy, however, uses "argumentum" in a very general way, without any qualifying phrase. The word might thus be used to denote the plot in the plays of the Old Comedy, which exhibited a certain unity and coherence. Aristotle expressly says that Crates was the first to introduce a plot of a definite kind, to *universalise*[1] his plot, and pass from the personal attack

---

[1] Poet. v. 1449 b. καθόλου ποιεῖν λόγους καὶ μύθους—"generalise his themes and plots" (Butcher).

characteristic of the Old Comedy. Andronicus gave a certain unity to pieces before disconnected, but Hendrickson would find it difficult to prove that Livy credits him with the precise innovation, which Aristotle attributes to Crates. It is strange, however, to find Livy associating the name of Andronicus with what was a mere development of native drama, while for Varro[1] he is the one, who had the glory of introducing Greek drama into Rome. Varro, always a careful investigator, is the more credible witness. Livy's narrative is here at fault, and either he or the critic, whom he follows, has got hold of an erroneous tradition.

Hendrickson would discover in the passage quoted from Horace a practically complete parallel with Livy's account of the rise of Roman drama, but there are some marked differences between the two writers. For both, drama has its origin in the Fescennine verses, but their opening standpoint is not the same. Horace is concerned with the Fescennine verses in their original home in the country, at the time of the harvest festival, while in Livy's opening stage, they are divorced from their original associations, and transplanted to the city, where they figure in the performances of the city-bred youths. Livy, too, as we saw, follows their fortunes in a second series of developments, when they were revived as "exodia," but of this there is nothing in Horace, unless the vague phrase "hodieque manent vestigia ruris"[2] can be referred to it. Still less can the second stage in each writer be said to be parallel. At this point in Horace, the Fescennine verses have evidently migrated from the country to the city,[3] and are now marked by the spirit of personal invective, characteristic of the Old Comedy. Their violence became so great, that the law intervened to restrain it. In Livy's second stage of "dramatic satire," we have, I believe, something wholly distinct from the Fescennine verses. It was

---

[1] Gellius, N.A. xvii. 21-42. Livy is thus not dependent upon Varro; cf. Michaut, op. cit. p. 101 *et seq.*

[2] Ep. II. i. 160.   [3] Cf. " per honestas domos," *ibid.* 149.

an advance upon them as a dramatic species, but was not an organic development[1] proceeding from them. For this reason, Livy makes a clear distinction between the voluntary actors in the one case, and the professional actors, who performed in the "saturae". It is significant that, when the Fescennine verses were revived, they were once again associated with the free-born youth, voluntary actors instead of professionals. Livy's "saturae" bear no traces of personal invective. There is no proof, as we saw, that his "solutus jocus" is identical with Horace's "saevus jocus," nor has the historian a word about the intervention of the law.

We reach the third stage in Horace, when the Fescennine verses were compelled by law "ad bene dicendum delectandumque".[2] Here, Hendrickson says, Horace has in mind the introduction of the New Comedy, the characteristics of which, according to Aristotle, are τῷ μὴ λύπειν τον ἀκουόντα τὲ και τέρπειν. There is an analogy of phrase between Horace and Aristotle, but is it sufficient to support the serious hypothesis advanced by Hendrickson? Moreover, Horace in the words quoted seems to have still in mind merely a further development of native drama in the Fescennine verses, and to think of Greek influence only in the lines which follow.[3] Livy in his third stage is concerned with the improvements made by Andronicus in the "saturae," which, as we saw, he regarded as distinct from the Fescennine verses. Horace proceeds to deal with the Greek invasion of the Roman stage in Tragedy as well as Comedy. Livy, if his words are interpreted in their natural meaning, is concerned only with a native development in Comedy, and displays no interest whatever in tragedy. The accounts in the two writers cannot thus be said to be parallel or derived from the same source.

[1] Michaut, op. cit. p. 71, takes the opposite view, but he seems not to take sufficiently into account Livy's clear distinction between the character of the actors in each case.
[2] Ep. II. i. 155.   [3] Ibid. 156 et seq.

Hendrickson, I believe, might have had better success in proving dependence on Aristotle in the case of Horace than in that of Livy. Unless, however, we are prepared to throw overboard the Fescennine verses in their opening stage, as described by Horace, it is not easy to reject the development he traces in these rude improvisations, originally associated with the harvest festival. The development he sketches in them is not an unnatural one. When they were taken from their original setting, and transferred to the city, they would naturally assume a higher artistic form, in which the rude banter of the verses in their earlier home was turned into personal invective directed against noble Roman families. Such violence raged unchecked, till it was finally restrained by the intervention of the law.

When Horace comes to deal with Satire, he is not so much interested in its origin, as he was in the origin of drama. Whatever opinion we may hold as regards Livy's "saturae," there is a clear tradition that, before Lucilius, Ennius and Pacuvius composed "saturae". Ennius, we are told by the scholiast,[1] left four books of Satires. We know from other sources[2] some of their subjects, and a few of their titles.[3] We know nothing of the Satires of Pacuvius beyond the fact that they resembled those of Ennius.[4]

Various explanations have been proposed by the grammarian Diomede of the origin of the word "satura," as applied to a literary genre, but most in favour are those that would derive it either from "satura lanx,"[5] a dish containing all kinds of

[1] Ad Hor. Sat. I. x. 46.

[2] Quintilian, IX. ii. 36, on dialogue between Life and Death; Gellius, N.A. II. xxix. 20; VII. ix. 2; Apul. Apol. 39, 6; cf. Nettleship, op. cit. p. 27; Teuffel-Schwabe, "History of Roman Literature," vol. i. p. 152.

[3] Gerlach, "Lucilii Reliquiae," Introd. p. 100.

[4] Diomede, "Gr. Lat." (ed. Keil), i. p. 485; cf. Teuffel-Schwabe, vol. i. p. 156. Festus speaks of a Satire of Nævius, cf. Lejay, op. cit. p. 97.

[5] *Vide* Michaut, op. cit. p. 58 *et seq.*; Nettleship, op. cit. p. 24; Kiessling, Introd. to Horace's Satires, p. 9.

meats, or "satura lex," a law that included in its scope various unrelated provisions. The dominant idea in the word is thus that of a medley.[1] But again, the question[2] has been raised what was the precise nature of the medley. Some (like Munck and Boissier) hold that the "satura" was a mixture of Etruscan and Roman elements, a combination of Etruscan dances and music with the native Fescennine verses. This is a view evidently based on the passage from Livy already discussed, and the "satura" is here nothing else than the "dramatic satire" of the historian. For others, it is a mixture of different "tones, forms, and subjects". Diomede furnishes a hint[3] as to its nature, when he says that formerly (i.e. before Lucilius) the name "satura" was applied to a "carmen, quod ex variis poematibus constabat," such as were the satires of Ennius and Pacuvius. This points to a number of poems, written in different metres within the limits of the same satire, the variety of metres being employed to mark a variety of subjects. This was the "older kind of satire,"[4] revived by Varro, who imitated Menippus of Gadara.[5] The Satires of Varro were a mixture of prose and verse in different kinds of metre. They were a medley of myth and history,[6] largely aspersed with Greek philosophy, and treating of such disparate subjects as poetry, grammar, and the general vices of the age.[7]

[1] Juv. i. 86, "nostri farrago libelli". [2] Michaut, op. cit. p. 67 et seq.
[3] Loc. cit. Quintilian, X. i. 95, distinguishes Varro's satire from the older satire, by saying it was "non sola carminum varietate mixtum".
[4] Quintilian, loc. cit. Lejay, op. cit. p. 108, takes the "prius saturae genus" to be that of Menippus, but what becomes then of Quintilian's boast, "Satura quidem tota nostra est"?
[5] Cic. Acad. Post. I. ii. 8: "Menippum imitati, non interpretati". Riese, "Varronis Sat. Men. Reliquiae," Introd. p. 8; Probus ad Virg. Eclog. vi. 31 (there quoted) says Varro was called Menippeus "a societate ingenii, quod is quoque omnigeno carmine satiras suas expoliverat"; cf. Riese, ibid. p. 15; Gerlach, op. cit. p. 102.
[6] Nettleship, op. cit. p. 35; Riese, op. cit. p. 22 et seq.; cf. Mommsen, Hist. vol. iv. p. 558 et seq.
[7] Gellius, N.A. vii. 16; ii. 18, 7; iii. 18, 5; xiii. 11, 22; xv. 19; Riese, op. cit. p. 38 et seq.

These Satires looked upon the foibles of the time from the philosophic standpoint, and moralised on life, but not with that vehemence and acrimony, which distinguished Satire in the hands of Lucilius. It is strange to find Horace making merely a passing reference[1] to the earlier phase of Satire, and reserving for Lucilius the glory of being the real founder[2] of this literary genre. The explanation is to be found in the novel character impressed by Lucilius on the work of his predecessors. In some books of his Satires at least, he preserved the variety of the old Satire by using different kinds of metres,[3] and possibly, too, he was aiming at variety by the mixture of Greek and Latin, which Horace regards as a defect in his works.[4] But, if we consider the work of Lucilius as a whole, it is clear that he left the impress of his genius indelibly marked upon Satire. Though Ennius had employed hexameters in his Satires, yet Lucilius was the first to write an entire book[5] of Satires in hexameters, thus giving metrical unity to his poems,[6] though still preserving a certain variety of subject.[7] Lucilius also employed dramatic metres, but his use of the hexameter was considered to be characteristic of him, and to be one of his great contributions to the art of writing Satire. It is evident that Horace regarded the hexameter[8] as the typically Lucilian

[1] Sat. I. x. 66. This assuredly refers to Ennius and the "turba seniorum," who preceded Lucilius. Vide Kiessling and Lejay, ad loc.

[2] Sat. I. x. 48, "Inventore minor". This (with Kiessling) I refer to Lucilius. If taken to refer to Ennius, it is difficult to explain Hor. Sat. II. i. 63. Lucilius, from the new character he gave to Satire, might well be regarded as the "inventor". For the significance of the word, vide Kiessling ad Hor. Sat. I. x. 48; cf. Hack, op. cit. p. 24.

[3] Gerlach, op. cit. pp. 109, 123, on the difficulty at times of determining the metre.

[4] Sat. I. x. 20.

[5] Books I.-XX., also XXX. were entirely in hexameters.

[6] Evanthius seems to have this in mind, when he says " Primus Lucilius novo conscripsit modo, ut poesin inde fecisset, id est unius carminis plurimos libros"; cf. Michaut, op. cit. p. 60.

[7] Gerlach, op. cit. p. 110; Lejay, op. cit. pp. 73, 106.   [8] Sat. I. x. 59.

metre, and it is clear, too, from his own practice, and from that of the other great masters of Roman Satire, Persius and Juvenal, that after Lucilius this metre came to be looked upon as the appropriate medium for Satiric writers. An even greater achievement of Lucilius was to have definitely stamped upon Satire the character of invective,[1] which it retained in the hands of Horace, Persius, and Juvenal, and which is still regarded as its very essence. Hence Horace could proclaim[2] the dependence of Lucilius on the writers of the Old Comedy. When he says that Lucilius differed from them only in employing a different metre, he clearly means, that he was indebted to them especially for what was most characteristic of them, their spirit of personal attack. Hence Diomede describes Lucilian Satire as "ad carpenda hominum vitia archaeae comoediae charactere compositum," and contrasts it with the older style of Satire, written by Ennius and Pacuvius. It was these innovations of Lucilius that enabled Horace to regard him as the "inventor" of Roman Satire, and as his own master in the art.[3] He breathed into it a spirit of his own, making it almost a new creation, so that Horace, considering his standpoint, was in a position to practically ignore the work of Ennius and Pacuvius, and pass over in silence the Menippean Satires of Varro. After Lucilius, Varro of Atax,[4] and "quidam alii"[5] attempted Satire, but their efforts met with no success.

[1] Hor. Sat. I. x. 3; Cic. Ad Fam. xii. 16; Persius, i. 114; Juv. i. 165.
[2] Sat. I. iv. 6 *et seq.*; cf. Persius, i. 123. Hendrickson, "A. J. Ph." 1894, p. 11, suggests that the comparison of Lucilius to the Old Comedy was first due to Varro. Nettleship, op. cit. p. 34, regards Horace's criticism as a complaint, but I cannot detect any trace of complaint in it; cf. Sat. I. x. 9 *et seq.*, where Horace enumerates the excellences of the Old Comedy worthy of imitation.
[3] Sat. II. i. 28, 34.
[4] *Vide* Prop. II. xxxiv. 85; Ovid, Am. I. xv. 21; Tristia, ii. 439; Quintilian, X. i. 87; Riese, op. cit. p. 261 *et seq.* for some fragments. There is nothing left of his Satires.
[5] Probably Nicanor, and L. Abuccius, "cujus Luciliano charactere sunt libelli," Varro, R.R. III. ii. 17.

Horace, while recognising the part played by Lucilius in the development of Roman Satire, has criticised[1] him severely for his want of form, his redundancy, the slovenliness of his verse, and his careless workmanship generally. He lacked the urbanity,[2] the incisiveness, the economy of language, which were the great glory of the writers of the Old Comedy. Lucilius had written for the average man,[3] not for the cultured few. Horace reversed the position, and while ignoring the common crowd, as is his wont, he appealed to the judgment of the educated,[4] and to a select circle of the initiated.[5] These latter were to be found especially in the literary coteries,[6] which were so characteristic of the Augustan Age, and had no little influence on the critical outlook of Horace. The prominence Horace gives to his own practice is clearly intended as a stricture on the course followed by Lucilius.

Horace lays down one very important principle in the course of his criticism of Lucilius. He says[7] that, if Lucilius had lived in the Augustan Age, he would have pruned and polished his verse, till it reached a far greater degree of excellence than it did. In putting forward this extenuating circumstance as an excuse for the crudeness of the poet, he shows that he realised the importance of the historical element in literary criticism. He recognises that literature has its periods of development clearly defined, that, at least as far as form is concerned, like the other arts, it must grow gradually from infancy to perfect manhood. This is a far-reaching principle in literary criticism, obvious indeed to the modern mind, but not so obvious to a

---

[1] Sat. I. iv. 8 *et seq.*; I. x. 1, 50.   [2] *Ibid.* x. 9 *et seq.*

[3] Cic. De Fin. I. iii. 7; De Or. II. vi. 25.

[4] Sat. I. x. 76; cf. Ep. II. i. 187; A.P. 248, 342.

[5] Sat. I. iv. 73; x. 81 *et seq.* Horace has no ambition to become hackneyed, or descend to the position of a school text. Cf. Sat. I. x. 75; Ep. I. xix. 37 *et seq.*; xx. 17; Persius, i. 29. In Juvenal's time he had become so, cf. Sat. vii. 226.

[6] Wight Duff, p. 612 *et seq.*; cf. Cic. Brutus, 283.

[7] Sat. I. x. 67 *et seq.*; cf. Quintilian, x. 1, 97.

critic in the time of Horace, though it had been already recognised by Cicero[1] in dealing with Roman oratory.

Moreover, in enumerating this principle Horace sets up the
Augustan Age[2] as the standard of excellence. It is the superior
polish and refinement of its verse,[3] that in Horace's eyes constituted its chief claim to pre-eminence. Assuredly, when
one compares not only the older poets, but the rough-hewn
hexameters of Lucretius with the marvel of achievement
wrought by Virgil, the claim was not excessive. Few years
separated these two poets, yet in these few years the Latin
language had reached its highest excellence as a poetic medium,
and Virgil could evoke from it new and sublime harmonies,
hitherto unheard by his countrymen.

Horace not only sets up the Augustan Age as a criterion of
worth, but, in laying such emphasis on the need of perfection
of form,[4] he makes a tacit appeal to his own practice. He
was himself a model of correctness, who valued above all
quality in poetry,[5] and polished his verse[6] with almost excessive care. The lesson, that he teaches most insistently,
is the necessity of the "limae labor,"[7] and of a rigorous self-
criticism, if one aspires to be a poet. We have seen the

---

[1] Brutus, 288, 294; cf. Haenni, "Die litterarische Kritik in Cicero's
'Brutus,'" p. 17 *et seq.*; Jebb, "Attic Orators," Introd. p. 67 *et seq.*,
on the criticism of Dionysius. The author of the "Dialogus" (chaps. 18,
19, 25) takes even higher ground, making oratory depend on social and
political conditions. It is thus the expression of the nation's life.

[2] Cf. A.P. 272.

[3] Note Horace's words used in criticism of the older poets—"nimis
antique," "dure," "ignave," "crasse," "illepide," Sat. I. iv. 9; Ep. II.
i. 66 *et seq.*

[4] In Literature generally, the Romans were inclined to insist particularly on mere form. Cf. the Roman conception of History as an
"opus maxime oratorium"; Cic. De Leg. i. 5; Or. xx. 66; Quintilian, X.
i. 31-3.

[5] "Nam ut multum non moror," Sat. I. iv. 13.

[6] Odes, IV. ii. 31, "operosa carmina".

[7] A.P. 290-2, 386 *et seq.*; Sat. I. x. 72; Ep. II. i. 167; II. ii. 109 *et
seq.*, 122.

literary activity, that prevailed in Horace's day, and this circumstance may have convinced him of the importance of laying down stringent rules for writing. But, moreover, the attention he pays to form springs from his general theory of poetry. Horace would not find a place in his Republic of Letters for the " mad poet,"[1] the creature of inspiration, who, dependent for success on the divine afflatus, ignored all technical rules. He raises the question [2] whether a poet is born or made. His answer is that both art and genius [3] are required to supplement each other, but he then proceeds to lay especial stress on the need of personal effort and study, if success is to be attained. The Greeks were endowed with genius,[4] the gift of the Muses, and were a people devoted before all else to the cult of the Beautiful. The Romans are essentially a practical people, immersed in the sordid things of life. If they would achieve success in poetry, they must pass through a preparatory course of severe training and stern self-discipline. From Horace's remarks, it follows logically that the "art" of poetry[5] can be acquired by patient industry. Though he recognises the existence of inspiration, it is difficult to determine if he had any clearly defined theory as to its meaning. In one passage,[6] he tells us that he is indebted to Apollo not only for his inspiration (*spiritus*) but for his art, possibly wishing to distinguish the spontaneous outburst of pure poetic thought from mere technical skill in versifying. Again, in the well-known Pindar Ode,[7] he strikingly contrasts the fire, and sublimity, and onward sweep of the Greek poet with his own

[1] A.P. 296, 455 *et seq.*; cf. Cic. De Div. i. 37, 80; Plato, Phædrus, 244-5.

[2] A.P. 408 *et seq.*

[3] Cf. the distinction frequently made by the Romans between " ars " and " ingenium," A.P. 295, 320; Cic. Ad Q. Fr. II. ix.; Ovid, Ars Am. I. xv. 14, 19 ; Tristia, ii. 424 ; Quintilian, I. viii. 8.

[4] A.P. 323.

[5] I.e. technique, all that appertains to expression.

[6] Odes, IV. vi. 29.   [7] *Ibid.* ii.

laboured efforts. In many passages, he speaks of being in-spired by a Muse[1] or by some god,[2] as by Bacchus when he is endeavouring to catch the spirit of the Greek dithyramb. But, at such times, Horace is merely the slave of literary tradition, and his own exquisitely polished verse shows little trace of being written under a divine afflatus.[3] In one of the Satires he refers to the question,[4] raised by some critics, whether Comedy has the right to be classed as poetry. The right was denied to it, as it was believed to lack the force and inspiration of true poetry, both in its language and subject-matter. His own Satires, though in verse, Horace will not allow to be honoured with the name of poetry,[5] as their affinity to prose can be detected, once they are freed from the restraints of metre. He quotes a passage from Ennius,[6] in which, torture it how you will, you can always discover the " disjecti membra poetae ". All this proves that Horace held that there were some intangible qualities in poetry, which did not depend on the technique of the verse, but the elaborate rules he lays down for composition tend to leave the impres-sion that perfection of technique should be the highest aim of the poet. It was a dangerous doctrine to propound in an age of indiscriminate poetising.[7] Moreover, in no other point does Horace, despite his aversion to them, show a closer af-finity to the Alexandrians, who were often inclined to neglect the soul of poetry in their efforts to attain perfection in externals.

[1] Odes, I. i. 31 *et seq.*; xii. 2 ; III. i. 3 ; iv. 2 ; IV. iii. 24 ; cf. Virg. Eclog. ix. 32.

[2] Odes, II. xix. 6 ; III. xix. 14, "attonitus vates " ; xxv. 1 ; Ep. I. xix. 4 *et seq.*; II. ii. 78 ; cf. Quintilian, XII. x. 24.

[3] Cf. Hack, op. cit. p. 33.

[4] Sat. I. iv. 43 *et seq.*; cf. Cic. Or. 67 ; Quintilian, X. i. 81, on the poetry of Plato's prose.

[5] Sat. I. iv. 39 ; II. vi. 17 ; Ep. II. i. 250.

[6] Sat. I. iv. 60 ; cf. Norden, " Ennius und Vergilius," pp. 15 *et seq.*, 53.

[7] Ep. II. i. 117, " Scribimus *indocti doctique* poemata passim ".

Horace again was treading on dangerous ground in urging those, who write,[1] to choose a subject suited to their powers. It was an excellent doctrine in its way, of which Horace himself was a living illustration, but it was capable of being misinterpreted in an age when so many aspired to the name of poet. No one, according to it, was debarred from success, provided he did not take on himself too great a burden. Horace in particular was one who recognised to the full his own limitations. He had been urged to sing the exploits of Augustus [2] and Agrippa,[3] but his answer in each case is the same, that, however great his will, his powers are not equal to the task. His genius is for lyric poetry, his ambition [4] is to be included in the ranks of the lyric poets. His songs [5] are of love and wine ; his lays are often mere sportive airy nothings, born of some passing fancy [6] or some momentary mood, and beyond these he refuses to go to handle an Epic theme.[7] Once,[8] when he was essaying such a task, Apollo reproved him, and warned him not to set sail in his tiny bark over the Etruscan sea. Varius,[9] who is endowed with the qualities of the Epic poet, will celebrate the great deeds of Agrippa, while Antonius,[10] or some of the poets on the staff of Tiberius will sing the glories of Augustus. It is possible, too, that Horace was deterred from attempting such a task by the difficulties of the purely historical Epic.[11] The turgidity and bombast of a writer like Furius Bibaculus,[12] who undertook to celebrate the Gallic victories of Julius Cæsar, must have made still more apparent the obstacles to its successful treatment. Virgil,

---

[1] A.P. 38 ; Hack, op. cit. p. 23, rightly takes this as springing from the doctrine of literary forms ; cf. Lejay, op. cit. Introduction to Sat. IV. p. 103.

[2] Sat. II. i. 11 ; Ep. II. i. 250 *et seq.*   [3] Ode, I. vi.

[4] Odes, I. i. 35.   [5] *Ibid.* vi. 17 ; II. i. 37 ; IV. i. 1.

[6] This, of course, is not inconsistent with subsequent elaboration.

[7] Odes, II. xii. 4 ; III. iii. 69.   [8] *Ibid.* IV. xv. 1 *et seq.*

[9] *Ibid.* I. vi. 1 *et seq.*   [10] *Ibid.* IV. ii. 33 ; Ep. I. iii. 7.

[11] *Vide* Patin, op. cit. vol. i. pp. 164 *et seq.*, 184.

[12] Sat. I. x. 36 ; II. v. 41.

great poet as he was, saw the difficulty of composing an Epic founded purely upon history, and, though he once had thought of singing of the exploits of Augustus, he abandoned the idea for a work of larger scope and wider horizon, in which legend and history could be woven into one great harmonious whole worthy of Imperial Rome. It is interesting to find in Tibullus [1] and Propertius [2] the same professions of inability to treat of Epic themes. It was thus characteristic of the leading poets of the Augustan Age to know their own limitations, and not to attempt a task too great for their powers. Horace's rule was excellent for those who were endowed with the gift of poetry, and could see how far their genius would carry them, but when combined with his insistent demand for finish in externals, it might easily allure men to attempt poetry,[3] who had little or no natural talent for the task, convinced that success depended on the observation of set rules.

The effect of setting up the Augustan Age as a standard and of assigning such importance to perfection of form, is seen especially in Horace's attitude to the older poets of Rome. The eternal question of the Ancients versus Moderns was then being hotly debated. Probably through the influence of Varro, whom Cicero calls " diligentissimus investigator antiquitatis,"[4] the older poets were then in high favour [5] with some of Horace's contemporaries. Varro, the " most learned of the Romans," as Quintilian styles him,[6] contributed much to the revival of antiquarian studies at Rome. He was a pupil of Ælius Stilo,[7] one of the foremost scholars of his time. When Julius

[1] Panegyr. Mess. 177 et seq. [2] III. iii. 15 ; cf. II. xxxiv. 59 et seq.
[3] Prof. Saintsbury, op. cit. p. 225, calls the Ars Poetica a plea for mediocrity in poetry, but Horace (A.P. 372) expressly guards against such an imputation. His critical rules are rather a plea for sanity in art, though in danger of being seriously misinterpreted.
[4] Brutus, 60. [5] Ep. II. i. 21 et seq., 50. [6] X. i. 95.
[7] Suet. De Gram. iii.; Cicero, Br. 205; Acad. I. ii. 8 ; iii. 9 (with Reid's notes) ; Gellius, N.A. I. xviii. 1 et seq. ; III. iii. 12 ; XVI. viii. 2 ; XIX. xiv. ; Riese, op. cit. Introd. p. 49.

Cæsar projected the building of Greek and Latin libraries,[1] Varro was intrusted with the task of organising them, and he had the unique distinction[2] of having his bust placed, while he was still alive, in the library "in Atrio Libertatis," the first public library erected in Rome, through the munificence of Pollio. We have unfortunately little left of his critical work,[3] which centred especially in the Roman drama, but his studies must have influenced the men of his own and the succeeding generation towards an admiration for the older poets of Rome. Over and above this, antiquity was in the air during the Augustan Age. The Emperor had revived not a little of ancient religious ceremonial, had encouraged a study of the Past, and had endeavoured to turn the current of men's thoughts back to the origins of Rome. Still, admiration for the Past did not blind him to the excellences of the Present. In the matter of style at least, he condemned the use of archaisms,[4] and reproved Tiberius for hunting up "obsolete and pedantic expressions". But the taste for archaic literature in Horace's day passed all reasonable bounds, when men proclaimed their admiration[5] not only for the older poets, but for such pieces of antiquity as the text of the Laws of the Twelve Tables and the Salian Hymn. Such admiration was in part, as we have said, engendered by the antiquarian researches of Varro and his school, but in part it was a symptom of that frequently recurring phenomenon, the struggle as to the relative merits of the Ancients and Moderns.[6] Persius comments[7] on the

---

[1] Suet. Julius Cæsar, 44.

[2] Pliny, N.H. vii. 30, 15 ; Suet. Oct. 29 ; Boyd, " Public Libraries and Literary Culture in Ancient Rome," p. 4.

[3] *Vide* Nettleship, op. cit. p. 51, for a list of Varro's critical works which is based principally on Gellius.

[4] Suet. Oct. 86.   [5] Hor. Ep. II. i. 23 *et seq.*, 86.

[6] Cf. Friedländer, op. cit. vol. iii. p. 5 *et seq.*

[7] Sat. i. 76; cf. Martial, xi. 90-5. Even Lucilius found Pacuvius unnatural ; cf. Gerlach, " Reliquiae," xxvi. 48 ; Introd. pp. 55, 65, 78 ; Gellius, XVII. xxi. 49.

taste for Accius and Pacuvius in his day. Under Vespasian there were many, who professed their predilection for the prose of Cato and the Gracchi, and the poets of the Punic Wars. Quintilian tells us [1] that there were some in his time, who preferred Lucilius not only to all other writers of Satire, but to all other poets. The author of the " Dialogus " says [2] that certain of his contemporaries ranked Lucilius above Horace, Lucretius above Virgil. The Younger Pliny furnishes clear evidence [3] of the same struggle in his own period, while in the reign of Hadrian the archaising party, the Ennianistae [4] as they were called, were once more influential.

Horace makes some interesting suggestions [5] as to the cause of the popularity of the ancient poets, especially among the older men of his generation. They do not, he says, wish to yield homage to the present race of poets, men younger than themselves, who had breathed a spirit into Roman poetry, to which they were strangers. He suggests, too, that the veneration felt for the older poets was due in part to their use as school-texts, [6] though modern conditions might not bear out this contention. But, making all due allowance for the extravagant admiration of some of his contemporaries for the older poets, it must be said that Horace, in his reaction against the archaising party, is unfair in his criticism of the Ancients. That party was strong, and its line of argument apparently was that, because the most ancient writers among the Greeks were the best, the same should hold good of Roman Literature. Horace might have made a more effective answer than he did to such an argument, especially in

---

[1] X. i. 93, 43.   [2] Dial. c. xxiii. 7 ; cf. xx. 19 ; xxv.
[3] Ep. vi. 21.
[4] Gellius, xviii. 5, 3 ; cf. Wendland, " Die Hellenistisch-Römische Kultur," p. 64.
[5] Ep. II. i. 83 et seq.
[6] Ibid. i. 69 et seq.; Suet. De Gram. ii., xxiv.; Wilkins, " Roman Education," p. 60.

view of his recognition of the principle of development in
literature. By the " most ancient writers among the Greeks "
were meant especially the writers of the best period of
Greek Literature, whose masterpieces have won the admiration
of every age. Horace could have replied that, before these
masterpieces were produced, a long period of striving was
necessary. A mighty chasm separates the reliefs in the
temple of Selinus, and the so-called Ptoan Apollo from the
great creations of Phidias and Praxiteles. Before the tragedies
of Sophocles could be written, Greece had to witness first the
crude efforts of Thespis. So in Roman Literature many years
of travail had to ensue before the great works of the Augustan
Age could be given to the world. Horace directs the greater
part of his Epistle to Augustus against the predilection for the
Ancients, which many then exhibited, but, in endeavouring to
reveal the defects of the older school, he is inclined to overlook its virtues. He quotes [1] the flattering judgments of contemporary critics on the older poets, but manifestly with
disapproval. We shall find [2] that in his own criticism of the
Ancients it is above all their crudeness, the lack of polish and
refinement in their verse, that evoke his condemnation. He
is indignant that not indulgence, but honour and rewards are
demanded by their admirers for the early Roman poets. He
deplores the fact that an occasional well-turned line, or a
graceful expression in Livius is enough to win favour for a
whole poem. He sets forth the terms of praise, in which
Ennius was regarded, while clearly disagreeing with them.
In all this, he shows himself a critic with a limited horizon,
devoid of wide sympathies. He measures the older poets by
the standard of perfection reached in his own age, and naturally finds them wanting, and is thus rendered blind to the
excellences, which many of them could lay claim to. Before
Horace, Cicero had shown a marked appreciation for the old

---

[1] Ep. II. i. 50 *et seq.*   [2] *Ibid.* 66, 72 *et seq.*

Tragedians,[1] and his frequent quotations from them have preserved for us some valuable fragments. Ennius in particular
was the one writer before Virgil, in whose verse the Roman
spirit of pride in Roman greatness and achievement, and of
unshakeable faith in the future destiny of Rome, found fullest
expression. His verse could not, in the nature of things, have
shown the smoothness, polish, and rhythmical qualities of the
Augustan poets. Horace censures [2] both him and Accius for
a certain looseness in their use of the Iambic trimeter, and he
reproves Ennius in particular for his carelessness in composition, and his general ignorance of the poetic art. Still, one
has but to read such a fragment of Ennius [3] as the opening
lines of his Medea, to see in him the germ of greater things, a
foreshadowing of that solidity and massive dignity of speech,
which, when combined with the refinement of the Augustan
Age, were to make the Latin language one of the noblest
monuments of the Roman people. Virgil, who was quick to
discern the virtues of Ennius, has many close imitations of
him,[4] appropriating at times almost whole passages from the
older poet, which his genius transmuted into pure Virgilian
gold. Ovid, again, shows a wider sympathy than Horace,
speaking of him as " Ennius ingenio maximo ".[5]   Though
Quintilian's judgment [6] might not be regarded as enthusiastic,
still it is clear that, in his day, Ennius was held in the same
veneration as some ancient temple, the sanctities of which had
never been eradicated, where amidst the ruins the memory of
old worships still lingered.

[1] Laelius, vii. 24 ; De Fin. I. ii. 4 ; De Off. I. xxxi. 114 ; Tusc. Disp.
II. xxi.; III. xix. 45 ; De Or. i. 198 ; ii. 193 ; Acad. I. iii. 10 ; cf. Gellius,
XII. ii. However, in Br. 258 he censures the style of Pacuvius.

[2] A.P. 258 *et seq.*

[3] Ribbeck, " Trag. Lat. Reliquiae," pp. 36, 248 ; Rhet. ad Her. ii. 22 ;
cf. Cic. De Fin. I. ii. 4 ; Wight Duff, op. cit. pp. 143-5.

[4] Macrob. Sat. VI. i. 8 *et seq.*, 60 ; ii. 16, 27 ; iii. 3 ; Norden, op. cit.
p. 153 *et seq.* ; Glover, " Studies in Virgil," p. 54.

[5] Tristia, ii. 423 ; Am. I. xv. 19 *et seq.* ; cf. Prop. III. iii. 6.

[6] X. i. 88.

Horace censures Plautus[1] for a certain looseness of plot, and finds fault[2] with Romans of preceding generations for their praise of the wit and metre of his comedies. Here again, he concentrates too exclusively on defects, and is unwilling to make allowance for the period, in which Plautus' plays were written. Plautus wrote in a rude unlettered age, and as far at least as form was concerned, even if he had been able, he had little incentive to rise above its requirements. Possibly, too, as Horace suggests,[3] pecuniary embarrassment frequently led in his case to haste in composition. He was indifferent to the perfection of his comedies as a whole, did not aim at rigid unity, but endeavoured by a succession of comic scenes, as a rule loosely jointed, and often issuing into broad farce, to hold the attention of an audience, which would have been blind either to subtlety of plot or refinement of language. Horace, once more applying the standard of his own age,[4] finds the dramatist's verse faulty, and his plays lacking in graceful and cultured wit, and will not even recognise in him the "comica virtus,"[5] which Julius Cæsar found wanting in Terence, but which Plautus possessed in a very remarkable degree.

Now, though Horace has no word of praise for the ancient poets, it may seem strange to find him defending and encouraging the revival of archaic words by the poets of his own day. Here he is in part following out his true instincts as a poet. Poetry, dealing generally with an ideal world, has in some measure to create a language of its own,[6] possessing a dignity and sublimity to which the language of mere prose cannot lay claim. It tends to give a new content to words in current use; it will recast an ordinary phrase, and frequently

---

[1] Ep. II. i. 170 *et seq.*   [2] A.P. 270 *et seq.*   [3] Ep. II. i. 175.
[4] A.P. 272-3; cf. Sat. I. x. 13.   [5] Suet. Life of Terence, v.
[6] On the language of poetry and on poetic licence, cf. A.P. 9; Cic. De Or. i. 70; iii. 153; Or. xx. 66; De In. i. 33; Quintilian, VIII. vi. 20; X. i. 27-9; Petr. Satyr. 118; Hardie, "Classical Essays," pp. 162 *et seq.*, 198.

revive archaic words,[1] hallowed by old memories and associations. We find Horace vehemently defending this privilege,[2] partly, as I have said, giving play to his instincts as a poet, but in part, too, from a desire to uphold the practice of Virgil, Varius, and the Augustan school of poetry. Of his intimacy with Virgil and Varius, there is little need to speak. Time and again[3] he couples their names together, and has for them only the most generous and unmeasured praise.[4] They it was, who gave him his first introduction to Mæcenas,[5] which was to ripen into lasting friendship. From the way in which he couples their names, and from the prominence he gives them, it is clear that they were the moving spirits of the younger school of poets, and of the literary circle, which had gathered round the great minister of Augustus. We have unfortunately nothing left of Varius but a few fragments,[6] by which to form a judgment of his genius. Horace praises his power[7] as an Epic poet, while Quintilian passes the highest eulogy[8] on his tragedy "Thyestes," which he regards as worthy of being compared with the work of any of the Greek tragedians. The only explicit piece of literary criticism of Horace[9] on the work of his great contemporary, Virgil, was delivered in his early years, and refers almost certainly to the Eclogues and the minor poems. What exactly Horace meant by the qualities (*molle atque facetum*), which he attributes to the Mantuan poet, is open to question. Possibly they stand for Virgil's " deep and tender sensibility,"[10] for the "glow and fire" of that Celtic vein,

[1] *Vide* Raleigh, " Style," p. 32 *et seq.* on the use of archaism.
[2] Ep. II. ii. 115 *et seq.*; cf. A.P. 47 *et seq.*
[3] Sat. I. v. 40; vi. 55; Ep. II. i. 246; A.P. 55.
[4] Sat. I. v. 41; cf. Odes, I. iii. 7.   [5] Sat. I. vi. 55 *et seq.*
[6] Macrob. Sat. I. ii. 19; VI. i. 39 *et seq.*; Virg. Eclog. iii. 8; Ribbeck, op. cit. p. 347; Wight Duff, op. cit. p. 614.
[7] Sat. I. x. 43; Odes, I. vi. 1.
[8] X. 98; cf. Hor. Odes, I. xvi. 17, possibly an echo of it; Dial. xii.
[9] Sat. I. x. 44.
[10] This is suggested by Mr. Garrod, " Oxford Book of Latin Verse," Introd. p. 18 *et seq.*; cf. " English Literature and the Classics," p. 156.

which is believed to be apparent in his genius. The epithet "facetum" struck Quintilian[1] as a strange one to apply to Virgil, but Quintilian had the Æneid with all its grandeur and sublimity before his mind, so much so that he understood by the epithet a "certain grace and cultured elegance". The epithets, however, might well stand for the tenderness and playfulness of the Eclogues, and of some of the erotic poems attributed to Virgil. But Horace's admiration for his great contemporary must have grown immeasurably as the Georgics, and still more as the Æneid appeared. Virgil's wonderful achievements in Roman poetry would inevitably have impelled Horace to defend his poems from the attacks of hostile critics. It is clear that in the passages I have quoted, in which Horace lays down rules for the language of poetry, we have echoes of one of the literary quarrels of the time. Men were found to disparage the genius of Virgil.[2] There were purists,[3] who objected to the use of archaisms and to the enrichment of the language by borrowing or by the coinage of new words. Virgil has frequent close imitations[4] of the older writers, and often revives[5] archaic words, inserting them with such skill in his verse as to make them appear new creations. Such happy combinations illustrate perfectly Horace's "callida junctura,"[6] which succeeds in giving an old word the appearance of novelty. Again, Horace defends[7] the enlargement of the

---

[1] VI. iii. 19; cf. Palmer's note ad Sat. I. x. 44; Pliny, Ep. v. 3, 6 (there quoted).

[2] On the "obtrectatores Vergilii," *vide* Suet. Life of Virgil, 43 *et seq.*; cf. Suet. Gaius, 34; Dial. xii. 24; Gellius, X. xvi.; Conington, Virgil, Introd. p. 29 *et seq.*

[3] For traces of purism among the Romans, cf. Cic. Br. 139, 261, 274; Dial. xxii. 21; Macrob. Sat. I. v. 2; Hardie, op. cit. p. 278.

[4] For examples, *vide* Macrob. Sat. Bk. VI.; cf. Quintilian, I. vii. 8; IX. iii. 14; Gellius, IX. ix. 2; XII. ii. 10; Sellar, "Virgil," p. 286; Norden, "Ennius und Vergilius," p. 4 *et seq.*

[5] Macrob. Sat. VI. iv. 2; Quintilian, VIII. iii. 24.   [6] A.P. 47, 242.

[7] Ep. II. ii. 115 *et seq.*; A.P. 48 *et seq.*; cf. Cic. De Fin. III. iv. 15; De Or. iii. 38, 153; Quintilian, VIII. iii. 30 *et seq.*

language by the coinage of new words or the adoption of
words recently created.   A writer of genius will always succeed
in creating a number of new words, or by setting the seal of
his approval on words current among the people, he can raise
them to the dignity of classic language.   Horace, however, sets [1]
up limitations to the coinage of new terms.   New or lately
coined words will always win acceptance, if they are derived
from a Greek source with slight modification (*parce detorta*).
The modification desired by Horace was probably nothing
more than the giving of Latin inflexional endings to words so
borrowed.   Virgil has a goodly number of words [2] taken from
the Greek, and sometimes he even retains the Greek endings.
Many of these words, as Macrobius shows, had already been
employed by earlier writers, but apparently the critics of the
younger school of poets ignored that fact in their anxiety to
damage its prestige.   A privilege granted to Cæcilius and
Plautus is denied to Virgil and Varius.[3]   Horace is so keen
on defending the practice of his contemporaries that he goes
into the philosophy of language.[4]   He shows that language is
in the last resort a matter of custom and convention, that it is
in a condition of perpetual flux, so that words are constantly
becoming obsolete and new terms are springing into use.
He would imply that no fixed or rigid rules can be formulated
to govern the growth of language, and that writers who, like
Ennius and Cato, Virgil and Varius, have in their respective
periods helped to enrich their native tongue are worthy of all
honour.

Horace again was at variance with some of his contemporaries in his attitude to the Alexandrian poets, and their
Latin imitators.   He is never tired of proclaiming his own

---

[1] A.P. 51 *et seq.*

[2] Macrob. Sat. V. xvii. 19; xxi. 1; VI. iv. 17 *et seq.*   [3] A.P. 54.

[4] *Ibid.* 60 *et seq.*; cf. Ep. II. ii. 118 *et seq.*; cf. Quintilian, X. ii. 13;
Seneca, Ep. LXIII. 2 *et seq.*

dependence on Greek sources [1] and on the early Greek poets. It is to the finest period of Greek poetry he has gone for his inspiration, and he reiterates this fact with such insistence, that one is forced to conclude that he wished above all to free himself from the suspicion of any taint of Alexandrianism. [2] In this also he was probably influenced by a desire to recall [3] his countrymen to the best models. His lyre is Greek, [4] the same lyre that has waked to music at the touch of Sappho and Alcæus. He is so intent upon establishing his kinship with the great lyric poets of Greece as to make claims to originality, [5] that are not always founded on justice, and that ignore the achievements of Catullus. Again, he speaks of Anacreon [6] as the source of his inspiration. In one of his latest Odes [7] he endeavours to show that lyric poetry has the power of conferring immortality as well as epic, though Homer will always hold the foremost place among the poets. It is not, however, to the Alexandrians that he goes for examples in proof of his contention, but to the representative lyric poets in the golden age of Greek Literature. In an interesting Ode [8] Horace, who had a narrow escape from death from a falling tree, pictures himself in the Under-world, where he sees Sappho and Alcæus engaged as in life in singing their lays, and Alcæus in particular the centre of an admiring throng. It is clear then where Horace's predilection lay, though we might expect from him a greater sympathy with the Alexandrians, considering that Virgil had fallen to some extent under their sway, especially under the

---

[1] Odes, II. xvi. 38; III. xxx. 15; cf. Hack, op. cit. p. 60.

[2] On Alexandrianism, *vide* Hardie, op. cit. p. 277 *et seq.*; Wendland, op. cit. pp. 55-7; Wight Duff, op. cit. p. 303 *et seq.*

[3] A.P. 268; cf. Nettleship, op. cit. pp. 69, 73.

[4] Odes, I. i. 34; xxvi. 11; xxxii. 5; IV. iii. 12; vi. 35.

[5] *Ibid.* I. xxvi. 10; III. xxx. 13; IV. ix. 3; Ep. I. xix. 32 (with Wilkins' note), *ibid.* 32. On the modifications introduced by Horace into the Greek metres, cf. Hardie, op. cit. p. 252 *et seq.*

[6] Odes, I. xvii. 18; cf. Epode xiv. 10.

[7] Odes, IV. ix.   [8] *Ibid.* II. xiii. 24 *et seq.*

sway of one of the greatest of them, Apollonius Rhodius, who influenced him [1] particularly in the Fourth Book of the Æneid, and in many isolated passages. Moreover, Horace and the Alexandrians had this in common that they set the highest value on perfection of technique, and on the elegance and polish of their verse. But even Horace, who attaches such importance to the "limae labor," must have found them too laboured, too lacking in freshness and spontaneity and the true inspiration of the poet. Their poetry endeavoured to catch the echoes of the older poets of Greece, and developed, as it mostly was, in the shadow of a great library, it sought to make affectation of scholarship and perfection of form a substitute for true poetic genius. For all this, it is difficult to understand the bitterness of Horace's sneer at Catullus,[2] who, though he drew his inspiration from the Alexandrians in some of his poems, yet in many others was wholly untouched by their influence, and exhibits a freedom and buoyancy combined with a depth of fire and passion unsurpassed in Roman Literature. Horace directs the same sneer against Calvus. We are unfortunately not in a position to estimate the genius of Calvus as a poet,[3] but he as well as Gallus [4] would be included among the "cantores Euphorionis," of whom Cicero speaks[5] so slightingly. It was probably their prettinesses and affectation that roused the hostility of Horace, who in his careful study of

---

[1] Macrob. Sat. V. xvii. 4; cf. Glover, "Studies in Virgil," pp. 51 et seq., 164-5; St. Beuve, "Étude sur Virgile," p. 278; Patin, op. cit. vol. i. p. 160 et seq.

[2] Sat. I. x. 19. Lejay, op. cit. p. 253, suggests that political reasons had something to do with Horace's antagonism to Catullus, Calvus, and Bibaculus, who were all strong anti-Cæsarians.

[3] Vide Prop. II. xxv. 4; xxxiv. 89. On his oratory, cf. Cic. Brutus, 284; Dial. 18; Quintilian, X. i. 115.

[4] Vide Prop. II. xxxiv. 91; Ovid, Am. I. xv. 29; Quintilian, X. i. 93.

[5] Tusc. Disp. iii. 43; cf. Ad Att. VII. ii. 1; Or. 161 on "poetae novi". On Euphorion, cf. Cic. De Div. II. lxiv. 133; Virg. Eclog. x. 50; Quintilian, X. i. 56; Wight Duff, op. cit. p. 308 et seq.

the older poets of Greece had been accustomed to more solid
fare.   In a well-known passage [1] Horace too seems to be having a sly thrust at Propertius, who took Callimachus as his
model, and claimed himself to be the Roman Callimachus. [2]
One might possibly argue that Horace's hostility to the Alexandrian school has been exaggerated, but the indications I
have mentioned, together with the poet's unceasing appeal to
the lyric writers of early Greece as his models, leave no doubt
as to the side on which his sympathies were ranged.

There was a type of criticism current in Horace's day, and
for its form owing not a little to Alexandria, which also provoked the condemnation of the poet.   When Horace shows disapproval [3] of the unmeasured praise bestowed upon the Ancients
by certain of his contemporaries, he condemns not merely the
partisan spirit thus displayed, but the style of criticism, in
which such eulogies were embodied.   There was a tendency [4]
in Roman criticism to become stereotyped, to degenerate into
mere formulæ, fixed and rigid, into which each writer was
made to fit as into a mould.   This tendency is well illustrated
by the classification [5] of the various styles in prose and poetry,
and by the creation of a number of terms in literary criticism,
which became, as it were, convenient labels to attach to the
writers under consideration.   Armed with such instruments
the critics endeavoured to express the merits of a writer in
some terse phrase, which, though it might seize on obvious
and salient characteristics, generally left his inmost and vital
qualities unapprehended.   Such criticisms readily became traditional, and, superficial as they were, had the effect of regu-

[1] Ep. II. ii. 100.

[2] Prop. IV. i. 64; cf. II. xxxiv. 31-2; III. i. 1; ix. 54; Ovid, Am. I. xv.
13; Tristia, ii. 367; Quintilian, X. i. 58.

[3] Ep. II. i. 50 *et seq.*

[4] Nettleship, op. cit. p. 54 *et seq.*; Haenni, op. cit. pp. 12-13; Saintsbury, op. cit. p. 337.

[5] Horace has such a classification in mind, A.P. 86; cf. Cic. Or. 20-1;
Quintilian, X. i. 44; XII. x. 58; Gellius, VII. xiv.

lating a writer's worth in the public mind, till some critic of independence appeared to impugn their value. Such style of criticism is common in Cicero, especially in the Brutus, where he deals with the Roman orators before his time, though in many of his judgments he shows great breadth of view, and much personal appreciation, untrammelled by the formulæ of a school. It is apparent again in Quintilian, whose pithy judgments of the Greek writers in particular frequently[1] do not even lay claim to originality. He is more independent in his estimate of Roman authors, but here also he sometimes merely reproduces criticisms, that had long been current among his countrymen. It is not improbable that the criticisms preserved for us by Horace[2] on the older poets of Rome owe their origin to Varro. The latter derived much of his criticism,[3] ultimately of course from Aristotle, but by way of the Alexandrian scholars, who had dealt largely in the type of criticism[4] I have described. Varro's own critical works[5] treated principally of the Roman drama. His antiquarian studies, as we saw, had no little influence in fostering the taste for the Ancients, which prevailed in the Augustan Age. Those short pithy criticisms, detailed by Horace, which set forth the excellences of the great representatives of Roman drama in its earliest period, may well have emanated from Varro or his followers, in their desire to extol the Ancients. Certain specimens of Varro's own criticisms on some of the Roman dramatists have been preserved,[6] and they bear a striking resemblance to those recounted by Horace.

[1] *Vide* In. Or. X. i. 53, 54, 58, 73.   [2] Ep. II. i. 50 *et seq.*
[3] *Vide* Michaut, op. cit. p. 117. Accius, the greatest critic before Varro, was influenced by the Pergamene school. On Accius, cf. Gellius, III. xi.; XX. iii. 3; also Suet. De Gr. ii.
[4] For their brief judgments on works of art, cf. Friedländer, op. cit. vol. ii. p. 327.
[5] Cf. such titles as De Actionibus Scenicis, De Comoediis Plautinis, Quaestiones Plautinae.
[6] Gellius, VII. xiv. 6; Fr. xv. Parmeno, Riese, op. cit. p. 191; Nettleship, op. cit. p. 52 (with quotation from Charisius).

It was characteristic also of this conventional criticism to endeavour to draw up canons of authors in the various literary forms. Side by side with the task of definitely branding a writer in some brief characterisation, the critics set themselves to form a kind of sacred circle in each literary genre, into which none but a chosen few were admitted. This method had been brought to perfection by the Alexandrian scholars,[1] and a canon of Greek writers had been formed by Aristophanes of Byzantium and his pupil Aristarchus.[2] Volcatius Sedigitus seems to have been the first Latin critic to follow the same method, by constructing a canon of Roman writers of comedy, which is preserved for us by Gellius.[3] Possibly Horace has something of the nature of a canon in mind when, speaking of the prevailing admiration for the old dramatists, he says,[4] "(Roma) habet hos *numeratque* poetas ad nostrum tempus Livi scriptoris ab aevo".

Horace gives several indications that there was a good deal of activity in dramatic writing, especially Tragedy, during his time. The strongest indication is the amount of space he devotes to the drama in the Ars Poetica, and the minute rules he lays down for its composition. The Romans had always shown a marked inclination towards Tragedy.[5] That species of drama was in harmony with the national character, with its grim determination, its dignity and seriousness. The conflict of strong natures, locked in a death struggle, must have appealed to the Romans, especially in the period when, through many tribulations, surmounting incredible obstacles, and beat-

---

[1] *Vide* Quintilian, I. iv. 3; X. i. 54, 59, 61, 73, 76; cf. Peterson, Introd. to Q. Bk. X. p. 34 *et seq.*; Dionysii De Imitatione, Reliquiae (ed. Usener), Epilogus, p. 129 *et seq.*; Jebb, "Attic Orators," vol. i. Introd. p. 65 *et seq.* for canon of Ten Orators, which probably came from Pergamum.

[2] Cf. Hor. A.P. 450; Quintilian, X. i. 54.

[3] N.A. xv. 24; cf. III. iii. 1; Suet. Life of Terence, v.; Nettleship, op. cit. pp. 50, 84; Usener, op. cit. p. 136 *et seq.*

[4] Ep. II. i. 61.

[5] *Ibid.* 166; cf. A.P. 287; Sellar, "The Roman Poets of the Republic," c. v.

ing down powerful rivals, they were building a world-Empire. The political strife during the last century of the Republic would find in the Tragic drama many examples of the vicissitudes of fortune, many counterparts of the tragedies in real life, which were enacted amidst the heated passions of the Civil Wars. Tragedy too was always a storehouse for the teacher of Rhetoric, its stately and sonorous diction being akin to the language of oratory. So we find Quintilian showing a high appreciation for Roman Tragedy, and decrying[1] the efforts of his countrymen in Comedy, which, being written in the language of every-day life, without " gravitas sententiarum, verborum pondera," afforded no assistance for the training of the orator. We have unfortunately little left to enable us to judge of the merits of the drama in the Augustan Age. Quintilian, as we have seen, is loud in his praises of the " Thyestes " of Varius and the " Medea "[2] of Ovid. We know too that Asinius Pollio[3] wrote tragedies, but not even a fragment of them remains. Augustus once began the composition of a tragedy[4] entitled Ajax, but, the Muse not being propitious, he abandoned the attempt. Horace, when writing[5] to Florus and inquiring about the literary activity of the staff of Tiberius (the *studiosa cohors* as he calls it), asks among other things if his friend Titius is engaged upon a tragedy. The "tearful compositions"[6] of the otherwise unknown Pupius were tragedies, we must presume, and indeed are so set down by the Scholiast. When Horace has delivered his judgment on certain qualities of the drama in his day, he has an uneasy

---

[1] X. i. 99.

[2] A few fragments are preserved; cf. Ribbeck, op. cit. p. 197.

[3] Hor. Odes, II. i. 9 ; cf. Sat. I. x. 42 (with reading *fata*); Virgil, Eclog. iii. 86; viii. 10; Dial. xxi. 31, For Severus, Gracchus, and Santra, cf. Ovid, Ex Ponto, IV. ii. 1; xvi. 9, 31; Ribbeck, pp. 195-6, 346. There are few references to writers of Comedy; cf. Hor. Sat. I. x. 42, on Fundanius. Porphyrion, Hor. Ep. I. x., calls Fuscus " Scriptor comoediarum ".

[4] Suet. Oct. 85 ; cf. Macrob Sat. II. iv. 2.

[5] Ep. I. iii.   [6] *Ibid.* i. 67 ; cf. Kiessling, ad loc.

feeling[1] that he may seem to be damning with faint praise a species of literature, which he himself has left untouched, but in which others have achieved success. He has clearly Tragedy in particular in view, drama that by its fictions can arouse all the emotions of pity, fear, anger, and allay them in turn, while the phrase, "cum recte tractent alii," points to activity in that direction amongst his contemporaries. The expression[2] that he uses in reference to the elder Piso, in commending his choice of a traditional subject, seems to indicate that he was actually engaged in writing a tragedy, and this hypothesis would, in part at least, account for the prominent position[3] given to the discussion of the Tragic drama in the Ars Poetica. All this would go to show that there was something like a revival of dramatic writing, especially Tragedy,[4] in Horace's day, though what particular line such a revival took we are not in a position to estimate with precision. Horace in recommending a subject offers[5] an alternative between a traditional subject[6] and an original theme, though he is careful to emphasise the difficulties that lie in the way of the latter's successful treatment. The traditional subject[7] probably continued to be most in favour. The Roman, who had his gaze fixed intently on a Greek model, would not readily abandon the beaten path to make a hazardous experiment in novelty. Horace, who had borne testimony to the difficulties of prospecting in some new field of the drama, has a special word

---

[1] Ep. II. i. 208 et seq.

[2] A.P. 128, "tuque rectius deducis".

[3] Vide Boissier, "L'Art Poétique et la Tragédie romaine," in Rev. de Phil. vol. xxii. p. 1 et seq.

[4] Horace also lays down (A.P. 220 et seq.) elaborate rules for the Satyric drama, which raises the presumption that it was not being neglected; cf. Michaut, op. cit. pp. 129 et seq., 404; Ridgeway, "The Origin of Tragedy," p. 50 et seq.

[5] A.P. 119 et seq.

[6] On traditional subjects, cf. Persius, Sat. i. 34; Arist. Poet. ix. 9; Butcher, op. cit. pp. 159, 331.

[7] Cf. the titles given in Ribbeck, op. cit. p. 195 et seq.

of praise[1] for those of his countrymen, who had attempted national subjects in Tragedy or Comedy.

Horace is interesting also in his remarks[2] upon the low ebb, which appreciation for the drama had reached in his day. He had already pointed out the extravagant admiration that existed among a section of his countrymen for the works of the Ancients, especially the writers of drama among them, but such admiration was apparently bestowed on their plays, principally for their literary' value, without much regard for their relation to the stage. But, among the playgoing public, indifference to or lack of insight into the merits of a drama were the prevailing characteristics, and Horace seems to suggest that such an attitude was the fate of all plays, whether of the Ancient or Modern school. The general public in Horace's time was of course much more cultured than in the days, when the plays of Plautus and Terence were produced. There are plenty of indications that the playgoers contemporary with these dramatists were for the most part a rude, unlettered throng, without refined tastes or intellectual interests. For one thing, the use by Plautus of the Prologue of mere exposition,[3] and crude tedious exposition at that, gives us a fair measure of the intelligence of his audience. No great modern dramatist, worthy of the name, would employ so clumsy and patent a device to make the exposition[4] essential to the understanding of the piece that is being enacted. Terence shows a higher sense of dramatic structure by making the exposition[5] of necessary details in the course of the play itself, and generally reserving his Prologues for literary polemics. But Terence

---

[1] A.P. 287 ; cf. Dial. c. 2 and 3 ; Ribbeck, p. 348 *et seq.* on Praetextatae ; Wight Duff, p. 232.

[2] Ep. II. i. 177 *et seq.*

[3] Some at least of the Plautine Prologues are genuine, and that is sufficient for my point.

[4] *Vide* Archer, " Playmaking," c. vii., on the question of Dramatic Exposition.

[5] Cf. Prologue to Adelphi, 22 *et seq.*

19

has to complain [1] bitterly at times of the want of appreciation shown by his audience, who will leave in the midst of the play, if there is a counter-attraction in the shape of a rope-dancer. In several of the Plautine Prologues,[2] the speaker of the Prologue has to strain his voice to make himself heard above the prevailing din, and is forced to frequently call for attention. One would expect better things in the Augustan Age, when there was a permanent theatre at Rome,[3] and when the arrangements for the accommodation of the audience were vastly superior to those that obtained, when the Drama was in its infancy.   Horace finds,[4] among Romans generally, a lack of critical taste, and among playgoers he complains [5] that the common people (*plebecula*) are so impervious to the appeal of the Drama, as to call for a bear or boxers in the midst of the performance of a piece.   Their aspirations did not rise above these, and unfortunately at Rome there were always plenty of sensations,[6] such as animal-baiting and gladiatorial shows, to satisfy such debased cravings.   Our poet complains,[7] too, that the din of the theatre is like the roaring of the Tuscan Sea. When he is giving reasons for the use of Iambics in dramatic verse,[8] with his eye probably on contemporary conditions, over and above the two reasons given by Aristotle, he gives as an additional reason that the Iambic (from the nature of its ictus) was more likely to be heard above the clamour of the audience.   He is particularly interesting when he proceeds to extend his strictures to the knights,[9] naturally the more intelligent and cultured portion of a Roman audience. Even their taste is depraved, and to pander to it, the play (Horace has here Tragedy particularly in mind) from being

---

[1] *Vide* Prologues to Hecyra.

[2] Cf. especially Prologues to Poenulus and Captivi.

[3] Besides the theatre of Pompey already existing, the theatres of Balbus and Marcellus were completed during the reign of Augustus.

[4] A.P. 263-4.   [5] Ep. II. i. 185.

[6] *Vide* Friedländer, op. cit. vol. ii. pp. 41 *et seq.*, 63.

[7] Ep. II. i. 200 *et seq.*   [8] A.P. 80.   [9] Ep. II. i. 187 *et seq.*

primarily an appeal to the intellect, aims principally at spectacular effect. In recent times the whole question of stage-production has been warmly debated. Some producers undoubtedly erred in subordinating dramatic interest to scenic effect, so that many are in favour of the simplest accessories by way of scenery, in order not to distract the mind by the mere accidents of display from the essential dramatic values of a piece. It is interesting then to find the same problem engaging the attention of a critic[1] in the Augustan Age. It is clear, too, from Horace that this lapse towards degeneracy in the art of the theatre was due in great measure to the Imperial position of Rome. Roman triumphs, captive kings, and the spoils of conquered provinces were represented on such occasions. The Romans were offered a pageant of Empire, by which they could come to a knowledge of the countries, over which the Roman standards held sway. Novelties of every kind from distant provinces appeared upon the stage, which became a miniature of the Imperial city itself, into which the arts[2] and wealth of foreign or subject races were pouring without cessation.

[1] Ep. II. i. 206; cf. *ibid*. I. vi. 40 *et seq.*; Plutarch, Lucullus, 39; Cic. Ad Fam. VII. i. 2.
[2] Ep. II. i. 203, "artes divitiaeque peregrinae".

INDEX.

ABT, A., 198, 200-4, 206-17, 219, 220, 247.
Agrippa, 25, 26, 30, 47, 223, 272.
Amelung and Holtzenger, 22.
Angelico, Fra, 236.
Antonius, M., 4, 5 *et seq.*, 17, 18, 28, 47, 51, 57, 64, 94.
Ara Pacis, 31, 52, 66, 73, 117, 118.
Archer, W., 289.
Arnim, Von H., 86, 87, 90, 100, 133, 135, 226.
Arnold, E. Vernon, 91.
Augustus, 2 *et seq.*, 18-26, 28-32, 43-53, 56-75, 93-5, 99, 100, 104, 106-8, 115-22, 125, 129, 141-3, 159, 161-3, 172, 179, 182, 185, 188, 196, 197, 223, 226, 227, 231, 245, 272-6, 290.

BAILEY, C., 198, 232, 233, 234, 236, 241, 242.
Balfour, A. J., 124.
Becker, W. A., 165, 176-9, 185-8, 190.
Belloc, H., 22.
Bergson, M., 82, 83.
Bevan, E., 14, 78, 103, 130, 222.
Bloch, G., 150, 154.
Boissier, G., 26, 35, 40, 43, 52, 53, 58, 60, 61, 68, 72, 73, 100, 136, 169, 232, 233, 236, 237, 241, 242, 253, 265, 288.
Bouché-Leclercq, 221, 222, 224, 225, 227, 230.
Bouchier, E. S., 24-6, 171.
Boyd, C. E., 67, 274.
Breiter, Th., 222, 223.
Bruns, 41, 69.
Bryce, Lord, 104.
Buecheler, F., 190, 232, 233, 236-9, 241.

Burne, C. S., 208, 211, 214, 216, 241, 243, 245, 246.
Butcher, S. H., 80, 83, 251, 261, 288.
Butler and Owen, 191.

CÆSAR, Julius, 11, 12, 17, 22-4, 28, 38, 45, 53, 57, 60-2, 106, 149, 155, 171, 173, 177, 187, 188, 190, 223, 272, 273, 278.
Cardinali, G., 145, 146, 147, 159, 160.
Carter, J. B., 35, 36, 49, 50, 57, 59, 63, 65, 67, 72, 75, 163, 221, 233.
Cicero, 16, 39, 42, 77-9, 84, 91, 92, 95, 97, 98, 101, 136, 166, 180, 181, 183, 186, 218, 222, 223, 230, 235, 245, 269, 276, 283, 285.
Cleopatra, 6 *et seq.*, 18, 106, 188.
Cohen, "Médailles Impériales," 9, 17, 21, 22, 53, 64.
Comparetti, D., 133.
Connington, J., 280.
Conway, R. S , 45.
Cornford, F. M., 35, 73, 133, 219, 226, 228, 229.
Cromer, Lord, 7, 19, 93, 104, 167, 169.
Cumont, F., 14, 35, 38, 41, 43, 54-6, 65, 104-7, 171, 199, 201, 204, 214, 221, 222, 224, 225, 228-30, 232, 236, 247.

DANTE, 235.
Daremberg and Saglio, 145, 151, 157, 201, 202, 204-10, 212, 213, 217.
Davis, W. S., 153.
De Coulanges, F., 232, 241.
De-Marchi, A., 60, 106.

Dessau, H., 164, 184, 189, 190, 215, 237, 244.
Diels, H., 50, 66, 72, 74, 107, 209, 247.
Dill, Sir S., 93, 104-7, 166, 171.
Döllinger, 35, 59, 67, 68, 107.
Dryden, J., 83.
Duff, J. D., 95.
Duff, J. Wight, 251, 268, 277, 279, 282, 283, 289.

Epicureanism, 40, 84, 94-9, 235, 238, 239.
Erman, A., 104, 105.
Euhemerus, 55.

Fahz, L., 200-3, 207, 208, 210, 211, 213-20.
Ferrero, G., 5, 6, 16-18, 20, 25, 30, 32, 33, 60, 68, 69, 70, 71, 72, 94, 128.
Figulus, Nigidius, 222, 223.
Fowler, Warde, 35, 36, 40, 42, 48, 50, 51, 53-7, 59-61, 63-5, 72, 74, 75, 77, 93, 100, 102, 107, 109, 111, 113, 114, 152-4, 163-5, 176, 199, 209, 222, 229, 230, 233, 236, 241-3, 246-8.
Frank, Tenney, 12, 19, 22, 33, 151, 170.
Frazer, J. G., 54, 72, 107, 208, 214, 216, 219, 246.
Friedländer, L., 66, 68, 98, 164, 167, 170, 171, 174-84, 187-9, 191, 192, 194, 215, 224, 235, 237, 274, 285, 290.
Furneaux, H., 23, 24, 71, 100, 103, 136, 155.
Furtwängler and Urlichs, 22, 66, 73, 118.

Gardner, E., 184.
Gardner, P., 14.
Garrod, H. W., 102, 128, 279.
Geikie, Sir A., 72, 175.
Gerlach, Fr., 82, 206, 258, 264, 265, 266, 274.
Glover, T. R., 39, 100, 105, 277, 283.
Gomme, G. L., 198, 205, 215, 246.
Gordon, G. S., 80, 82, 83.
Gracchi, 147, 148, 155, 156, 227, 275.

Granger, F., 205.
Greenidge and Clay, 147, 148, 155.
Greenidge, A. H. J., 12, 43, 51, 163, 169.
Griffith-Thomson, Papyri, 208, 210, 214.
Gummerus, H., 152.

Hack, R. K., 253, 254, 266, 271, 272, 282.
Haddon, A. C., 209, 210, 214-6.
Hadrian, 20, 237, 275.
Haenni, P. R., 269, 284.
Halliday, W. R., 218, 219, 244-6.
Hardie, W. R., 278, 280, 282.
Harrison, J. E., 204, 214, 236.
Haselbach, Von, 215.
Heitland, W. E., 93, 102, 147, 153, 169, 176, 222, 226.
Hendrickson, 256, 257, 259-64, 267.
Hermes, 146, 253, 256.
Hill, G. F., 6, 9, 15, 17, 21, 22, 50, 72.
Hogarth, D. G., 14.
Huelsen, Ch., 21, 48, 53, 67, 233.

Jebb, Sir R. C., 80, 215, 269, 286.
Jerome, St., 171.
Jevons, F. B., 35, 198, 205, 214, 241.
Jones, Stuart H., 45, 61, 152, 155, 170, 171, 177, 178, 182, 184, 185, 187-90, 193, 206.

Keightley, T., 194.
Kiessling, A., 89, 210, 249, 253, 256, 264, 266, 287.
Kukula, R. C., 72, 162.

Lanciani, R., 206, 246.
Lecky, 39, 86, 93, 153, 161, 165, 167, 224.
Lejay, P., 249, 255, 260, 264-6, 272, 283.
Leges Juliae, 5, 69-71, 73.
Leland, C. G., 113, 207, 209.
Lemuria, 242, 243.
Leo, 256.
Lindsay, W. M., 235.
Lucas, C. P. Sir, 7, 169, 170.

MÆCENAS, 1, 2, 29, 131, 138, 140, 143, 206, 207, 225, 279.
Mahaffy, J. P., 14, 78.
Mahan, Admiral, 5.
Marius, 37, 149.
Martha, C., 85, 97.
Masson, J., 85.
Mayor, J. B., 65, 66.
Meredith, G., 82.
Meyer, E., 146.
Michaut, G., 255, 257-60, 262-6, 285, 288.
Michelangelo, 235, 236.
Milton, quoted, 134.
Molière, 83.
Mommsen, Th., 6, 14-18, 20, 22, 24, 25, 26, 28-30, 32, 33, 37, 146, 147, 148-52, 155, 156, 265.
Murena, Licinius, 4, 33, 81.
Murray, G., 39, 54, 109, 110, 133, 198, 225.

NETTLESHIP, H., 100, 114, 251, 252, 264, 265, 267, 274, 282, 284-6.
Niese, 146.
Norden, E., 56, 128, 202, 218-20, 222, 229, 230, 231, 253, 271, 277, 280.

OMAR KHAYYÀM, quoted, 99.
Orelli, 239.

PAIS, E., 146.
Palmer, A., 89, 280.
Palmer, J., 83.
Panætius, 90, 91, 92.
Papyri, 200-3, 207, 208, 210, 211, 213, 214, 217, 219, 247.
Parentalia, 242.
Patin, M., 251, 272, 283.
Peet, T. E., 243.
Pelham, H., 19, 48, 50, 60, 61, 68, 69, 122, 152, 157.
Peterson, W., 286.
Pompeius, Gn., 15, 16, 190.
Posidonius, 56, 90, 130, 222, 230, 235.

RALEIGH, W., 279.
Reid, J. S., 79, 84, 101, 136, 273.
Révue de Philologie, 253, 288.

Ribbeck, O., 277, 279, 287-9.
Richmond in " Essays Presented to Wm. Ridgeway," 64.
Richter, F., 248.
Ridgeway, W., 54, 205, 233, 241, 243, 288.
Riese, A., 176, 177, 265, 267, 273, 285.
Rousseau, 102.
Rushforth, G. McN., 9, 25, 26, 31, 58, 60, 62, 117.

SAINT-BEUVE, 45, 283.
Saintsbury, G., 251, 273, 284.
Sandys, J. E., 180.
Scipionic Circle, 37, 91.
Sellar, W. Y., 38, 153, 280, 286.
Sibylline Books, 36, 40, 65, 66, 72.
Stock, St. George, 86, 88, 133.
Stoicism, 39, 55, 84 et seq., 99, 133-6, 167, 222, 226, 228.
Storr-Best, L., 154.
Strong, A., 54, 55, 59, 60, 63, 66, 73, 75, 108, 109, 116-18, 133, 224, 230, 231, 233, 237, 241.
Sulla, 15, 38, 149.
Swoboda, A., 223.

TABELLAE DEFIXIONUM, 215, 244.
Taylor, L. Ross, 58, 105, 107, 171.
Teuffel-Schwabe, 264.
Tiberius, 21, 32, 33, 143, 182, 183, 193, 251, 272, 287.
Toutain, J., 54, 57, 58, 105, 106, 171, 198, 199, 201, 215, 222, 232.
Tylor, E. B., 244.

USENER, H., 286.

VARIUS, 252, 272, 279, 281, 287.
Varro, 49, 152, 163-5, 168, 192, 193, 223, 262, 265, 267, 273, 274, 285.
Verral, A. W., 2, 3, 18, 25, 81.
Virgil, 44, 45, 49, 95, 96, 100, 106, 112, 120, 128, 150, 153, 169, 179, 194, 196, 211, 222, 229, 234-6, 240, 252, 259, 269, 272, 275, 277, 279, 280-2.

WALLON, H., 164.
Walters, H. B., 178, 182, 184, 185, 190.
Wendland, P., 14, 35, 38, 67, 103, 130, 133, 275, 282.
Wickham, E. C., 18, 27, 72, 132.
Wilkins, A. S., 10, 131, 275, 282.

Wissowa, G., 35, 45, 50, 55, 57-63, 65-7, 72, 105, 107, 111, 248.

ZELLER, E., 78, 84, 86.8, 90, 93, 100, 130, 131, 133, 135, 224, 226.